Lecture Notes in Computer Science 4916

Commenced Publication in 1973
Founding and Former Series Editors:
Gerhard Goos, Juris Hartmanis, and Jan van Leeuwen

T0223145

Stefan Leue   Pedro Merino (Eds.)

Formal Methods for Industrial Critical Systems

12th International Workshop, FMICS 2007
Berlin, Germany, July 1-2, 2007
Revised Selected Papers

 Springer

Volume Editors

Stefan Leue
University of Konstanz
Department of Computer and Information Science
78457 Konstanz, Germany
E-mail: stefan.leue@uni-konstanz.de

Pedro Merino
University of Málaga
Department of Computer Science
Campus de Teatinos, 29071, Málaga, Spain
E-mail: pedro@lcc.uma.es

Library of Congress Control Number: 2008926951

CR Subject Classification (1998): D.2.4, D.2, D.3, C.3, F.3

LNCS Sublibrary: SL 2 – Programming and Software Engineering

ISSN   0302-9743
ISBN-10   3-540-79706-8 Springer Berlin Heidelberg New York
ISBN-13   978-3-540-79706-7 Springer Berlin Heidelberg New York

Springer is a part of Springer Science+Business Media

springer.com

© Springer-Verlag Berlin Heidelberg 2008
Printed in Germany

Typesetting: Camera-ready by author, data conversion by Scientific Publishing Services, Chennai, India
Printed on acid-free paper   SPIN: 12266005   06/3180   5 4 3 2 1 0

Preface

The FMICS 2007 workshop was affiliated with the Computer-Aided Verification (CAV) conference and held at the Park-Inn Hotel Alexanderplatz in Berlin, Germany, July 1–2, 2007.

The aim of the FMICS workshop series is to provide a forum for researchers who are interested in the development and application of formal methods in industry. In particular, these workshops are intended to bring together scientists and practitioners who are active in the area of formal methods and interested in exchanging their experience in the industrial usage of these methods. These workshops also strive to promote research and development for the improvement of formal methods and tools for industrial applications.

The topics for which contributions to FMICS 2007 were solicited included, but were not restricted to, the following:

- Design, specification, code generation and testing with formal methods
- Verification and validation of complex, distributed, real-time systems and embedded systems
- Verification and validation methods that aim at circumventing shortcomings of existing methods with respect to their industrial applicability
- Tools for the design and development of formal descriptions
- Case studies and project reports on formal methods-related projects with industrial participation (e.g., safety critical systems, mobile systems, object-based distributed systems)
- Application of formal methods in standardization and industrial forums

The workshop included five sessions of regular contributions and three invited presentations, given by Charles Pecheur, Thomas Henzinger and Gérard Berry. At the workshop, a participants' proceedings volume was made available to all participants. This LNCS volume reports on the presentations given at FMICS 2007 in archival form. The papers included in this volume were selected after a second round of peer reviewing by the FMICS 2007 Program Committee from those papers accepted for presentation at FMICS 2007. Out of the 31 submissions to FMICS 2007, 15 papers were accepted for presentation at the workshop, and revised versions of all accepted papers are included in this volume.

FMICS 2007 attracted 33 participants, some of which are members of the FMICS working group, from 14 different countries.

Following a tradition established over the past few years, the European Association of Software Science and Technology (EASST) has offered an award to the best FMICS paper. The Program Committee decided to confer the FMICS 2007 best paper award to the paper "An Approach to Formalization and Analysis of Message Passing Libraries," written by Robert Palmer, Michael DeLisi, Ganesh Gopalakrishnan and Robert M. Kirby.

Further information about the FMICS working group and the next FMICS workshop can be found at: http://www.inrialpes.fr/vasy/fmics.

We wish to thank the members of the Program Committee and the additional reviewers for their careful evaluation of the submitted papers during both rounds of reviewing. We also appreciate the effort of all members of the Program Committee in making judicious choices and engaging in constructive discussions during the electronic program selection meeting. We are very grateful to the local organizers of the CAV conference for their organizational support, and to the University of Dortmund for allowing us to use their Online Conference Service.

February 2008   Stefan Leue
                                                                 Pedro Merino

Organization

Program Committee

Per Bjesse (Synopsys, USA)
Lubos Brim (Masaryk University, Czech Republic)
Marsha Chechik (University of Toronto, Canada)
Darren Cofer (Rockwell Collins, USA)
Stefania Gnesi (ISTI-CNR, Italy)
Patrice Godefroid (Microsoft Research, USA)
Michael Goldsmith (Formal Systems, UK)
David Harel (Weizmann Institute of Science, Israel)
Connie Heitmeyer (Naval Research Laboratory, USA)
Leszek Holenderski (Philips, The Netherlands)
Joost-Pieter Katoen (RWTH Aachen, Germany)
Roope Kaivola (Intel, USA)
Stefan Kowalewski (RWTH Aachen, Germany)
Salvatore La Torre (Universita' degli Studi di Salerno, Italy)
Martin Leucker (TU München, Germany)
Stefan Leue (University of Konstanz, Germany), Co-chair
Radu Mateescu (INRIA Rhone-Alpes, France)
Pedro Merino (University of Malaga, Spain), Co-chair
David Parker (University of Oxford, UK)
Charles Pecheur (Université Catholique de Louvain, Belgium)
Francois Pilarski (Airbus, France)
Andreas Podelski (University of Freiburg, Germany)
Jakob Rehof (University of Dortmund, Germany)
John Rushby (SRI International, USA)
Don Sannella (University of Edinburgh, UK)
Ina Schieferdecker (Fraunhofer FOKUS, Germany)
Anna Slobodova (Intel, USA)
Jaco van de Pol (CWI, The Netherlands)
Farn Wang (National Taiwan University, Taiwan)
Willem Visser (SEVEN Networks, USA)

Additional Reviewers

David Aspinall (University of Edinburgh, UK)
Dave Berry (University of Edinburgh, UK)
Jesse Bingham (Intel, USA)
Iavor S. Diatchki (Galois Connections Inc., USA)
Alessandro Fantechi (DSI-UNIFI, Italy)

Table of Contents

Verification of Embedded Software:
From Mars to Actions

Charles Pecheur

Catholic University of Louvain, Belgium
charles.pecheur@uclouvain.be
http://www.info.ucl.ac.be/~pecheur

Embedded controllers are more and more pervasive and feature more and more advanced capabilities. For space applications in particular, the development of autonomous controllers is seen as a critical technology to enable new mission objectives and scale down operating costs. On the flip side, the validation of intelligent control software poses a huge challenge, both due to the increased complexity of the system itself and the broad spectrum of normal and abnormal conditions in which it has to be able to operate. This talk will follow our journey in applying some modern, analytical verification technologies and tools to the validation of autonomy software, in the context of space applications, at NASA Ames Research Center in California. This route will take us from the concrete, practical dependability requirements for space-bound software that motivated the work down to the deeper, broader issues in formal methods that emerged as part of that work.

Our work has focused on analysing model-based approaches to fault diagnosis, as exemplified by NASA Ames' Livingstone system. We developed two lines of verification tools for model-based diagnosis applications, and experimented with those tools on real-size problems taken from NASA applications. Under different angles, both approaches stem from model checking principles. Verifying diagnosis systems and models has led to considering the issue of diagnosability: given a partially observable dynamic system, and a diagnosis system observing its evolution over time, how to verify (at design time) whether the system provides sufficient observations to determine and track (at run-time) its internal state with sufficient accuracy. This kind of question can be reduced to a state reachability problem, which can be solved using (symbolic) model checking. In turn, diagnosability can be phrased as a particular temporal and epistemic property ("the diagnoser always knows the faults"), and we have carried experiments in applying a generic temporal-epistemic model checker to our diagnosis applications. Finally, epistemic models and logics themselves can, under some assumptions, be reduced to labelled transition systems and action-based temporal logics. We implemented this reduction and added support for this logics in NuSMV, thereby leveraging NuSMV's language, features and ecosystem to the analysis of epistemic (and, more broadly, action-based) properties.

S. Leue and P. Merino (Eds.): FMICS 2007, LNCS 4916, p. 1, 2008.
© Springer-Verlag Berlin Heidelberg 2008

Synchronous Design and Verification of Critical Embedded Systems Using SCADE and Esterel

Gérard Berry

Esterel Technologies, France
Gerard.Berry@esterel-technologies.com
http://www.esterel-technologies.com

SCADE (Safety Critical Application Design Environment) is a design environment dedicated to safety-critical embedded software applications. It is widely used for avionics, railways, heavy industry, and automotive applications. For instance, most critical systems of the Airbus A380 have been developed with SCADE. The core element is the Scade synchronous formalism, which can be viewed as a graphical version of Lustre coupled with synchronous hierarchical state machines. The Scade to C compiler is certifiable at level A of DO-178B avionics norm, which removes the need for unit-testing the embedded C code and brings big savings in the certification process. The SCADE tools encompasses a simulator, a model coverage analyzer, a formal verifier, a display generator, and gateways to numerous other prototyping or software engineering tools. Esterel Studio is a similar hardware modeling, design, and verification environment based on the Esterel v7 formal synchronous language. Esterel Studio is used by major semiconductor companies to specify, verify, and synthesize complex hardware designs. It can generate both an optimized circuit and a behaviorally equivalent software model from a single formal specification. It also supports simulation and formal verification, which is widely used in production applications. We discuss the advantages and limitations of the underlying synchronous concurrency model. We explain why the same core science and technology can be applied to such different domains, however with quite different integration in global system-level design flows according used in the different industries.

S. Leue and P. Merino (Eds.): FMICS 2007, LNCS 4916, p. 2, 2008.
© Springer-Verlag Berlin Heidelberg 2008

Static Analysis of the Accuracy in Control Systems: Principles and Experiments

Eric Goubault[1], Sylvie Putot[1], Philippe Baufreton[2], and Jean Gassino[3]

[1] CEA, LIST, Boîte courrier 65, GIF-SUR-YVETTE CEDEX, F-91191 France
{eric.goubault,sylvie.putot}@cea.fr
[2] Hispano-Suiza
philippe.baufreton@hispano-suiza-sa.com
[3] IRSN
jean.gassino@irsn.fr

Abstract. Finite precision computations can severely affect the accuracy of computed solutions. We present a complete survey of a static analysis based on abstract interpretation, and a prototype implementing this analysis for C code, for studying the propagation of rounding errors occurring at every intermediary step in floating-point computations. In the first part of this paper, we briefly present the domains and techniques used in the implemented analyzer, called FLUCTUAT. We describe in the second part, the experiments made on real industrial codes, at Institut de Radioprotection et de Sûreté Nucléaire and at Hispano-Suiza, respectively coming from the nuclear industry and from aeronautics industry. This paper aims at filling in the gaps between some theoretical aspects of the static analysis of floating-point computations that have been described in [13,14,21], and the necessary choices of algorithms and implementation, in accordance with practical motivations drawn from real industrial cases.

Keywords: Static analysis, floating-point computations, control systems.

1 Introduction

The use of floating-point arithmetic as a computable approximation of real arithmetic may introduce rounding errors at each arithmetic operation in a computation. Even though each of these errors is very small, their propagation in further computations, for example in loops, can produce a dramatic imprecision on a critical output. We propose an analysis that computes for each variable an over-approximation of the difference between a same computation in real and in floating-point arithmetic. Moreover, we decompose this difference over the operations that introduced errors, thus pointing out the operations responsible for the main losses.

Principal contributions. This paper essentially surveys the different abstract interpretation domains and techniques used in the static analyzer FLUCTUAT. The emphasis is not put on the theoretical details of the main domain used for

S. Leue and P. Merino (Eds.): FMICS 2007, LNCS 4916, pp. 3–20, 2008.

abstracting floating-point values, which can be found in [14]. But it describes the main techniques and answers to the difficulties we had to address in the practical use of these domains in an analyzer. Also, a large part is dedicated to some examples of the analysis which was led on industrial examples.

Related work. Few complete static analyzers of C programs are fully described in the literature. This paper tries to match some of the available descriptions of the ASTREE analyzer [1,2] which is probably the most complete analyzer today, with respect to the number of techniques and domains implemented, in particular. Also, some commercial abstract interpreters like CodeSonar [24] and PolySpace [25] are now available. All these tools analyze run-time errors mostly, whereas we analyze a subtle numerical property, namely the discrepancy introduced by the use of floating-point numbers instead of real numbers, in C programs. This requires very fine and specific abstract domains, and the difficulty lies mostly in the numerical subtleties of small parts of a code, and not in the size of the program.

Overview. This paper is divided in two parts. In Section 2, we present the abstract domains and main techniques used in the FLUCTUAT analyzer. In subsection 2.1, we briefly introduce the abstract domain for representing floating point variables, which is described in more details in [14]. Then in subsection 2.2, we detail how this domain is extended to integer variables, and the specificities and difficulties of handling integers. We then describe in subsection 2.3, the simple aliasing model we are using, when it comes to abstract pointers, structures and arrays. The iteration strategy which is used to solve the semantic equations (and in particular specific widening operators), is described in subsection 2.4. Finally, some assertions in a language specific to the analyzer, allow us to specify properties of variables, such as set of possible input values, but also more subtle properties such as bounds on the gradient of an input over iterations in a loop. These are presented in subsection 2.5.

We then discuss in Section 3 some experiments conducted with FLUCTUAT on industrial codes. We first describe the analysis of some programs developed at Hispano-Suiza in the aeronautics industry. We first concentrate on some interesting specific sub-functions, and then come to a full control application. In a second part, we describe the analysis of a code from the nuclear industry that IRSN has to expertise.

2   Abstract Domains and Techniques Used in FLUCTUAT

2.1   Floating-Point Variables

General principles. The analysis bounds at each operation the error committed between the floating-point and the real result. It relies for this on a model of the difference between the result x of a computation in real numbers, and the result f^x of the same computation using floating-point numbers, expressed as a sum of error terms

$$x = f^x + \bigoplus_{\ell \in L \cup \{hi\}} \omega_\ell^x . \tag{1}$$

We assume that a control point of a program is annotated by a unique label $\ell \in L$. In this relation, a term w_ℓ^x, $\ell \in L$, denotes the contribution to the global error of the first-order error introduced by the operation labeled ℓ. It expresses both the rounding error committed at label ℓ, and its propagation due to further computations on variable x. Errors of order higher than one, coming from non-affine operations, are grouped in one term associated to special label hi. We let $\mathcal{L}$ be the union of L and hi.

Let $\mathbb{F}$ be either the set of single or double precision floating-point numbers. Let $\uparrow_\circ : \mathbb{R} \to \mathbb{F}$ be the function that returns the rounded value of a real number r, with respect to the rounding mode $\circ$. The function $\downarrow_\circ : \mathbb{R} \to \mathbb{F}$ that returns the roundoff error is then defined for all $f \in \mathbb{R}$, by $\downarrow_\circ (f) = f - \uparrow_\circ (f)$. The result of an arithmetic operation $\Diamond^{\ell_i}$ contains the combination of existing errors on the operands, plus a new roundoff error term $\downarrow_\circ (f^x \Diamond f^y) \varepsilon_{\ell_i}$. For addition and subtraction, the existing errors are added or subtracted componentwise, and a new error $\downarrow_\circ (f^x + f^y)$ is associated to control point ℓ_i:

$$x +^{\ell_i} y = \uparrow_\circ (f^x + f^y) + \bigoplus_{\ell \in \mathcal{L}} (w_\ell^x + w_\ell^y) + \downarrow_\circ (f^x + f^y) .$$

The multiplication introduces higher order errors, we write:

$$x \times^{\ell_i} y = \uparrow_\circ (f^x f^y) + \bigoplus_{\ell \in \mathcal{L}} (f^x w_\ell^y + f^y w_\ell^x) + \sum_{(\ell_1, \ell_2) \in \mathcal{L}^2} w_{\ell_1}^x w_{\ell_2}^y + \downarrow_\circ (f^x f^y) .$$

We refer the reader to [10,19] for more details on this domain.

Unstable tests. Our approach is that of abstract interpretation [7], and all control flows due to sets of possible inputs are considered. But there is one specific difficulty due to floating-point computations. Indeed, in tests, the branch followed by the floating-point and the corresponding real value of a variable can be different, we then call them unstable tests (as in [26]). Consider for example the following portion of code, supposing input x is in interval [1,3] with an error equal to 1.0e-5:

```
if (x <= 2) x = x+2;
```

Then, for x equal to 2 for example, the floating-point result after this test is 4, whereas the result of this program if it were executed on the real semantics would be 2.00001. But handling this divergence in control flow in the general case would be complicated and costly, and quickly very imprecise. For example here, if we consider the different control flows, we find the floating-point value of x in $[2, 4]$, with an error in interval $[1.0e^{-5}, 2]$. Without any additional relation between values and errors, this result is highly imprecise.

We thus made the choice in the Fluctuat analyzer to make the assumption that the real and floating-point flows take the same branches. The result given here at the end of the program would thus be $x = [2, 4]$ with an error equal to $1.0e^{-5}$ (if we neglect the additional rounding error due to the addition).

However, when the analyzer detects, as is the case here, that the control flows may be different, it issues a warning.

Relational domain. A natural abstraction of the coefficients in expression (1), is obtained using intervals. The machine number f^x is abstracted by an interval of floating-point numbers, each bound rounded to the nearest value in the type of variable x. The error terms $\omega_i^x \in \mathbb{R}$ are abstracted by intervals of higher-precision numbers, with outward rounding. However, results with this abstraction suffer from the over-estimation problem of interval methods. If the arguments of an operation are correlated, the interval computed with interval arithmetic may be significantly wider than the actual range of the result.

We thus proposed and implemented a relational domain, relying on affine arithmetic [5,22] for the computation of the floating-point value f^x. Affine arithmetic uses affine correlation between real variables, and allows us to get much tighter results than classical interval arithmetic (the concretisation forms zonotopes: center-symmetric bounded convex polytopes). It relies on a representation of a quantity x by an affine form, which is a polynomial of degree one in a set of noise terms ε_i:

$$\hat{x} = \alpha_0^x + \alpha_1^x \varepsilon_1 + \ldots + \alpha_n^x \varepsilon_n, \quad \text{with } \varepsilon_i \in [-1,1] \text{ and } \alpha_i^x \in \mathbb{R}. \tag{2}$$

Each noise symbol ε_i stands for an independent component of the total uncertainty on the quantity x, its value is unknown but bounded in [-1,1]; the corresponding coefficient α_i^x is a known real value, which gives the magnitude of that component. The sharing of noise symbols between variables expresses implicit dependencies. The full semantics is described in [14], and linearizes floating-point expressions dynamically (and not statically as in [20]). The semantics is memory-efficient: it needs only a small factor of the size that an (economic) interval analysis would take. No a priori decided packing of variables [2] is needed since the representation of relations is implicit [14]. Nevertheless, we use a sparse representation of the global environment, akin to the one described in Section 5 of [1].

The coefficients α_i^x have no meaning relevant to our analysis, the decomposition is a mean for a more accurate computation. This is different from expression (1), where coefficient ω_ℓ^x represent the contribution of control point ℓ to the total rounding error. However, they can be used for an analysis of the sensibility of a program to an input: when an input is taken in a small interval, a new noise symbol ε_i is created. The evolution of the corresponding α_i^x in further computations indicates how this initial uncertainty is amplified or reduced [23].

These affine forms allow us to represent results of real arithmetic. The analysis must be adapted to the case of floating-point arithmetic, where symbolic relations true in real arithmetic do no longer hold exactly. We thus decompose the floating-point value f^x of a variable x resulting from a trace of operations, in the real value of this trace of operations r^x, plus the sum of errors δ^x accumulated along the computation, $f^x = r^x + \delta^x$. The real part is computed using affine arithmetic, and the error is computed using three intervals that respectively bound the error on the lower and upper bounds of the set of real values r^x, and the maximum error on all this set. Without going into too much detail, we can say that these errors on bounds allow us to improve the estimates for the floating-point bounds, compared to using the maximum error. But the maximum error is still needed at each step to estimate the results of further computations.

This domain for the values of variables, is of course more expensive than interval arithmetic, but comparable to the domain used for the errors. And it allows us to accurately analyze non trivial numerical computations, as we will show in Section 3. We also plan to introduce a relational computation for errors, along the lines of [16]. First ideas on these relational semantics were proposed in [13], [21]. The relational semantics for the value f^x is described in detail in [14], with in particular the lattice operations such as join and meet.

2.2   Integer Variables

We implemented modular integer arithmetic semantics, and a domain consisting of value (coded by affine forms) plus sum of errors is used as for floating-point variables. For example, when adding one to the greatest integer that can be represented in the `int` type, say `INT_MAX`, the value of the result is the smallest integer represented by an `int`, say `INT_MIN`, and an error of `INT_MAX-INT_MIN+1` is associated to this variable. Conversions between integers and floating-points are supported, and the errors are propagated.

Bitwise operations. Some attention must be paid to the propagation of errors on operands in order to avoid losing too much precision. Indeed, the behavior of the `and`, `or` and `xor` operators is non affine with respect to the operands. In the general case, the errors on the operands x and y are propagated as follows:

- we compute the result of $\diamond$ on the sets of floating-point values, $f^z = f^x \diamond f^y$,
- we compute the result of the same operation on the interval bounds for the real values, $r^z = r^x \diamond r^y$, with $r^x = f^x + \sum_l \omega_l^x$ and $r^y = f^y + \sum_l \omega_l^y$,
- then the propagated error on z is $r^z - f^z$, and it is associated to the label of the current operation.

There are two consequences. First, we lose the decomposition of errors on operations executed before bitwise operations. Second, the larger the intervals f^x and f^y, the more over-approximated the propagated errors are. We thus propose an option of the analyzer to locally subdivide one of these intervals in the propagation of errors: the cost of a bitwise operation is approximately multiplied by the number of subdivisions, but this cost is in general negligible compared to the full analysis, and the results can be greatly improved.

Error terms are agglomerated for the same reason for the division and modulo operators on integers. The error is also computed as the difference between the floating-point interval result and the real interval result: local subdivisions can again greatly improve the estimation of errors.

Conversions. The semantics for the conversion between floating-point numbers, and with integers differ by the meaning we give to each:

- in the conversion from double precision to single precision floating-point numbers, we consider the difference between the initial double precision value and the result of the conversion, as an error on the result.
- in the conversion from a floating-point number to an integer, we consider that the truncation is wanted by the user, and is thus not an error. A new error can be introduced by such a conversion only when the floating-point number exceeds the capacity of the integer type. However, all errors are grouped in one integer term corresponding to the label of the conversion.
- in the conversion from an integer to a floating-point number, most of the time no precision is lost, and the sum value plus errors is transmitted as is. However, this is not always the case, and an error still has to be added in some cases: for example a 32 bits integer with all bits equal to 1 cannot exactly represented by a single precision floating-point number, which mantissa is represented on 23 bits.

We encountered some other cast operations that we included in the set of instructions understood by the analyzer, such as the ones used to decode and encode IEEE 754 format, directly by bitwise operations. Take for instance the following piece of code (assuming 64 bits little endian encoding for `double`):

```
double Var = ...; signed int *PtrVar = (signed int *) (&Var);
int Exp = (signed int) ((PtrVar[0] & 0x7FF00000) >> 20) - 1023;
```

We cast variable `Var` into an array of 32 bits types. Then we extract the first 32 bits of the 64 bits word. The rest of the manipulation of the program above, masks the bits of the mantissa, and shifts the value, to get in `Exp` the binary exponent in IEEE754 format of the value stored in `Var`.

In the interpretation of this case by FLUCTUAT, all error terms are agglomerated in one corresponding to the label of the cast, and local subdivisions of the values can be applied to improve the bounds for the errors, as for bitwise operations.

2.3 Aliases and Arrays

Our alias and array analysis is based on a simple points-to analysis, like the ones of [18], or location-based alias analyses. An abstract element is a graph of locations, where arcs represent the points-to relations, with a label (which we call a selector) indicating which dereferencing operation can be used. Arrays are interpreted in two different ways, as already suggested by some of the authors in [9]: all entries are considered to be separate variables (called "expanded" in [1]) or the same one (for which the union of all possible values is taken - called "smash" in [1]). These abstractions have proven sufficient typically for SCADE generated C programs.

2.4 Iteration Strategy

Loops. The difficulty in loops is to get a good over-approximation of the least fixpoint without too many iterations of the analyzer. For that, we had to design adapted iteration strategies:

- in the case of nested loops, a depth first strategy was chosen: at each iteration of the outer loop, the fixpoint of the inner loop is computed,
- a loop is unfolded a number of times (similar to the "semantic loop unrolling" of [1]), before starting Kleene iterations (unions over iterations),
- some particularities of our domain require special care in loops: for example, noise symbols are potentially introduced at most operations, and there are new noise symbols for each iteration of a loop. But we can choose to reduce the level of correlation we want to keep, and for example keep correlations only between the last n iterations of a loop, where n is a parameter of the analyzer. Also, we can choose to agglomerate or not some noise symbols introduced in a loop when getting out of it. This allows us to reduce the cost of the analysis while keeping accurate results.
- acceleration techniques (widenings) adapted to our domain had to be designed. In particular, widenings are not always performed at the same time on integer or floating-point variables, and on values or error terms. Also, we have designed a widening specially adapted to floating-point numbers, by gradually reducing the precision of the numbers used to bound the terms: this accelerates the convergence of Kleene iteration compared to iteration with fixed precision, and allows us to get very accurate results. This should be thought of as an improved method than the "staged widening with thresholds" of [1], in the sense that thresholds are dynamically chosen along the iterations, depending on the current values of the iterates. After a number of these iterations, a standard widening is used.

To illustrate this last point (progressive widening by reduction of the precision), let us consider the fixpoint computation of

```
while () x = 0.1*x;
```

with no unrolling of the loop, starting from $x_0 \in [0, 1]$. With our simple (non relational) semantics, we have, with $ulp(1)$ denoting the machine rounding error around 1,

$$x_1 = [0, 1] + \delta \varepsilon_2, \quad \delta = 0.1[-ulp(1), ulp(1)]$$
$$x_2 = [0, 1] + (0.1\delta + \delta)\varepsilon_2$$
$$x_n = [0, 1] + (\sum_{k=0}^{n} 0.1^k)\delta \varepsilon_2.$$

If real numbers are used to compute the error term, without any widening the computation does not terminate even though the error term remains finite. Now if floating point numbers are used to bound the error term, the convergence depends on the number of bits used to represent the mantissa. For simplicity's sake, let us consider $\delta = [-1, 1]$, and radix 10 numbers. With 3 significant digits, a fixpoint is got in 4 iterations:

$$\omega_1 = \delta = [-1, 1]$$
$$\omega_2 = \uparrow_\infty ([-0.1, 0.1] + [-1, 1]) = [-1.1, 1.1]$$

$$\omega_3 = \uparrow_\infty ([-0.11, 0.11] + [-1, 1]) = [-1.11, 1.11]$$
$$\omega_4 = \uparrow_\infty ([-0.111, 0.111] + [-1, 1]) = \uparrow_\infty [-1.111, 1.111] = [-1.12, 1.12]$$
$$\omega_5 = \uparrow_\infty ([-0.112, 0.112] + [-1, 1]) = \uparrow_\infty [-1.112, 1.112] = [-1.12, 1.12]$$

More generally, we can show that with N significant digits, a fixpoint is got in N+1 iterates. Thus reducing the precision of numbers accelerates the convergence towards a (larger) fixpoint.

Of course, this is a toy example, in practice the fixpoint is computed by unrolling the loop a certain number of times before beginning the unions, which here solves the problem. But we are confronted with this kind of computations in the general case. And in more complicated examples, when the optimal unrolling was not chosen, this widening allows us to still compute an interesting fixpoint.

Interprocedural analysis. In critical embedded systems, recursion is in general prohibited. Hence we chose to use a very simple interprocedural domain, with static partitioning, based on [17].

2.5   Assertions

A number of assertions can be added to the analyzed C source code, to specify the behavior of some variables of the program. For a single precision floating-point variable x, the assertion:

```
x = __BUILTIN_DAED_FBETWEEN(a,b);
```

indicates that x can take any floating-point value in the interval $[a, b]$. The same assertions exist to define the range of double precision or integer variables.

One can also specify an initial error together with the range of values for a variable. For example,

```
x = __BUILTIN_DAED_FLOAT_WITH_ERROR(a,b,c,d);
```

specifies that variable x of type float takes its value in the interval $[a, b]$, and that is has an initial error in the interval $[c, d]$.

In some cases, bounds on the values are not sufficient to describe accurately the behavior of a system: we thus added an assertion that allows us to bound, in a loop indexed by an integer variable i, the variation between two successive values of an input variable x:

```
for (i=i0 ; i<N ; i++)
x = __BUILTIN_DAED_FGRADIENT(x0min,x0max,gmin(i),gmax(i),xmin,xmax,i,i0);
```

In this assertion, i_0 is the value of variable i at first iteration. The value of x at first iteration is in the interval [x0min,x0max], the difference between two successive iterates is in the interval [gmin(i),gmax(i)], which bounds may depend on the iterate, and the value of x is always bounded by [xmin,xmax]. Thus $x(i_0) =$[x0min,x0max], and for all $i \in \{i_0, \ldots, N\}$, we have $x(i) = (x(i-1)+[\text{gmin}(i),\text{gmax}(i)]) \bigcap [\text{xmin},\text{xmax}]$. Our relational domain (subsection 2.1) is specially well adapted to dealing with these relations between iterates in a loop. An example of the use of this assertion is given in the worst-case scenario part of example presented in subsection 3.2.

Subdivisions of inputs. In the example `SqrtR` of subsection 3.1, even with the relational domain, non-linearities of the studied iterative scheme produce too much imprecision, and the solver of the abstract equations does not prove the termination of the analyzed algorithm. A solution to this is to restrict the range of values of the inputs, for which we want to analyze the program, so that we are close enough to linear behaviors. This is done in FLUCTUAT by subdividing the domain of some inputs whose ranges are already bounded by assertions of the type `__BUILTIN_DAED_FBETWEEN`. The user can select one or two such variables to be subdivided by pointing in the program the corresponding assertions.

FLUCTUAT analyzes independently the program as many times as we subdivide some of the inputs. Suppose we subdivide n times an input variable x which has range, defined by an assertion, in $[a, b]$: the analyzer will analyze the program with x in $[a, a + \frac{b-a}{n}]$, then in $[a + \frac{b-a}{n}, a + 2\frac{b-a}{n}]$, ..., $[a + (n-1)\frac{b-a}{n}, b]$. Hence it does not need more memory than needed for one analysis, but takes about n times the duration of one analysis, where n is the number of subdivisions. In the case when we subdivide two such assertions, the subdivisions are completely independent, hence leading to a quadratic factor time increase of the analysis. We chose not to offer the user the possibility to subdivide the values of more than two input variables because it would lead to too slow analyses. This would become reasonable only for parallel versions of FLUCTUAT.

This kind of subdivision cannot be used for an assertion in a loop, because it would be equivalent to choosing at all iterates of the loop the values of x to be in the same sub-interval. Indeed, subdividing independently all iterates would be far too costly, and maybe not either what is really intended by the user. We thus proposed the special assertion `__BUILTIN_DAED_FGRADIENT` for these cases of reactive programs, where inputs are acquired cyclically over time.

3 Experiments on Control Systems

3.1 Hispano-Suiza

The Full Authority Digital Engine Control, better known as a FADEC, is one of the largest electronic control units on an aircraft. It continuously processes and analyzes key engine parameters, to make sure the engine operates at maximum potential. The following test cases for FLUCTUAT are extracted from pieces of code which have been written during the development of reusable libraries, designed for the FADEC. They are representative of the code of the FADEC, and some of them present some hard numerical difficulties for static analyzers.

Experiments on elementary symbols. We examined several elementary symbols used in applications at Hispano-Suiza. Elementary symbols are manually developed and coded independently from SCADE which is used as a design tool. Among these symbols was the following code (slightly changed for convenience), which is intended to return `Output` equal to the square root of `Input` by a Householder method.

```
void SqrtR (double Input)
{    double xn, xnp1, residu, _EPS, Output;
     int i, cond;
     _EPS = 0.000001;
     Input = __BUILTIN_DAED_DOUBLE_WITH_ERROR(0.1,20.0,0,0);
     if (Input <= 1.0)
        xn = 1.0;
     else
        xn = 1.0/Input;
     xnp1 = xn;    residu = 2.0*_EPS*(xn+xnp1);
     i = 0;
     while (fabs(residu) > _EPS * (xn+xnp1))
     {
        xnp1 = xn * (1.875 + Input*xn*xn*(-1.25+0.375*Input*xn*xn));
        residu = 2.0*(xnp1-xn);
        xn = xnp1;
        i++;
     }
     Output = 1.0 / xnp1;
     should_be_zero = Output*Output - Input;
}
```

This involves the iteration, until some residue is less than a small value _EPS=e^{-6}, of a fifth-order polynomial. *The number of iterates for the algorithm to converge is thus not given by the syntax of the program and must be the result of an accurate analysis.* Also, to this short program was added a last computation should_be_zero = Output*Output - Input; that enables a functional proof of the algorithm. Indeed, if variable should_be_zero is proved (both as a real and as a floating-point number) to be close to zero, this proves that the algorithm really computes something that is close to the square root of Input, for all values of Input in the given range [0.1,20].

When Input is in [0.1, 20] as above, FLUCTUAT with 100000 subdivisions converges to a finite and precise estimate of the floating-point value of Output and of the number of iterates of the studied algorithm. Indeed, it finds Output to be in [$3.16e^{-1}, 4.48$] with global error in [$-2.56e^{-13}, 2.56e^{-13}$]. And the number of iterates in the main loop i is found to be within 1 and 6 for the floating-point version of the Householder algorithm. This number of iterates is an exact result, as can be confirmed by using FLUCTUAT in the symbolic execution mode for Input equal to 1 and to 20 respectively (or alternatively, by checking the execution of the real binary file). Also, the analyzer reports an unstable test for the stopping condition of the loop. Indeed, the number of iterations of the Householder algorithm before convergence may be different with the floating-point semantics and with the real semantics! And if we took constant _EPS too small, the algorithm in real numbers would still terminate, while the analyzer would prove that the floating-point algorithm does not always terminate (see

[12] for more details). Note that no other static analyzer we know of is able to find even a good approximation of the floating-point enclosure of Output.

When perturbing the input by an error, for example in the range $[-e^{-8}, e^{-8}]$ and still subdividing 100000 times, we find in 603 seconds and 4Mb of memory on a 1 Ghz laptop PC, the same floating-point enclosure, and a global error in $[-3.06e^{-6}, 3.06e^{-6}]$ which is mainly due to the initial error of the order of e^{-8}. This shows the good behavior of the algorithm. Even though the results on the global error seem satisfying, we hope to be able to improve them a lot with a new relational domain on the error terms, as sketched in [13].

In fact, FLUCTUAT does not need to subdivide equally for all ranges of the input. For instance, with Input restricted to [16,20], it needs only 133 subdivisions to converge. Whereas, with Input restricted to [0.1,1], it needs about 4500 subdivisions. Hence a dynamic subdivision mode is planned for a future version.

Finally, let us consider the fonctional proof of the algorithm: that is, we no longer consider only the relevance of the floating-point implementation compared to the scheme in real number, but also measure the quality of the approximation of the square root by this algorithm. In order to get good results here, we need the fully relational version of Fluctuat which is only partially implemented. We thus considered only a reduced range [16, 20] for Input, so that a fixed number of 6 iterations for the Householder algorithm corresponds to the number of iterations needed to reach the stopping criterion of the loop for this range of Input. We then prove (with subdivisions of Input), that the real value of should_be_zero is in the range $[-4.e^{-15}, 4.e^{-15}]$. This allows us to conclude that the algorithm, for this range of Input, computes in real number a result which is not further from the actual square root than $6.5e^{-8}$. The analyzer also bounds the error between the real and the floating-point value of should_be_zero in $[-5.e^{-14}, 5.e^{-14}]$. Then the approximation of the square root actually computed is not further from the result of the algorithm in real number than $2.5e^{-07}$. In fact, with more subdivisions, we could prove that the real value is even smaller, but the computation time becomes unreasonable for such a small program. However, the computation of the error remains stable when we subdivide the input, which leads us to think that it may be a tight over-approximation of the error.

These results all indicate a good behavior of the algorithm for Input in the range $[0.1, 20]$. However, this function was designed to be used for Input in $[1e^{-50}, 1e^{50}]$. Symbolic execution shows that the algorithm is much less satisfying for this extended range, and may need up to 95 iterations, which is too large for practical use, because of timing constraints. Since then, the algorithm for the square root has been changed.

Representative code. The following test case for FLUCTUAT is extracted from pieces of SCADE code which have been generated during the development of a military engine controller. The control law named asservxn2 is aimed to control the speed of the Low-Pressure Compressor. Therefore, the control loop should be stable inside the whole flight domain, including the fuel flow wf32cb and the motor regime xn2. The code is 2358 lines long in C (44 functions, among which filters, interpolators, integrators), uses complex nested compound

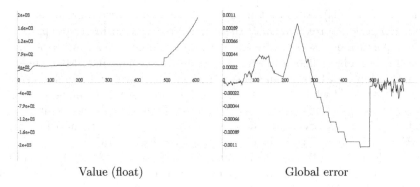

Value (float)	Global error

Fig. 1. Evolution of the fuel flow `wf32cb` for a given target motor regime

structures containing arrays and pointers, and has 167 integer variables and 269 floating-point variables known at the end of the main function (and many more local variables).

We have first used the static analyzer as an abstract interpreter (hence delivering information about precision loss) on the test scenarios that have been used to certify the program. As an example, the first test scenario consists in showing that the rotation regime `xn2` is well controlled by the command on the flow `wf32cb`. FLUCTUAT has been run in symbolic execution mode (i.e. with the semantics described in Section 2.1, but on one control flow only) on the sequence of 2500 consecutive inputs, on a 50 seconds duration. The scenario corresponds to a target low pressure regime shown in Figure 2 for the first 650 inputs. The control program computes the fuel flow necessary to reach this regime, see Figure 1. As shown in the excerpt of the test scenario, the motor regime is well controlled by `wf32cb`: when `wf32cb` increases, `xn2` increases as well until it reaches its target value `xn2cs`, in which case `wf32cb` stabilizes. At iteration 500, the target regime is increased and the control begins. The error in the command `wf32cb` is shown to be always bounded by 10^{-3} in absolute value, which indicates a good (relative) precision of the control algorithm.

Other similar tests have been carried out. We are in the process of studying the code for more general inputs (i.e. for ranges of target motor regimes), in a similar manner as done in next section (using gradient constraints on the inputs). It is to be noted though that the control mechanism uses an integrator, which is known to be hard to analyze, see for instance [12].

3.2   Institut de Radioprotection et Sûreté Nucléaire (IRSN)

Computer systems are increasingly used for safety purposes in nuclear reactors. For example, on the latest French power reactor series, software is used to perform safety functions including critical ones like protection. The Protection System does not control the process but monitors it, by continuously acquiring parameters like water pressure, temperatures in different pipes, neutron flux, and so on. From these inputs, the system computes tens of values using classical

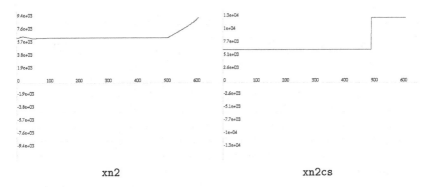

xn2   xn2cs

Fig. 2. Evolution of the motor regime **xn2**, and of its target **xn2cs**

data processing techniques: filters, arithmetic and logic operations, non-linear functions, thresholds. The system then checks that these computed values remain within the authorized domain. If not, it has to automatically shutdown the reactor within half a second, and to trigger safety systems like water injection or spraying, depending on the nature of the incident.

The following test case (mean-square filter), was taken from a representative piece of code that IRSN has to give expertise on, for the French nuclear certification body. Several key process parameters are sampled every 50 milliseconds by the protection system, which stops the reactor if a given threshold is exceeded. Unfortunately, the readings are affected by noise, which could delay a necessary stop or, on the contrary, cause a spurious one. Simply reducing the actual power of the plant below the threshold to provide a noise margin is not adequate for obvious economic reasons. On the other hand a spurious stop is also undesirable because it induces strong promptings to the mechanical structures and prevents the plant to produce electricity for several hours. Thus, a least-square linear regression filter is applied to improve the estimate of the most sensitive parameter. It is important however to make sure that this filtering step does not add too much numerical error due to rounding, we thus used FLUCTUAT to bound the error committed in it, and study the propagation of existing errors.

The filter is adaptive, that means its depth D_k can vary at each cycle k, according to a formula depending on the signal value. The input sample $(i_k)_k$ is in an interval $[1e^2, 1.5e^8]$, and is transformed to give the input of the filter, by $Y_k = \log(ai_k + b)$. In this transformation, only ranges are known for parameters a and b, with nominal values.

Worst-case scenario. We first consider a reduced version of the filter, using the fact that the filter can be written in such a way that outputs are independent, except that the depth of the filter depends on the previous values. It can be shown that, with the parameters used, the depth of the filter is always bounded and the inputs are in the maximum possible range $Y_k \in [8.42, 22.4]$. We thus study a worst-case scenario, that allows us to get bounds for the values and errors on the output that hold true for any step of the filter.

- We first suppose all inputs are independent and can take any value in this range at any step, using assertion Yk = __BUILTIN_DAED_FBETWEEN(8.42,22.4); Then we get with the relational domain, the following enclosures of the filtered value O, and of a value S related to the variation speed:

$$O = [3.912, 26.907] + [-1.91e^{-4}, 1.91e^{-4}]\varepsilon$$
$$S = [-0.350, 0.350] + [-5.37e^{-6}, 5.37e^{-6}]\varepsilon$$

In these two expressions, the first interval bounds the floating-point value, the second one bounds the rounding error, the filter being implemented using single precision floating-point numbers.
- In order to have a more representative model of the inputs, we then used the assertion on the gradient to limit the variation between two successive inputs: we still take the range of inputs equal to $[8.42, 22.4]$, but also bound the difference between two successive inputs by $[0, 0.01]$, by

```
for (int k=1 ; k<=N ; k++)
  Yk = __BUILTIN_DAED_FGRADIENT(8.42,22.4,0,0.01,8.42,22.4,k,1);
```

Then we get, with the relational domain, much tighter enclosures:

$$O = [8.33, 22.5] + [-1.91e^{-4}, 1.91e^{-4}]\varepsilon$$
$$S = [-1.18e^{-5}, 0.01] + [-5.34e^{-6}, 5.34e^{-6}]\varepsilon$$

The error is of the same order as previously, but now the bounds for the value of the output are very close to the input bounds, and we get back the information on the variation speed.

Complete filter. We now want to study more closely the behavior of the output. We choose here a plausible scenario for the inputs, that is a sampling of function $i(x)$ defined by

$$x \leq 0 : i(x) = 1.e^2,$$
$$x > 0 \text{ and } i(x) \leq 1.5e^8 : i(x) = i(0) * 2^{50*x/60}.$$

Interval ranges are given for the coefficients of the transformation, and we add a perturbation to the input of the filter thus obtained. We present in Figures 3 and 4, the results got with FLUCTUAT, for the evolution over time of the bounds on the values and errors on the input Y_k of the filter, and of its output. The error on the input is due partly to the logarithm computation, partly to the addition of a perturbation depending on previous inputs. For the time being, we have parameterized the error due to the logarithm computation, which is not yet specified in the IEEE 754 norm.

The output is approximately in the same range as the input. We represent in Figure 4 right, the evolution of the depth of the filter: the depth at a given time depends on the values of the parameters and does not have one fixed value. The error on the output is overestimated (no relational analysis for errors here), but we can still observe that the error is not too much amplified. We can also note that its variation is related to the variation of the filter depth.

Finally, we can note that the magnitude of the maximum error on the output, is of the same order as the magnitude on the output obtained with the worst-case scenario. This confirms the relevance of the worst-case analysis.

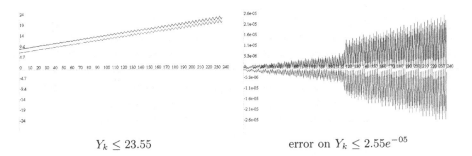

$Y_k \le 23.55$ \qquad\qquad\qquad error on $Y_k \le 2.55e^{-05}$

Fig. 3. Evolution of the filter input over time

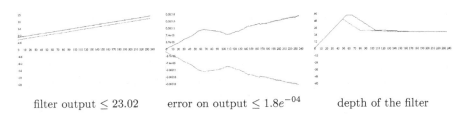

filter output ≤ 23.02 \qquad error on output $\le 1.8e^{-04}$ \qquad depth of the filter

Fig. 4. Evolution of the filter output over time

3.3   Linear Filters

Linear filters are a key element of all control systems. We study in this paragraph the outputs S_i of a second order linear filter:

$$S_i = 0.7E_i - 1.3E_{i-1} + 1.1E_{i-2} + 1.4S_{i-1} - 0.7S_{i-2},$$

where $S_0 = S_1 = 0$ and E_i are independent inputs in the range $[0,1]$. These inputs are thus modelled in our relational domain (see section 2.1 or [14]) by

$$\check{E}_i = \hat{E}_i = \frac{1}{2} + \frac{1}{2}\varepsilon_i,$$

with independent noise symbols $\varepsilon_i \in [-1,1]$. We first consider the output S_i of this filter for a fixed number of unfoldings, e.g. $i = 99$. Fluctuat gives an affine form for the real value of the output S_i

$$\hat{S}_{99} = \check{S}_{99} = 0.83 + 7.81e^{-9}\varepsilon_1 - 2.1e^{-8}\varepsilon_2 - 1.58e^{-8}\varepsilon_3 + \ldots - 0.16\varepsilon_{99} + 0.35\varepsilon_{100};$$

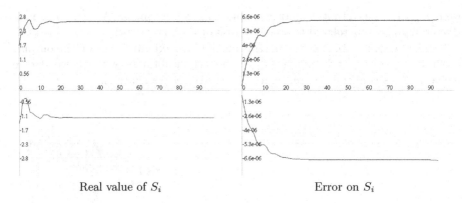

Real value of S_i Error on S_i

Fig. 5. Concretization of S_i for i between 1 and 100

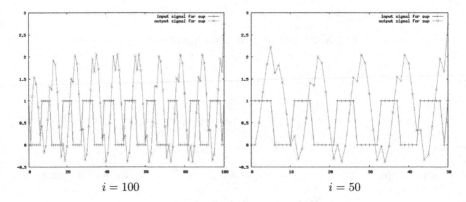

$i = 100$ $i = 50$

Fig. 6. Input sequence that maximizes S_i, and Output sequence, for $i = 100$ and $i = 50$

whose concretization gives an exact (under the assumption that the coefficients are computed exactly) enclosure $S_{99} \in [-1.0907188500, 2.7573854753]$. The enclosures of the value of successive S_i for i lower or equal to 100 are represented figure 5 (left graph). We also represent on the same figure (right graph) the error on the outputs computed with our new relational domain for the errors, also relying on affine arithmetic.

The coefficients of the affine form allow us to deduce the sequence of inputs E_i leading to the max (or min) of the enclosure of the value of S_{99}: take $E_i = 1$ if the corresponding coefficient multiplying ε_{i+1} is positive, $E_i = -1$ otherwise. For example, the input sequence E_i that maximizes S_{100} is represented figure 6 (left graph), together with the outputs S_i, for i between 1 and 100. These sequences, even for such a simple filter, would not be easy to find manually. The input sequence that maximizes S_{50} is represented figure 6 (right graph). This input sequence is fairly different from the first 50 inputs of the input sequence maximizing S_{100}: indeed, the successive maximum values of the S_i are not reached for the same sequence of inputs.

Note that the exact enclosure of the filter actually converges towards $S_\infty = [-1.09071884989..., 2.75738551656...]$, and therefore the signal leading to the maximal value of S_{99} is a very good estimate of the signal leading to the maximal value of S_i, for any $i \geq 99$.

All this generalizes to linear recursive filters of any order, and can be partly extended to the case of non linear filters (see [15]). The next question to be considered is to find input sequences that maximize the error on the output instead of the value. This is left for future work.

4   Conclusion and Future Work

We have shown in this paper how we designed a static analyzer for bounding the imprecision error in numerical programs. This design relied on a careful study of the semantics of the IEEE754 standard, of numerical convergence of the kind of iterative schemes we encountered in control systems, and of specificities of the programming of these systems (SCADE generated code in general). Some real industrial examples were given, which were simple enough to explain in a few pages. The analyzer has already been used (on a low-end PC with 512Mb of memory) for code of the order of 10 thousand lines of C code, and seems to scale up well.

In the future, we plan to invest more on domains dealing precisely with integrators, which make precision analysis hard to carry out, see [12] for example. We also plan to experiment with relational domains for error computations as briefly sketched in [13,16]. We also would like to improve the precision of the least fixed point computation of the abstract equations in our tool, using policy iteration mechanisms, see [6,8]. Last but not least, our abstract domain can be adapted to under-approximations as well, see [15]. A combination of under- and over-approximations will indeed allow us to assess the quality of the results, and give some indications in some cases that the control system under analysis is definitely not implemented in a sufficiently accurate way.

References

1. Blanchet, B., Cousot, P., Cousot, R., Feret, J., Mauborgne, L., Miné, A., Monniaux, D., Rival, X.: Design and Implementation of a Special-Purpose Static Program Analyzer for Safety-Critical Real-Time Embedded Software. In: Mogensen, T.Æ., Schmidt, D.A., Sudborough, I.H. (eds.) The Essence of Computation. LNCS, vol. 2566. Springer, Heidelberg (2002)
2. Blanchet, B., Cousot, P., Cousot, R., Feret, J., Mauborgne, L., Miné, A., Monniaux, D., Rival, X.: A Static Analyzer for Large Safety-Critical Software. In: Proc. PLDI 2003 (2003)
3. Bourdoncle, F.: Abstract Interpretation by dynamic partitioning. Journal of Functional Programming 2(4), 407–435 (1992)
4. Bourdoncle, F.: Efficient chaotic iteration strategies with widenings. In: Pottosin, I.V., Bjorner, D., Broy, M. (eds.) FMP&TA 1993. LNCS, vol. 735. Springer, Heidelberg (1993)

5. Comba, J.L.D., Stolfi, J.: Affine arithmetic and its applications to computer graphics. In: SIBGRAPI 1993 (1993)
6. Costan, A., Gaubert, S., Goubault, E., Martel, M., Putot, S.: A policy iteration algorithm for computing fixed points in static analysis of programs. In: Etessami, K., Rajamani, S.K. (eds.) CAV 2005. LNCS, vol. 3576. Springer, Heidelberg (2005)
7. Cousot, P., Cousot, R.: Abstract interpretation frameworks. Journal of Logic and Symbolic Computation 2(4), 511–547 (1992)
8. Gaubert, S., Goubault, E., Taly, A., Zennou, S.: Static Analysis by Policy Interation on Relational Domains. In: De Nicola, R. (ed.) ESOP 2007. LNCS, vol. 4421. Springer, Heidelberg (2007)
9. Goubault, E., Guilbaud, D., Pacalet, A., Starynkévitch, B., Védrine, F.: A Simple Abstract Interpreter for Threat Detection and Test Case Generation. In: WAPATV 2001 (2001)
10. Goubault, E.: Static analyses of the precision of floating-point operations. In: Cousot, P. (ed.) SAS 2001. LNCS, vol. 2126. Springer, Heidelberg (2001)
11. Goubault, E., Martel, M., Putot, S.: Asserting the precision of floating-point computations: a simple abstract interpreter. In: Le Métayer, D. (ed.) ESOP 2002 and ETAPS 2002. LNCS, vol. 2305. Springer, Heidelberg (2002)
12. Goubault, E., Martel, M., Putot, S.: Some future challenges in the validation of control systems. In: Proceedings of ERTS 2006 (2006)
13. Goubault, E., Putot, S.: Weakly Relational Domains for Floating-Point Computation Analysis. In: NSAD 2005 (2005)
14. Goubault, E., Putot, S.: Static Analysis of Numerical Algorithms. In: Yi, K. (ed.) SAS 2006. LNCS, vol. 4134. Springer, Heidelberg (2006)
15. Goubault, E., Putot, S.: Under-approximations of computations in real numbers based on generalized affine arithmetic. In: Riis Nielson, H., Filé, G. (eds.) SAS 2007. LNCS, vol. 4634. Springer, Heidelberg (2007)
16. Goubault, E., Putot, S.: Automatic analysis of imprecision errors in software (2007), http://www.di.ens.fr/~goubault/papers/abstract.pdf
17. Jones, N.D., Muchnick, S.S.: A flexible approach to interprocedural flow analysis and programs with recursive data structures. In: POPL 1982 (1982)
18. Landi, W., Ryder, B.: A safe approximate algorithm for inter-procedural pointer aliasing. In: Proceedings of PLDI. ACM, New York (1992)
19. Martel, M.: Propagation of roundoff errors in finite precision computations: a semantics approach. In: Le Métayer, D. (ed.) ESOP 2002 and ETAPS 2002. LNCS, vol. 2305. Springer, Heidelberg (2002)
20. Miné, A.: Relational Abstract Domains for the Detection of Floating-Point Run-Time Errors. In: Schmidt, D. (ed.) ESOP 2004. LNCS, vol. 2986. Springer, Heidelberg (2004)
21. Putot, S., Goubault, E., Martel, M.: Static Analysis-Based Validation of Floating-Point Computations. In: Alt, R., Frommer, A., Kearfott, R.B., Luther, W. (eds.) Numerical Software with Result Verification. LNCS, vol. 2991. Springer, Heidelberg (2004)
22. Stolfi, J., de Figueiredo, L.H.: An introduction to affine arithmetic. TEMA Tend. Mat. Apl. Comput. 4(3), 297–312 (2003)
23. Goubault, E., Putot, S.: Fluctuat user manual (2007) (available upon request)
24. Grammatech Inc. CodeSonar, overview, http://www.grammatech.com/products/codesonar/overview.html
25. PolySpace Technologies. PolySpace for hand-written code, http://www.polyspace.fr/products.htm
26. LIP6. The CADNA Library, http://www-anp.lip6.fr/cadna/Accueil.php

Application of Static Analyses for State Space Reduction to Microcontroller Assembly Code

Bastian Schlich, Jann Löll, and Stefan Kowalewski

Embedded Software Laboratory, RWTH Aachen University,
Ahornstr. 55, 52074 Aachen, Germany
{schlich,loell,kowalewski}@cs.rwth-aachen.de
http://www-i11.informatik.rwth-aachen.de/

Abstract. This paper describes how static analyses can be applied to microcontroller assembly code to tackle the state explosion problem arising from explicit state model checking. It presents difficulties, which occur when trying to apply static analyses to microcontroller assembly code, caused by, for example, interrupts, hardware dependency, recursions, and indirect control. Enhancements of two reduction techniques (namely Dead Variable Reduction and Path Reduction) and their underlying static analyses are detailed, which make these techniques applicable to microcontroller assembly code. A short case study is presented in which five programs are used to demonstrate the state space reductions that can be achieved using these two techniques.

1 Introduction

Microcontrollers are often used in safety-critical systems. Extensive testing of such applications is not always possible due to fast time to market, uncertain environments, etc. Model checking has been recognized by industry as a promising tool for the analysis of such systems. First, proprietary models were created by hand for model checking. Then, model checking of source code (C, C++, Java, etc.) became more and more popular. Currently, model checking of assembly code (machine code) [1, 2, 3, 4, 5] is getting into focus of research.

Model checking assembly code has quite some advantages. Assembly code is the code that is later on deployed to the hardware. It is no longer an intermediate representation as, for example, C code. Hence, all errors can be found which are introduced during the complete development process, including errors in the compiler, errors that are not visible in the intermediate representation (e.g., reentrance problems), and errors in the usage of hardware features. The model checker does not have to account the behavior of the compiler used. Furthermore, all assembly constructs have a clean and well documented semantics and are easier to handle than, for instance, some C constructs (dynamic memory allocation and pointer arithmetic). Moreover, the source code of the program is not needed, and complete applications including external libraries can be checked.

Nevertheless, model checking of assembly code has two disadvantages that have to be handled. First, it adds hardware dependency to the analysis, that

S. Leue and P. Merino (Eds.): FMICS 2007, LNCS 4916, pp. 21–37, 2008.

means, the analysis has to be adapted for every new microcontroller. Second, the state spaces tend to be bigger than when model checking intermediate representations as more details are involved. To use model checking of assembly code effectively, these two disadvantages have to be tackled.

We developed an explicit state, on-the-fly, Computation Tree Logic (CTL) [6] model checker called *[mc]square*[1], which is able to model check assembly code for certain microcontrollers (ATMEL ATmega16, 32, etc. and Infineon XC 167). To ease the disadvantage of hardware dependency, an architecture was implemented in *[mc]square* that could easily be extended to other microcontrollers [7].

In this paper, it is described how the problem of bigger state spaces is concerned. Two reduction techniques are used to address the state explosion problem (Dead Variable Reduction and Path Reduction). Both were used in other model checkers before (see Sect. 7), but they could not be transferred one-to-one to *[mc]square* as the assembly language contains constructs making the use of an intraprocedural static analysis approach infeasible (e.g., indirect data accesses, indirect control, recursions, communication via global variables). Dead Variable Reduction applied in *[mc]square* uses an Interprocedural Live Variable Analysis, which is combined with a stack analysis and an analysis determining the status of the global interrupt flag, both using the method of abstract interpretation. Without these, Dead Variable Reduction would not work for the assembly code used. Path Reduction is not conducted completely statically because some constructs found in assembly code need to be handled dynamically during state-space creation (e.g., indirect jumps and nondeterminism). Hence, some analyses are done statically before model checking, and others are done dynamically during model checking.

This paper is structured as follows. First, a short introduction to *[mc]square* is given and some basics are explained. Next, the problems at hand are described in detail. Then, the two reduction techniques are introduced in depth. Subsequently, a small case study demonstrating the reduction effect of Dead Variable Reduction and Path Reduction is presented. In the end, a conclusion is drawn, and future work is presented.

2   Introduction to *[mc]square*

[mc]square is a discrete, explicit state, CTL model checker used to verify assembly programs for specific microcontrollers. It takes as input a file in Executable and Linking Format (ELF) (the program) and a formula given in CTL (the specification). Beside model checking, the tool also checks hardware specific properties as maximum stack size, occurrence of stack collisions, and undesired use of hardware features (e.g., write to reserved registers). Counterexamples and witnesses are shown in the assembly code, in the C code (if the C file was provided), as a state space graph, and in the Control Flow Graph (CFG) of the assembly code. In this section only a short introduction to *[mc]square* is given

---

[1] http://www-ill.informatik.rwth-aachen.de/mc_square.html

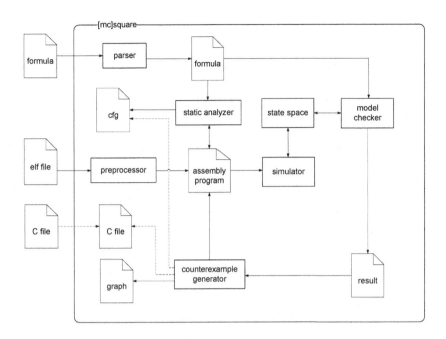

Fig. 1. Process used in *[mc]square*

as this paper concentrates on static analyses used in this tool. More details can be found in [3, 7, 8].

The process used in *[mc]square* is shown in Fig. 1. First, the user has to provide the property he wants to check encoded as a CTL formula. This formula is translated into a formula object, which is used by the static analyzer and the model checker component. Furthermore, the user has to provide the program as an ELF file. ELF is a hardware independent standard for binary files used by most compilers. If the C code file of the program is available, the user can optionally provide this file as it can be used by *[mc]square* to present counterexamples and witnesses.

Next, the elf file is transformed into human-readable assembly code, and the static analyzer starts working on this assembly code. During the analysis, information from the formula object are used (atomic propositions) to preserve the validity of the annotations applied to the assembly code. These annotations are used during state space creation to minimize the state space. Furthermore, the CFG of the assembly code, used to show counterexamples and witnesses, is created by the static analyzer. Details of the static analyzer are described in Sect. 3, 4 and 5.

The state space is built on-the-fly during model checking. States are only created when they are needed by the model checker component. Building of the state space (encoded as a Kripke structure) is done by the simulator component. The simulator is not an ordinary simulator. It natively supports nondeterminism (caused by timers and input from the environment) and builds an over-approximation of the real state space to limit the problem of state explosion and to preserve the validity of the model-checking result.

Whenever the state space requires successors of a state, it uses the simulator to create these successors. To do so, it gives the state to the simulator, and then the simulator creates all possible successors of this state (over-approximation) and returns them. A state may have several successors due to possible occurrences of interrupts, input from the environment, or expiration of timers. For example, executing an add instruction usually creates just one successor. If in a state in which an add instruction is executed one interrupt is active, this state already has two successors. In one successor the interrupt handler is entered (interrupt occurred), and in the other successor the add instruction is executed (interrupt did not occur). Another example is an instruction reading input from the environment by means of an Input/Output (I/O) port. If the complete port is used for input (controlled by other registers), this state has 256 successors because an I/O port used in an ATmega16 is 8 bit wide, and hence, 256 different values can be read from the environment through this port.

A state in *[mc]square* consists of the complete SRAM including all registers, I/O registers, variables, etc. and some additional fields required by the model checker (e.g., fields for formula values, list of successors, and fields needed for state-space creation which are not part of the SRAM). In case of the ATmega16 a state has up to 2 KB of data. Therefore, it is important to create as few states as possible (still preserving a safe over-approximation) and to use every technique available that helps to save memory (e.g., lossless compressions, hard disk model checking).

To minimize the problem of state explosion, the simulator uses different abstraction techniques during the creation of the state space(e.g., lazy stack evaluation, lazy interrupt evaluation, path reduction, dead variable reduction). All these options lead to the creation of fewer states. Some create an over-approximation, while others omit the creation of states which are not possible or irrelevant (still preserving a safe over-approximation). In case the over-approximation is too coarse to show the given property, the user can deactivate some options to create a finer over-approximation of the state space. This causes the state space to grow, but it also makes the state space more accurate and therefore, rules out paths which are infeasible in the real system. In case all options are deactivated, the simulator behaves as the real hardware except that the simulator abstracts from real-time as considering time would lead to real-time model checking (see [9]), which would significantly increase the size of the state spaces. Certain options are activated and deactivated automatically by *[mc]square* depending on the properties checked and the algorithm used.

Another feature that helps to minimize the number of states is the hardware dependency of the simulator. For instance, the simulator can exclude occurrences of interrupts and expiration of timers whenever interrupts and accordingly timers are deactivated. A general purpose model checker could not do this because it does not know the underlying hardware.

Model checking works as follows. The model checker gets the initial state from the state-space component and begins to check particular parts of the provided formula in this state. Depending on the structure of the formula and the result of this check, it requests successors of the current state from the state space. If these states were not yet created, the state space uses the simulator to build the successors as described above. Then, model checking continues using the successor states. This process continues until a goal state (proving or disproving the truth of the formula) is reached or the complete state space is build, and hence, the formula can be evaluated completely. The on-the-fly, CTL model checking algorithm implemented in *[mc]square* is taken from [10]. A first version of this algorithm was presented in [11].

After model checking is finished, the counterexample generator takes the result and builds a counterexample or a witness depending on the formula and the outcome of the model-checking process. Then, it presents the counterexample/witness in the assembly code, in the C code (if it was provided), as a state space graph, or in the CFG of the assembly code. In all these representations the user can step forward and backward through the traces and follow the evaluation of the different values of, for example, registers and variables. Thereby, it is easier for the user to understand the result of the model checking process and to locate possible errors.

3   Challenges Applying Static Analysis to Assembly Code

This section describes the challenges that arise when applying Dead variable Reduction (DVR) and Path Reduction (PR) to assembly programs checked by *[mc]square*. Both reduction techniques were already implemented in other model checkers (see Sect. 7) using intraprocedural static analyses. The techniques used could not be transferred one-to-one to *[mc]square* because the assembly code checked with *[mc]square* contains features that cannot be handled using intraprocedural static analyses. Other model checkers obtained the information for both reduction techniques entirely statically. Again, this is not possible in *[mc]square* because of some constructs present in the assembly code. During all analyses hardware specific details (interrupts, condition of special registers as the status register and the stack pointer, etc.) have to be taken into account.

In the assembly language used, functions are not explicitly declared in header files. Every location of an assembly program can be reached via a `call` statement. All program fragments reachable by a `call` are defined to be functions. As recursions are used in the assembly programs at hand, functions could not be handled by inlining or bounded call-strings. Handling functions by assuming that they change all variables is also not appropriate as this over-approximation would be too coarse to obtain usable results. Additionally, all memory locations (e.g., registers, I/O registers, and variables) in the assembly language are globally accessible at every program location. Hence, interprocedural analyses have to be used to preserve soundness of the results obtained.

The assembly language does not contain parallel processes, but it contains interrupts. Interrupts can intercept the main process at any point whenever they are activated. The main process can only be continued when control is returned from the interrupt handler. Thereby, interrupts can communicate at every program location with the main process and can change all memory locations. This makes data flow analysis even more difficult (see Sect. 4). Interrupts are handled the same way as functions are handled, but special analyses are applied in DVR to obtain a more accurate set of locations where occurrences of interrupts are possible.

Furthermore, the assembly code contains indirect loads and stores. Currently, these are addressed by an over-approximation assuming that at the corresponding location all variables are accessed. In the future, this should be improved by an abstract interpretation collecting all possible values of pointers. Presence of indirect control halts the analyses used for DVR as the Live Variable Analysis cannot deliver reliable results using an incomplete CFG. In the future, an abstract interpretation should be used to gather all possible targets of the indirect control statements. The analyses utilized for PR can handle indirect control. However, indirect control is not often present in the assembly code used as only some library functions add indirect control to the assembly code. In the following two sections, DVR and PR are detailed.

4   Dead Variable Reduction

Dead Variable Reduction copes with the state-explosion problem by reducing the number of states generated during state-space construction. If two states differ only in the value of a dead variable, i.e. the variable is not in the set of live variables, then both can be seen as equivalent and can be joined into one state. In [mc]square 0 is assigned to a variable when it becomes dead. Hence, states that differ only in the value of a dead variable will be merged. To preserve the validity of the model-checking results, variables used within the formula (specification) are not reset.

For the Dead Variable Reduction a Live Variable Analysis (LVA), which is a static data flow analysis, is needed to compute the set of live variables. As defined in [12], a variable v is alive at the exit of a program location l if there exists a path π from l to a location l' where v is used, and if π does not contain a location l'' where v is re-defined. The LVA determines via a worklist algorithm for each program location the set of variables that may be alive at the exit of that location [12]. The worklist algorithm presented in [12] computes the Maximal Fix Point Solution of the data-flow equation.

After the sets of live variables are determined, for each location the set D of dying variables has to be identified. This is done by successively comparing the sets of live variables of two consecutive program locations l and l'. The variables that are alive at l and are no longer alive at l', die at l. After that, the variables contained within the formula have to be removed from each set

```
                                    0x23: in R1 SREG
0x23: PUSH R1                       0x24: PUSH R1
0x24: in R1 PORTA                   ...
0x25: out PORTB R1                  0x3c: POP R1
0x26: POP R1                        0x3d: out SREG R1
```

Fig. 2. Use of a working register   **Fig. 3.** Restoring the value of SREG

D. Then, every program location is annotated with its corresponding set D indicating the variables which can be reset by the simulator.

The application of LVA to microcontroller assembly code programs involves some problems, which are not captured by the standard approaches. In the following subsections, three distinct problems arising when analyzing microcontroller assembly-code and their solutions are described in detail.

4.1 Stack Analysis

In assembly code the stack is used to temporary save the contents of working registers used within a function. In the beginning, the contents of these registers are put onto the stack, and in the end of the function, the contents of these registers are taken back from stack and written into the corresponding registers. Hence, for the data-flow analysis it looks as if this function reads and writes these registers, although this function does not use the values of these registers.

The stack analysis is used to check two things. First, it is used to check which registers are really read within a function. This check supports the data-flow analysis to, for example, identify working registers. Second, it checks whether the respective values are written into their corresponding registers at the end of the function (e.g., the value of R1 is written back to R1). This second check is, for instance, used during the analysis of the global interrupt flag to find out, whether the global interrupt flag is changed by a function or not, that is, the corresponding function does or does not activate interrupts (see Sect. 4.2).

Due to the dynamic nature of stacks, the size and contents of the stack at a specific program location can only be determined during run-time. In Fig. 2 an example is shown which demonstrates the use of working registers. Register R1 is only used as a temporary variable, and in the end of this function it contains the same value as in the beginning of this function. A standard, static data flow analysis cannot recognize this.

To solve this problem, and hence, to get a more accurate data-flow analysis, an abstract interpretation is used to determine for each program location the set of possible stack configurations. The abstract interpretation observes all accesses to the stack (push, pop, change of stack pointer, and write accesses into the memory area of the stack) and determines if at the end of the function the original values of the working registers are restored. If the stack analysis fails due to an infinite number of possible stack configurations (e.g., caused by loops), manual change of the stack pointer, etc., it has to be assumed that this function changes the contents of all working registers used within this function.

In the example shown in Fig 2 the stack analysis correctly recognizes that at location 0x26: POP R1 the original value of R1 is restored.

4.2 Global Interrupt Flag

The global interrupt flag (bit within the SREG register) defines whether all interrupts are activated or not. Without an analysis that determines the value of the global interrupt flag, it has to be assumed that interrupts are active at every program location. If an interrupt handler reads a certain register and is active at any program location, this register can never be reset by the DVR. To get more precise results, an abstract interpretation is applied that determines the status of the global interrupt flag for each program location. This abstract interpretation observes all accesses to the SREG register done via calls to cli() and sei() and direct/indirect write accesses. Whenever the analysis fails to show that interrupts are deactivated, it is assumed that they are activated (safe over-approximation).

Without the stack analysis described in Sect. 4.1, this analysis would not be as accurate as it is because the current status of the SREG is saved onto the stack in the beginning and restored at the end of every interrupt handler and some functions. Hence, these functions would activate interrupts because a standard, static data-flow analysis would not know the value that is written into the SREG at the end of the function.

The example shown in Fig. 3 demonstrates how this analysis benefits from the stack analysis. Here, the stack analysis can assure that 0x3c: POP R1 restores the value of R1 saved at 0x24: PUSH R1, and hence, that the original value of the SREG is restored. If the stack analysis would fail, 0x3d: out SREG R1 would activate interrupts.

4.3 Interprocedural Live Variable Analysis

The data-flow equation for LVA can be solved intraprocedural by the worklist algorithm described in [12]. Due to the presence of function calls (and interrupts) in the assembly code, this intraprocedural approach has to be enhanced to deal with function calls. As explained before, the standard approaches to do this (inlining, call-strings, and assuming that all variables are manipulated by a function) are not appropriate.

As described before, functions are all program fragments which can be reached via call statements. Additionally, interrupts are also handled like functions. In the assembly language used, functions do not have formal parameter values. Communication with functions is done via global variables, registers (globally accessible), the stack, or indirect loads and stores from and to a memory area indicated by a pointer. The latter case is seldom used and leads to an over-approximation in this approach as indirect loads/stores access all memory locations. Most common case is the usage of global variables and registers.

To handle functions (including interrupt handlers), a static behavior is defined for them (context insensitive). The behavior of a function regarding the LVA is a set containing all memory locations (e.g., global variables and registers) that the function reads. The behavior of a function regarding a Reaching Definitions Analysis is a set of memory locations that are written by the function. In the worst case, this approach leads to an over-approximation of the behavior of a function assuming that all memory locations are accessed, but in most cases, just a few memory locations are accessed. This analysis benefits from both analyses described before because without theses analyses the results obtained during the LVA would be too inaccurate to be used for DVR.

The LVA algorithm works as follows. In the first step every function (including main and interrupt handlers) is analyzed alone and call instructions (including occurrence of interrupts) within a function are ignored. The result of this step is for every function the set of memory locations read by the function. This set is called the initial behavior of a function. In this step, the results obtained from the stack analysis are used to accurately determine the memory locations read by the function.

In the next step, calls are analyzed. If a function f calls a function p, the behavior of function p is added to the behavior of the call site within function f. This may change the behavior of function f. If the behavior of f is changed, all functions which call f are analyzed again (propagate behavior). This is done until a fixed point is reached. During this step, results obtained from the global interrupt flag analysis are used to properly identify program locations where interrupts can occur. At all these locations, interrupts are handled as calls to the corresponding interrupt handler (behavior is added at these locations).

In the last step, the set of variables alive at the call location of a function p are given to p to set them alive for complete p. This is needed as these variables have to be alive after p is handled. The behavior of the function is not changed as the variables added are not read by the function. The result of this analysis is for each program location a set of variables alive at that location.

5   Path Reduction

Path Reduction (PR) was described by Yorav and Grumberg in [13]. Is is used to compress single successor paths (computational paths which consist of states having only single successors) into a single step (only the first and the last state of this path are stored) to reduce memory consumption. The disadvantage of this method is that it only preserves CTL*-X, i.e. validity of the neXt operator (X) is not preserved.

First, program locations which satisfy certain conditions are determined by means of a static analysis. These program locations are called Breaking Points (BP) in [13]. Then, during state-space creation, only states that are generated from breaking locations are stored. In [13] all breaking points could be identified statically. In /mc/square some of these breaking points have to be determined dynamically during state space creation due to, for example, indirect control, indirect data accesses, and nondeterminism. Details are given in the following.

Yorav and Grumberg defined the following locations l to be breaking:

1. l is the initial or terminating program location,
2. l is associated with the program location of an assignment that changes a variable used within the formula,
3. l i associated with the program location of a non-deterministic assignment,
4. l is the head of a "while" statement,
5. l is labeled by a procedure call, or is the statement immediately following a procedure call,
6. l is labeled by a communication statement (**send** or **receive**), or is the statement following a communication.

The first and the second condition can be check statically in *[mc]square*, too. The third condition cannot be checked statically in *[mc]square* because non-determinism is not indicated by certain statements in the assembly language. Different memory location can introduce nondeterminism and are accessed via diverse statements. A memory location can change back and forth between non-deterministic and deterministic behavior (e.g., input port is switched to output or a timer is deactivated). Hence, a static analysis would over-approximate too much. Therefore, the third condition is checked dynamically during state space creation in *[mc]square* (every state having more than one successor is stored).

The fourth condition needs some special treatment because in the assembly language used there exists no while statement. This condition is needed to guarantee termination during state-space building. If there is a loop consisting only of single successors, it would not be possible without this condition to detect revisits, and hence, the state-space creation would not terminate. To avoid this, one location of each loop has to be breaking. In *[mc]square* all locations are defined to be breaking that have more than one predecessor in the CFG. A location has more than one successor in the CFG if it is the target of a jump or branch instruction. Most of these targets can be found by a static analysis. Only the targets of indirect jumps cannot be found during static analysis, and thus, *[mc]square* identifies them dynamically during state-space creation. Thus, in every loop there is at least one location that is breaking. As not every of these target locations is part of a loop, some locations are unnecessarily breaking (over-approximation), but the runtime overhead needed to detect only real loops would be considerably higher.

The fifth condition is checked completely statically in *[mc]square*. All locations containing a call or indirect call statement and the succeeding locations are marked to be breaking.

The last condition is not directly applicable to the assembly language used. The assembly language does not contain parallel processes, but it contains interrupts which show a similar behavior (described in Sect. 3). There are no communication statements which control the communication between the main process and the interrupt handlers. Whenever an interrupt is active, it can communicate with the main process. To represent this behavior in this analysis, each location where interrupts may occur has to be breaking. There are two differences to the handling of call statements: The succeeding location is not made blocking because interrupts return to the location where they occurred, and locations where interrupts may occur are marked during run-time. This sounds as PR would not bring too much benefit, but interrupts are only active within parts of the program and inactive during most interrupt handlers. That is, interrupt handlers are long, single successor paths which are particularly addressed by PR. This is shown in the next section.

6   Case Study

In this section, a case study is described, which uses five different programs to show the effect Dead Variable Reduction and Path Reduction have on the size of state spaces. It was conducted on a Server equipped with an AMD Opteron processor with 1.8 GHz, 16 GB main memory, and a hard disk with a capacity of 120 GB. As *[mc]square* is completely written in Java, it can be used with any operating system.

During this case study, all other options/optimizations were turned off in order to interpret the results without any side-effects between different options.

The five programs chosen for this case study were all written by students in lab courses, during diploma theses, or in exercises. None of these programs was written to be model checked afterwards. These programs were really used on the ATMEL ATmega16 microcontroller. The results of the case study are shown in Tab. 1. The first line shows the results for every program without applying static analysis. The second and the third line show the results using Dead Variable Reduction and Path Reduction respectively. The last line demonstrates the result when applying both analyses. The column *states stored* reflects the number of states that are stored in the state space. The column *states created* presents the number of states that are created during model checking including revisits. The column *size of state space* shows the size of the hash table representing the state space in memory. The last column shows the complete time needed for applying static analysis, building state space, and doing model checking.

The first program called *light switch* is a simple program utilized to demonstrate basic microcontroller functions. It consists of 72 lines of C code (162 lines of assembly code), uses two timers, but does not use interrupts. In this program DVR lowers the number of states stored by 11.57%. PR lowers the number of states stored by 70.65%, but it increases the number of states created by 101.28%. This happens because of long single successor chains of which only the last state is stored. To recognize revisits, the complete chain has to be visited again. For this small example this has no effect on runtime. Using both analyses together, leads to 77.29% less states stored than when using no analysis. The savings of both analyses do not add up completely, but the combination has a noticeable effect. The savings in number of states stored directly carry over to savings in size of the state space in main memory.

Table 1. Comparing effect of DVR and PR using five different programs

Program	Analysis used	# states stored	# states created	State space size[MB]	Time needed[s]
light switch	none	7,367	10,608	2.27	0.531
	DVR	6,515	9,635	2.01	0.422
	PR	2,162	21,352	0.70	0.438
	both	1,673	19,764	0.56	0.688
plant	none	801,616	854,203	184.55	49
	DVR	801,616	854,203	184.55	49
	PR	54,788	1,297,080	12.85	49
	both	54,788	1,297,080	12.85	49
reentrance problem	none	107,649	110,961	23.45	7.25
	DVR	107,649	110,961	23.45	7.90
	PR	6,631	122,999	1.43	4.86
	both	6,631	122,999	1.43	5.00
traffic light	none	35,522	38,110	8.52	2.21
	DVR	35,522	38,110	8.52	2.56
	PR	2,873	55,083	0.72	2.33
	both	2,873	55,083	0.72	2.53
window lift	none	10,100,400	11,196,174	2,049	379
	DVR	2,341,728	2,754,314	725.89	74
	PR	520,331	18,444,220	161.88	332
	both	119,331	5,123,942	44.49	93

The next program called *plant* controls a fictive chemical plant. It consists of 73 lines of C code (225 lines of assembly code), uses one timer and two interrupts. DVR has no effect in this program because the same variables are used throughout the hole program including the interrupt handlers. Therefore, this program has no location where a variable becomes dead, and hence, DVR cannot save anything. PR lowers the number of states stored by 93.17% and increases the number of states created by 51.85%. It means that either the number of revisits is smaller compared to the light switch program or the length of single successor chains is shorter. As the savings in number of states created directly carry over to savings in size of the state space in memory, a significant decrease in memory usage can be observed. It drops from 185 MB to 13 MB.

The program called *reentrance problem* is used to demonstrate the reentrance problem. A variable i is accesses both in the main process and in the interrupt leading to invalid values of i. It is a very small program consisting of only 37 lines of C code (148 lines of assembly code) and it uses one interrupt. As in the previous described program, DVR has no influence due to the same causes. Again, PR has a significant influence and stints 93.84% of the states stored. The number of states created is only increased by 10.85% due to fewer revisits and shorter single successor chains as in the other programs.

Traffic light is a program written by students in a lab course. As the name says, it is used to control the operation of a traffic light. It comprises of 85 lines of C code (155 lines of assembly code) and uses two interrupts and one timer.

Once again, DVR has no effect. PR shows the same performance as before with a slightly lower increase in number of states created than observed in the *plant* program.

The last program called *window lift* was inspired by a real automotive task. A controller for a power window lift used in a car was implemented. The program we chose for this case study contains 115 lines of C code (289 lines of assembly code) and uses three interrupts and two timers. DVR already has a noticeable effect in this program as 76.82% states less have to be stored. Also, the time used drops from 379 seconds to just 74 seconds. In the combination of both analyses only 119,331 states have to be stored but 5,123,942 states have to be created. This is due to many revisits and long single successors chains. Time needed does not drop significantly due to the high number of revists. Comparing the case PR only and the case where both reduction techniques are used shows that DVR does not significantly reduce the number of states stored, but it lowers the number of states created, and hence, helps to lower the time needed.

Summarizing, it can be seen that PR reduces the number of states stored drastically in every case. In some cases (e.g., *window lift* and *plant*) time needed does not drop due to repeated revisits. It is a trade-off between time and space. As space is our main difficulty, from our point of view this analysis should be used whenever possible. Since we do not use the X operator in our specifications, the loss of validity of the X operator (see [13]) is not a problem for us.

The result of DVR is not that clear. In some examples it helped to save space and to decrease time (due to less states created), but whenever there is a tight coupling between data variables across functions and/or interrupt handlers, this option does not have an effect. Another problem is that variables which are part of the formula cannot be reduced. If there is a formula involving many variables, the effect of DVR is decreased even more. This analysis should always be used because it can only have a positive effect or no effect. A negative effect is not possible.

Both reduction techniques can be always used in combination because the combination yields the same or even better results than the application of one of the techniques alone.

The other options/optimizations applied in *[mc]square* often help to, for example, ease the effect that was observed in *window lift* or *plant* (increase in number of states created) applying PR. Nevertheless, they were not used in this case study because the combination of all methods makes it difficult to examine the effect of a new analysis.

7   Related Work

As this paper concentrates on the static analysis that is implemented in *[mc]-square*, only related work regarding the static analysis is presented. Details of related work regarding model checking can be found in [3, 7, 8].

In [13] DVR and PR were described for a parallel version of the *while* language and implemented for the model-checking tool *Murphi*. The language used in

Murphi is comparable to the parallel *while* language. In the language used, every process has its own local variables, global variables do not exist. Communication is done at fixed program locations by means of send and receive statements. For DVR, function calls are handled by inlining the body of the method at each call location. Hence, the static analysis used can be done intraprocedural. The so-called breaking points (see Sect. 5) used for PR can be determined completely statically. The language used does not contain indirect control.

In his master's thesis [14] Mr. Quiros adapted the approach described in [13] to a bytecode language used in a specific virtual machine. This bytecode language is similar to the parallel *while* language as it has no indirect control and the communication between processes is conducted at fixed program locations. The only important difference for static analysis is that the bytecode language has local and global variables, but they are easily distinguishable as different instructions are used to access global and local variables respectively. The DVR is only applied to local variables because the static analysis in this approach is done intraprocedural as in [13]. The breaking points used in the PR analysis are determined completely statically, too.

Spin [15] uses both, DVR and PR. It works on a language called *Promela* which is similar to the two languages described before regarding these two reduction techniques. That means, method calls are handled by inlining, communication is conducted at certain program locations, and indirect control is not present. Both analyses are done statically via an intraprocedural approach before model checking.

In contrast, *[mc]square* works on assembly code including indirect control, indirect data accesses, recursions, interrupts, and globally accessible memory. This makes intraprocedural approaches and inlining infeasible. Restricting DVR to local variables is not possible as all variables are globally accessible. In *[mc]square*, breaking points cannot be determined completely statically as some constructs can only be handled dynamically during runtime (e.g., nondeterminism, indirect control and interrupts).

A different approach for DVR used in the model checking tool *Estes* is described in [16]. PR is not used in the *Estes* model checker. DVR is done dynamically during state-space creation to exploit run-time information. Due to the dynamic nature of the approach, the results are in certain situations more accurate, but increase the run-time. The user has to provide some information to use the DVR (e.g., description of the behavior of the environment, addresses of main function, interrupt handler starting points and interrupt handler ending points). This is not needed in *[mc]square*.

8   Conclusion and Future Work

This paper describes two static analyses used in *[mc]square* to tackle the state-explosion problem. Both analyses are already used in some other model checkers (e.g., *Spin*, *Estes* and *Murphi*), but could not be transferred one-to-one to *[mc]square* because the underlying analyses are done completely statically using intraprocedural approaches. Due to the peculiarities of the assembly language used (e.g., only global variables, indirect control, interrupts, and recursions), interprocedural analyses have to be used in *[mc]square*. The preparation of the program for PR could not be done completely statically due to interrupts and indirect control. Some of the so-called breaking points have to be determined during model checking because a static determination of these points would lead to a too coarse over-approximation (having no effect at all).

The results of the DVR are comparable to the results achieved in other model checking tools, although the analysis has to be performed interprocedural (including pointers, etc.). However, PR has a bigger influence on the size of the state spaces than in other model checkers. This is due to the nature of the assembly language (similar results observed in [14]). Programs written in assembly language tend to have many long, single successor chains, which need not to be stored completely (e.g., single C instruction is compiled into six assembly instructions). Another source for long, single successor chains are interrupts. In most cases an interrupt handler cannot be intercepted by another interrupt, and hence, it is a long, single successor chain, which can be reduced very efficiently.

Both reduction techniques can be used to lower the size of state spaces. DVR can be used in any case as it does not have any negative effect. PR can only be used whenever the X operator (CTL*-X preserving) is not needed. The negative effects of using PR (increase in number of created states due to revisits) can be eased by some other abstraction techniques implemented in *[mc]square*. From our point of view, it is better to trade time in for space, since memory requirements are a bigger problem.

At present, *[mc]square* is able to handle up to 68,000,000 states in memory (16 GB main memory) and up to 670,000,000 using hard disk model checking. Hence, there is still some performance reserve for programs more complex than used in the case study. The biggest program checked had about 4,500 lines.

To further improve the static analyses used to support model checking, the interrupt analysis has to be improved. To do this, two things have to be done before. First, the analyses have to be implemented using more details of the underlying hardware. At present, the over-approximation is in some cases too coarse (e.g., whenever an I/O register is written, all I/O registers are written). To improve this approximation the different I/O registers can be clustered. Within such a cluster the I/O registers influence each other, but clusters do not influence other clusters. Hence, whenever an I/O register is written, only the I/O registers of the same cluster are written. Second, the pointer analysis has to be improved. The idea is to use abstract interpretation during the Reaching Definitions Analysis to collect all possible values of pointers. Currently, whenever an indirect load occurs, all variables are read.

Another analysis that should be added is pruning of interrupts. This is an analysis similar to the Partial Order Reduction used in *Spin*. This analysis lowers the number of possible interleavings between the main process and interrupt handlers.

Summarizing, it can be said that reduction techniques using static analyses (in particular DVR and PR) can be used to tackle the state-explosion problem in explicit state model-checking. Significant improvements can be observed when using DVR and PR for model checking of assembly code. As described above, the impact, PR has in this specific domain, is even bigger than in model checkers working on intermediate languages.

References

1. Mehler, T.: Challenges and Applications of Assembly-Level Software Model Checking. PhD thesis, Universität Dortmund (2005)
2. Mercer, E.G., Jones, M.D.: Model checking machine code with the gnu debugger. In: SPIN Workshop on Model Checking of Software, San Francisco, USA (August 2005)
3. Schlich, B., Kowalewski, S.: [mc]square: A model checker for microcontroller code. In: Margaria, T., Philippou, A., Steffen, B. (eds.) Proc. 2nd Int'l Symp. Leveraging Applications of Formal Methods, Verification and Validation (IEEE-ISoLA 2006) (2006); To appear in: IEEE proceedings
4. Schlich, B., Rohrbach, M., Weber, M., Kowalewski, S.: Model checking software for microcontrollers. Technical Report AIB-2006-11, RWTH Aachen University (August 2006)
5. Balakrishnan, G., Reps, T., Melski, D., Teitelbaum, T.: Wysinwyx: What you see is not what you execute. In: Verified Software: Theories, Tools, Experiments. Springer, Heidelberg (to appear, 2007)
6. Clarke, E.M., Grumberg, O., Peled, D.A.: Model Checking. The MIT Press, Cambridge (1999)
7. Schlich, B., Kowalewski, S.: An extendable architecture for model checking hardware-specific automotive microcontroller code. In: Schnieder, E., Tarnai, G. (eds.) Proc. 6th Symp. Formal Methods for Automation and Safety in Railway and Automotive Systems (FORMS/FORMAT 2007), Braunschweig, Germany, GZVB, pp. 202–212 (2007)
8. Schlich, B., Kowalewski, S.: Model checking c source code for embedded systems. In: Margaria, T., Steffen, B., Hinchey, M.G. (eds.) Proc. IEEE/NASA Workshop on Leveraging Applications of Formal Methods, Verification, and Validation (IEEE/NASA ISoLA 2005), Maryland, USA, NASA, September 2005, pp. 65–77 (2005); NASA/CP-2005-212788
9. Larsen, K.G., Larsson, F., Pettersson, P., Yi, W.: Efficient verification of real-time systems: Compact data structure and state-space reduction. In: Proc. 18th IEEE Real-Time Systems Symposium (RTSS 1997), pp. 14–24. IEEE Computer Society, Washington, DC, USA (1997)
10. Heljanko, K.: Model checking the branching time temporal logic ctl. Research Report A45, Helsinki University of Technology (May 1997)
11. Vergauwen, B., Lewi, J.: A linear local model checking algorithm for ctl. In: Best, E. (ed.) CONCUR 1993. LNCS, vol. 715, pp. 447–461. Springer, Heidelberg (1993)
12. Nielson, F., Nielson, H.R., Hankin, C.: Principles of Program Analysis. Springer, New York (1999)
13. Yorav, K., Grumberg, O.: Static analysis for state-space reductions preserving temporal logics. Form. Methods Syst. Des. 25(1), 67–96 (2004)

14. Quirós, G.: Static byte-code analysis for state space reduction. Master's thesis, RWTH Aachen University (March 2006)
15. Holzmann, G.J.: The engineering of a model checker: The gnu i-protocol case study revisited. In: Dams, D.R., Gerth, R., Leue, S., Massink, M. (eds.) SPIN 1999. LNCS, vol. 1680, pp. 232–244. Springer, Heidelberg (1999)
16. Lewis, M., Jones, M.: A dead variable analysis for explicit model checking. In: Proc. 2006 ACM SIGPLAN Symp. Partial evaluation and semantics-based program manipulation (PEPM 2006), pp. 48–57. ACM Press, New York (2006)

Checking the TWIN Elevator System
by Translating Object-Z to SMV

Sören Preibusch[1] and Florian Kammüller[2]

[1] German Institute for Economic Research
Mohrenstraße 58, 10117 Berlin
spreibusch@diw.de
[2] Technische Universität Berlin
Fakultät IV: Elektrotechnik und Informatik
Franklinstraße 28-29, 10587 Berlin
flokam@cs.tu-berlin.de

Abstract. In the context of large scale industrial installations, model checking often fails to tap its full potential because of a missing link between a system's specification and its functional and non-functional requirements, like safety. Our work bridges this gap by providing a translation from the formal specification language Object-Z to the SMV model checker input language to combine their advantages.

This paper focuses on the translation of the object-oriented features of Object-Z: operation promotion and communication between objects. We demonstrate the feasibility of our approach using the example of the TWIN Elevator system and embed the translation process in the industrial software production workflow.

1 Introduction and Related Work

Software development for industrial purposes differs from application development by the nature of the constructed software products and by the nature of the production process. Industrial software enables the effective and efficient usage of large installations and equipment in aviation, power generation, logistics, medical treatment, and production lines. These systems are typically safety-critical; disturbance of their well-functioning may cause personal or physical damage.

Model checking techniques are used to check properties of these systems; they provide reliable results by including a system's whole state space in mathematical proofs of correctness.

A variety of model checking tools has emerged along with different input languages. As a standardized input format does not exist yet, interoperability between users and re-use of specification is hampered. The lack of established authoring tools and intuitive means to structure large specifications are additional drawbacks. The ability to use Object-Z as a common input language would allow to overcome these difficulties. Object-Z [4] is an object-oriented extension of the

S. Leue and P. Merino (Eds.): FMICS 2007, LNCS 4916, pp. 38–55, 2008.

standardized specification language Z [5]. It has well understood semantics [13] and benefits from tool support [2], Section 5.

Advantages of Combining Object-Z and SMV. Coupling Object-Z as a system specification language with model checking support manifests advantages when compared to purely verifying Z specifications [19]. These advantages originate the specification phase and the checking phase in the workflow.

Whereas a Z specification defines a single state space, Object-Z's classes with their separate namespaces are especially handy for specifying medium- to large-scale software systems [12]. The object-oriented specification paradigm is well adapted to distributed and embedded systems; communicating objects reflect the spatial separation of different components. Unlike Z, Object-Z supports specifying concurrent systems. Multiple instantiation of the same class provides for easy scalability where Z would have required a manual enumeration of each instance.

Moreover, translating Object-Z to SMV enables the use of general-purpose model checking tools. Those profit from a larger community and ongoing research resulting in performance enhancements.

Finally, there is a difference between Z and SMV in the nature of the properties that may be expressed (and thus checked). Z and Object-Z specifications are limited to first order predicate logic whereas SMV is designed for temporal logic expressed in CTL or LTL formulas. Those temporal formulas are naturally checked against the specification; in contrast, Z checkers usually only perform type checks or well-formedness checks.

Previous Work has provided model checking support for the base language Z [14]. However, its authors have seen the extension to Object-Z as future work. Especially the object-oriented features make this a non-trivial task. [18] describes a translation procedure from Object-Z to SMV using ASM as an intermediate language. Then again, this works lacks considering the semantics of an Object-Z specification as a description of a system embedded in an environment. Hence, the translation of operations is problematic. Inter-object communication is hard to follow and distributed operations operators are not covered. Moreover, that work does not preserve the structure of an Object-Z specification but instead flattens the top-level structure provided by classes and modules.

Our contribution is twofold. First, on a concrete level, we present a specification of the TWIN elevator system in the formal specification language Object-Z. We provide a step-by-step translation to an equivalent (Cadence) SMV program [9]. Second, on an abstract level, we elaborate general rules for the translation process, focusing on the object-oriented features of Object-Z: operation promotion and communication between objects. In addition, we sketch how the translation can be integrated rewardingly in the workflow of industrial software production processes.

The remainder of this paper is organized as follows. The following Section portrays the TWIN elevator system by ThyssenKrupp. Section 3 is the core of the paper. It presents the commented TWIN's specification in Object-Z along with the SMV equivalents and general translation rules. The resulting SMV program is enriched by temporal formula stating fairness and safety requirements that are successfully checked. Section 5 embeds the translation process in the industrial software development process prior to concluding in Section 6 with a summary and outlook.

2   TWIN Elevator System Case Study

The idea of having an elevator with two independent cabins operating in the same shaft dates back to the 1930s. However, first attempts to build this efficient transportation system failed and the engineering of a control system has been an unsolved problem for almost a century. Only in 2002 ThyssenKrupp installed the first TWIN elevator system at Stuttgart University.

In a TWIN elevator system, two cabins are arranged one above the other; they run independently in the same TWIN shaft – also at different speeds. A safety distance is kept, depending on the speeds involved. The cabins can move in different directions, which means that they can also move toward each other [17]. Because the TWIN cabins cannot sidestep, each TWIN installation comprises at least one conventional shaft to serve routes that would result in a crossing of the TWIN cabins (Fig. 1).

A prospective passenger communicates his destination level no longer within the elevator cabin, but instead by Destination Selection Control (DSC) terminals mounted on each floor. The control system then selects one of the cabins capable to serve the call.

The informal specification of safety requirements of ThyssenKrupp has been the basis for their formal expression by means of formal specification and model checking [7]. In [7], we developed a detailed SMV program to check the TWIN's well-functioning and provide evidence for the scalability of model checking procedures. However, the crafting of an SMV program that large is unrealistic to be carried out in an industrial

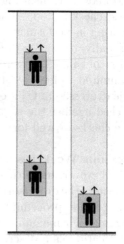

Fig. 1. Minimal TWIN installation (schematic view): a TWIN shaft with two cabins on the left and conventional shaft on the right

context. In contrast, it is more likely that Object-Z specifications are used and developed already in an early project stage.

The earlier results also act as a benchmark for our translation process in that applying model checking on an SMV program resulting from an automated translation should not perform worse than on the hand-made SMV program.

In addition, the duo of this paper and the first TWIN case study is an example for abstraction. The TWIN specification developed in the next section is just detailed enough to examine fairness and safety requirements.

3   Translating Object-Z Specifications to SMV Programs

3.1   Fundamental Object-Z Concepts

In Object-Z, graphical *schema* notation enables the concise structuring of state and operation specifications and modularizes them into classes. Any schema consists of a declaration part and a predicate part enabling abstract specification of invariants, pre-conditions and post-conditions. Classes in Object-Z encapsulate a state and an initial schema, as well as operation schemas specifying the methods of an object oriented class. In addition, Object-Z features specific class constructs for visibility, constant declarations, polymorphism, and inheritance.

The idea of instantiation of an object o of a class C is naturally represented by the declaration of a variable $o : C$ where o then denotes the identity of an object. Object-Z has a reference semantics [13] and the common object-oriented dot notation, e.g. $o.m$ to annotate the invocation of an object's feature.

The so-called *schema calculus* comprises operators enabling composition of operations to create new operations, especially in the context of modular systems. In Object-Z operations are composed by conjunction $\wedge$, non-deterministic choice $[\!]$, sequential composition $\S$, and parallel composition $\|$.

In Section 3.3, we will piecewise present the TWIN's specification in *Object-Z* along with explanations of the newly introduced Object-Z features. We outline the corresponding translation rule and present the (one or more) resulting SMV code fragments. We have partitioned large classes; the splits are clearly signed (. . . / [cont'd]). Where appropriate, we skip over specification parts that would not contribute to introduce new translation rules. In addition to this paper, the unsplit and unabridged versions are available online [10],[11].

3.2   Directness and Structure Preservation

Our translation from Object Z to SMV is *direct* in that it identifies concepts of Object-Z, like propositional logic, basic types, and the class concept, with almost directly corresponding features of SMV. Where appropriate, the missing semantics is added in the translation process using additional definitions, constraints, or other constructions as we will see. The striking advantage of this direct translation is that it is quite obviously *structure preserving*, i.e. the structure of the Object-Z classes and SMV modules correspond one to one and the initial and state schemas of Object-Z have distinct representations in SMV code chunks. Although the granularity of the operations cannot be preserved, one can show that the translation distributes over the constructs of SMV used for operation representation.

3.3   Translation Rules

Type Definitions and Constants. Types and constants used within the Object-Z specification are defined at its beginning. Types can be defined by enumerating their values or as an integer sub-range. We define a type for the cabin status and for the storeys.

Expressions in the constant definition are evaluated once during the translation process; static evaluation is correct as – by definition – Object-Z constants do not change their values. Definitions for the boolean constants are added. In SMV, truth values are represented by integers.

$CabinStatus$ ::= vacant | busy
$Level$ ::= $(1 .. 12)$

$LevelGround = min\ Level$
$LevelTop = max\ Level$

```
typedef CabinStatus {vacant, busy};
typedef Level 1..12;

#define LevelGround 1
#define LevelTop 12

#define true 1
#define false 0
```

Classes. Following the object-oriented paradigm, classes are the top-level structuring mechanism in Object-Z. They provide a scope for variables and may contain operations that change the variables' values by state transition. Our specification comprises four classes: A *Call* class, acting as a datatype for calls with the attributes *from* and *to* coding the route's endpoints, a *Cabin* class for cabins in a conventional shaft or in a TWIN elevator shaft, a class for the *DSC*, and a class for the *TWIN_System* itself.

A class' state variables are noted inside an Object-Z box. Variables are typed and can instantiate classes. In SMV, modules provide a similar scoping mechanism.

Call

$from : Level$
$to : Level$

```
module Call() {
  from : Level;
  to : Level; }
```

Initial schema. An Object-Z class can include an *INIT* schema, assembling predicates that must hold in the initial state. Initially, a cabin is vacant and its target level is the current level so that there is no induced call. The current level is initialized upon instantiation in the *TWIN_System* class. Cabins in a TWIN shaft have *has_other_cabin* set to true and the variables *other_curr_level* and *other_target_level* referring to the other cabin in the same shaft. Therefore, a TWIN cabin is aware of the other cabin's position – an information needed when deciding whether the cabin may accept a call or not.

The predicates over the initial state are translated to an active initialisation in SMV.

```
┌─ Cabin ──────────────────────────────────────────────────────────┐
│  ┌──────────────────────────────┐ ┌─ INIT ──────────────────────┐ │
│  │ curr_level : Level           │ │ target_level = curr_level   │ │
│  │ target_level : Level         │ │ status = vacant             │ │
│  │ status : CabinStatus         │ └─────────────────────────────┘ │
│  │ other_curr_level : Level     │                                 │
│  │ other_target_level : Level   │                                 │
│  │ has_other_cabin : 𝔹          │                                 │
│  └──────────────────────────────┘                                 │
│                                                                   │
│  . . .                                                            │
└───────────────────────────────────────────────────────────────────┘
```

```
module Cabin() {
  curr_level : Level;
  target_level : Level;
  status : CabinStatus;
  other_curr_level : Level;
  other_target_level : Level;
  has_other_cabin : boolean;

  init(target_level) := curr_level;
  init(status) := vacant;
```

State Transitions: Precondition and Stimulus. In Object-Z, state transitions are realized by named operations that change the values of the state variables enumerated in their Δ-lists. Below a horizontal line, predicates over the variables' values before the state transition are noted (precondition of the operation). The primed variable names refer to the variables' values after the operation's execution (postcondition).

The operations MoveUp and MoveDown realize the state transition of the cabin with regard to its current level. The operations' preconditions assure that the cabin moves in the direction of its target level and does not run out of the shaft.

For each operation, we introduce two defined boolean variables in the SMV program. These variables do not add to the state vector and thus do not impact on the performance of verification. The SMV variable *operationname_pre* has the truth value of the precondition. It is hereby also a translation of the Object-Z expression "pre *operationname*" that represents the truth value of the operation's precondition.

The variable *operationname_stimulus* indicates whether there is a call of the operation from the environment. According to the semantics of Object-Z [12], the specified system is embedded in an environment that may evoke an operation. Unless this evokation occurs, the state transition specified by the operation does not take place. This is in contrast to SMV, where each possible state transition is executed. Hence, the variable *operationname_stimulus* acts as an additional guard.

```
 ┌─ Cabin [cont'd] ──────────────────────────────────────────────────
 │  ...
 │  ┌─ MoveUp ──────────────────────┐   ┌─ MoveDown ─────────────────────┐
 │  │ Δ(curr_level)                 │   │ Δ(curr_level)                  │
 │  │                               │   │                                │
 │  │ curr_level < LevelTop         │   │ curr_level > LevelGround        │
 │  │ curr_level < target_level     │   │ curr_level > target_level       │
 │  │ curr_level' = curr_level + 1  │   │ curr_level' = curr_level − 1    │
 │  └───────────────────────────────┘   └────────────────────────────────┘
 │  ...
 └───────────────────────────────────────────────────────────────────
```

```
/* operation MoveUp */
MoveUp_pre : boolean;
MoveUp_pre := (curr_level < LevelTop) & (curr_level < target_level);

MoveUp_stimulus : boolean;


/* operation MoveDown */
MoveDown_pre : boolean;
MoveDown_pre := (curr_level > LevelGround) & (curr_level > target_level);

MoveDown_stimulus : boolean;
```

All operations possibly changing a state variable can be identified by examining their Δ-lists. For each state variable, the influencing operations are collected; their respective precondition and stimulus variables guard the state transition in SMV.

The general schema has the form:

```
next(variable) := case{
  op1_pre & op1_stimulus : op1_postpredicate;
  op2_pre & op2_stimulus : op2_postpredicate;
  ...
  default : variable; }
```

The last alternative (`default`) results in the variable to remain unchanged if none of the operations is executed.

```
next(curr_level) := case{
  MoveUp_pre & MoveUp_stimulus : curr_level + 1;
  MoveDown_pre & MoveDown_stimulus : curr_level - 1;
  default : curr_level; };
```

Communication variables. Communication variables can be defined in the local scope of an operation. Output variables are decorated with an exclamation mark, input variables with a question mark. Communication variables in opposite directions with the same basename are identified when operations are combined (see below on page 46).

The cabin's operation *AcceptCall* may record a *new_call?* for the cabin if the cabin is currently vacant (first precondition). In addition, if the cabin is a TWIN cabin (*has_other_cabin* is true), it can only accept the call in case call processing would not result in a crash with the other cabin (second precondition).

If the cabin has accepted the call, its *status* is set to busy and the call's attribute *to* is taken as the cabin's new *target_level*. If the cabin has finished a call, its *status* is set to vacant.

In the translation to SMV, the communication variable *new_call?* is prefixed with **in** (**out** for output communication variables) and with the operation name, to provide for a local scope.

Cabin [cont'd] _____

. . .

AcceptCall _____
$\Delta(status, target\_level)$
$new\_call? : Call$
_____
$has\_other\_cabin = \text{false} \vee$
$(new\_call?.to - other\_target\_level) \times$
$(curr\_level - other\_curr\_level) > 0$
$status = \text{vacant}$
$status' = \text{busy}$
$target\_level' = new\_call?.to$

FinishCall _____
$\Delta(status)$
_____
$curr\_level = target\_level$
$status = \text{busy}$
$status' = \text{vacant}$

. . .

```
/* operation AcceptCall */
AcceptCall_pre : boolean;
AcceptCall_pre := (has_other_cabin = false) |
  ( (AcceptCall_in_new_call.to - other_target_level) *
    (curr_level - other_curr_level) > 0 ) & (status = vacant) ;

AcceptCall_stimulus : boolean;

AcceptCall_in_new_call : Call;

/* operation FinishCall */
FinishCall_pre : boolean;
FinishCall_pre := (curr_level = target_level) & (status = busy);

FinishCall_stimulus : boolean;

next(target_level) := case{
  AcceptCall_pre & AcceptCall_stimulus : AcceptCall_in_new_call.to;
  default : target_level; };

next(status) := case{
  AcceptCall_pre & AcceptCall_stimulus : busy;
  FinishCall_pre & FinishCall_stimulus : vacant;
  default : status; };
```

Operation Promotion and Communication. Operations defined by operation schemas may be used to define new operations by composition. These "operation promotions" are placed inside a class. A new operation op can be defined by:

- conjunction: $op \mathrel{\widehat{=}} op1 \wedge op2$
  both $op1$ and $op2$ are executed
- (non-deterministic) choice: $op \mathrel{\widehat{=}} op1 \mathbin{[\!]} op2$
  one of $op1$ and $op2$ is arbitrarily chosen and executed. If the precondition of one of the compounding operations is not fulfilled, the operation is removed from the choice.
- parallel composition: $op \mathrel{\widehat{=}} op1 \parallel op2$
  both $op1$ and $op2$ are executed with bi-directional communication
- sequential composition: $op \mathrel{\widehat{=}} op1 \mathbin{\S} op2$
  both $op1$ and $op2$ are executed with forward communication only

The operators for operation composition can be combined and several operations can be combined at once.

Communication between operations is realized by matching the communication variables. Bi-directional communication means that the values of communication variables with the same basename are identified. Forward communication means that only the output variables of the first operation are matched with the input variables of the second operation. An operation lacking communication variables does not participate in communication. In general, communication variables need not match; the unmatched communication variables of the composed operations are then simply unified in the signature of the combined operation. In the case of the choice operator, the unified signatures of the involved constituent operations must be identical.

Operation Promotion: Choice. We define a new operation *Move* as the choice between the operations *MoveUp*, *MoveDown*, and *FinishCall* depending on whether the cabin's current level is below, above, or equal its target level. In case the current level equals the target level, the call has been processed.

Analogously to operations defined by operation schemas, two boolean variables for stimulus and precondition are introduced in the translation. The precondition of the promoted operation is calculated by combining the preconditions of the compounding operations (see Table 1).

Table 1. Operation operators overview

Operator	Precondition escalation (SMV)	Stimulus propagation	Communication
$\wedge$	conjunction (&)	conjunction	none
$[\!]$	disjunction (|)	exclusive disjunction	none
$\parallel$	conjunction (&)	conjunction	bi-directional
$\S$	conjunction (&)	conjunction	forward

```
__ Cabin [cont'd] _____
 ...
  Move ≙ MoveUp [] MoveDown [] FinishCall
_____
```

```
Move_pre : boolean;
Move_pre := MoveUp_pre | MoveDown_pre | FinishCall_pre;
```

```
Move_stimulus : boolean;
```

The non-deterministic choice between two operations susceptible to be chosen (i.e. whose preconditions evaluate to true) is realized in SMV by assigning a set of values to a variable. This assignment is understood as that one value of the set is arbitrarily chosen each time and assigned to the variable.

We use SMV's construct of guarded set membership when enumerating the set elements: *cond* ? *elem* means that *elem* is included in the set if *cond* evaluates to true.

```
Move_choice : {1,2,3};
Move_choice := {
  (MoveUp_pre) ? 1,
  (MoveDown_pre) ? 2,
  (FinishCall_pre) ? 3 };
```

The stimulus from the promoted operation propagates to the compounding operations as defined in Table 1. The arbitrary choice between the set values assures that the stimulus propagates to only one of the compounding operations:

```
MoveUp_stimulus :=
  (Move_stimulus & Move_choice = 1);
```

```
MoveDown_stimulus :=
  (Move_stimulus & Move_choice = 2);
```

```
FinishCall_stimulus :=
  (Move_stimulus & Move_choice = 3);
```

Recapitulative Example: the *DSC* class. So far we know how to translate Object-Z classes, state variables, operations, and communication variables to SMV. We now apply these rules to translate the small *DSC* class.

The Destination Selection Control (DSC) terminal registers the passenger's ride request. The calls are communicated to the cabins; the storey where the DSC is mounted (*location*) is the call's *from* attribute. The translation to SMV follows the principles established above.

```
__ DSC _____
 _____       __ PlaceCall _____
 | location : Level            |        | Δ()                                |
 |_____|        | new_call! : Call                   |
                                        |_____|
                                        | new_call!.from = location          |
                                        |_____|
_____
```

```
module DSC() {

  /* state variables */              /* operation PlaceCall */
  location : Level;                  PlaceCall_pre : boolean;
                                     PlaceCall_pre := true;
  PlaceCall_stimulus : boolean;

  PlaceCall_out_new_call : Call ;
  PlaceCall_out_new_call.from := location; }
```

Multiple Instantiation. The class *TWIN_System* models the TWIN elevator system. It instantiates the previously defined class *Cabin* thrice – once for a conventional cabin and twice for the TWIN cabins. In each storey, a DSC is mounted, resulting in a functional mapping from a *Level* to a *DSC* object.

TWIN_System
> $dscs : Level \rightarrow DSC$
> $twin\_lower, twin\_upper, conventional : Cabin$
>
> $\forall\, l \in \text{dom}\, dscs \bullet dscs(l).location = l$
> $\dots$

$\dots$

```
module TWIN_System() {

  /* state variables */
  dscs : array Level of DSC ;
  forall(l in Level)
    dscs[l].location := l;

  twin_lower, twin_upper, conventional : Cabin;
```

Operation Promotion: Conjunction. We combine the *Move* operations of all cabins in the *TWIN_System* to a single operation *MoveCabins*. Since all cabins move independently, we use an operation operator without communication but with conjunctive stimulus propagation: the 'and' operator $\wedge$.

TWIN_System [cont'd]
> $\dots$
>
> $MoveCabins \mathrel{\widehat{=}} twin\_lower.Move \wedge twin\_upper.Move \wedge conventional.Move$
> $\dots$

```
  /* operation promotion MoveCabins */
  MoveCabins_pre : boolean;
  MoveCabins_pre := twin_lower.Move_pre | twin_upper.Move_pre |
    conventional.Move_pre;
```

```
MoveCabins_stimulus : boolean;

twin_lower.Move_stimulus := MoveCabins_stimulus;
twin_upper.Move_stimulus := MoveCabins_stimulus;
conventional.Move_stimulus := MoveCabins_stimulus;
```

A priori, a call may be processed by any of the available cabins. Any of the cabins capable of processing the call may accept it (see the operation *AcceptCall* in the *Cabin* class). Therefore, we use a non-determistic choice ⫿. The call accepting by the cabins occurs in parallel (∥) with the call placing by the DSCs. We use a 'distributed' choice (⫿) between the *PlaceCall* operations of all *DSC* objects.

Distributed Operation Promotion. The distributed choice operator in Object-Z provides a non-deterministic choice over a range of objects whose methods are enabled. In SMV, the distributed precondition escalation is realized by applying the boolean precondition combination operator over an array constructed of all individual operations' preconditions: `f [expr(var) : var in Type]` applies the operator `f` (`|` or `&` according to Table 1) distributively over all expressions `expr(var)`.

The set of choice alternatives is constructed analogously by using SMV's iterative construction capabilities: the expression `expr(var)` is included in the set `{expr(var) : var in Type, cond(var)}` if `cond(var)` evaluates to true.

Finally, the stimulus propagation iterates over all DSC object's *PlaceCall* operations indexed by `l in Level`. We observe another structure preservation property in that the distributivity is preserved and an explicit enumeration of all *DSC* instances is not necessary during the translation process.

┌─ *TWIN_System* [cont'd] ───┐
│ $\cdots$
│
│ $DistributeCalls \mathrel{\widehat{=}} \llap{\lceil} \rceil\, l : Level \bullet dscs(l).PlaceCall \parallel$
│ $(twin\_lower.AcceptCall \;\llap{\lceil}\rceil\; twin\_upper.AcceptCall \;\llap{\lceil}\rceil\; conventional.AcceptCall)$
│ $\cdots$
└──┘

```
/* operation promotion DistributeCalls */
DistributeCalls_pre : boolean;
DistributeCalls_pre := |[dscs[l].PlaceCall_pre : l in Level ] &
  (twin_lower.AcceptCall_pre | twin_upper.AcceptCall_pre |
  conventional.AcceptCall_pre);

DistributeCalls_stimulus : boolean;

DistributeCalls_choice : {1,2,3};
DistributeCalls_choice := {
  (twin_lower.AcceptCall_pre) ? 1,
  (twin_upper.AcceptCall_pre) ? 2,
  (conventional.AcceptCall_pre) ? 3 };
```

```
DistributeCalls_choice_2 : Level;
DistributeCalls_choice_2 := { l : l in Level, dscs[l].PlaceCall_pre};

twin_lower.AcceptCall_stimulus :=
  (DistributeCalls_stimulus & DistributeCalls_choice = 1);

twin_upper.AcceptCall_stimulus :=
  (DistributeCalls_stimulus & DistributeCalls_choice = 2);

conventional.AcceptCall_stimulus :=
  (DistributeCalls_stimulus & DistributeCalls_choice = 3);

forall(l in Level)
  dscs[l].PlaceCall_stimulus :=
    (DistributeCalls_stimulus & DistributeCalls_choice_2 = 1);
```

Matching Communication Variables. The parallel operator $\parallel$ results in a communication between the chosen *PlaceCall* operation and the chosen *Accept-Call* operation as described on page 46: `AcceptCall_in_new_call` is assigned the value of `PlaceCall_out_new_call` in case the *DistributeCall* operation is stimulated. The communication is conditioned over the choice ($[]$) only with regard to the outputting operation (realized by `DistributeCalls_choice_2` in the translation to SMV). It must not be conditioned with regard to the choice of the receiving operation: because choosability depends on an operation's precondition, which in turn may depend on an input variable, a circular definition would occur.

```
/* operation promotion DistributeCalls - communication */
twin_lower.AcceptCall_in_new_call := case {
  DistributeCalls_stimulus :
    dscs[DistributeCalls_choice_2].PlaceCall_out_new_call; };

twin_upper.AcceptCall_in_new_call := case {
  DistributeCalls_stimulus :
    dscs[DistributeCalls_choice_2].PlaceCall_out_new_call; };

conventional.AcceptCall_in_new_call := case {
  DistributeCalls_stimulus :
    dscs[DistributeCalls_choice_2].PlaceCall_out_new_call; };
```

Finally, we combine the TWIN system's two tasks (cabin movement and call management) in a single *Operate* operation.

TWIN_System [cont'd]
...
$Operate \;\hat{=}\; MoveCabins \wedge DistributeCalls$

```
/* operation promotion Operate */
Operate_pre : boolean;
Operate_pre := true;

Operate_stimulus : boolean;

MoveCabins_stimulus := Operate_stimulus;
DistributeCalls_stimulus := Operate_stimulus;
```

Adding the main module. SMV requires one main module in each program. All top-level modules are instantiated once in this module. Also, the stimulus for all operations not used to construct any other operation inside the Object-Z specification is set to true to assure that a 'running' system is checked. As we aim at an automated mechanical translation procedure, it is noteworthy that these operations are easy to enumerate.

```
module main() {
  system : TWIN_System();
  system.Operate_stimulus := true; }
```

4   Model Checking the Translation with SMV

After the Object-Z specification has been translated in SMV, one can enrich the program by (temporal) formulas expressing crucial system requirements. As an illustration, we express requirements regarding fairness, correct call processing, and safety in SMV:

For each cabin, the **Fairness** properties state that a call will be finished: always, if the cabin is busy, it will be vacant in the future:

```
Fairness_1 : assert
  G (system.twin_lower.status = busy) ->
    F (system.twin_lower.status = vacant);
Fairness_2 : assert
  G (system.twin_upper.status = busy) ->
    F (system.twin_upper.status = vacant);
Fairness_3 :
assert
  G (system.conventional.status = busy) ->
    F (system.conventional.status = vacant);
```

The **Processing** properties assure that the call termination is only achieved if the cabin really reaches its target level.

```
Processing_1 : assert  G (system.twin_lower.status = busy)
  U (system.twin_lower.curr_level = system.twin_lower.target_level);
Processing_2 : assert  G (system.twin_upper.status = busy)
  U (system.twin_upper.curr_level = system.twin_upper.target_level);
Processing_3 : assert  G (system.conventional.status = busy)
  U (system.conventional.curr_level = system.conventional.target_level);
```

For the TWIN shaft, the `Safety` property would be violated in case of a crash. It requires the upper TWIN cabin to always stay above the lower TWIN cabin.

```
Safety : assert
  G (system.twin_upper.curr_level > system.twin_lower.curr_level);
```

The assertions are noted in the SMV `main` module, thence prefixed with `system.` to reference the objects. One can place assertions in any module; we opted for the `main` module to emphasize on the separation between the specified system and the requirements towards it.

All properties together were successfully checked within seconds on standard desktop hardware. SMV allocated 34881 BDD nodes. Experiments showed that the time necessary to check the properties is only marginally influenced by the number of storeys.

To leverage this verification potential during the software development process, we have automated the translation process in a web-based prototype (called ZOË) and sketch its workflow embedding in the next section.

5   Workflow Embedding

The industrial software development process exhibits specifities that require fitted management and tools. The engineering of complex software systems on a large scale usually involves many developers, possibly from different backgrounds. Tightly coupled heterogenous components in an installation are developed by cross-functional teams. Each of the team members is an expert in one domain of the software's functionality. Documentation along the process is crucial and the documents regularly are one of the manufacturer's deliverables. For this reason, the documents need to be well presented, with appropriate languages and notations, so that they can be understood accurately and used effectively [8].

However, domain-specific language dialects across departments often hamper a holistic documentation and complicate the cooperation inside the development team. Requirements are typically expressed in a different language than the system description (e.g. CTL formula for safety requirements vs. Object-Z as a common language for the functional specification) and inspectors may also be an external party not involved in the software development process.

A unifying formal methods approach can conciliate between these different formalisms and promises advances in product and process quality: the software will better fulfill its requirements and adherence to delivery dates and budget will be improved. Similar endeavors have been undertaken in the Alloy project [16]. The Alloy Analyzer is a tool that checks properties on a model, visualizes, and simulates it. However, the Alloy Analyzer is a 'model finder' that finds any model satisfying a logical formula, rather than checking a formula on an operationally specified model.

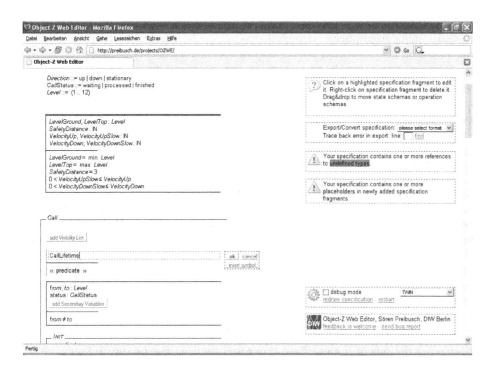

Fig. 2. The ZOË Workspace

Our portrayed translation from an Object-Z specification to a checkable software model bridges the described gap and brings together domain-experts from functionality specification and requirements checking. Functional and non-functional requirements can be checked as demonstrated exemplarily in the previous section. In case an error is found, a counterexample is generated and the detected discrepancy between the required and the actual behaviour can be traced back to the original specification because of the structure-preservation. If, for instance, a property is breached subsequent to a state transition, the operations causing the state transition are enumerated. The manual workload is reduced and applicability of formal methods is thereby extended.

To support the workflow, we have developed a web-based authoring environment for Object-Z specifications, ZOË, see Fig.2. The translation process described in this paper is implemented as a prototype fully integrated with our front end tool ZOË.

A domain-expert can develop the specification inside his browser, and the web-based infrastructure supports collaborative engineering. In contrast to previous tool support, no special software installations or plugins are needed. The editor and the translator are implemented using HTML, CSS and JavaScript – available with any current browser. The editor alleviates the expert's tasks as it allows an interactive specification development. The formulated Object-Z specification can be exported by means of output/formatter plugins.

The checked model can be refined to an executable program, so that end-to-end quality assurance can be achieved [1]. The refinement may be carried out based on the generated SMV program as the translation produces an easily readable output: variable names are maintained and so is the specification's inherent structure.

The on the fly checking of the fairness and safety properties of our TWIN case study provides evidence for applicability also for larger systems.

6   Conclusion and Discussion

We have established and explained rules for translating an Object-Z specification to a corresponding SMV program. These rules make full use of the close correspondence between many important features of Object-Z and SMV whilst being careful not to identify syntactical similarities whose semantics do not match. Besides propositional logic and basic datatypes, one major correspondence we identified is that of prestate and poststate. We cover the object-oriented concepts of Object-Z and non-deterministic choice, and we successfully cope with object communication and operation promotion.

Object-Z is a powerful specification formalism and it is generally not possible to represent it in its entirety in the input language of SMV. However, using simple restrictions of infinite base types and limiting the predicate language to equations and simple quantified expressions, we arrive at a useful subset of the original specification language that can be verified automatically with standard model checking techniques.

The resulting translation enables the further application of model checking techniques to verify the specified system's correct behaviour. We therefore embed the translation procedure in the industrial software production process and have developed appropriate web-based tool support.

Our method's suitability is attested by its application to the cutting-edge TWIN elevator case-study. Starting from a concise system specification in Object-Z, we employ the translation algorithm to optain a checkable TWIN model. Fairness and safety requirements are verified on this model within seconds.

The approach we take in this work is pragmatic but sound. Although soundness is not formally verified, it is fairly evident as we exploit natural similarities between state based specification in Object-Z and the state model of SMV. The integration of temporal logics and Object-Z semantics is furthermore based on well-established results [3], [15].

A very important point in favour of our approach to translating Object-Z into SMV directly, that makes it stand out in comparison to other similar endevours, is its *shallowness* [6]: the concepts of the application are identified in a one-to-one fashion with concepts of the formal target language. Here the application is Object-Z and the formal target language is SMV. The striking advantage of shallowness is that we inherit the full expressiveness of the target language and hence the full power of any available support.

References

1. Amnell, T.: Code Synthesis for Timed Automata. Thesis, Uppsala University (2003)
2. The Community Z Tools project (2006), http://czt.sourceforge.net/
3. Derrick, J., Smith, G.: Linear temporal logic and Z refinement. In: Rattray, C., Maharaj, S., Shankland, C. (eds.) AMAST 2004. LNCS, vol. 3116. Springer, Heidelberg (2004)
4. Duke, R., Rose, G.: Formal Object-Oriented Specification Using Object-Z. Cornerstones of Computing. MacMillan (2000)
5. International Organization for Standardization: ISO/IEC 13568:2002: Information technology – Z formal specification notation – Syntax, type system and semantics, http://www.iso.ch/iso/en/ CatalogueDetailPage.CatalogueDetail?CSNUMBER=21573
6. Kammüller, F.: Interactive Theorem Proving in Software Engineering. In: Habilitationsschrift, Technische Universität Berlin (2006)
7. Kammüller, F., Preibusch, S.: An Industrial Application of Symbolic Model Checking – The TWIN-Elevator Case Study. In: Informatik Forschung und Entwicklung. Springer, Heidelberg (accepted for publication, 2007)
8. Liu, S.: Formal Engineering for Industrial Software Development. Springer, Heidelberg (2004)
9. McMillan, K.: Symbolic Model Checking. Kluwer Academic Publishers, Dordrecht (1995)
10. Preibusch, S.: TWIN Elevator System, Concise Object-Z Specification (2007), http://preibusch.de/projects/TWIN/Concise_OZ
11. Preibusch, S.: TWIN Elevator System, Concise Object-Z Specification (Translation to SMV) (2007), http://preibusch.de/projects/TWIN/Concise_OZ_Translation_SMV
12. Smith, G.: The Object-Z Specification Language. In: Advances in Formal Methods. Kluwer Academic Publishers, Dordrecht (2000)
13. Smith, G., Kammüller, F., Santen, T.: Encoding Object-Z in Isabelle/HOL. In: Bert, D., P. Bowen, J., C. Henson, M., Robinson, K. (eds.) B 2002 and ZB 2002. LNCS, vol. 2272. Springer, Heidelberg (2002)
14. Smith, G., Wildman, L.: Model Checking Z Specifications Using SAL. In: Treharne, H., King, S., C. Henson, M., Schneider, S. (eds.) ZB 2005. LNCS, vol. 3455. Springer, Heidelberg (2005)
15. Smith, G., Winter, K.: Proving temporal properties of Z specifications using abstraction. In: Bert, D., P. Bowen, J., King, S. (eds.) ZB 2003. LNCS, vol. 2651. Springer, Heidelberg (2003)
16. Software Design Group, MIT Computer Science and Artificial Intelligence Laboratory. The Alloy Analyzer (2007), http://alloy.mit.edu/
17. ThyssenKrupp Elevator. TWIN Report (2005), http://www.twin.thyssenkrupp-elevator.de/?&L=1
18. Winter, K., Duke, R.: Model Checking Object-Z using ASM. In: Butler, M., Petre, L., Sere, K. (eds.) IFM 2002. LNCS, vol. 2335. Springer, Heidelberg (2002)
19. The World Wide Web Virtual Library: The Z notation. Tool support (2005), http://vl.zuser.org/#tools

Introducing Time in an Industrial Application of Model-Checking

Lionel van den Berg, Paul Strooper, and Kirsten Winter

University Queensland, Queensland, Australia
{pstroop,kirsten}@itee.uq.edu.au

Abstract. The safety of many industrial systems is directly related to time. Model checking has been used to verify that safety requirements are met by a model of the system. In many cases, however, time is excluded to limit the state space explosion. Two approaches to include time constraints are either to use model checking for timed systems, or to integrate an explicit model of time using standard model checking. This paper presents a case study using the latter approach. We have worked closely with one of Australia's largest railway companies, Queensland Rail, on a real industrial environment to produce models to verify the safety of railway interlockings. Our models are written and optimised for the symbolic model checker NuSMV. In this paper we introduce time into our existing models and examine time in the context of level crossings. We also present quantitative data to show the feasibility of the approach.

Keywords: model checking, real-time system, railway interlockings.

1 Introduction

Model checking is a useful technique for verifying industrial systems. One problem faced when modelling systems is time. A variety of model checkers are available, of which some, such as NuSMV [3], do not explicitly support time, while others, such as UPPAAL [1] and KRONOS [5], do. In this paper we refer to a model checker that does not support time as a *standard* model checker. The choice of which tool to use when modelling a real-time system may appear obvious, but there can be good reasons for choosing a tool that does not support time. Often significant resources have been devoted to developing models for a tool that does not support time. Rather than re-modelling the entire system, it can be preferable to extend the given untimed model to integrate time explicitly.

Queensland Rail (QR) is one of Australia's largest railway companies. QR's railway interlocking systems provide numerous non-trivial verification challenges. We use the symbolic model checker NuSMV to tackle some of these, namely a subset of the safety requirements for *control tables*. A control table specifies how the components of a railway interlocking are supposed to behave. Incorrect or missing entries in the control table can cause safety violations. Initially our models could only be used to verify small interlockings. However, after significant optimisations and fine-tuning of both the model and the model checker [11], we are now able to check a subset of the safety requirements of all QR's interlockings.

S. Leue and P. Merino (Eds.): FMICS 2007, LNCS 4916, pp. 56–67, 2008.

Our original models do not include time and consequently only a subset of the requirements for control tables could be verified. Some of the operational functionality of a railway interlocking, however, relies on time. Incorrect time specifications can lead to safety violations. For this reason we have integrated time into our models. Our investigations were based on the fact that the existing approach uses NuSMV. The interlocking models have been designed and optimised for the NuSMV model checker, and a significant investment has been made to build accurate representations of QR's railway interlockings. NuSMV does not support time at the model-checking level, but does support real-time temporal logics such as RTCTL [9]. It was therefore necessary for us to integrate time into our models explicitly.

This paper describes our approach and uses level crossings as an example of functionality in which time is a significant factor. Section 2 lays out the background on the operation of railway interlockings. In particular, level crossings and control table specifications are required to understand the remainder of the paper. Our models without time are also described. Section 3 introduces an explicit model of time and Section 4 describes a model of level crossings with its timing aspects. In Section 5 we evaluate runtime statistics comparing untimed models with timed models and examine the statistics in terms of the size of the interlocking. Section 6 discusses related work and we conclude in Section 7.

2 Background

Railway interlockings are safety-critical systems. Queensland Rail uses control tables to specify the behaviour of railway interlockings. Specifically, control tables define the control and operation of all signalling equipment including signals, points, level-crossing lights and gates. A correct control table ensures the safety of an interlocking. However, incorrect or missing entries can cause safety violations, such as collisions and derailments.

Figure 1 shows a sample track layout. It is split horizontally such that the top two dotted lines on the right match up with bottom two dotted lines on the left. Points, for example *799*, are movable components that can be set normal allowing the train to proceed in the same direction at high speed, or set reverse allowing the train to change tracks at lower speed. The current state of a point is referred to as the *lie of the point*. Tracks, for example *41C*, are indicated between the small lines that are perpendicular across the large lines. Each track has a maximum permitted speed, determined by track geometry and operational requirements, and a length. Signals, for example *61* (representing a signal for a main route) and 21 (representing a signal for a shunt route), are similar to traffic lights and can be set to stop (red), proceed (green) or some other aspect warning the driver that a signal ahead may be at stop. The current state of a signal is referred to as the *aspect of the signal*. A route, not shown on the track layout, is defined as a path traversing tracks between two signals. The details of shunt routes, which are used to join and separate trains, are not relevant for this paper. Track segments, for example *72Ca*, give a track and a direction. Track

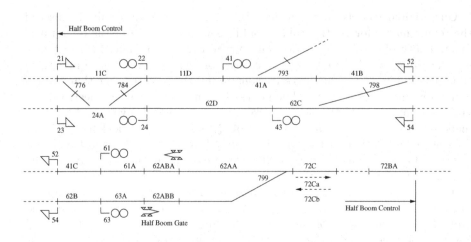

Fig. 1. An example track layout

segments are not part of actual QR railway interlocking design. We have added them to our models to express both the location and direction of trains and to model train movement.

Our original models considered two control tables: points control and signal control. The points control table specifies the requirements for moving the points. For a train to be permitted to travel along a route, the route must be *locked* for this train. The signal control table specifies the requirements for locking routes. That is, if a request is made for using a particular route, the table will specify the requirements to be satisfied for granting the request. These requirements include a set of tracks required clear (i.e., not currently occupied by a train), a set of points required normal or reverse, and routes that have to be locked normal or reverse. The conditions under which signalling equipment is held by the route are also included, such as the tracks that must be occupied and cleared before the route is available for use by another train.

Level crossings throughout Queensland are provided with protection ranging from signs only (passive) to those crossings that are protected with flashing lights and/or boom gates which may also be co-ordinated with the roads traffic light system. This paper considers crossings that use flashing lights and boom gates to protect road traffic, pedestrians and trains against collisions. There are two primary requirements in the implementation of level-crossing protection [14]:

1. Motorists and pedestrians must be provided a minimum warning time of 28 seconds.
2. Gates must be open for a minimum time of 20 seconds between consecutive operations of level-crossing protection.

The operational sequence for activating the level-crossing control and providing the necessary warning times is displayed in Figure 2. Pedestrians and motorists must be provided with 28 seconds of warning. Once the operational

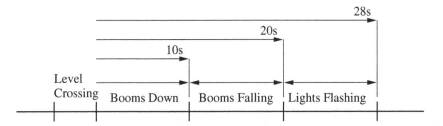

Fig. 2. Level crossing operation sequence

sequence is initiated, lights flash for eight seconds before the booms begin to fall. Half-boom gates take 10 seconds to fall and should be detected down for at least 10 seconds before the train reaches the crossing. Figure 2 describes this behaviour and illustrates when each of the events occur as a function of time.

A level crossing is labelled in Figure 1. A *level-crossing control table* is the specification of the behaviour of level crossings. It includes the conditions under which the warning sequence should be initiated and the half boom gates lowered and held down. In Figure 1 the half boom gates close the tracks $62ABA$ and $62ABB$ and the half boom control sequence (i.e., the sequence of control tracks) starts at the right and left end of the track-layout as indicated in the figure. The lowering sequence is initiated when a control track becomes occupied. The lowering sequence is also subject to the lie of points and aspects of signals between the train and level crossing as specified in the level-crossing control table. For example, the boom-gates should lower if track $41A$ is occupied unless point 793 is set reverse. These conditions are described in the level-crossing control tables.

An expression from the level-crossing control table corresponding to the track layout in Figure 1 might have the following form:

$$[\{(11C \text{ or } 776R \text{ or } 784R)\ 11D \text{ or } 41+\}(41A \text{ or } 798R) \text{ or } 793R]$$
$$(62C \text{ or } 798N)\ 41B\ 41C$$

It shows the tracks required clear which are subject to the lie of points and aspects of signals. A signal identifier followed by a $+$ indicates the signal should be red. A point identifier followed by either R or N describes whether the point should be reverse or normal respectively. Identifiers or brackets/braces not separated by a symbol or keyword are conjoined.

When checking control tables without considering time, we use a generic model which is to be instantiated for a specific verification area, which represents a subset of the track layout [18]. At a minimum, a verification area must contain one route and all of its opposing routes that affect the use of the route. Our models comprise a model of the interlocking design and one or two trains. Trains have a location and a direction indicated by the track segment they are occupying. They are well-behaved, meaning that they move through a track layout according to the lie of points and aspects of signals. We include a model of points (set *normal* or *reverse*), and routes and their locking (locked *normal* or *reverse*). A boolean input variable, *move*, is used to indicate whether or not a train is allowed to move or not (even though it will only move if *move* is true and the surrounding signalling equipment permits this). Each train is associated with a variable, *currentRoute*, of enumerated type, indicating the route that the train is using. The railway control centre places requests to set routes, points and cancel signals. The behaviour of the control centre is modelled using an input variable, *request*, of enumerated type.

To model trains and their behaviour causes a major increase in the model's complexity. Therefore, it is beneficial to restrict the number of trains in the model as much as possible. Extensive testing showed that it is sufficient to consider a *one-train model* and a *two-train model*. A one-train model assumes that only one train is in the system whereas a two-train model considers two trains running in the system. We were able to show that the one-train model is sufficient to detect all errors that cause derailment and some errors in which a route is set that opposes the *currentRoute* of the train. The two-train model has proved to be sufficient to detect front and rear collisions, and possible side swipes.

3   Introducing Time

When introducing explicit time into our interlocking model we use a discrete time model similar to the work described by Lamport [13]. Each transition in our model represents the passing of one second. Each track segment in the verification area is assigned a *duration*, which is the minimum time it takes for a train to occupy and clear the segment when travelling at the maximum permitted speed (*duration = segment length / maximum permitted speed*). Using the notation of [13] we have a *count-up timer* for each train in the model. Timers are ordinary integer variables. They are used to record how long a train has been occupying its current track segment. Each timer can be assigned values from zero to the time it takes to cross the track segment with the greatest *duration*. When a train first occupies a track segment, its count-up timer is set to zero and is incremented by one each iteration. It continues to increment until it reaches the value of the *duration* for its current track segment.

Although the count-up timer stops when it reaches the track segments *duration*, the train does not have to move onto the next track immediately. The *move* variable also determines if a train can move. It is therefore possible for the model checker to explore paths in which the train occupies a track segment for any time greater than or equal to the corresponding *duration* thus modelling trains travelling at lower than the maximum speed.

4   Modeling the Level-Crossing

The operation of level-crossing protection is modelled using two integer variables, *sequenceStatus* and *gateStatus*, and a boolean variable, *gateOpening*. We also introduce a guard, *lower_gates*, which is a boolean that is true when the level-crossing control table requires the half boom gates to be lowered, and false at all other times.

The variable *sequenceStatus* is a count-up timer. It is initialised to zero before any transitions occur and has a range of zero to the maximum warning time that is to be provided to motorists and pedestrians (28 seconds). When the conditions in the control table indicate that the warning sequence should be started, the *sequenceStatus* variable begins to increment until it reaches its maximum value or *lower_gates* becomes false. When *gateOpening* is true or *lower_gates* is false, *sequenceStatus* is returned to zero. This behaviour is defined in Algorithm 1.

Algorithm 1. Transition conditions for the *sequenceStatus* variable

---

if gateOpening $\vee$ ¬lower_gates
    sequenceStatus = 0
else if sequenceStatus < 28 $\wedge$ lower_gates
    sequenceStatus = sequenceStatus + 1
else
    sequenceStatus = sequenceStatus

The value of *sequenceStatus* has the following interpretation (see Figure 2):

- Values 1-8 indicate that motorists and pedestrians are being warned.
- Values 9-18 indicate that the boom gates are being lowered.
- Values 19-28 indicate that the gates are being held down for the minimum time of 10 seconds.

The variable *gateStatus* is a counter, that counts both up and down. The value of *gateStatus* indicates the current stage of the boom gates. It ranges from 0 to 10; if the gates are fully open then *gateStatus* is 0, if the gates are fully closed the counter is 10. Initially, *gateStatus* is 0, the gate is open.

If *gateOpening* is true, then *gateStatus* will decrement until it reaches 0 (and the gate is fully open). The variable *gateStatus* will increment when *sequenceStatus* is greater than or equal to 8, provided it is less than its maximum value and *gateOpening* is false (the gate is closing). If *gateOpening* is false and *gateStatus* is greater than 0 but *lower_gates* is false, *gateStatus* will also decrement (the gate is half closed and since the condition for lowering the gate are not satisfied it will be opened again). This is required as there is a one transition delay when *gateOpening* changes from false to true. The default case is for *gateStatus* to remain unchanged. This behaviour is defined in Algorithm 2.

Algorithm 2. Transition conditions for the *gateStatus* variable

---

if gateStatus > 0 $\wedge$ gateOpening
    gateStatus = gateStatus - 1
else if gateStatus < 10 $\wedge$ ¬gateOpening $\wedge$ sequenceStatus ≥ 8
    gateStatus = gateStatus + 1
else if ¬gateOpening $\wedge$ gateStatus > 0 $\wedge$ ¬lower_gates
    gateStatus = gateStatus - 1
else
    gateStatus = gateStatus

The variable *gateOpening* is initialised to false. If *gateOpening* is true, it will transition to false only if *gateStatus* is 0, that is, the gates are fully open. If it is false, it will transition to true if *gateStatus* is greater than zero and the conditions in the level-crossing control table indicate that the boom gates are not required closed. The default case is for *gateOpening* to be false. This behaviour is defined in Algorithm 3.

Algorithm 3. Transition conditions for the gateOpening variable

---

if gateOpening
    if gateStatus = 0
        gateOpening = false
    else
        gateOpening = true
else
    if gateStatus > 0 ∧ ¬lower_gates
        gateOpening = true
    else
        gateOpening = false

Safety properties can be expressed as simple invariants. Figure 1 includes crossing tracks *62ABA* and *62ABB*. Our model creates track segments *62ABAa*, 62ABAb, 62ABBa, *62ABBb* and includes the train position variable *trainPosition*. The resulting invariant for the NuSMV model-checker is formalised as follows

$$\neg((trainPosition = 62ABAa \ \lor \ trainPosition = 62ABAb \ \lor$$
$$trainPosition = 62ABBa \ \lor \ trainPosition = 62ABBb) \ \land$$
$$sequenceStatus < 28)$$

The invariant states that the train should not be occupying the level-crossing track segments if the operational sequence has not been activated for 28 seconds.

5   Evaluation

One-train and two-train untimed and timed models were tested on an interlocking in the Queensland Rail network. The verification area generated is of medium size. It consists of 25 tracks, 9 points, 15 signals and 28 routes. NuSMV 2.4.1 RC2 was used to run the models using a Dell PowerEdge 2850 server with 2 Intel Xeon 3192 MHz dual core processors and 4 Gb memory running CentOS. The version of NuSMV used allows the user to provide a variable ordering, transition ordering and a threshold.

The chosen orderings and threshold are based on previous work [11], where we have spent considerable time and effort to define a domain-specific variable and transition ordering that is very good (if not optimal) for the QR models when using the NuSMV model checker. When using NuSMV's implemented heuristics for finding a good transition ordering, large QR models could not be verified.

To make use of our customised transition ordering the NuSMV code had been changed in order to allow for user input to determine the transition order. Our optimised transition order has the effect that now the model checking process terminates in a reasonable time for every QR model, even the large models. These efforts are one of the main reasons for why we have introduced an explicit notion of time in the NuSMV models, rather than starting from scratch with a model checker that supports the notion of time.

To ensure our previous optimisations were still relevant for the timed models, all the experiments reported in this paper were run with three configuration options (c.f. Tables 1 and 2):

- Option 1: Using NuSMV with a user-defined variable ordering and NuSMV defaults for transition ordering and clustering.
- Option 2: Using NuSMV with a user-defined variable ordering and transition ordering and NuSMV default threshold.
- Option 3: Using NuSMV with a user-defined variable ordering, transition ordering and a threshold of 10000.

Table 1 includes a comparison of results running the untimed and timed one-train models using various parameters in NuSMV. A model of the level crossing was not included in these models. The results show that the memory use for the timed model is only slightly higher than the untimed model. The run-time, however, is significantly greater in the timed model. The difference when using parameters of Options 1, 2, and 3 (see Tables 1 and 2) is insignificant for memory use but more significant in terms of run-time. For our requirements, a long run-time is less important than memory use. It is acceptable to have a longer run-time as long as the model will terminate.

Table 1. One-train untimed and timed models without level crossings

	Option 1		Option 2		Option 3	
	Time (seconds)	Memory (Mb)	Time (seconds)	Memory (Mb)	Time (seconds)	Memory (Mb)
Untimed	5	12.98	5	12.94	4	12.74
Timed	28	13.96	20	13.72	18	13.83

Table 2 includes a comparison of results running the untimed and timed two-train models using various parameters in NuSMV. The untimed model uses an invariant stating that two trains can not occupy the same track at the same time while traveling in different directions, that is, the same track but different track segments. The timed model uses the invariant as formalised in Section 4. The results show that the memory use and run-time for the timed model with level crossings is significantly worse than the untimed model. Option 2 and 3 helped significantly reduce the run-time and memory use of both models. The run-time and memory use of the timed model using Option 3 is very good for this medium-sized interlocking.

Table 2. Two-train untimed model without level crossings and timed model with level crossings

	Option 1		Option 2		Option 3	
	Time (seconds)	Memory (Mb)	Time (seconds)	Memory (Mb)	Time (seconds)	Memory (Mb)
Untimed	507	115	558	107	396	62
Timed	8928	576	4484	409	2821	383

To test the value and effectiveness of adding time and level crossings to our model we injected errors manually by removing tracks in the level-crossing control table. Models were built and run on the faulty control tables. Counterexamples were produced for missing tracks that are closer than 28 seconds from the level crossing. Tracks that are further than 28 seconds provided sufficient time for the gates to close and no error was detected. For example, a missing entry for track *41C* can be detected but not a missing entry for track *11*C.

These results are not surprising, but they do show that it is difficult to detect a missing entry if the error does not violate a safety condition, such as *11C* missing. At this stage we do not have a model of the approach section of the level crossing, the conditions specifying when the half boom gates should be held down due to a second train approaching. Our work has, however, proved that time can be used in an industrial setting and it can successfully detect errors.

6   Related Work

Many authors have investigated supporting time at the model-checking level. The tools KRONOS [5] and UPPAAL [1] use Büchi automata extended with real-timed variables to model clocks as an input notation. They support a number of timed logics, like timed CTL (TCTL) and metric temporal logic (MTL) [12], which allow quantitative temporal reasoning over dense time. Others have also proposed including time at the model-checking level [17][16][15].

Our reason for not using a model checker for timed systems is that we extend an existing model, given in SMV input notation, which in our case provides a simpler solution than re-modelling everything in a new notation. For our purposes, the expressiveness of invariants, CTL and integer-valued time variables are sufficient. Our work shows the results and feasibility of using an explicit time model in a real industrial system.

Our work is similar to that of Lamport [13], who showed that real-time systems can be modelled using discrete time models and verified using standard model checking. In Lamport's work, time is represented using a variable *now* that is incremented by a *Tick* action. Timing bounds on actions are specified using the concept of timers: *count-up* and *countdown* timers are integer variables that are incremented and decremented, respectively, by the *Tick* action, and *expiration* timers which are left unchanged by the *Tick* action but are used as a boundary when set in relation to *now*. Lamport describes a discrete time model of the leader algorithm using a TLA+ specification to show that time can be modelled effectively in this way.

In our work, it is sufficient to use timer variables only, to measure the time a train occupies a particular track. We do not need to include an explicit representation of overall time, like *now* in [13]. We use *count-up* and *countdown* timers as well as a timer that functions as both, a *count-up* and *countdown* timer.

Clarke et al. [4] discuss discrete time with a high-level description of an aircraft control system, but do not include a detailed analysis of how to model such a system. They also introduce clocks for continuous real-time systems and support these at the model-checking level. While our timers are similar to clocks, they are specific to our models and are defined explicitly in the model.

Brinksma and Mader [2] introduced an approach for checking process control programs and the derivation of optimal control schedules using the model checker SPIN [10]. This work utilises *variable time advance* as a time-abstraction technique. This allows to abstract from intermediate states in which only time advances and "jump" to a state in which the next relevant event occurs. In our model, however, such an abstraction would not be sound since during the time steps that it takes for a train to move to the end of a track, other relevant changes can occur in the system. Those would be lost.

The Symbolic Analysis Laboratory (SAL) [6] tool suite has also been utilised to verify timed systems, which combine real-valued and discrete state variables. In Dutertre and Sorea [8] different specification approaches are presented, which range from a direct encoding of timed automata and a novel modelling approach based on event calendars [7]. The verification techniques rely on induction and abstraction to support the SAL symbolic model-checking tools. For our models so far abstraction and induction has not been necessary since the NuSMV model checker terminates in reasonable time.

7   Conclusion

Although time is a critical component of many safety-critical systems, we have found limited discussion of model checking timed systems in an industrial setting. In particular, the explicit representation of time has not been targeted. Tools such as UPPAAL and KRONOS support time at the model-checking level using clocks. They support timed logics such as TCTL and MTL. However, when considerable initial effort has been spent on an untimed model using a standard model checker, it seems preferable to keep the setting and to extend the given models using an explicit model of time.

Our results show that time can be successfully modelled explicitly using standard model checking. This is achieved by representing time as integer variables for timers and counters. We presented an approach that models time explicitly using the NuSMV model checker. We compared models of Queensland Rail's railway interlockings that did not include time with their timed extensions. We also built timed models which included a model of level crossings, for which time is a critical factor. Our results show that for a medium-sized railway interlocking we can achieve reasonable run-times and memory usage. Adding the model of the level crossing was the most significant factor that increased run-time and memory use, however this was to be expected as it required additional variables.

A lesson to be learned for us is that *"model checking real-time systems is (or can be) really simple"* [13] if the focus on time is limited to short periods and only discrete time steps are considered. In our example, we only need to count the time steps that it takes for a train to run over a particular track and the time it takes to lower the gates, etc. At the end of these periods the counters can be reset and, thus, are not assigned high values. This way, introducing time is just introducing another state variable of limited range. Due to our optimisation effort on the variable and transition orderings for QR interlocking models (as reported in [11]) the NuSMV model checker can still handle the timed version of those models.

References

1. Behrmann, G., David, A., Larsen, K.G.: A tutorial on UPPAAL. In: Bernardo, M., Corradini, F. (eds.) SFM-RT 2004. LNCS, vol. 3185, pp. 200–236. Springer, Heidelberg (2004)

2. Brinksma, E., Mader, A.: Verification and optimization of a PLC control schedule. In: Havelund, K., Penix, J., Visser, W. (eds.) SPIN 2000. LNCS, vol. 1885, pp. 73–92. Springer, Heidelberg (2000)

3. Cimatti, A., Clarke, E., Giunchiglia, F., Roveri, M.: NuSMV: A new symbolic model verifier. In: Halbwachs, N., Peled, D.A. (eds.) CAV 1999. LNCS, vol. 1633, pp. 495–499. Springer, Heidelberg (1999)

4. Clarke, E.M., Grumberg, O., Peled, D.A.: Model Checking. MIT Press, Cambridge (1996)

5. Daws, C., Olivero, A., Tripakis, S., Yovine, S.: The tool KRONOS. In: Alur, R., Sontag, E.D., Henzinger, T.A. (eds.) HS 1995. LNCS, vol. 1066, pp. 208–219. Springer, Heidelberg (1996)

6. de Moura, L., Owre, S., Rueß, H., Rushby, J., Shankar, N., Sorea, M., Tiwari, A.: SAL 2. In: Alur, R., Peled, D.A. (eds.) CAV 2004. LNCS, vol. 3114, pp. 496–500. Springer, Heidelberg (2004)

7. Dutertre, B., Sorea, M.: Modeling and verification of a fault-tolerant real-time startup protocol using calendar automata. In: Lakhnech, Y., Yovine, S. (eds.) FORMATS 2004 and FTRTFT 2004. LNCS, vol. 3253, pp. 119–214. Springer, Heidelberg (2004)

8. Dutertre, B., Sorea, M.: Timed systems in sal. Technical Report SRI-SDL-04-03, SRI Intenational (2004)

9. Emerson, E.A., Mok, A.K., Sistla, A.P., Srinivasan, J.: Quantitative temporal reasoning. Real-Time Systems 4(4), 331–352 (1992)

10. Holzmann, G.J.: The SPIN Model Checker. IEEE Transactions on Software Engineering 23(5), 279–295 (1997)

11. Johnston, W., Winter, K., van den Berg, L., Strooper, P., Robinson, P.: Model-based variable and transition orderings for efficient symbolic model checking. In: Misra, J., Nipkow, T., Sekerinski, E. (eds.) FM 2006. LNCS, vol. 4085, pp. 524–540. Springer, Heidelberg (2006)

12. Koymans, R.: Specifying real-time properties with metric temporal logic. Real-Time Syst. 2(4), 255–299 (1990)

13. Lamport, L.: Real-time model checking is really simple. In: Borrione, D., Paul, W. (eds.) CHARME 2005. LNCS, vol. 3725, pp. 162–175. Springer, Heidelberg (2005)

14. Queensland Rail Signal and Operational Systems. Signalling Principles - Brisbane Suburban Area. Technical Report S0414, Queensland Rail Technical Services Group (1998)

15. Sathawornwichit, C., Katayama, T.: A parametric model checking approach for real-time systems design. In: APSEC 2005: Proceedings of the 12th Asia-Pacific Software Engineering Conference (APSEC 2005), pp. 584–594. IEEE Computer Society Press, Los Alamitos (2005)

16. Campos, S.V., Clarke, E.: Real-Time Symbolic Model Checking for Discrete Time Models. In: Rus, T., Rattray, C. (eds.) Theories and Experiences for Real-Time System Develpment. AMAST Series in Computing. World Scientific Press, Singapore (1994)

17. Henzinger, T.A., Nicollin, X., Sifakis, J., Yovine, S.: Symbolic Model Checking for Real-Time Systems. In: 7th. Symposium of Logics in Computer Science, pp. 394–406. IEEE Computer Society Press, Los Alamitos (1992)

18. Winter, K., Johnston, W., Robinson, P., Strooper, P., van den Berg, L.: Tool support for checking railway interlocking designs. In: Cant, T. (ed.) Proc. of the 10th Australian Workshop on Safety Related Programmable Systems (SCS 2005), vol. 55, pp. 101–107. Australian Computer Society, Inc (2005)

Integration of Formal Analysis into a Model-Based Software Development Process

Michael Whalen[1], Darren Cofer[1], Steven Miller[1], Bruce H. Krogh[2],
and Walter Storm[3]

[1] Rockwell Collins Inc., Advanced Technology Center
400 Collins Rd, Cedar Rapids, IA 52498
[2] Carnegie Mellon University, Dept. of Electical & Computer Engineering
5000 Forbes Ave., Pittsburgh, PA 15123
[3] Lockheed Martin Aeronautics Company, Flight Control Advanced Development
P.O. Box 748, Ft. Worth, TX 76101
{mwwhalen, ddcofer, spmiller}@rockwellcollins.com,
krogh@ece.cmu.edu, walter.a.storm@lmco.com

Abstract. The next generation of military aerospace systems will include advanced control systems whose size and complexity will challenge current verification and validation approaches. The recent adoption by the aerospace industry of model-based development tools such as Simulink® and SCADE Suite™ is removing barriers to the use of formal methods for the verification of critical avionics software. Formal methods use mathematics to *prove* that software design models meet their requirements, and so can greatly increase confidence in the safety and correctness of software. Recent advances in formal analysis tools have made it practical to formally verify important properties of these models to ensure that design defects are identified and corrected early in the lifecycle. This paper describes how formal analysis tools can be inserted into a model-based development process to decrease costs and increase quality of critical avionics software.

Keywords: Model checking, Model-based development, Flight control, software verification.

1 Introduction

Emerging military aerospace system operational goals will require advanced safety-critical control systems with more demanding requirements and novel system architectures, software algorithms, and hardware implementations. These emerging control systems will significantly challenge current verification tools, methods, and processes. Ultimately, transition of advanced control systems to operational military systems will be possible only when there are affordable V&V strategies that reduce costs and compress schedules. The AFRL VVIACS program documented these challenges in detail [1].

Current software validation and verification for critical systems centers on testing of English-language requirements. While testing is currently the only way to examine

S. Leue and P. Merino (Eds.): FMICS 2007, LNCS 4916, pp. 68–84, 2008.
© Springer-Verlag Berlin Heidelberg 2008

the behavior of a system in its final operational environment, it is incomplete and resource intensive. The incompleteness of testing is due to the extremely large *state space* of even small control systems.

To illustrate, the number of possible states of a program with ten 32-bit integers is 10^{96}, which exceeds the number of atoms in the universe (around 10^{80}). To exhaustively test such systems is clearly impractical. Extremely large numbers of tests must be run to gain confidence in the correctness of programs, and these test suites are still insufficient to determine whether or not a system meets its requirements.

Further complicating the issue is that the requirements for the system are usually specified in English. It is often the case that these requirements are ambiguous, incomplete, and inconsistent, meaning that developers may legitimately disagree as to whether the system meets its requirements, or even that it is not possible to implement a program that meets all of the requirements.

While the benefits of formal methods have been understood for over twenty years, their use has been hampered by the lack of specification languages acceptable to practicing engineers and the level of expertise required to effectively use formal verification tools such as theorem provers. Over the last few years these hurdles have been greatly reduced by two trends: 1) the growing adoption of model-based development for safety-critical systems; and 2) the development of powerful verification tools that are easier for practicing engineers to use. The result will be a revolution in how safety-critical software is developed.

Lockheed Martin, Rockwell Collins, and Carnegie Mellon University are working together under AFRL's Certification Technologies for Advanced Flight Critical Systems (CerTA FCS) program. Our team is tasked with determining the applicability of formal methods to avionics verification concerns for next-generation control systems. Rockwell Collins has built a set of tools that translate Simulink models into the languages of several formal analysis tools, allowing "push button" analysis of Simulink models using model checkers and theorem provers. The project is split into two phases which analyze *finite* and *infinite* state models, respectively.

This paper describes the process used and the results obtained in the first phase of the project, in which we successfully and cost-effectively analyzed large finite-state subsystems within a prototype UAV controller modeled in Simulink. During the analysis, over 60 formal properties were verified and 10 model errors and 2 requirements errors were found in relatively mature models. These results are similar to previous applications of this technology on large avionics models at Rockwell Collins [2][3][10].

To use formal methods most effectively, some changes must be made to the traditional development cycle, and formal analysis should be considered when creating requirements and designing models. This paper focuses on processes and techniques for using formal methods effectively within the design cycle for critical avionics applications.

2   Formal Methods in a Model-Based Development Process

Model-Based Development (MBD) refers to the use of domain-specific modeling notations such as Simulink or SCADE that can be analyzed for desired behavior before a digital system is built. The use of such modeling languages allows a system engineer to create a model of the desired system early in the lifecycle that can be executed on the desktop, analyzed for desired behaviors, and then used to automatically generate code and test cases. Also known as *correct-by-construction* development, the emphasis in model-based development is to focus the engineering effort on the early lifecycle activities of modeling, simulation, and analysis, and to automate the late life-cycle activities of coding and testing. This reduces development costs by finding defects early in the lifecycle, avoiding rework that is necessary when errors are discovered during integration testing, and by automating coding and the creation of test cases. In this way, model-based development significantly reduces costs while also improving quality.

Formal methods may be applied in a MBD process to prevent and eliminate requirements, design and code errors, and should be viewed as complementary to testing. While testing shows that functional requirements are satisfied for specific input sequences and detects some errors, formal methods can be used to increase confidence that a system will *always* comply with particular requirements when specific conditions hold. Informally we can say that testing shows that the software *does* work for *certain test cases* and formal, analytical methods show that it *should* work for *all* cases. It follows that some verification objectives may be better met by formal, analytical means and others might be better met by testing.

Although formal methods have significant technical advantages over testing for software verification, their use has been limited in industry. The additional cost and effort of creating and reasoning about formal models in a traditional development process has been a significant barrier. Manually creating models solely for the purpose of formal analysis is labor intensive, requires significant knowledge of formal methods notations, and requires that models and code be kept tightly synchronized to justify the results of the analysis.

The value proposition for formal methods changes dramatically with the introduction of MBD and the use of completely automated analysis tools. Many of the notations in MBD have straightforward formal semantics. This means that it is possible to use models written in these languages as the basis for formal analysis, removing the incremental cost for constructing verification models. Also, model checkers are now sufficiently powerful to allow "push-button" analysis of interesting properties over large models, removing the manual analysis cost. If a property is violated, the model checker generates a counterexample, which is simply a test case that shows a scenario that violates the property. The counterexamples generated by model checkers are often better for localizing and correcting failures than discovering failures from testing and simulation because they tend to be very short (under 10 input steps) and tailored towards the specific requirement in question.

The Rockwell Collins translation framework is illustrated in Figure 1. Under a five year project sponsored in part by the NASA Langley Research Center, Rockwell Collins developed highly optimizing translators from MATLAB Simulink and SCADE Suite™ models to a variety of implicit state model checkers and theorem provers. These automated tools allow us to quickly and easily generate models for verification directly from the design models produced by the MBD process. The counterexamples generated by model checking tools can be translated back to the MBD environment for simulation. This tool infrastructure provides the means for integration of formal methods directly and efficiently into the MBD process.

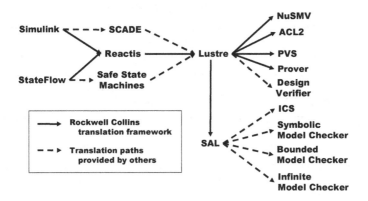

Fig. 1. Rockwell Collins model translation framework

There are at least two different ways that model checking can be integrated into a MBD process. First, it can be performed as part of the traditional verification process in a traditional waterfall model in addition to testing. This was the approach used in the first phase of the CerTA FCS project. In this approach, the model checker simply provides a significantly more rigorous verification step to ensure that the model works as intended. However, if this step is performed late in the development cycle, much of the benefit of early detection and quick removal of defects is lost.

A better approach for integrating model checking technology is to include formal analysis as an extension of a spiral development process. In an MBD process, it is common during the model design phase to use simulation as a "sanity check" to make sure that the model is performing as intended with respect to some system requirements of interest. When performed at the subsystem level, model checking allows a much more rigorous analysis based directly on the requirements of the system. If the subsystem requirements have been captured as "shall" statements, it is usually the case that these statements can be easily re-written as formal properties. Although model checking is a rigorous application of formal methods, for many kinds of models it does not require a significant amount of manual effort.

The spiral approach was used in a previous effort during the model development process for a complex cockpit displays application [2]. After each modification of the design, Simulink models were re-analyzed against a large set of requirements in a matter of minutes. By the end of the project, the model had been proven correct against all of their requirements (573 formal properties) and 98 errors had been corrected.

The guidance in this paper focuses on the use of *implicit state model checkers*, because this is the most mature of the "push-button" analysis tools, and these tools were the focus of Phase I of the CerTA FCS project. In order to reap the maximum benefit of formal analysis, models must be designed for analysis, much as they are designed for autocode or test case generation in current processes. The rest of this section provides guidelines for determining whether implicit state model checking is an appropriate technique for the model being constructed, and for using model checking successfully within the development process.

Implicit state model checkers are designed to analyze models with discrete variables that have relatively small domains: Boolean and enumerated types, or relatively small subranges of integers. The performance of the tools is primarily determined by four things: 1) the number of inputs to the model, 2) the number of latches (delays) in the model, 3) the size of each variable (number of bits), and 4) the complexity of the assignment equations for the variables. Implicit state model checkers do not have the ability to analyze models with real or floating point variables.

There are four primary questions in determining the applicability of implicit state model checkers in an MBD process.

- Does tool support exist (or can it be created) to automatically translate the MBD notation to the notation of the analysis tool? A handful of tools have model checking support built into the tool (e.g., Esterel Technologies SCADE, i-Logix State-Mate), and several more academic and commercial projects support translation into analysis tools from Simulink and Stateflow.
- If the model contains large-domain integers or floating point numbers, can these be abstracted or restructured away from the "core" of the model? Implicit state model checkers cannot reason about floating point numbers, and do not scale well with large-domain integers. However, it is often the case that there is a complex mode logic "core" that can be analyzed separately via model checking, while the surrounding code that manages the floating point or large-domain integers can be analyzed using other means.
- Can the model be partitioned into subsystems that have intrinsically interesting properties and that are of reasonable size? Model checking has been shown to be very effective at verification and validation of large software models in a model-development process. However, there are scalability limits for implicit state tools that limit the size of models that can be analyzed effectively. In Section 5, we describe strategies for structuring requirements such that requirements over the entire model are entailed by simpler obligations over subsystems within the model.
- Can the requirements be formalized? Traditional English requirements documents are often well-suited to formalization [3], so this may not be a significant a barrier to use. Also, designers tend to have an intuitive notion of the expected behavior of a subsystem, and when formalized, these properties can form excellent documentation about the behavior of a model.

If the answers to each of these questions is 'yes', then implicit state model checking is an efficient and low-cost approach for analyzing the behavior of models.

3   Changes to the Verification Process

In our experience, the introduction of model checking changes the nature of the verification process. Instead of focusing on the creation of test vectors, the focus is on the creation of *properties* and *environmental assumptions*. The properties are translations of natural language requirements into a formal notation, and the environmental assumptions are constraints on the inputs of the model that describe the intended operating environment for the model.

Figure 2 illustrates the difference between a test-based process and analysis-based verfication. In a test-based verification process, test cases must be developed for each requirement. Each test case defines a combination of input values (a test vector) or a sequence of inputs (a test sequence) that specifies the operating condition(s) under which the requirement must hold. The test case must also define the output to be produced by the system under test in response to the input test sequence.

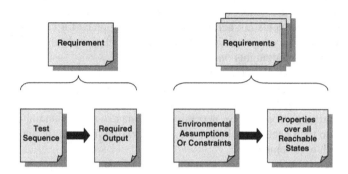

Fig. 2. Test-based verification (left) vs. Analysis-based verification (right)

An analysis-based verification process may be thought of in the same way. We normally consider a group of requirements, with related functionality for a particular subsystem. The environmental assumptions or constraints specify the operating conditions under which the requirements must hold. The properties define subsystem behaviors (values of outputs or state variables) that must hold for all system states reachable under the specified environmental assumptions.

The essential difference is one of precision: model checking requires the specification of *exactly* what is meant by specific requirements and determines *all* possible violations of those requirements at the subsystem level. This precision can be challenging, because an engineer is no longer allowed to rely on an intuitive understanding to create test vectors. Also, in some cases, the notation used for properties (such as CTL and LTL [4]) can be confusing, though there are a variety of notations (including the MBD languages themselves!) that can be used to mitigate this difficulty. Also, *precise* is not the same as *correct*. If a property is incorrectly written, then obviously a formal analysis tool may be unable to uncover incorrect behavior within a model. Therefore, it is very important that properties are carefully written and reviewed to ensure that they match the intuitive understanding of the requirement.

The fact that a model checker generates a counterexample from the set of *all* possible violations of a property often leads to 'nonsensical' counterexamples in which the model inputs change in ways that would be impossible in the real environment. In order to remove these counterexamples that will not occur in the real system, it is sometimes necessary to describe environmental constraints that describe how the inputs to the model are allowed to evolve. On the bright side, these constraints serve as a precise description of the environmental assumptions required by the component to meet its requirements.

We next describe specific changes to the verification process to facilitate the use of model checking tools.

Creating Formalizable Requirements

There are many different notations and tools used for capturing requirements in the avionics domain. These notations include traditional structured English "shall" statements, use cases, SCR specifications [5], CoRE documents [6], and others. Most avionics systems still use "shall" statements as the basis of their requirements. In our experience, shall statements are actually a good starting place for creating formalized requirements. Their prevalence indicates they are a natural and intuitive way for designers to put their first thoughts on paper.

The problem with shall statements has been that inconsistencies, incompleteness, and ambiguities are not found until the later phases of the project. The process of formalizing the requirements into properties helps remove the problem of ambiguity. When formalizing a property, by necessity, one must write an unambiguous statement. The issue then becomes whether the formalization matches the intention of the original English requirement.

Inconsistencies can be detected in several ways. First, if all requirements are formalized, then it is not possible to simultaneously prove all properties over a model if the set of properties are inconsistent. With additional translation support, it is also possible to query a model checker to determine whether *any* model can satisfy all of the properties simultaneously. There are also current research projects to define metrics for requirements completeness over a given formal model using model checking tools [7], but this research is not yet usable on an industrial scale.

Testable requirements are also analyzable, so this is a good starting point for determining whether requirements are suitable for analysis. On the other hand, there are classes of requirements that are not testable but are, in fact, analyzable. For example, requirements such as:

- the system shall *never* allow behavior x,
- given y, the system shall *always eventually* do z

can be analyzed formally, but are not suitable for testing as they require an unbounded number of test cases.

Other system requirement techniques such as use cases are also possible sources of properties. While more structured than shall statements, as practiced today use cases normally lack a precise formal semantics and suffer from the same problems of inconsistency, incompleteness, and ambiguity as shall statements. While not part of this experiment, it seems reasonable that it should be possible to express use cases as a sequence of properties describing how the system responds to its stimuli, and to verify these sequences through simulation and formal analysis. In this way, the consistency and completeness of use cases could be improved in the same manner as was done for shall statements.

Creating Environmental Assumptions

One significant change when moving from a testing-based verification process to a formal process is that much more attention must be focused on environmental assumptions for the system being analyzed. Often, there are a significant number of environmental assumptions that are built into the design of the control software that cause it to fail when those assumptions are violated, and these assumptions are often not well documented. In testing, it is usually the case that the tester has an intuitive understanding of the system under test and is unlikely to create test scenarios where the plane is "flying upside-down and backwards". The model checker, on the other hand, will often find requirements violations that occur under such scenarios if environmental constraints that rule out impossible conditions are not stated explicitly.

It is often not possible to verify interesting safety properties on a large model in a completely unconstrained environment. As part of the analysis process, we examine the environmental assumptions in the requirements document to create constraints on the possible values of inputs into the system. Each of the model checking tools that we have examined supports *invariants* that allow engineers to specify constraints on the behavior of the environment. Here, "environment" means any inputs or parameters that can affect the behavior of the model being verified, and invariants are restrictions on these environmental variables. These invariants should be as simple as possible so as to not impact unduly the efficiency of the verification algorithm, but they must be sufficiently complex to assure that the specification is being evaluated for the relevant conditions. For example, for specifications for a controller model that are related to the closed-loop behavior of the system, the appropriate invariant may require the creation of a "plant model" representing a reactive environment that responds dynamically to the controller outputs.

Although invariants are necessary to prove "interesting" properties over subsystems, they are also dangerous to the soundness and applicability of the analysis. If conflicting invariants are specified, then there are *no states that satisfy the invariants*, so all properties are trivially true. Similarly, if invariants restrict the set of allowed inputs so that it is a subset of the possible inputs to the real system, then our analysis will be incomplete. Finally, just because constraints are specified in the requirements document does not mean that the environment, which can include other subsystems, will actually obey these constraints.

Therefore, although we formalize the invariants in this step *we do not use them in our initial model checking analysis.* If the initial subsystem analyses return counterexamples, we analyze the counterexamples to see whether they are due to violations of our invariants or due to incorrect behavior within the model. Even if counterexamples are due to invariant violations, we prefer to strengthen the model behavior, when possible, to deal with abnormal environments rather than use system invariants. If it is determined that there is no good way to handle abnormal environments within the model, then we finally begin to use the invariants derived from the environmental assumptions.

It is worth noting that such environmental assumptions were precisely the cause of the Arianne V disaster [8], when an assumption about the lateral velocity of the rocket shortly after liftoff was violated when the control software was reused from the Arianne IV, causing it to fail catastrophically. By requiring developers to make their assumptions about the operating environment explicit and precise, a formal analysis process can help to eliminate this type of error.

Interpreting Counterexamples

One of the benefits of using a model checker in the verification process is the generation of counterexamples that illustrate how a property has been violated. However, for large systems it can be difficult and time consuming to determine the root cause of the violation by examining only the model checker output. Instead, the simulation capabilities of the MBD tools should be utilized to allow playback of a counterexample.

Both Simulink and SCADE have sophisticated simulation capabilities that allow single-step playback of tests and easy "drill down/drill up" through the structure of the model. These capabilities can be used to quickly localize the cause of failure for a counterexample. Third-party tools such as Reactis [11] for Simulink also allow a "step back" function so that it is possible to rewind and step through a sequence of steps within a counterexample, adding to the explanatory power of the tool.

When a counterexample is discovered, it is classified by its underlying cause and appropriate corrective action taken. The cause may be one or more of the following:

- Modeling error
- Property formalization error
- Incorrect/missing invariants for the subsystem
- High-Level requirements error

4   Changes to the Modeling Process

Flight control models, such as the Lockheed Martin operational flight program (OFP) model analyzed in our CerTA FCS project, are too large to be efficiently analyzed by current model checkers. There are several development practices that should be adopted within a MBD process to create models that are suitable for analysis. These practices will yield models that will be simpler to analyze.

Partitioning the System

The first step in analyzing the model is to divide the requirements and model into subsystems that can be automatically analyzed. *Analysis partitions* are created by splitting the original model into different subsystems and assigning a set of system requirements that will be analyzed on the subsystem (Figure 3). After the subsystems have been created, each subsystem is separately analyzed. The result of the analysis process may require changes to the subsystem under analysis, to another subsystem, or to the system-level requirements or environmental assumptions.

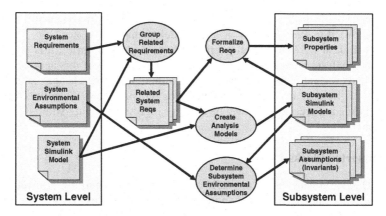

Fig. 3. Process for creating analysis partitions

There are several steps necessary to create the analysis partitions.

Group Related Requirements. To create analysis partitions, we first try to group system requirements into sets that can be checked against a portion of the system Simulink model. In our experience with the WM and the FCS 5000 [3], it is usually the case that the properties naturally partition into sets that are functionally related to one another, and that the truth or falsehood of these property sets can be determined by examining a relatively small portion of the entire Simulink model.

Create Analysis Models. After grouping the properties, we split the system model into reasonably-sized analysis models that are sufficient to check one or more of the requirements groups. We would like to make each subsystem small enough that it is quick to analyze using our BDD-based model checking tools.

Formalizing Requirements. The next step in analyzing the model involves formalizing the functional and safety requirements as properties. For a synchronous system where the requirements are specified as "shall" statements over system inputs and outputs, this process is often straightforward. In [2], [3], and [10], we described the process of translating these informal statements into safety properties in more detail.

The system requirements document is not the only source of properties to be analyzed. Properties also emerge from discussions with developers about the functionality of different subsystems, or even from a careful review of a particular implementation detail of the Simulink model. In some cases, these properties can be thought of as validity checks for particular implementation choices, but on occasion they lead to additions to the system requirements document.

Using Libraries

The construction of analysis partitions can be simplified by splitting the original model into *libraries*. Both Simulink and SCADE support packaging of subsystems into libraries, which are really just additional "source" files for the model. Just as it makes sense to construct a large C program using several source files (for various reasons, including version control), it makes sense to construct models using library files.

If a Simulink or SCADE model is created from a set of libraries, it is possible to generate the analysis models with very little effort. A benefit of this approach is that the subsystems within the libraries can evolve without requiring changes to the analysis models, as long as the subsystem interfaces remain stable. Therefore, once the analysis models are created, they can be used for regression testing without any additional effort.

Using Supported Blocks

Most MBD environments were originally constructed for the purpose of modeling and simulation, or for autogeneration of source code, and not for design analysis. It is usually necessary to restrict the use of certain constructs within a MBD language that complicate the semantics of the language, or that have potentially undefined behavior outside of the simulation environment. Some languages, such as SCADE, were built for formal analysis, and so almost all features of the SCADE environment (i.e., all aspects that do not involve use of a 'host' language, such as C, to implement functionality) can be formally analyzed. Simulink contains an extremely wide range of block sets with varying levels of formality. None of the current model checking tools for Simulink/StateFlow support all of the block sets that can be used within the language.

The Rockwell Collins translation tools support a wide range of Simulink/StateFlow constructs. This toolset is tailored for critical avionics software, and is able to analyze all of the blocks used in the OFP model.

Structuring for Analysis

Design choices that lead to code-bloat or poorly cohesive systems also affect the performance of the model checker. A rule of thumb is that the larger the number of blocks within a model, the longer it will require to analyze. Therefore, model re-factoring is not only a useful design activity, but often necessary to successfully analyze large subsystem models.

In our experience, we have re-factored models in which some piece of functionality (e.g., display application placement) is replicated (e.g., left-side and right-side display application placement) by "copy and paste reuse". By properly packaging the functionality into subsystems, we can split the analysis task into independent parts, leading to much faster analysis.

Similarly, when creating the analysis models, it is possible to indirectly analyze subsystem coupling by examining the complexity of invariants between the outputs of one subsystem and the inputs of another subsystem. If complex invariants are required to prove properties about a subsystem, then it is likely that the subsystem is tightly coupled to the subsystem that generates the outputs. These cases should be examined to determine if it is possible to re-factor the design to simplify the analysis invariants.

Structuring for Predicate Abstraction

If models contain several large-domain integers and/or real numbers, they will not be analyzable by current tools. However, it is often the case that these variables can be factored out of modules that contain the complex behavior that would benefit most from formal analysis. The idea is to either abstract the conditions that involve numeric constraints or the ranges of the constants and variables involved in the conditions.

Subsystems that compute system modes often contain a handful of large-domain integers that are used for comparisons in conditions within the mode computation, e.g., *Altitude > PreSelectAlt + AltCapBias*. If the ranges of these integers are large, e.g., zero to 50000 feet, analysis may become intractable, even though they only influence a few conditions within the logic. In this case, it is much simpler for formal analysis if the original comparisons in the mode logic are replaced with Boolean inputs representing the result of the comparison (e.g., *Altitude_Gt_PreSelect_Plus_AltCapBias*). This input is then computed by an external subsystem which can be separately (and usually trivially) checked for correctness. This kind of model factoring is called *predicate abstraction* [9], and can reduce the analysis time required from hours to seconds in the original subsystem.

If the model contains a significant number of variables and the constraints involving those variables are related, or if it uses the variables to compute numeric outputs, predicate abstraction is less useful. In these cases, it is often possible to perform domain reductions in order to scale the ranges so as to be able to analyze the models successfully.

Reducing State through Type Replacement

A primary limiting factor when using the model checker is the size of the state space. In this section, we describe strategies to reduce the size of the model state space in order to apply implicit state model checking technology.

Using Generic Types. The implicit state model-checking tools that we use are unable to reason about real numbers. Fortunately, it is often the case that the interesting safety-related behavior is preserved by replacing real-valued variables by integers for the purpose of analysis [9]. We have used a simplified version of predicate abstraction, which attempts to reduce the domain of a variable while preserving the interesting traces of the system behavior, i.e., the ones that can lead to a counterexample. The idea is to preserve enough values such that all conditions involving real numbers will be completely exercised.

From a design-for-analysis perspective, both Simulink and SCADE support a notion of generic types that allow models to be constructed that can use either integers or reals. The only place where the types must be specified is at the "top-level" inputs. If models are constructed using library blocks, then very little effort is required to derive analysis models from the original models.

Limiting Integer Ranges. To efficiently model-check a specification, we would like to determine the minimal range necessary to represent the behavior of each variable in the model. This is because the performance of BDD-based model checkers is directly correlated to the ranges of the variables in the model. The Rockwell Collins translation tools currently allow a high degree of control over the integer range of each variable within the model. It is possible for the user to specify both the default range of all integer variables within the model, and also to set the ranges for individual variables within the model. This allows us to trim unreachable values of variables and reduce the system state space. If we inadvertently eliminate a reachable value, the model checker will detect this and the variable range can be corrected.

5 Analysis Results

In this section, we discuss the application of the process described here to the analysis of finite-state models from the Lockheed Martin OFP Simulink model. In this analysis we focused on the Redundancy Manager (RM) component of the OFP.

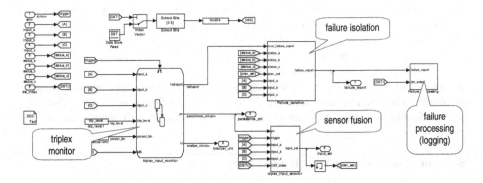

Fig. 4. Simulink model for triplex voter subsystem of the Redundancy Manager

Redundancy Manager Verification Results

The redundancy manager model originally consisted of two main subsystems: *triplex_voter,* which implements sensor fusion and failure detection for a triply redundant sensor, and *reset_manager,* which implements the pilot and global failure reset functionality for the sensors and control surfaces for the aircraft. The triplex_voter (see Figure 4) contains a fault monitor that detects failed sensors, failure isolation logic to prevent failed sensors from influencing the output, and a sensor fusion function to synthesize the correct sensor output. It also contains a fault logging function called the fault history table (FHT) that introduces a significant amount of state but is functionally isolated from the rest of the voter. Therefore, we factored this FHT functionality into a third subsystem, *failure processing.*

These models contained a mix of Simulink and StateFlow subsystems, and initially the triplex voter model contained floating-point inputs and outputs. Some of the more complex model features used were data stores with multiple reads/writes within a step, triggered and enabled subsystems with merge blocks, boundary-crossing and directed acyclic transitions through junctions, variables that were used both as integers and as bit flags, bit-level operations (shifts, masks, and bit-level ANDs and ORs), and StateFlow truth tables and functions. As shown in Table 1, during the course of our analysis we derived three analysis models from the RM model, checked 62 properties and found 12 errors. The complete analysis of all the properties using the NuSMV model checker takes approximately 7 minutes.

Table 1. Model size and analysis results for Redundancy Manager

Subsystem	Number of Simulink subsystems / blocks	Reachable State Space	Properties	Confirmed Errors
Triplex voter without FHT	10 / 96	$6.0 * 10^{13}$	48	5
Failure processing	7 / 42	$2.1 * 10^4$	6	3
Reset manager	6 / 31	$1.32 * 10^{11}$	8	4
Totals	23 / 169	N/A	62	12

As an illustration of the properties analyzed for the Redundancy Manager, one requirement states that:

A single frame miscompare shall not cause a sensor to be declared failed.

A miscompare occurs when one of the three sensors disagrees with the other two sensors by more than a predefined tolerance level. This requirement states that a transient error on one of the sensors will not cause the sensor to be declared failed.

In the RM model, failures are recorded in the *device status table* (DST), and the sensor values are input to the model as input_a, input_b, input_c. From the requirements, we create variables representing when a sensor value miscompares with the other sensor values:

```
DEFINE
     a_miscompare :=
             (abs(input_a - input_b) > trip_level) &
             (abs(input_a - input_c) > trip_level) &
             (abs(input_b - input_c) <= trip_level);
     b_miscompare := ...
     c_miscompare := ...
```

These variables state that a sensor miscompares if it is outside of tolerance (trip_level) with the other two sensors and the other two sensors are within tolerance of each other. In a single frame miscompare, the sensor does not miscompare in the current frame but does miscompare in the next frame. In this case, the sensor must not be marked failed in the next frame.

Given these definitions, we can encode the property in CTL as follows:

```
AG((!a_miscompare) ->
     AX(failure_report != a_failed));
AG((!b_miscompare) ->
     AX(failure_report != b_failed));
AG((!c_miscompare) ->
     AX(failure_report != c_failed));
```

This property was violated in the original triplex voter model. The root cause of this error is that the model used a single counter to record the number of consecutive miscompares to determine whether to fail a sensor. If one sensor miscompares for several frames and then another sensor miscompares for a single frame at the failure threshold, then the second sensor will be declared failed.

This error was corrected by creating separate persistence counters for each input so that miscompares for one sensor will not cause another sensor to be declared failed.

Effort Required

The total effort required to perform the formal analysis was 399.8 hours. As shown in Figure 5, we broke down the analysis time along two axes: the phases of the analysis process and the type of effort. The three main phases of the analysis process are:

- **Preparation:** This task described the effort necessary to extend the analysis tools and condition the models for analysis.
- **Initial Verification:** This task described the effort necessary to perform the initial formal analysis of the models.
- **Rework:** This task described the effort necessary to fix the models and complete the analysis.

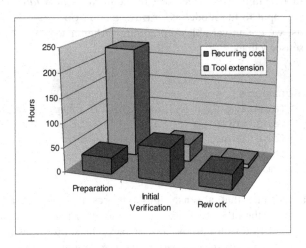

Fig. 5. Categorization of verification effort

We identified two types of effort: tool modification (one-time tasks extending the capabilities of the tools for this project) and verification activites (tasks that would be carried out for each application). The largest effort for this project was tool modification, extending the Rockwell Collins translators to handle the subset of Simulink / StateFlow used by Lockheed Martin in the CerTA FCS models. This is a non-recurring cost that can be amortized in future analysis projects. This tool modification effort occurred both during the preparation phase (the initial tool up) and in the initial verification phase (where additional tool optimizations were discovered to speed the analysis).

The majority of the one-time tool modification costs occurred during preparation, when we were extending the translation tools to handle the additional blocks used in the CerTA FCS models. The remaining tool modifications costs were due to a handful of bugs in the tool extensions that were found during the verification effort.

The verification activities, which represent recurring costs, were fairly evenly distributed between the preparation, initial analysis, and rework. A significant fraction of the verification time went towards model preparation because the models were not initially constructed for analysis, so several of the "design for analysis" steps detailed in Section 4 had to be performed. Had the formal analysis been integrated into the design cycle, much of this work would have been unnecessary.

After the initial verification and rework effort on the original model, Lockheed Martin provided a modified version of the triplex voter with 10 additional requirements. Since the model had already been structured for automatic translation and analysis, only minor changes were needed. There included addition of input and output ports, definition of appropriate type replacements, and specification of the new properties. In this case, six of the new properties failed due to a single logic error in the new design. The modifications, verification, and results analysis were accomplished in approximately eight hours. This further illustrates the potential for cost savings.

6 Conclusion

This paper describes how formal methods (model checking) can be successfully injected into an avionics software development cycle and how this can lead to early detection and removal of errors in software designs. As a demonstration, we applied this technology to one of the major subsystems of an existing Lockheed Martin Aeronautics Company operational flight plan model, analyzing 62 properties and discovering 12 errors. These results are similar to previous applications of this technology on large avionics models at Rockwell Collins.

In this effort, we performed model checking as an augmentation of the traditional verification process after the models had been developed. In this approach, the model checker provides a verification step that is significantly more rigorous than simulation to ensure that the model works as intended. The total (recurring) time required for analysis was approximately 130 hours, of which about 70 hours were required to prepare the models and perform the initial verification.

Although we were successful, we believe that formal verification can have an even greater impact if its use is anticipated from the outset in the design process. In this paper, we described how model checking can be integrated into the design cycle for models to yield additional benefits. The changes to the development process focused on designing models for analysis and regular use of the model checker during design. The former change significantly reduces the time required to prepare models for analysis, and the latter allows bugs to be found very early in the development cycle, when they are cheapest to fix.

In the next phase of the CerTA FCS project, we will attempt to analyze models that contain large-domain integers and reals. This will be a significant challenge, and will involve investigating new model checking algorithms and theorem provers. On the model checking side, we will be investigating tools that use two recent checking algorithms: k-induction and interpolation, which can be used to analyze the behavior of models containing large-domain integers and reals. Unfortunately, these model check-ing algorithms have a significant restriction in that they only analyze models contain-ing linear arithmetic. Therefore, we will also be investigating the use of theorem provers that can analyze arbitrarily complex non-linear models, but require greater expertise on the part of users.

Acknowledgments. This work was supported in part by AFRL and Lockheed Martin Aeronautics Company under prime contract FA8650-05-C-3564.

References

1. Buffington, J.M., Crum, V., Krogh, B.H., Plaisted, C., Prasanth, R., Bose, P., Johnson, T.: Validation & verification of intelligent and adaptive control systems (VVIACS)*. In: AIAA Guidance, Navigation and Control Conference (August 2004)
2. Whalen, M.W., Innis, J.D., Miller, S.P., Wagner, L.G.: ADGS-2100 Adaptive Display & Guidance System Window Manager Analysis, NASA Contractor Report CR-2006-213952 (February 2006)
3. Miller, S., Heimdahl, M.P.E., Tribble, A.C.: Proving the Shalls. In: Proceedings of FM 2003: the 12th International FME Symposium, Pisa, Italy, September 8-14 (2003)
4. Clarke, E., Grumberg, O., Peled, P.: Model Checking. The MIT Press, Cambridge (2001)
5. Heitmeyer, C., Jeffords, R., Labaw, B.: Automated Consistency Checking of Requirements Specification. ACM Transactions on Software Engineering and Methodology (TOSEM) 5(3), 231–261 (1996)
6. Faulk, S., Brackett, J., Ward, P., Kirby Jr, J.: The CoRE Method for Real-Time Require-ments. IEEE Software 9(5), 22–33 (1992)
7. Chockler, H., Kupferman, O., Vardi, M.Y.: Coverage metrics for formal verification. In: Geist, D., Tronci, E. (eds.) CHARME 2003. LNCS, vol. 2860, pp. 111–125. Springer, Heidelberg (2003)
8. Lions, J.L.: Arianne 5 Flight 501 Failure Report by the Inquiry Board, ESA Technical Re-port No. 33-1996 (July 1996)
9. Choi, Y., Heimdahl, M.P.E., Rayadurgam, S.: Domain reduction abstraction. Technical Report 02-013. University of Minnesota (April 2002)
10. Tribble, A.C., Lempia, D.D., Miller, S.P.: Software Safety Analysis of a Flight Guidance System. In: Proceedings of the 21st Digital Avionics Systems Conference (DASC 2002), Irvine, California, October 27-31 (2002)
11. Reactive Systems, Inc, Reactis Home Page, http://www.reactive-systems.com

Formal Verification with Isabelle/HOL in Practice: Finding a Bug in the GCC Scheduler

Lars Gesellensetter, Sabine Glesner, and Elke Salecker

Institute for Software Engineering and Theoretical Computer Science,
Technical University of Berlin, FR 5-6, Franklinstr. 28/29, 10587 Berlin, Germany
{lgeselle, glesner, salecker}@cs.tu-berlin.de
http://pes.cs.tu-berlin.de/

Abstract. Software bugs can cause tremendous financial loss and are a serious threat to life or physical condition in safety-critical areas. Formal software verification with theorem provers aims at ensuring that no errors are present but is too expensive to be employed for full-scale systems. We show that these costs can be reduced significantly by reusing proofs and by the checker approach. We demonstrate the applicability of our approach by a case study checking the correctness of the scheduler of the popular GCC compiler for a VLIW processor where we indeed found an error.

1 Introduction

Software systems are becoming increasingly important in our daily lifes, especially in safety-critical areas. This raises the question whether these systems work as they are supposed to. Formal verification is a way of guaranteeing correct behavior. In this paper, we investigate how program transformations, e.g. as performed in compilers, can be formally verified by using theorem provers, in particular Isabelle/HOL. Formal software verification with theorem provers completely ensures that no special cases have been overlooked and that the system behaves according to its specification. However, formal verification is very expensive because most proofs of software correctness are conducted in higher-order logic and require user interaction. To overcome this serious limitation, we seek to reduce these costs, e.g. by reusing formalizations and proofs (which is by far not state of the art in formal software verification). Moreover, we work on methods to automatically compose correctness proofs for larger systems from the correctness proofs of their subsystems. Finally, we also work on the clever combination of verification and checking methods, which, in combination, still guarantee formally correct results while at the same time significantly reducing the overall verification costs.

In this paper, we focus on the problem of verifying scheduling, in particular the scheduling process for VLIW[1] processors in compilers, a transformation that

---

[1] VLIW = very long instruction word.

S. Leue and P. Merino (Eds.): FMICS 2007, LNCS 4916, pp. 85–100, 2008.

analyzes data dependencies and puts data-independent instructions in instruction groups that can be executed in parallel. Our formalization relies on the observation that only essential data dependencies exist in suitable intermediate program representations of compilers. These data dependencies define a partial order on the instructions. We have directly adapted this point of view by formalizing a semantics for compiler intermediate languages based on partial orders. We regard scheduling as a process of inserting further dependencies into this order. As long as the order relation remains acyclic and contains the original relation, scheduling is correct. A particular advantage of our proof formalization is that it is naturally divided into two parts: the more general part formalizing partial orders and the insertion of new dependencies, and the specific part about the concrete VLIW scheduling. This separation enables us to reuse the more general part of our formalization and the corresponding correctness proofs for other scheduling problems as well.

Our correctness proof formalized in Isabelle/HOL provides us with a formally verified criterion that every correct schedule must fulfill and that can be used to verify the results of a given scheduler implementation. Moreover, by using Isabelle's code generation facilities, we generate a checker from our proof formalization that checks this formally verified criterion for each run of the scheduler, cf. Figure 1. If the checker states that the criterion is fulfilled, then the schedule

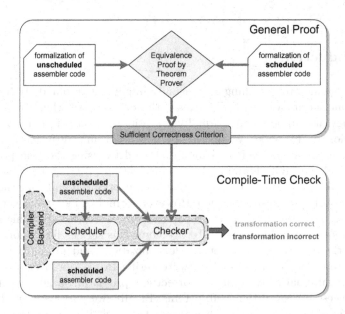

Fig. 1. Our Checker Approach

has been verified. This checker can be attached to any compiler implementation. If connected appropriately to the compiler (i.e. if it receives the program before and after scheduling), it tells for each run of the compiler whether the input program was scheduled correctly. Thus we do not know that the scheduler is correct for all cases. But for all translated programs, we can tell if they were correctly transformed. In the positive case, we then have a formal proof for their correctness, provided by an instantiation of our general correctness proof, formulated in Isabelle/HOL.

From a program analysis point of view, VLIW processors are particularly interesting because they allow the compiler to exploit its global view on programs – in contrast to the only limited overview that, say, a superscalar processor has on the directly succeeding instructions. However, these optimizations are error-prone, a fact also demonstrated by a bug in the VLIW scheduler of the GCC that we found with our checker during the case study.

This paper is organized as follows: In Section 2, we summarize foundations of our work concerning static single assignment (SSA) intermediate representations in compilers as well as scheduling in VLIW processors. Section 3 presents our Isabelle/HOL formalization and proof for the correctness criterion of scheduling results. In Section 4, we show how this criterion can be used to generate a checker, which has been used in our case study summarized in Section 5. We discuss related work in Section 6 and give our conclusions in Section 7.

2 Background

2.1 Static Single Assignment (SSA) Representations

Static single assignment (SSA) form has become the preferred intermediate representation for handling all kinds of program analyses and optimizing transformations prior to code generation [CFR+91]. Its main merits comprise the explicit representation of def-use-chains and, based on them, the ease by which further data-flow information can be derived. In SSA form, every variable is assigned statically only once. SSA form can be obtained by suitable duplication and renaming of variables and is very well-suited for optimizations. As most intermediate representations, SSA form is based on basic blocks. Basic blocks are maximal sequences of operations that do not contain branches or jumps. Within basic blocks, computations are purely data-flow driven because an operation can be executed as soon as its operands are available. The control-flow of the program connects the individual basic blocks.

While SSA form is usually used for high-level intermediate representations within a compiler, its concept is general and can also be applied to the assembler level. Here SSA form means that each register is assigned only once in a basic block. The identification of basic blocks is trivial for assembler code, basic block borders are given by jump labels or jump instructions. In this paper, we concentrate on the verification of the data-flow driven parts of SSA computations and their scheduling into VLIW code.

2.2 Scheduling for VLIW Processors

Scheduling is a compiler optimization that (re-)arranges the instructions to improve runtime performance. The improvement is achieved mainly by:

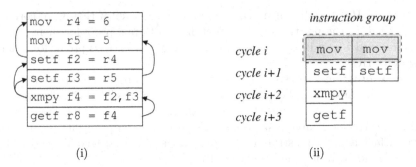

Fig. 2. Scheduling for VLIW Processors: (i) Instruction Sequence (ii) Schedule

- hiding instruction latencies: instead of waiting for a result, the processor executes other instructions that do not depend on it
- exploiting resources: on a parallel processor, several instructions can be executed at the same time

The scheduler takes the instructions of the program and defines at which processor cycle each instruction should be executed. It is important that the scheduler transforms the program correctly, i.e. that the program behavior is not changed. To this end, the scheduler has to ensure that no instruction is executed before the values it needs are available.

In case of VLIW processors, multiple instructions can be assigned to one cycle. Thus, the scheduler plays a key role in achieving efficient code since the amount of parallelism exploited depends heavily on the schedule. As opposed to superscalar processors, which are also parallel but reorder instructions dynamically at program run-time, VLIW processors leave the code unchanged. So the scheduler has to take care that dependent instructions are not put in the same cycle since this cannot be detected by the processor and will lead to incorrect behavior.

Most schedulers perform scheduling not at program but at *basic block* level. Because of the *SSA* form, only data dependencies have to be considered within a basic block. Thus instructions can be rearranged arbitrarily by the scheduler as long as no data dependencies are violated.

As an example of scheduling, consider Fig. 2. On the left hand side, the assembler code for an integer multiplication on the Intel Itanium is shown (Fig. 2(i)). The operands are put in registers r4 and r5, respectively. The considered processor is only able to multiply floating point registers (xmpy), so the integer values have to be transferred from integer registers to floating point registers (setf) and back again (getf). The result of the multiplication is available in r8. Note the data dependencies between the instructions, indicated by arrows. From this information, the scheduler can find an optimal order of the instructions, as shown in Fig. 2(ii). We refer to the set of instructions that are executed in the same cycle (i.e. the lines in Fig. 2(ii)) as *instruction group*. This program will serve as running example throughout this paper.

3   Formalization in Isabelle/HOL

A formal semantics of the involved programming languages is a basic requirement for each formal verification of transformations performed by compilers. Different formalizations are possible, as long as all properties are reflected that are required to prove semantic equivalence between a program and its transformed version. We have developed an Isabelle/HOL formalization for SSA form that is based on very abstract principles and has only few SSA specific parts [BGLM05]. With this formalization we could prove the correctness of code generation from SSA form. In this paper we present an extension of this formalization for scheduled code and a correctness proof for scheduling algorithms. Formalization and proof are based on a reuse of the SSA-independent parts and on proofs of our previous formalization. With this work we demonstrate the reusability of our previous formalization and its corresponding proofs.

In Section 3.1 we summarize the most important parts of the formal semantics for SSA form (see [BGLM05] for the detailed description). In Section 3.2, we present our new formalization of VLIW schedules. Finally, in Section 3.3 we describe in detail the correctness criterion that relates our formalization with realistic schedulers and will be used by our checker. We conclude by addressing the issue of reusing our formalization.

3.1   Partial Orders

Evaluation of SSA basic blocks only needs to consider data dependencies. Such data-flow driven computations induce partial orders. Constant functions and input values of a basic block correspond to elements of the partial order without predecessors. Elements with predecessors denote operations that directly or indirectly need results of other operations for their computation. Based on this observation we have formalized partial orders as a self-contained part and developed our semantics for SSA starting from it.

To formalize partial orders, we introduce the notion *relational set* by defining the type *RelSet*. A relational set is a pair with a carrier set of an arbitrary but fixed type, denoted $'a$ in Isabelle/HOL, as its first and a relation over the type $'a$ as its second component. A relational set fulfills the predicate *sane* if all elements occurring in the field of the relation are elements of the carrier set.

---

types $'a\,RelSet = \,'a\,set \times ('a \times 'a)\,set$
constdefs *sane* :: $'a\,RelSet \Rightarrow bool$
$sane\,RS \equiv \forall a\,b\,.\,(a,b) \in snd\,RS \longrightarrow a \in fst\,RS \wedge b \in fst\,RS$

A *strict finite partial order* (*sfpo*) is a relational set that is *sane*, has a finite carrier set and a transitive and irreflexive relation. Antisymmetry of the relation follows from transitivity and irreflexivity. The function *sfpo_union* takes a relational set $rs = (c, rel)$ and a set of pairs r as parameters and returns a "larger" relational set $rs' = (c, rel')$ with $rel' = (rel \cup r)^{+}$.

$$\textbf{constdefs } sfpo :: {}'a\,RelSet \Rightarrow bool$$
$$sfpo\,RS \equiv finite\,(fst\,RS) \wedge sane\,RS \wedge trans\,(snd\,RS) \wedge irrefl\,(snd\,RS)$$
$$\textbf{constdefs } sfpo\_union :: {}'a\,RelSet \Rightarrow ({}'a \times {}'a)\,set \Rightarrow bool$$
$$sfpo\_union\,rs\,r \equiv (fst\,rs, (snd\,rs \cup r)^{+})$$

A concrete SSA representation is formalized by the data structure *ssa_graph*. It is defined as a record that specifies the nodes of the SSA graph (*base*), what kind of instruction a node represents (*function*) and all its predecessors (*plist*). This formalization abstracts from concrete details and can be instantiated with formalizations of concrete instruction sets or intermediate representations.

$$\textbf{record } {}'a\,ssa\_graph = base :: nodeId\,set$$
$$plist :: nodeId \Rightarrow nodeId\,list$$
$$function :: nodeId \Rightarrow ({}'a\,valueType\,list \Rightarrow{}' a\,valueType)$$

To relate our model for SSA graphs to strict finite partial orders we have defined the function *rel*. It computes all dependencies between the nodes of a given SSA graph (i.e. the partial order on the instructions).

$$\textbf{constdefs } rel :: {}'a\,ssa\_graph \Rightarrow (nodeID \times nodeID)\,set$$
$$rel\,G \equiv \{\,(y, x)\,|\,y \in set\,(plist\,G\,x)\}$$

Evaluation of a basic block is defined by an inductive set *evalssa*. This set is defined by two parameters, *ssa_graph* and additional dependencies between instructions in the SSA graph, given as pairs of node IDs. *evalssa* contains pairs (*instruction*, *value*), where *value* represents the value to which *instruction* is evaluated. A pair is in the result set if three conditions are fulfilled:

- *instruction* is an element of the carrier set (i.e. the instruction belongs to the basic block)
- all predecessors of *instruction* are already in the result set (i.e. all operands on which the instruction is based are calculated)
- the additional dependencies (resulting from the transformation to machine code) must be respected if present.

$$\textbf{consts } evalssa ::$$
$$[\,{}'a\,ssa\_graph\,,\,(\,nodeId \times nodeId\,)\,set\,]\,\Rightarrow\,(\,nodeId \times {}'a\,valueType\,)\,set$$
$$\textbf{theorem } evaluation\_correctness :$$
$$[sfpo(base\,(ssaG), rel\,ssaG);\,sfpo(sfpo\_union(base\,(ssaG), rel\,ssaG)\,eval\_order)]$$
$$\Longrightarrow evalssa\,ssaG\,eval\_order = evalssa\,ssaG\,\{\}$$

The inductive set *evalssa* together with the evaluation order specified by it is the basic definition for our main theorem *evaluation_correctness*. With this theorem, we show that additional dependencies *eval_order* do not change the result set of the evaluation function *eval_ssa* as long as they do not destroy the partial order property of a basic block $ssaG$. Hence, a linear sequence of instructions can be considered a correct transformation of a basic block to machine code if all data-flow dependencies are respected.

3.2   Schedule and Instruction Groups

We consider scheduling algorithms operating on basic block level. Assuming basic blocks in SSA form, we use the definitions from the previous section to represent the input of the scheduler.

We represent the result that we get from the scheduler as a list of disjoint sets denoting instruction groups ($disjointSetList$). The cycle associated to an instruction group corresponds to the position in the list. Thus information about the chronology of execution of instruction groups is preserved. The fact that each instruction is assigned to exactly one cycle is formalized as the predicate $isDisjointToAllListelements$. Furthermore, we specify that each instruction group is a finite set of instructions with at least one element.

---

consts $disjointSetList :: (a'\,set)\,list \Longrightarrow bool$
primrec $disjointSetList\,[] \qquad = True$
$\qquad disjointSetList\,(X\#xs) = isDisjointToAllListelements\,X\,xs\,\wedge$
$\qquad\qquad\qquad\qquad finite\,X \wedge X \neq \{\} \wedge disjointSetList\,xs$

We establish a relationship between our specifications for schedules and partial orders by a function which transforms the former into the latter model. This corresponds directly to our way of mapping ssa_graphs to partial orders. The function $setList2RelSet$ takes as its argument a list with sets as list elements and calculates a relational set. The first component of the result tuple is the union of all list elements calculated by the function $getSetElements$. The function $setList2Rel$ generates a relation for a list of sets ls, such that a pair (a, b) is in the result set iff $\exists i, j < length\,ls \,.\, i < j \wedge a \in ls!i \wedge b \in ls!j$ (i.e. an instruction a is scheduled before another instruction b) using the function $makeTupel$. This function computes for a set A and a list ls all pairs (c, d) with $c \in A$ and $d \in ls!i$ with $0 \leq i < length\,ls$[2].

---

consts $makeTupel :: \,'a\,set \Rightarrow (\,'a\,set\,list) \Rightarrow (\,'a \times' a)\,set$
primrec $makeTupel\,A\,[] \qquad = \{\}$
$\qquad makeTupel\,A\,(x\#xs) = A <*> x \cup makeTupel\,A\,xs$
consts $setList2Rel :: \,'a\,set\,list \Rightarrow (\,'a \times' a)\,set$
primrec $setList2Rel\,[] \qquad = \{\}$
$\qquad setList2Rel\,(x\#xs) \quad = case\,xs\,of\,[] \Rightarrow \{\}$
$\qquad\qquad\qquad\qquad\qquad | \,(y\#ys) \Rightarrow makeTupel\,x\,xs \cup setList2Rel\,xs$
constdefs $setList2RelSet :: (\,'a\,set)\,list \Rightarrow \,'a\,RelSet$
$setList2RelSet\,ls \equiv ((getSetElements\,ls), (setList2Rel\,ls))$

---

[2] A note on Isabelle/HOL notation: $ls!i$ returns the list element at index i. $X <*> Y$ computes the Cartesian product of sets X and Y.

In this section, we have introduced the specifications on which our correctness proof is based. *Strict finite partial orders* and *disjointSetLists* represent input and output of a scheduling algorithm, namely SSA basic blocks and VLIW instruction groups. In the next section, we show how these definitions are used in the proof for verifying results from scheduling algorithms.

3.3   Proof

Our formalization for SSA form as well as our formalization for schedules can be mapped onto the more abstract formalization of strict finite partial orders (cf. Fig. 3). The intuition behind this approach is that a schedule just as an SSA graph implies a partial order on the set of the instructions that it contains. Elements without predecessors in the partial order correspond to the instructions that are executed in the first cycle. Instructions that are associated to a later cycle have all instructions of the previous cycles as direct or transitive predecessors. Scheduling, as well as machine code generation, is considered as the introduction of additional dependencies between the instructions. Its result can only be correct if a similar criterion as for machine code generation is fullfilled.

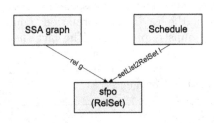

Fig. 3. Formalizations and corresponding Relations

To reuse the correctness proof for machine code generation we prove that the dependency relation of a list of instructions is a strict finite partial order if the list fulfills the *disjointSetList* predicate. This proof is done by separate lemmas for each property of a strict finite partial order (i.e. irreflexivity, transitivity, finiteness, saneness).

---

lemma *is_irrefl* : *disjointSetList ls* $\Longrightarrow$ *irrefl*(*setList2Rel ls*)
lemma *is_trans* : *disjointSetList ls* $\Longrightarrow$ *trans*(*setList2Rel ls*)
lemma *is_finite* : *disjointSetList ls* $\Longrightarrow$ *finite fst*((*setList2RelSet ls*))
lemma *is_sane* : *disjointSetList ls* $\Longrightarrow$ *sane*(*setList2RelSet ls*)
lemma *is_sfpo* : *disjointSetList ls* $\Longrightarrow$ *sfpo*(*setList2RelSet ls*)

Based on these lemmas we define the notion of a *well-formed* schedule. To represent instructions in a schedule, we use the type *nodeId = nat*, and for a schedule the type *schedule = (nodeId set) list*. We call a schedule *well-formed* if it fulfills the predicate *disjointSetList*.

---

constdefs *well_formed_schedule* :: *schedule* $\Rightarrow$ *bool*
well_formed_schedule sched $\equiv$ (*disjointSetList sched*)

The assumptions of the main theorem *correct_scheduling* formalize the criterion that must be met by a correct result obtained from a scheduling algorithm and that can be checked by an independent checker. These assumptions are:

- the set of instructions in the schedule must be the same as in the input program
- all data dependencies must be respected
- additional dependencies induced by the scheduling must not destroy the existing partial order

These conditions ensure that all values are computed. They also ensure that instructions are not executed before their operands are available (i.e. additional dependencies introduced by the scheduler must be respected too). If this criterion is satisfied, we can evaluate the set of instructions and consider the additional dependencies inserted by the scheduler. The results we get are the same as we would get by evaluating without them. Our dependency checker implementation verifies this criterion for each performed transformation.

Our correctness criterion is also necessary. If it does not hold, then at least one of the assumptions of theorem *correct_scheduling* is not valid. If the set of instructions is not the same in the original and scheduled version, then the predicate *base ssaG = instructions* does not hold. If some instructions are repeated in the scheduled code, then the predicate *well_formed_schedule* is violated. If the instructions are the same but not all of their data dependencies are respected, then *rel ssaG ⊆ datadependencies* is not valid. In this case, some data dependencies are not respected in the scheduled program which will lead to wrong results.

> **theorem** *correct_scheduling* :
> ⟦ *sfpo*(*base ssaG, rel ssaG*); (* *good basic block* *)
> *well_formed_schedule sched*; (* *instructions not repeated* *)
> *instructions = getSetElements sched*;
> *base ssaG = instructions*; (* *same instructions in basic block and schedule* *)
> *datadependencies = setList2Rel sched*;
> *rel ssaG ⊆ datadependencies*; (* *schedule respects datadependencies* *)
> *eval_order = datadependencies − (rel ssaG)* (* *deps introduced by scheduler* *)
> ⟧ ⟹ *evalssa ssaG eval_order = evalssa ssaG* {}

The main proof was done almost automatically by built-in tactics of the theorem prover. We only had to transform the assumptions with the above-presented lemma *is_sfpo*. In [BGLM05], we claimed that the general principle of our SSA formalization would allow us to reuse the proof and consequently reduce costs. Our new results are evidence of this reusability.

Our previous formalization consisted of 110 lemmas (200 lines of proof code (lopc)). Half of the lemmas consider properties of the abstract part of partial orders and only 25 lemmas the SSA specific properties. In the presented formalization (30 lemmas/220 lopc) we only had to prove properties that connect the added data structures for VLIW scheduling to the abstract part of our previous work. Because of the relation between the new specific formalization and the abstract one, the main correctness proof is also valid for the new formalization. The statistics demonstrate the reduced efforts for verification.

4   Dependency Checker

With the results of the previous section, we have proved that a schedule is valid
if all instructions are retained and if the data dependencies of the unscheduled
code are contained in the partial order induced by the scheduling. In this section,
we show how this result can be brought into practice, in order to verify that a
given scheduler generates a correct schedule.

Since the verification of an entire program (in our case, the scheduler) is very
hard to achieve, we follow the *checker approach* [BK95] (cf. lower part of Fig. 1).
We add an independent program, the checker, which takes after each run of
the scheduler its input and output, and checks whether the criterion yielded
by our formal correctness proof is fulfilled. We have used Isabelle's feature of
automatic generation of ML code [BN00] and extracted such a checker from our
formalization. With this verified checker we establish the formal correctness for
each actual positive program run. Thus we sacrifice general correctness of the
scheduler implementation, but in return we get a simpler subproblem which is
efficiently solvable.

Figure 1 pictures our approach: We have designed a formalization of both
unscheduled and scheduled assembler code, as described in the previous chapter.
Then, we have proved both representations as semantically equal w.r.t. the evaluation order. This yielded a criterion, which is sufficient for the correctness of the
scheduling. Having established this result, we extract a checker from the formalization, which checks whether the criterion holds for a given pair of unscheduled
and scheduled assembler code. This checker is supposed to augment an existing
assembler and watch its input and output. With this extended assembler, we can
tell for each invocation of the assembler whether the generated machine code is
a valid translation of the input assembler program. The checker approach has to
be distinguished from testing approaches. If a program passes all tests, we still
do not know whether the test conditions were sufficient. On the contrary, with
the checker approach, the result is known to be correct by a formal proof.

In the following we describe how we realised the checker approach presented
above. We consider schedulers working on basic block level (remember that basic
blocks can be directly identified in the input program, cp. Sect. 2.1), i.e., they
must not change the block structure of the program or move instructions from
one block to another. Thus, the blocks appear in the same order in input and
output of the scheduler. In addition, the machine code must be in SSA form,
i.e., in each block at most one assignment is allowed for each register. This can
easily be achieved for arbitrary machine code by register renaming (remember
that the SSA property must only hold locally for each basic block).

The main function of the checker is *checkProgram*. It receives the unscheduled
and the scheduled program as a list of basic blocks. An unscheduled block is
a set of instructions, while the scheduled variant consists of a list of instruction groups. We process the lists in conjunction block by block (remember that
the order of the blocks is the same in both programs). First we generate the
partial order for both the unscheduled and scheduled block by *generateDDG*
and *generateScheduleOrder* respectively. Each pair of unscheduled block and the

```
func checkProgram(prog: Block list, schedule: ScheduledBlock list) : bool
(* checks whether a program was scheduled correctly *)
   for each bb ∈ prog, s ∈ sched do
      ddg = generateDDG(bb)
      scheduleOrder = generateScheduleOrder(s)
      if not checkBlock( (bb,ddg),(s,scheduleOrder)) then return invalid
   return valid
```

Fig. 4. Algorithm for the checker

corresponding scheduled block is then checked by *checkBlock* w.r.t. the criterion yielded by our proof. If one check fails, we return *invalid*, otherwise *valid*.

The function *checkBlock* checks the correctness of the schedule at basic block level. It has been extracted from the corresponding function in our Isabelle formalization.

```
constdefs checkBlock :: 'a RelSet ⇒ 'a RelSet ⇒ bool
checkBlock bb sbb ≡ spoC bb ∧          (* check partial order properties *)
                    spoC sbb ∧
                    fst bb = fst sbb ∧  (*check equality of instruction sets*)
                    snd bb ⊆ snd sbb   (*check subsetrelation of dependencies*)
```

This function checks whether our criterion is fulfilled: we must first check, that both unscheduled and scheduled block fulfill the partial order predicate. We must then check that each instruction is scheduled exactly once, i.e. that no instruction is duplicated or omitted. This means that both unscheduled and scheduled block have to contain the same instructions. In the final step we must check whether the partial order of the unscheduled block is a subset of the partial order of the scheduled one. If all conditions hold, the block has been correctly scheduled. Otherwise an error occurred.

To use Isabelle's code extraction feature we had to add same supplementary definitions. First we had to instruct the code generator to compile sets into lists. This can be done with a specific Isabelle theory. Further on the predicates which define the partial order (*sane, irrefl, trans, sfpo*) had to be redefined. All of them except the *sfpo* predicate use quantifiers in such a way, that the code generator cannot compile the definitions into executable code and must for this reason be redefined. We give an example for the *sane* predicate.[3]

```
constdefs sane :: 'a RelSet ⇒ bool
sane RS ≡ ∀ a b . (a,b) ∈ snd RS ⟶ a ∈ fst RS ∧ b ∈ fst RS
constdefs saneC :: 'a RelSet ⇒ bool
saneC RS ≡ ∀ (a,b) ∈ snd RS . a ∈ fst RS ∧ b ∈ fst RS
```

---

[3] *saneC* refers to the redefined definition.

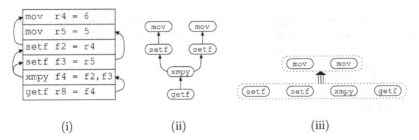

(i)   (ii)   (iii)

Fig. 5. Case study for the GNU assembler **gas**: (i) Our running example (ii) The resulting *data dependency graph (DDG)* (iii) The incorrect schedule produced by **gas** (thick edges subsume dependencies between all instructions of the related groups)

The *sfpo* predicate claims finiteness for the considered sets. The code generator compiles sets into lists which fulfill finiteness by definition. For this reason we can omit this condition. We have proved equivalence between modified an unmodified definitions hence using them for code generation is correct.

We have also extracted ML code for the *generateScheduleOrder* function, which corresponds directly to the *setList2RelSet* function in our formalization. The *generateDDG* is currently manually written. Since we did not yet formalize the concrete assembly language, it cannot be extracted from our formalization. At the moment we are extending our formalization accordingly. Afterwards the checker will be completely extracted from the formalization (despite low-level functionality like file I/O and parsing).

In this section we have described our checker approach. The essential parts of the checker are automatically generated from our formalization, using the code generation facilities of Isabelle. This gives us a verified checker. We have used our generated checker in a case study examining results of the GCC scheduler for the Intel Itanium, a processor with VLIW architecture.

5   Case Study: Checker for GCC

In a case study, we have used our generated checker for the Intel Itanium processor, a VLIW processor that can execute up to six instructions per cycle. The checker is invoked as a stand-alone program on an unscheduled and a scheduled assembler file. This enables it to be easily integrated in a tool chain to ensure the correctness of an arbitrary scheduler.

We have taken a collection of simple programs, which were designed as a test suite for compiler development. Each program, in assembler form, has been fed into the gcc assembler to generate the binary program. For all the assembler files we considered, the basic blocks were already in SSA form (i.e. all registers were assigned only once). Hence no additional preprocessing of the code was needed.

We have used our checker to check the correctness of the scheduler contained in the GCC assembler **gas**. We have used the **gas** provided with the current **binutils** version 2.17 (May 2006) [GNU06]. In our experiments, we have discovered that the assembler creates invalid schedules for certain floating point operations. Consider Fig. 5, showing the results for our running example. Figure 5(ii) shows the DDG of the input program, and Fig. 5(iii) shows the incorrect schedule produced by the GNU assembler. Clearly, the dependencies of the setf, xmpy and getf instructions have been ignored. This leads to undefined results. With our checker, the violated dependencies were reported correctly. The output of the checker could be used to correct the scheduled program manually.

Note: Further investigation of the error has yielded this explanation: The GCC assembler utilizes a definition of instruction classes for identifying the data dependencies of the instructions. From the class, it is known which resources are read or written. This definition table seems to have been directly taken from the official Itanium Specification ([Int06, p. 3:371, Table 5-5]). The error appears because the xmpy instruction is simply not in the class *floating point instruction*, hence the official Intel Itanium specification is incomplete. We have a possible explanation why this instruction may have been overlooked. xmpy is a so-called *pseudo-op* and will be mapped onto the xma (multiply-add) instruction at execution time (f_2, f_3, f_4 denote arbitrary floating point registers, f0 is a constant register with the value 0.0):

$$\text{xmpy } f_2 = f_3, f_4 \quad \Rightarrow \quad \text{xma } f_2 = f_3, f_4, \text{f0}$$

For xma, the dependencies are reported correctly. So if assembler programs were rewritten by replacing xmpy with xma appropriately, this error would not occur. We found no reports on the error. After posting the bug to the GNU developer's newsgroup, the bug was acknowledged, and both the GNU assembler as well as the Itanium specification were assured to be corrected.

6 Related Work

Formal verification is part of several related research projects. Especially the programming language Java has been under consideration. For example, the formal verification of the translation from a subset of Java to Java byte code and formal byte code verification was investigated in [Str02, KN03] using the theorem prover Isabelle/HOL [NPW02]. Furthermore, the type safety of a subset of Java [NvO98] and also of a subset of C++ [WNST06] has been proved in Isabelle/HOL. Another interesting work is the formal verification of the protocol controlling the traffic through the Elb tunnel in Hamburg [OST+02], also by using a theorem prover.

Early work on formal correctness proofs for compilers [Moo89] was carried out in the Boyer-Moore theorem prover considering the translation of the programming language Piton. Recent work has concentrated on transformations taking place in compiler frontends. [Nip98] describes the verification of lexical analysis in Isabelle/HOL. Further related work on formal compiler verification was done in the german Verifix project [GDG+96, GGZ04] focusing on correct compiler construction. [DvHG03] considers the verification of a compiler for a Lisp subset in the theorem prover PVS. [Ler06] proved the correctness of a compiler from a

C like language to PowerPC assembly code with the Coq proof assistant. From the formalization he could extract the verified compiler.

The checker approach was initially proposed for algebraic problems by [BK95] and applies generally to the verification of program results. In [MN98], this approach was used to augment the popular LEDA library (for combinatorial computation) with checkers, and as a result the reliability of the library was significantly enhanced. The approach of proof-carrying code (PCC) [Nec97] serves a different purpose than ours as it shows the safety of separately delivered executable code. Hence, PCC concentrates on the verification of necessary but not sufficient correctness criteria. The approach of program checking has been proposed by the Verifix project [GDG$^+$96] and has also become known as translation validation [PSS98, Nec00], recently also for loop transformations [GZB04]. For an overview and for results on program checking in optimizing backend transformations cf. [Gle03].

[FH02] also investigate the verification of scheduling VLIW code. In contrast to our work, two programs are checked for equivalence by simulating their dynamic behavior by symbolic execution. This requires a detailed model of the considered processor. While their approach can be applied to more general code transformations, its correctness has not been shown by a formal proof.

Verification of scheduling in hardware synthesis has been investigated in [KMS$^+$06]. In this approach, specifications of the systems are given as finite state machines. An algorithm is presented that can check two finite state machines for equivalence. In contrast to our work, parallelization is not an issue.

7   Conclusions

In this paper, we have shown that software verification with theorem provers can be used for full-scale applications as the GCC scheduler. This is important not only in safety-critical applications because software users are more and more interested in an increase in the reliability and not only in the efficiency of software. Based on a formal proof for the correctness of scheduling results and Isabelle/HOL's code generation facilities, we have generated a checker that ensures the correctness of scheduling results. By applying this checker to results of the GCC Itanium scheduler, we have found a bug resulting in incorrectly compiled programs.

Moreover, we have shown that formal verification costs can be reduced significantly if we manage to reuse proofs. We achieved this goal by splitting a proof into a more general part and a specific application-dependent part. By reusing the general part, we could save verification cost considerably, as we have shown in our proof statistics (lines of proof code in general and reused specific parts). In general, we are also aiming at methods to automatically compose correctness proofs for larger systems from the correctness proofs of their subsystems, a task to be accomplished in further work.

Acknowledgements. We would like to thank the anonymous reviewers for their constructive comments and suggestions, and Stefan Berghofer for his help on

Isabelle's code generation facilities. This work was supported by the German Science Foundation (DFG) and by the ARTIST2 NoE.

References

[BGLM05]   Blech, J.O., Glesner, S., Leitner, J., Mülling, S.: Optimizing Code Gener-
           ation from SSA Form: A Comparison Between Two Formal Correctness
           Proofs in Isabelle/HOL. In: Compiler Optimization meets Compiler Ver-
           ification (COCV 2005). Elsevier ENTCS, pp. 1–18. Elsevier, Amsterdam
           (2005)

[BK95]   Blum, M., Kannan, S.: Designing programs that check their work. J.
           ACM 42(1), 269–291 (1995)

[BN00]   Berghofer, S., Nipkow, T.: Executing higher order logic. In: Callaghan, P.,
           Luo, Z., McKinna, J., Pollack, R. (eds.) TYPES 2000. LNCS, vol. 2277,
           pp. 24–40. Springer, Heidelberg (2002)

[CFR+91]   Cytron, R., Ferrante, J., Rosen, B.K., Wegman, M.N., Zadeck, F.K.: Ef-
           ficiently Computing Static Single Assignment Form and the Control De-
           pendence Graph. ACM Trans. on Prog. Lang. and Systems 13(4) (1991)

[DvHG03]   Dold, A., von Henke, F.W., Goerigk, W.: A Completely Verified Real-
           istic Bootstrap Compiler. Int. Journal of Foundations of Computer Sci-
           ence 14(4), 659–680 (2003)

[FH02]   Feng, X., Hu, A.J.: Automatic formal verification for scheduled VLIW
           code. In: Languages, Compilers and Tools for Embedded Systems
           (LCTES/SCOPES 2002), pp. 85–92. ACM Press, New York (2002)

[GDG+96]   Goerigk, W., Dold, A., Gaul, T., Goos, G., Heberle, A., von Henke, F.W.,
           Hoffmann, U., Langmaack, H., Pfeifer, H., Ruess, H., Zimmermann, W.:
           Compiler Correctness and Implementation Verification: The Verifix Ap-
           proach. In: Gyimóthy, T. (ed.) CC 1996. LNCS, vol. 1060, Springer, Hei-
           delberg (1996)

[GGZ04]   Glesner, S., Goos, G., Zimmermann, W.: Verifix: Konstruktion und Ar-
           chitektur verifizierender Übersetzer (Verifix: Construction and Architec-
           ture of Verifying Compilers). it - Information Technology 46, 265–276
           (2004)

[Gle03]   Glesner, S.: Using Program Checking to Ensure the Correctness of Com-
           piler Implementations. Journal of Universal Comp. Science 9(3), 191–222
           (2003)

[GNU06]   The GNU Project. GNU binutils version 2.17 (2006),
           http://www.gnu.org/software/binutils/

[GZB04]   Goldberg, B., Zuck, L., Barrett, C.: Into the Loops: Practical Issues in
           Translation Validation for Optimizing Compilers. In: Compiler Optimiza-
           tion meets Compiler Verification (COCV 2004). Elsevier ENTCS. Else-
           vier, Amsterdam (2004)

[Int06]   Intel Corporation. Intel Itanium architecture software developer's man-
           ual: Volume 3: Instruction set reference. Revision 2.2 (January 2006)

[KMS+06]   Karfa, C., Mandal, C., Sarkar, D., Pentakota, S.R., Reade, C.: A formal
           verification method of scheduling in high-level synthesis. In: 7th Int. Sym-
           posium on Quality Electronic Design (ISQED 2006), pp. 71–78. IEEE,
           Los Alamitos (2006)

[KN03]   Klein, G., Nipkow, T.: Verified Bytecode Verifiers. Theoretical Computer Science 298, 583–626 (2003)

[Ler06]   Leroy, X.: Formal certification of a compiler back-end or: programming a compiler with a proof assistant. In: POPL 2006: Conference record of the 33rd ACM SIGPLAN-SIGACT symposium on Principles of programming languages, pp. 42–54. ACM Press, New York (2006)

[MN98]   Mehlhorn, K., Näher, S.: From algorithms to working programs: On the use of program checking in leda. In: MFCS, pp. 84–93 (1998)

[Moo89]   Moore, J.S.: A Mechanically Verified Language Implementation. Journal of Automated Reasoning 5(4), 461–492 (1989)

[Nec97]   Necula, G.C.: Proof-Carrying Code. In: 24th ACM SIGPLAN-SIGACT Symposium on Principles of Programming Languages (POPL 1997) (1997)

[Nec00]   Necula, G.C.: Translation Validation for an Optimizing Compiler. In: Programming Language Design and Implementation (PLDI 2000) (2000)

[Nip98]   Nipkow, T.: Verified Lexical Analysis. In: Grundy, J., Newey, M. (eds.) TPHOLs 1998. LNCS, vol. 1479, pp. 1–15. Springer, Heidelberg (1998)

[NPW02]   Nipkow, T., Paulson, L.C., Wenzel, M.T.: Isabelle/HOL. LNCS, vol. 2283. Springer, Heidelberg (2002)

[NvO98]   Nipkow, T., von Oheimb, D.: Java$_{light}$ is Type-Safe – Definitely. In: 25th ACM Symposium on the Principles of Programming Languages. ACM Press, New York (1998)

[OST$^+$02]   Ortmeier, F., Schellhorn, G., Thums, A., Reif, W., Hering, B., Trappschuh, H.: Safety Analysis of the Height Control System of the Elbtunnel. In: Anderson, S., Bologna, S., Felici, M. (eds.) SAFECOMP 2002. LNCS, vol. 2434, pp. 296–308. Springer, Heidelberg (2002)

[PSS98]   Pnueli, A., Siegel, M., Singerman, E.: Translation validation. In: Steffen, B. (ed.) ETAPS 1998 and TACAS 1998. LNCS, vol. 1384, pp. 151–166. Springer, Heidelberg (1998)

[Str02]   Strecker, M.: Formal Verification of a Java Compiler in Isabelle. In: Voronkov, A. (ed.) CADE 2002. LNCS (LNAI), vol. 2392, pp. 63–77. Springer, Heidelberg (2002)

[WNST06]   Wasserrab, D., Nipkow, T., Snelting, G., Tip, F.: An operational semantics and type safety proof for multiple inheritance in C++. In: OOPSLA, pp. 345–362 (2006)

Computing Worst-Case Response Times in Real-Time Avionics Applications

Murali Rangarajan[1] and Darren Cofer[2]

[1] Honeywell Aerospace Advanced Technology
3660 Technology Dr., Minneapolis MN 55418
`murali.rangarajan@honeywell.com`
[2] Rockwell Collins Inc., Advanced Technology Center
400 Collins Rd. NE, Cedar Rapids IA, 52498
`ddcofer@rockwellcollins.com`

Abstract. The work in this paper builds upon our prior work to analyze properties of applications running on top of the Deos real-time operating system. We describe how a control application's worst-case response time to an event can be "computed" using the model checker SPIN. We lay out the steps involved in reusing our existing models for this analysis, and our solution to reducing the memory required to perform the analysis. This work highlights the benefit of expanding the use of formal models, and the necessity of changing existing abstractions (such as the timer model in this work) to reflect changed verification goals.

Keywords: Model checking, software verification, real-time, flight control.

1 Introduction

Researchers in the avionics industry have been applying formal methods for the verification of safety-critical software for several years. Our past work has applied model checking and theorem proving tools to verification of time partitioning and other key properties of the Deos real-time operating system. Deos is the foundation for the Primus Epic avionics suite [1]. Previous publications have described many aspects of this work [4,9], most of which have been based on use of the SPIN model checker [6].

The work in this paper builds upon our prior work and focuses now on properties of applications running on top of the Deos RTOS. We describe how the worst-case response time to an event can be "computed" using SPIN. We lay out the steps involved in reusing our existing models for this analysis, and our solution to reducing memory consumption as part of this process. This work highlights the benefit of expanding the use of existing formal models, and the necessity of changing existing abstractions (such as the timer model in this work) to reflect changed verification goals.

The key property described in this paper is the worst-case response time for a producer-consumer type of application. Techniques such as Static Timing Analysis [7] are commonly used to determine worst-case response times. These techniques are ineffective when attempting to compute the worst-case response time across multiple threads, preemptions, OS scheduling, interrupt processing, etc. Our goal was to achieve similar

S. Leue and P. Merino (Eds.): FMICS 2007, LNCS 4916, pp. 101–114, 2008.
© Springer-Verlag Berlin Heidelberg 2008

worst-case paths for a specific configuration of applications running on Deos. The results from our analysis can be combined with Worst Case Execution Time analysis [8,5] of applications to obtain end-to-end real-time performance characteristics. This paper focuses on the identification of the critical path in the worst-case response time. The work has not been validated on real avionics software due to a lack of funds for that work at this time. This work has similar goals to that described by Colin and Puaut [3] on the RTEMS RTOS. An alternative approach to our timer design is to use Discrete-Time Spin [2]. Our decision not to use DT-Spin was due to our need for maximum flexibility in modeling time and in specifying properties using time.

Our model checking work has been based on the Deos model shown in Figure 1. This model includes separate processes for user (application) threads, the Deos kernel, and a platform timer. This model provides only a simplistic model of application behaviors. Application threads may nondeterministically:

- Be created
- Complete for period
- Delete themselves
- Wait for next interrupt, if enabled to do so.

In addition, the scheduler can stop threads (when they run out of time or are preempted) and resume threads, possibly giving them slack time. The time at which any of these events occurs is determined by the platform process.

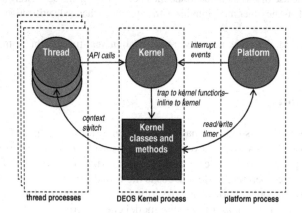

Fig. 1. Structure of Deos model in SPIN

The model was intended to follow the source code implementation as faithfully as possible. This fine-grained model was too large to be verified exhaustively with any of the advanced scheduling features enabled. The only configuration that can be exhaustively checked with this model is one with three basic application threads: one Main thread that dynamically creates two slower User threads, none of which are interrupt service routines (ISR) or slack consumers, and no mutex locking is enabled. Consequently, we have relied on estimation techniques (SPIN's supertrace) for most of the configurations analyzed. The size of the model has also motivated our work on distributed model checking for large systems.

Our goal in the current task has been to augment this model to include richer application behaviors so that timing properties of Deos applications interacting with the scheduler could be verified. A necessary first step must therefore be to reduce the size of the Deos model.

After discussions with Deos users, we have decided to model a representative application that should be very useful to application programmers. Currently, there is no way for application programmers to compute the worst case response times to events. For example, if sensor data is made available by a thread, there is no way to determine the upper bound for the time in which a consumer thread will read and process that data (Figure 2). Determination of response time is complicated by the presence of interrupt threads and by priority inheritance when using mutexes. Furthermore, the selection of the tick rate for the system (the fastest thread period) impacts the response time. A higher tick rate can reduce response time to interrupts at the cost of higher overhead, which can delay other tasks.

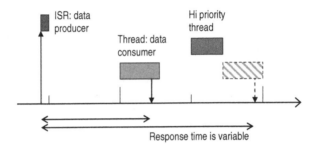

Fig. 2. Producer to consumer response time

Developers now bypass this problem by strictly scheduling all the threads in a specific order (producers followed by consumers) ahead of time using Deos's *schedule-before* relationship. However, this rigid approach defeats the flexibility provided by the dynamic scheduling capability of Deos. By being able to predict the worst case response time ahead of time, the developers will have the flexibility to consider other scheduling relationships or to not specify any specific schedule. Therefore, we will be demonstrating how we can use our Deos model to predict the worst case response time for a hand-constructed application running on top of Deos.

We organized the application verification task into the following steps, which will be described next:

- Simplify the Deos model to reduce its size (section 2).
- Implement a discrete-time platform/timer model (section 3).
- Create the producer-consumer application model (section 4).
- Verify the worst case response time (section 5).

The final section of the paper (section 6) presents future directions for this work.

2 Simplified Deos Model

To enable the application to be modeled with more detail we had to reduce the memory requirements of the basic Deos model. The main limitation now is memory consumption by the SPIN verifier. SPIN is written and optimized for 32-bit machines so its addressable memory is limited to 4GB. Therefore, we have worked to reduce the size of our model without sacrificing any behaviors that would impact application functionality.

Some of the main factors that impact memory usage in SPIN are:

- Size of the state vector. This is a fixed size collection of bits that encodes the model state at any instant. Each unique state must be stored in a structure of this size.
- Number of states stored. As SPIN searches the state space of the model it stores new states for comparison and identification of cycles.
- Depth of traces explored. SPIN conducts a depth-first search (DFS) of the state space and maintains the current trace on a DFS stack.

We have made a number of changes to the Deos verification model to reduce each of these factors. We have done this by retaining all the relevant scheduler functionality, but eliminating as much of the implementation-specific data as possible.

Our starting point was a Deos model in which the code for handling mutexes was present, but was not exercised. Similarly, code for utilizing slack time and code for interrupt threads were present, but none of the threads in the model were slack-enabled or interrupt threads. This model also included the scheduler overhead time computations.

The same exhaustively verifiable configuration was retained for all the tests so as to enable easier comparisons of performance improvements. This configuration consists of a main thread that dynamically creates two non-slack-enabled user threads (actually the threads create themselves) as shown in Figure 3. All the tests were conducted with partial order reduction and state compression enabled. The verification parameters for the last test were optimized to obtain the best memory performance that can be obtained from this model.

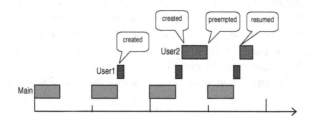

Fig. 3. System configuration used for model size comparison

The changes made to the Deos model were accomplished in five main steps. The first step was to remove the mutex code, since it does not have a significant impact on our application. This also includes all the data variables required for implementing mutexes resulting in a smaller state vector. In addition, this step also included the merging of the platform (the timer) with the scheduler. This allowed us to eliminate two communication channels used for synchronization, thus simplifying the model and speeding up verification. The modified model structure is shown in Figure 4.

The second step was to remove data structures and variables that are purely implementation dependent. For example, the priority lists that are used to efficiently handle the threads in their various states were replaced by a collection of flags. The priority lists served two purposes. The first was to identify the next highest priority thread to be scheduled in constant time. The second was to provide some measure of fairness by scheduling interrupted threads prior to scheduling threads that were not interrupted within the current period. Replacing the priority lists with flags had two consequences. The first was that, in order to identify the next eligible thread for scheduling, the model had to loop over all the threads in the system. This O(n) approach in the model is acceptable because we are not measuring real time, but rather the model time, which is not impacted by this change. However, this did result in a small increase in the number of states in the model, and a resulting increase in the memory usage. The second consequence was that the model no longer provided the fairness as provided by Deos. Again, this did not impact our analysis because, the fairness was never guaranteed by the OS, and the model we were using (see section 4) had only one user thread that could be interrupted, rendering any notion of fairness superfluous.

The third step was to include as much of the model within atomic blocks that can be executed without interleaving. Elimination of some of the communication channels in the first step allowed us to include more model code with atomic blocks. The code to be placed within atomic blocks was identified by hand, based upon our knowledge of the working of the model. The key to this step was the knowledge that only one thread can be executing at any one time, irrespective of whether that thread was within a kernel call or within user code.

The fourth step was to reuse as many of the temporary variables as possible to reduce the size of the state vector. The required analysis and model changes were done by hand.

The final step was to tune the verification parameters (such as the expected size of the state space) to minimize the memory required to complete the verification. Results from analysis of the model after each of these steps are summarized in Figure 5.

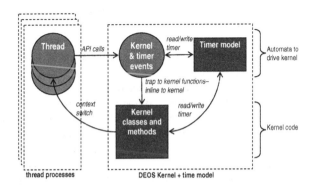

Fig. 4. Structural changes to model

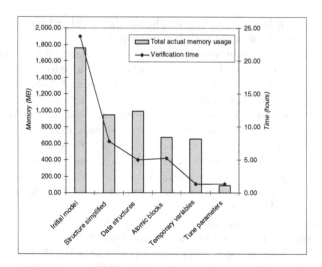

Fig. 5. Results of changes to reduce size of Deos model

Memory required for the basic model configuration was reduced by an order of magnitude as a result of these simplifications. Furthermore, it is now possible to exhaustively verify configurations that include both slack enabled threads and at least one interrupt thread.

3 Discrete-Time Model

With the simplified scheduler model we now have some margin to include additional application behavior. We want to be able to determine the worst case response time for a producer-consumer type of application. Accurate measurement of response time in the application requires some changes in our model of time.

Formerly, we have used a discrete-event model of time. In this model there are a small number of events involving the elapsing of time which may occur. Some of those events may be eligible to occur next, depending on the value of the tick timer and the time remaining on the thread timer. One of the eligible events is selected, the timers are adjusted to elapse time to correspond to the occurrence of the selected event, and the actions associated with the event are executed.

In the discrete-event model, time is advanced in jumps of varying size (Figure 6, top). To reduce the number of options for computing the size of the jumps, the discrete-event model limited the time elapsed when a thread completes voluntarily to be either zero, half, or all of the maximum possible time available before the next event.

To achieve better resolution we have switched to a discrete-time model. In the discrete-time model, time is always advanced by one unit (corresponding to one *tick*). Depending on the resulting state of the timers an event (a tick or timer interrupt, for example) may be enabled, the currently running thread may complete voluntarily, or nothing may happen (Figure 6, bottom). Pseudo-Promela code for each of these models of time is shown in Figure 7.

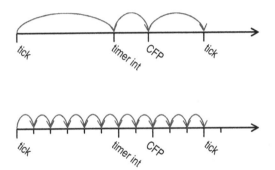

Fig. 6. Discrete-event (top) vs. discrete-time (bottom) model

To better understand the behavior of the different scheduler models and obtain some insight into their structures, we ran a series of verifications comparing search depth to the number of states discovered. SPIN's search depth limit was gradually increased and the number of states reachable within that depth was recorded. For the simplified discrete-event model, the results are shown in Figure 8. This model was found to have 175,853 states with a maximum search depth of 31,569 steps.

Several observations can be drawn from Figure 8. First of all, note that the number of transitions in the model is not much greater than the number of states ("states stored" in Spin's vocabulary). This indicates that most of the states occur in long non-branching paths. Second, note that the number of states discovered increases rapidly with depth and then levels out. However, it is interesting that the number of states is not monotonically increasing. There are many intervals in with the search depth increases but fewer states are reached.

```
If

:: [tick_time ≤ remaining_time] ->

    advance time to next tick;;

    tick interrupt;

:: [tick_time > remaining_time] ->

    advance time to next timer interrupt;

    timer interrupt;

:: get_remaining_time ->

    advance time arbitrary amount
(0/half/all);

    read timer;

:: true ->

    platform interrupt;

fi
```

```
decrement timers;

if

:: [tick_time = 0] ->

    tick interrupt;

:: [remaining_time = 0] ->

    timer interrupt;

:: get_remaining_time ->

    read timer;

:: true ->

    platform interrupt;

fi
```

Fig. 7. Simplified comparison of discrete-event (left) vs. discrete-time (right) model

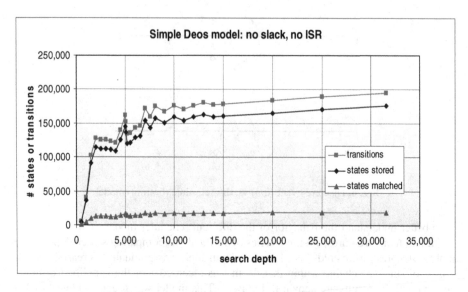

Fig. 8. States vs. depth for the discrete-event Deos model

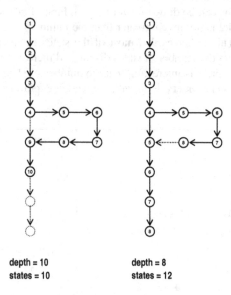

Fig. 9. For non-exhaustive depth-first searches, a greater depth limit may yield fewer reachable states

Figure 9 illustrates how this may happen. Spin performs a depth-first search of the state space. If there are multiple paths between two states, it may be that the model checker chooses the longer path and, consequently, may not be able to search much beyond the second state. However, if the search depth is limited then the second state may only be reachable by the shorter path and the model checker will be able to reach more states that lie beyond it. Note that if the verification is exhaustive then this situation cannot occur.

Considering the Deos scheduler model, it is not surprising that we should find this behavior. For example, between two start-of-period events there are a number of different sequences of intermediate events that may occur. Some paths are shorter and others are longer, depending on the number of threads that have been created at that time.

Figure 10 shows the states vs. depth plot for the discrete-time version of the model including a slack-enabled thread. This model has 1,084,643 states, reachable at a depth of 55,268. This time note that there are nearly twice as many transitions as states, indicating a more connected state space graph. The same characteristic leveling off of states reached with increasing depth is evident.

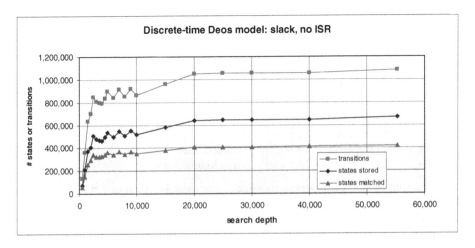

Fig. 10. States vs. depth for the discrete-time Deos model

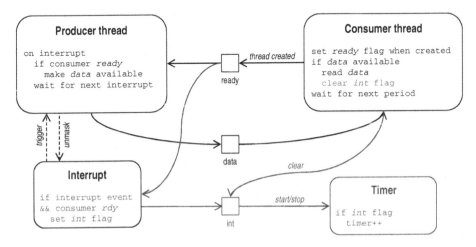

Fig. 11. Producer-consumer application model (additional verification instrumentation is the bottom half of the figure, also shown in blue)

4 Producer-Consumer Application Model

With the simplified discrete-time version of the scheduler model now in place, we are ready to add the producer-consumer application model. The application consists of two separate threads: an interrupt-triggered producer thread and a periodic consumer thread. The producer is triggered to run by the occurrence of an interrupt event corresponding to I/O activity in the system. If the consumer has been created and is ready to start receiving data, the producer fetches the data, formatting and buffering it for the consumer thread. The consumer runs periodically to compute some control action making use of the data provided by the producer. The model is illustrated in Figure 11.

In addition to the basic application behavior, we also need some additional instrumentation to gather the information needed for the response time verification (the bottom half of Figure 11). A timer has been added to measure the time between the occurrence of the interrupt event and the time that the data is consumed.

Configuration data (the Deos registry entries) for the producer-consumer application are as follows:

- Period P0: 15 ms
- Period P1: 45 ms
- Main thread (M): P0, 2 ms
- Consumer (U1): P1, 3 ms
- Producer (U2): P0, 4 ms, slack enabled, ISR
- Reserved system slack (not given to Main): 3 ms

Normalized to the fastest period, this means that there is a total of 7 ms of scheduled time out of 15 ms, with 3 ms of reserved slack and 5 ms necessary for various overhead operations. When the main thread starts, it is automatically given all of the available (non-reserved) time, so it starts with a budget of 7 ms. When the consumer thread (U1) is created, its normalized budget of 1 ms is deducted from Main's budget, and when the producer (U2) is created, its budget of 4 is deducted.

Main and Consumer execute periodically at their respective periods of 15 ms and 45 ms. Interrupts may occur at any time, triggering the scheduling and execution of ISR thread Producer. Producer may run multiple times in every period P0, up to a total running time of 4 ms, after which it may request slack time. Any thread may complete early in its period and yield its remaining time as slack.

5 Verification of Response Time

The final step is the actual verification of the worst case response time. We used the following procedure. For the configuration constructed, the timer will count up between the occurrence of the interrupt event and the time the consumer reads the data. We have added an assertion in the consumer claiming that after the data is read the value on the timer will be less than some target value. If there is a sequence of events resulting in a greater response time than the target, then Spin will find it. We then increase the target response time value and try again until a successful verification is achieved.

Before we started our analyses, we estimated the worst case response time to be used as an initial guess and came up with a value of 54. The consumer thread executes in every period, and the data for the consumer is made available (and the timer started) only after the consumer is created. Therefore, the delay would be maximized if the following scenario were to occur. The consumer is created at the beginning of its period (the slower period, duration = 3×15 = 45). Soon thereafter, an interrupt occurs and the timer is started. The consumer can run only in the period following the period in which it is created. Therefore, in the next period, the Main thread (budget of 2) and the interrupt thread (budget of 4 plus slack time of 3) consume their full budgets before the consumer gets to run. This brings the total delay to 45 + 2 + 4 + 3 = 54.

Using supertrace verification mode, the assertion int_timer ≤ max_int_delay in the consumer produced errors for values of 55, 56, 57, and 58 at depths between 5000 and 8000. However, no error was found for max_int_delay of 59 up to a search depth of 50,000. The worst case response time must therefore be 59 ms.

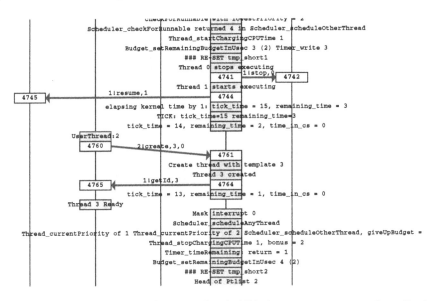

Fig. 12. Consumer created 1 ms after start of period P1; interrupt event occurs immediately after

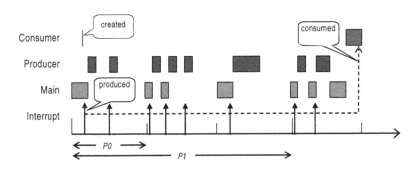

Fig. 13. Worst case response time from first interrupt to consumer

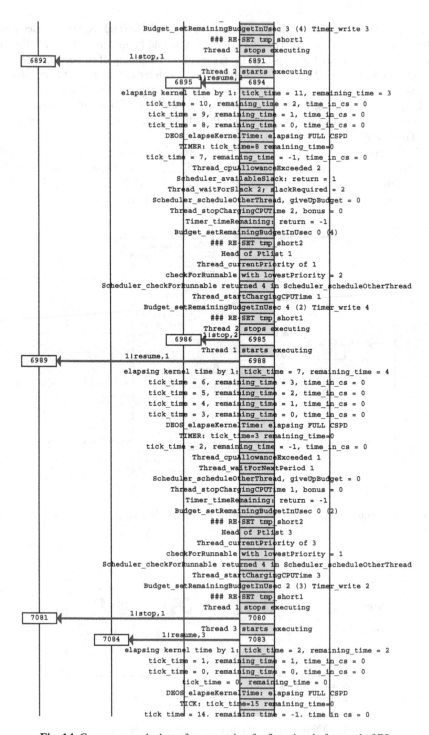

Fig. 14. Consumer reads data after executing for 3 ms just before end of P0

Message sequence charts in Figure 12 and Figure 13 show a worst case response scenario. As expected, the consumer thread (UserThread 2) is created 1 ms after the start of its period P1. The masking of the interrupt that occurs immediately afterward indicates that the interrupt has occurred, starting the timer.

Jumping ahead to the next start of P1, we see in Figure 13 that the main thread runs and is pre-empted twice by the producer ISR thread. After both thread runs, exhausting both their base budgets (6 ms) and the available slack (5 ms), the consumer finally gets to run. In this case the consumer doesn't get to read the data and stop the timer until 2 ms after it is run, just before the end of the current P0. The total elapsed time is then 44 ms (an entire P1, less 1 ms) + 15 (the entire next P0) = 59 ms. The complete scenario is illustrated in Figure 14.

6 Conclusions and Future Work

We have described in this paper the steps taken to formally verify a timing property for a sample Deos application. To accomplish this several steps were taken to reduce the size of the Deos scheduler model. While the simplifications result in some loss of faithfulness to the source code implementation, we have been careful to preserve the functionality of the model. The resulting savings in both memory consumption and verification time have allowed us to include in the model richer application behaviors. The producer-consumer application analyzed was found to have a worst case response time somewhat greater than that predicted before the analysis. The approach presented in this paper applies to multiple consumers too, so long as the last consumer determines the actual response time.

Another advantage of having a more compact model is the ability to exhaustively verify advanced scheduling features in Deos. For example, configurations with slack-enabled threads and interrupt threads could not previously be exhaustively verified and we had to resort to approximation techniques, such as Spin's supertrace. With our memory-optimized model, we were able to successfully re-verify models (that were previously verified using supertrace verification) exhaustively with both slack and ISR threads.

Other possibilities for future exploration include:

- Further reduction in the size of the state vector by using the embedded C code features of SPIN.
- Comparison of deterministic and nondeterministic ordering of threads within a priority level to assess the impact on response time and other performance measures.
- Incorporation of more complex application behaviors.

Acknowledgement

This work was funded in part by NASA Langley Research Center under cooperative agreement NCC-1-399.

References

1. Binns, P.: A robust high-performance time partitioning algorithm: The Digital Engine Operating System (DEOS) approach. In: 20th Digital Avionics System Conference Proceedings (October 2001)
2. Bosnacki, D., Dams, D.: Discrete Time Promela and Spin. In: Ravn, A.P., Rischel, H. (eds.) FTRTFT 1998. LNCS, vol. 1486, p. 307. Springer, Heidelberg (1998)
3. Colin, A., Puaut, I.: Worst-Case Execution Time Analysis of the RTEMS Real-Time Operating System. In: Proc. of the 13th Euromicro Conference on Real-Time Systems, Delft, The Netherlands, pp. 191–198 (June 2001)
4. Cofer, D., Rangarajan, M.: Formal Modeling and Analysis of Advanced Scheduling Features in an Avionics RTOS. In: Sangiovanni-Vincentelli, A.L., Sifakis, J. (eds.) EMSOFT 2002. LNCS, vol. 2491, Springer, Heidelberg (2002)
5. Eisinger, J., Polian, I., Becker, B., Metzner, A., Thesing, S., Wilhelm, R.: Automatic Identification of Timing Anomalies for Cycle-Accurate Worst-Case Execution Time Analysis. In: DDECS 2006, pp. 15–20 (2006)
6. Holzmann, G.J.: The Model Checker Spin. IEEE Trans. on Software Engineering 23(5), 279–295 (1997)
7. Lavagno, Martin, Scheffer: Electronic Design Automation For Integrated Circuits Handbook, ISBN 0-8493-3096-3
8. Puschner, P., Burns, A.: A Review of Worst Case Execution Time Analysis. Guest Editorial, Real Time Systems 18(2/3), 115–127 (2000)
9. Ha, V., Rangarajan, M., Cofer, D., Rueß, H., Dutertre, B.: Feature-based decomposition of inductive proofs applied to real-time avionics software. In: International Conference on Software Engineering (ICSE 2004), pp. 304–313 (May 2004)

Machine Checked Formal Proof of a Scheduling Protocol for Smartcard Personalization

Leonard Lensink, Sjaak Smetsers, and Marko van Eekelen

Institute for Computing and Information Sciences
Radboud University Nijmegen
The Netherlands
{L.Lensink, S.Smetsers, M.vanEekelen}@cs.ru.nl

Abstract. Using PVS (Prototype Verification System), we prove that an industry designed scheduler for a smartcard personalization machine is safe and optimal. This scheduler has previously been the subject of research in model checked scheduling synthesis and verification. These verification and synthesis efforts had only been done for a limited number of personalization stations. We have created an executable model and have proven the scheduling algorithm to be optimal and safe for any number of personalization stations. This result shows that theorem provers can be successfully used for industrial problems in cases where model checkers suffer from state explosion.

Keywords: verification, theorem proving, cyclic scheduling, simulation, PVS.

1   Introduction

Formal methods provide the kind of rigor in software engineering that is needed to move the software development process to a level comparably to other engineering professions.

There are many kinds of formal methods that can be employed at different stages of the development process. In the specification phase, a model can be constructed using some kind of formal language. This model can be used as a starting point for model based testing. Model checking, which proves properties for the entire state space of a finite part of the formal model by means of an exhaustive test, can eliminate a lot of errors. Both model based testing and model checking can be performed automatically. Theorem proving can be used for full verification of models that can have an infinite number of states. However, employing theorem proving is considerably more costly than the earlier mentioned methods.

Formal verification of models is gaining ground within the industrial world. For instance, Cybernétix participated in the AMETIST project, in order to improve the quality of their systems. This project's aim was to develop modeling methodology supported by efficient computerized problem-solving tools for the modeling and analysis of complex, distributed, real-time systems. A personalization machine was one of the case studies supplied by Cybernétix. This machine

S. Leue and P. Merino (Eds.): FMICS 2007, LNCS 4916, pp. 115–132, 2008.

consists of a conveyor belt with stations that personalize blank smartcards. The number of stations is variable.

The AMETIST participants modeled the machine in several model checking environments: Spin, Uppaal and SMV. However, within these systems, the models were checked and proven optimal and safe with respect to an ordering criterion for only a limited number of personalization stations. The most important reasons why it is interesting to look at the case study using other formal methods besides model checking are:

- In some production configurations the number of stations exceeds the amount of stations the model has been checked for. So there is not yet complete assurance that the scheduling algorithm is indeed safe and optimal for actually used configurations.
- Model checking is limited to a finite state space. Although there are methods allowing model checking to abstract away from the data or even to employ inductive reasoning on the model, so far no one has generalized to N stations. A stronger result would be to prove that for any number of stations, the scheduling algorithm is safe and optimal.
- Using a theorem prover to prove that a suitable invariant is correct usually gives more insight into why the machine satisfies its safety and optimality properties, instead of just checking them automatically.

In this paper we will present a formalized model of the machine in PVS (Prototype Verification System) [ORS92]. This is an environment for precise specification and verification of models. The specification language is based on simply typed higher order logic, but the type system has been extended with subtypes and dependent types. PVS also employs decision procedures to assist the user in a verification effort. These procedures take care of the bureaucracy associated with a formal proof and are usually able to discharge obvious proof obligations automatically. The specification language also allows for simulations and other means of animating the model if the model is composed out of an executable subset of the specification language.

We will come up with an invariant and use PVS to prove that this invariant holds for the model. This invariant is strong enough to prove all safety criteria and to prove that the algorithm guarantees optimal throughput for any number of personalization stations. We will also provide a simulation package. This makes it possible to verify that the model behaves as one would expect from a regular machine and which could form the basis of software that actually runs the machine.

In this article we present the smartcard personalization machine in section 2. The model of the machine is decribed in section 3 and we show by means of a simulation that this model is valid in section 4. Then, in section 5, the invariant is presented, followed by its proof in section 6. Safety and optimality are deduced from that invariant in section 6.1. A summary of related work by other people is given in section 7. An overview of future work can be found in section 8. All code and proofs referred to in this paper are available.[1]

---

[1] http://www.cs.ru.nl/~leonard/papers/cybernetix/cybernetix.tar.gz

2   Personalization Machine

A smart card personalization machine takes blank smart cards as input and programs them with personalized data. Subsequently, the cards are printed and tested. Typically, a machine has a throughput of several thousands of cards per hour. The machine has a conveyor belt transporting the cards. There is an uploader station putting cards onto the belt and an unloader station taking them off again. Directly above the belt are posts that can manipulate the cards, either by lifting them off the belt, like personalization stations, or by processing the cards while they remain on the belt, like graphical treatment stations. An example configuration is given in figure 1.

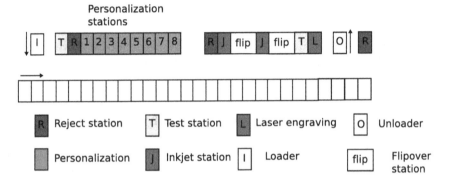

Fig. 1. Example of a standard configuration

There are different kinds of operations possible on the cards:

- Personalization stations program the chip on the card. These stations are able to detect if a card is defective. Cards need to be lifted into a personalization station by a lifting device.
- Graphical treatment stations are either laser engravers or inkjet stations. They can graphically personalize the cards. Graphical treatments happen while the card remains on the belt.
- Flipover stations can turn cards over to allow a graphical treatment of both sides of a card.
- Test stations determine whether the chip that is on the card functions properly.
- Rejection stations are used to extract cards that have been judged to be defective.

Due to the high number of cards that need to be personalized and the way the machine is structured, there are several requirements that need to be met by the smartcard personalization system:

- The output of the cards should happen in a predefined order, since further graphical treatment of the card may depend on the kind of personalization that has been received by the card. In the remainder of the paper we shall refer to this requirement as safety.
- The throughput of the machine should be optimal.
- The machine should allow for defective cards to be replaced.
- The system should be configurable and modular. The number of personalization and graphical treatment stations can vary according to the needs of the customers. Neither is the placement of the stations fixed. This means that the personalization stations can be spaced or appear interleaved with graphical treatment stations.

Cybernétix has developed and patented a scheduling protocol called "Super Single Mode". This particular scheduling protocol puts each time unit a new blank card on first position of the belt for N consecutive time units, where N is the number of personalization stations. After N time units, it leaves the first position of the belt empty for one time unit and then repeats itself by putting N new cards on the belt followed by leaving one slot empty.

3   PVS Model of the Personalization Machine

In the previous section, we have given a general description of the personalization machine. In this section we will discuss the model we have developed.

The personalization machine is modeled as a conveyor belt that transports cards underneath a set of M personalization stations. Each of these stations can pick up and drop cards onto the conveyor belt. The belt is synchronized with the personalization stations in order to enable picking up and dropping the cards.

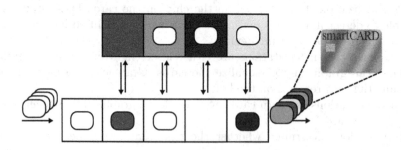

Fig. 2. A simplified machine with 4 stations

Since we are interested in the scheduling mechanism, the model that has been constructed can ignore several aspects of the machine, similarly to other studies [GV04, Ruy03, HKW05].

- For the scheduling algorithm it is not relevant how the cards end up on the belt or how they are taken off. This means that the loader and unloader can be safely omitted from the model.
- We assume that no cards are defective. This means that there is no need to model neither the testing stations nor the stations that take rejected cards off the belt. Although this reduces the interest of the example, only the study by Gebremichael [GV04] addressed the failed cards by creating a special "faulty" card mode. This can be added to the generalized model without too much effort in a later stage.
- The graphical treatment and flipover stations have also been omitted. These stations do not take cards off the belt, so they can not interfere with the ordering on the belt. Also, the processing time is magnitudes smaller than the processing time of the personalization stations. They have a negligible impact on the throughput of the system.
- The loading and offloading time of the personalization stations is also much smaller than the personalization time and not included into the model.

When the machine is started, the belt and all the personalization stations are empty. In figure 3 we show the transition of a four station personalization machine through time. At each transition, the belt is moved one slot and

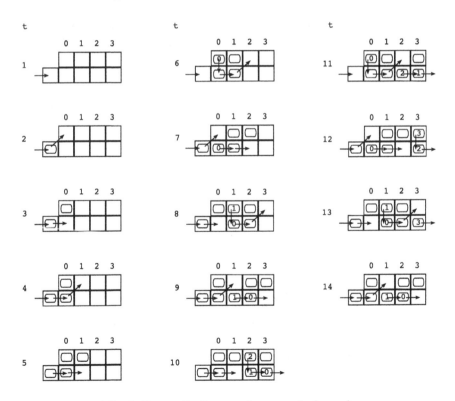

Fig. 3. Personalization run in super single mode

subsequently the cards are dropped or lifted from the slots when needed. The arrows indicate the move a card is about to make. The numbers above the stations indicate the kind of personalization produced by that station and can also be found on the card after a station has finished personalizing and has dropped the card back onto the conveyor belt.

At first, when the time that has passed is smaller than 9, the system is in an initial state where all the stations fill up with cards being processed. At t=9, the system starts a cycle that lasts for five transitions. As one can see in figure 3, the state at t=14 is the same as at t=9. The state of the machine as depicted in figure 2 can be found in the table at t=12.

Our aim in constructing a PVS model is to verify that the scheduling algorithm satisfies the following criteria:

- The personalized cards should leave the machine in the order of the occurrence of the personalization stations. Cards personalized by station 0 should appear at the last slot on the belt before the card personalized by station 1. No other sorting mechanism may exist in the system.
- The throughput of the machine should be optimal.

3.1   The Belt

The model encodes the conveyor belt using an algebraic data type. A slot on the belt can either contain no card: empty, contain a smartcard that has yet to be personalized: new_card, or contain a personalized card: personalization. The personalization is modeled as a natural number that corresponds to the relative position of the personalization station with respect to the conveyor belt. This means that cards leaving the left most station get 0, and the rightmost M.

In PVS, algebraic data types are specified by providing the *constructors* as well as *recognizers* and *accessors*. The constructors empty, new_card and personalization are used to build the objects of that data type. The recognizers (empty?,new_card? and personalization?) are used to determine of which kind an expression of the slot type is and the accessor number can be used to extract the personalization_nr, in case of a personalization.

```
slot : DATATYPE
BEGIN
empty : empty?
new_card : new_card?
personalization (number : personalization_nr) : personalization?
END slot
```

The conveyor belt is modeled as an array of $1 + M$ of these slots. Each slot is indexed by a natural number from 0 up to M. In PVS, these restrictions on values which can be held by an object can be expressed elegantly using *dependent* types: types dependent on values. For example, the (finite) subset $\{0, \ldots, M\}$ of the natural numbers can be described as below(n:nat) : TYPE = { m : nat | m < n }. In this case, the predicate on the natural numbers is below(1+M).

```
beltposition : TYPE = below(1+M)
```

3.2   The Stations

The relevant information to model a personalization station is whether a station is programming a card and if so, how far the personalization process has progressed. A timer is used to model this. The value 0 is assigned to a station to indicate that a station is empty and not working on a card. Once a station starts personalizing, the value is increased to 1 and incremented each time slot until it reaches the time needed to complete the personalization process. At that time, the machine will start looking whether it can drop the card or not. Theoretically, the machine can keep incrementing the timer as long as the card has not been dropped. Therefore, we model the timer by a natural number.

```
timer : TYPE = nat
```

Since we have one less personalization station than there are slots on the belt, the stations are modeled as an array of M of these timers.

```
stationposition : TYPE = below(M)
```

3.3   The Machine

The entire machine is rather straightforward. The machine is viewed as an array of M stations combined with an array of $1 + M$ belt-slots. A global timer is used to synchronize actions on the belt and in the stations. In PVS this is modeled using a record type:

```
machine_state : TYPE =
  [# stations : [stationposition → timer],
     belt : [beltposition → slot],
     global_timer : global_timer
  #]
```

In figure 4 the machine as earlier depicted in figure 2 is shown as a representation of the PVS model.

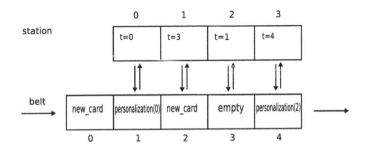

Fig. 4. Model of the simplified machine from figure 2

The behavior of the machine is described by a function f_next. This function transforms a machine state into the next machine state by operating the belt slots and stations for each position and by increasing the global timer. The next state of a station and belt at a certain position is determined by the content of the previous belt slot or the previous station.

- In the case of a station, the next state can only be determined by the content of the belt that is situated to the left and below the station. In the model they are indexed by the same position number.
- In the case of the belt, the next state at a certain position is determined by the content of either the station directly above the belt or the previous belt position. Both are indexed by the position minus one.

The f_next function constructs the next state out of the current state by creating a new record of type machine_state:

```
f_next(ps:machine_state) : machine_state =
  (# stations := f_operate_station(ps)
  , belt := f_operate_belt(ps)
  , global_timer := global_timer(ps)+1
  #)
```

The behavior of the machine is best described by discerning three different situations:

1. *We have an empty station and a new card is available on the previous slot on the belt.* In this case, we move the card from the belt into the station and start personalizing. As a consequence, the belt position becomes empty and the station's timer is started.
2. *The timer in the station indicates that the card has been personalized and there is an empty spot on the belt.* This means the personalized card, which is designated by its position, can be dropped onto the belt, leaving an empty station. At the same time the timer is reset.
3. *If none of the above applies* the contents of the belt are just shifted one position. *If the station at the position is personalizing* we adjust the timer by one tick to denote the progress of time.

The function operating on each station checks whether the timer of the station needs to be started, reset or increased, depending on whether it is done personalizing cards or ready to take in a new card:

```
f_operate_station(ps:machine_state)(spos:stationposition) : timer =
LET station = station(ps)(spos), belt = belt(ps)(spos) IN
IF empty?(station) ∧ new_card?(belt)
THEN start_timer
ELSIF done?(station) ∧ empty?(belt)
THEN  reset_timer
ELSIF ¬ empty?(station)
THEN increase_timer(station)
ELSE  wait(station)
ENDIF
```

The function that operates the belt reacts to basically the same conditions as the previous function with exception of the first belt position. There the cards must be scheduled according to the scheduling algorithm:

```
f_operate_belt(ps:machine_state)(bpos:beltposition) : slot =
  IF bpos=0
  THEN schedule(global_timer(ps))
  ELSE
    LET station = station(ps)(bpos-1), belt = belt(ps)(bpos-1) IN
    IF empty?(station) ∧ new_card?(belt)
    THEN lift
    ELSIF done?(station) ∧ empty?(belt)
    THEN drop(bpos)
    ELSE move_belt(belt)
    ENDIF
  ENDIF
```

The behavior of the system strongly depends on the time a personalization station needs to finish. If the personalization time exceeds the number of personalization stations, the safety property will not be satisfied, because it will mean that a blank card will reach the end of the conveyor belt before one of the stations will be able to pick it up. If the personalization time is smaller than M, there will not be an empty spot available to drop the card. This spot will only arrive after M time units, so it makes sense to have the personalization end at that time.

```
done?(t:timer) : bool = t=M
```

3.4 The Scheduler

The scheduler is a process that puts the cards onto the first spot of the conveyor belt in a cyclic fashion. It places M new cards on the belt followed by an empty spot. In order to keep track of when an empty space should be left on the belt, the global timer is used:

```
schedule(global_timer:global_timer) : slot =
  IF mod(global_timer,1+M) = 0
  THEN empty
  ELSE new_card
  ENDIF
```

4   Validating the Model

In section 3, we developed a model of the personalization machine. When modeling a system, the key question is whether it faithfully represents the original machine. In order to show this is indeed the case we need to be able to execute our model and make a visual representation that mimics the behavior expected from a personalization machine. This approach provides us with several benefits:

- To prove the safety property of the machine an invariant is needed. Visualizing the behavior makes is easier to determine this invariant.
- Secondly, if we have an appropriate API to drive the belt and sensors, the executable model means that we can generate code to run the machine. No manual translation from model to code is necessary. This eliminates a possible source of errors.
- Finally, visualizing the behavior of the model allows us to verify that the model behaves as expected.

PVS allows for animation of its specifications by means of a ground evaluator [vHPPR98]. The evaluator extracts executable Common Lisp code from the PVS functional specifications. Semantic attachments enable a safe connection of user defined Lisp functions to uninterpreted PVS functions. A library, PVSio [Muñ03], extends the ground evaluator with a library of predefined functions to handle all kinds of imperative languages features.

Since we have written the model in PVS, using only functional specifications, it is directly executable by PVS' ground evaluator. On top of the executable model it is possible to add IO as a side-effect of the original statements. Functions that produce side-effects must be modeled as Boolean functions that always return true. By conjoining those functions with the original model they will be executed alongside the executable model. We define a simulation function that takes as arguments how many times the transition should take place and the starting state. As a side effect, the state of the machine is printed to the standard output so we can observe the machine as time progresses.

```
f_step(ps:machine_state)(p:nat) : RECURSIVE void =
   print_state(ps) ∧
   (
   IF (p=0)
   THEN println("End of simulation")
   ELSE f_step(f_next(ps))(p-1)
   ENDIF
   )
MEASURE pn
```

The function print_state(ps0) prints the state variables to the standard output.

Although no machine experts were involved in validating this particular model, the models from the original AMETIST project were. The PVS model is close enough to these models to validate it against its expected behavior. We have simulated behavior for machines of several sizes and as an example show the validation of a conveyor belt with four personalization stations. What should be expected is earlier depicted in figure 3. A # denotes a new card, a * denotes a station that is personalizing, ˆan empty station, ! shows a station that is done personalizing, while the natural numbers stand for personalized cards. In figure 5 we show the output generated by a simulation run of the model for a four station machine.

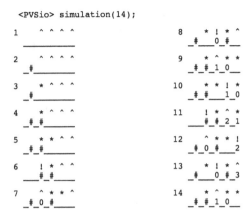

Fig. 5. A simulation run in PVSio

A comparison of figure 5 with figure 3 shows that the simulation behaves as expected.

5   The Complete State Invariant

In section 4 we have shown by means of a simulation that the model behaves as expected for four stations. The next step is to prove that the model satisfies the safety and optimality requirements:

- Concerning the safety property: The machine must maintain the order of the personalization stations in its generated output order. This can be split up in two requirements.
  - First, only personalized cards or empty spaces should be present at the last slot of the belt.
  - Secondly, once a personalized card n, where $0 \le n < M$, is present at the final position on the belt, the next card has to be personalization $mod(n+1, M)$ or a sequence of empty slots until the next card is personalization $mod(n+1, M)$.
- Concerning the optimality property: The machine must personalize as many cards as possible per time unit. The optimum is reached if all personalization stations are occupied and personalizing all of the time. This means that once the cyclic phase of the machine is entered, two properties should hold:
  - If a station is empty, then it must immediately be able to load a new card and start personalizing.
  - If a station is done personalizing, an empty space should immediately be available to drop the card.

We can formulate the safety property slightly more specific, because we know that only one empty spot is scheduled each cycle. This means that there can be only one empty spot in the output position once the cyclic phase of the machine has been reached. As a consequence, we can conclude that the order in which the

personalized cards leave the machine must be linearly related to the value of the
global_timer. We have established that the relation between the value of the
global_timer and the value of the personalized card, number(belt(ps)(M)),
however, we do not know yet at what time exactly mod(global_timer(ps),1+M)
will be equal to personalized card 0. There might be a phase transposition. We
call this c.

Assuming we have M personalization stations the first property can be specified formally as:

empty?(belt(ps)(M))
∨ (personalization?(belt(ps)(M)) ∧
    ∃ c: mod(global_timer(ps)+c,1+M) = number(belt(ps)(M)))

The second property can be formally specified as:

∀ pos: ∃ ps': global_timer(ps') = global_timer(ps)+1 ∧
(empty?(station(ps)(pos)) ⇒ start?(station(ps')(pos))) ∧
(done?(station(ps)(pos)) ⇒ empty?(station(ps')(pos)))

Trying to prove these two properties directly turns out to be futile. In order
to prove them we need to come up with an invariant that is stronger than the
safety and optimality properties. More particularly, in this invariant must be
expressed that whenever a station has finished personalizing, an empty spot will
be available to deposit the personalized card.

We assume the machine starts with an empty belt and all stations empty.
After an initialization phase, the machine will end up in a cyclic state until the
machine is shut down. In the initialization phase, the stations and belt positions
remain empty, until an empty card reaches them.

The graphical representation of the state of the personalization machine, de-
vised to validate the working of the system can also be put to good use in deriving
the invariant needed to prove the relevant properties.

In figure 6, the first observation we make is that the cyclic phase propagates
through the positions at the rate of one position every two time units. After two
time units the first position satisfies the stable (cyclic) invariant, while the rest
of the belt still is in its initial state. After four time units, the first two positions
satisfy the invariant, while the remaining part of the belt and stations are still
in their initial state, and so on:

p_invariant(ps:machine_state) : bool =
  ∀ bpos : IF 2*bpos+1 ≥ global_timer(ps)
            THEN p_init(ps)(bpos)
            ELSE p_stable(ps)(bpos)
            ENDIF

The initial invariant is simply that the timer of the station at position *pos*
is 0 and consequently the station is empty, as well as the corresponding belt
position.

p_init(ps:machine_state)(bpos:beltposition) : bool =
  (bpos ≤ M-1 ⇒ station(ps)(bpos) = 0) ∧ empty?(belt(ps)(bpos))

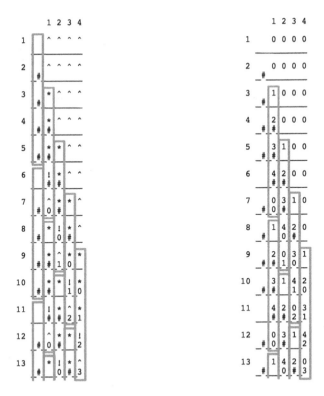

Fig. 6. Cyclic invariant propagation   **Fig. 7.** State of the stations

Observations on the stations of the personalization machine allow us to conclude that the timer of a station is related to the value of the global timer. As seen in figure 7, the value of a station neatly increases in time with a phase difference according to its position: station(bpos) = mod(global_timer - 2*(bpos+1),1+M)

The relationship between the global timer and the contents of the belt at a certain position are slightly more complex. In order to clarify that relationship, the state of the stations is removed from the representation in figure 8.

We replace some of the symbols we have used with a numerical representation. From this representation as in figure 9 we can derive the following property for the content of the belt:

belt = mod(global_timer(ps)-bpos-1,1+M) ∧
IF belt = bpos THEN empty
ELSIF belt > bpos THEN new_card
ELSE personalization(number(belt))
ENDIF

Combining and rewriting the above results we obtain an invariant for the entire system:

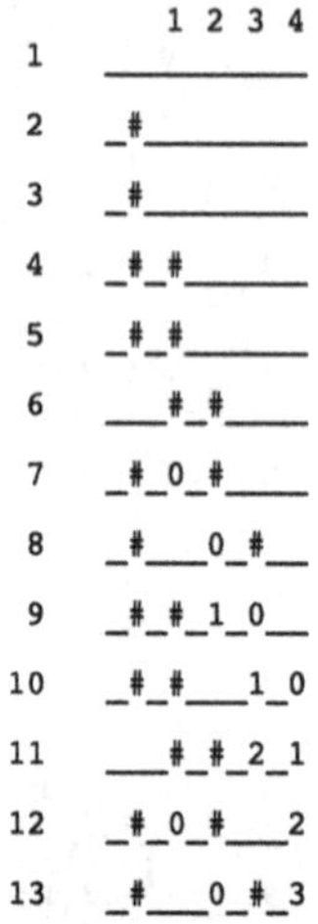

Fig. 8. State of the belt

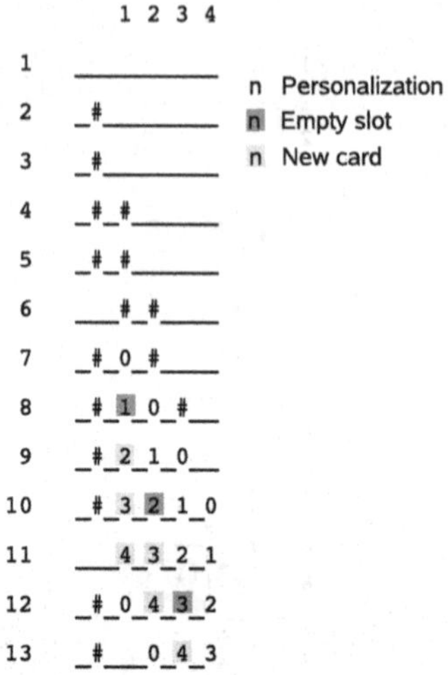

Fig. 9. State of the belt with selected numerical representations

```
p_stable(ps:machine_state)(pos:beltposition) : bool =
(pos ≤ M-1 ⇒ mod(global_timer(ps)-2*(pos+1),1+M) = station(ps)(pos))
∧
LET timer = mod(global_timer(ps)-2*pos-1,1+M), belt = belt(ps)(pos) IN
IF timer = 0
THEN  empty?(belt)
ELSIF timer < 1+M-pos
THEN new_card?(belt)
ELSE personalization?(belt) ∧ number(belt) = timer-1-M+pos
ENDIF
```

Since it contains complete information of the state of the machine at any given time, it should be possible to prove that this invariant (if it is correct) holds. We call this the *complete state invariant*. From this invariant, we can then directly deduce the properties we want to prove.

6   Proof of the Complete State Invariant

After specifying the invariant in PVS, we will now prove that the invariant holds in the initial state and does not change with each consecutive state change. We define the following theorem within PVS:

```
invariant: THEOREM
p_invariant(ps_init) ∧ (p_invariant(ps) ⇒ p_invariant(f_next(ps)))
```

Proving the invariant to hold is done by case distinctions on the invariant, as well as case distinctions on the functions f_operate_belt and f_operate_station.

These distinctions then invariably lead to some equation that can be proven correct using modulo arithmetic or to a contradiction within the assumptions. In the standard library of PVS, there are a number of lemmas that are sufficient to discharge all of the modular proof obligations. To provide better understanding, we describe a part of the proof in detail: We want to prove that the transition in the first part of the f_operate_station function does not invalidate the invariant. The relevant part of the function is:

```
[..]
  IF empty?(station(ps)(pos)) ∧ new_card?(belt(ps)(pos))
  THEN start_timer
[..]
```

Where start_timer returns the timer value of 1.

It has to be shown that the invariant still holds if empty?(station(ps)(pos)) and new_card?(belt(ps)(pos)) then station(f_next(ps))(pos) = 1 is added to the assumptions. This simplifies the invariant to two items that have to be proven:

- First, 2*pos+1 < 1+global_timer(ps). This can be derived from the fact that the p_init(ps) part of the invariant has to be false. The value of station(ps)(pos) is one, while the invariant states that it is zero when 2*pos+1 >= 1+global_timer(ps).
- Secondly, filling out the invariant further with the knowledge that the timer of the station at position pos is one and assuming that we can prove the first of our proof obligations the part of the invariant that remains is:

  mod(1+global_timer(ps)-2*pos,1+M) = 1

Because we know that at time global_timer(ps) we had a new card at the previous position, the invariant adds to the assumptions:

  mod(global_timer(ps)-2*pos,1+M) < 1+M-pos

From this assumption, using modulo arithmetic it is deducible that:

  global_timer(ps) ≥ 2*pos

There are two possible cases left:

- Either global_timer = 2*pos. Then, again using modulo arithmetic, it is easy to prove that mod(1+global_timer(ps)-2*pos,1+M) = 1.
- Otherwise, 2*pos > global_timer(ps). Then we know that the stable part of the invariant holds at global_timer(ps).
  This means: mod(global_timer-2*pos,1+M) = 0. This can be proven using modulo arithmetic.

The other situations where personalized cards are dropped in empty slots or the card on the belt is just moved to the right and the timer in the station is optionally increased are slightly more complicated, but revolve around a number of case distinctions as well. The total proof, which is surely not optimized, needs about 250 proof commands in PVS to be performed completely. Creating the model, deriving the invariant and proving the invariant to hold, took about a month for a PhD student, relatively inexperienced with PVS.

6.1 Safety and Optimality

Now that we have established that the invariant holds at all times, we will prove that the safety and optimality properties follow directly from the invariant:

- The safety property meant that the personalized cards leave the personalization part of the machine in order of the kind of personalization they have received. Once the invariant has been proven to hold, it follows directly that at the end of the conveyor belt (at position M), the following holds:

    ```
    empty?(belt(ps)(M))
    ∨ (personalization?(belt(ps)(M)) ∧
        mod(global_timer(ps),1+M) = number(belt(ps)(M)))
    ```

    Since `global_timer(ps)` is ordered, `mod(global_timer(ps)),1+M)` is ordered as well.
- The optimality property implied that the scheduling protocol needs to have the highest throughput per cycle. This derives immediately from the fact that if we have 1+M consecutive cards, the machine will not be able to personalize all the cards. This will violate the safety requirements. Therefore, the highest throughput per cycle is reached by leaving only one empty slot after M consecutive cards.

7 Related Work

The Cybernétix case study has been the subject of several research papers. Kugler and Weiss wrote an article about how to interactively derive scheduling algorithms for production lines using Live Sequence Charts [HKW05]. In it, they use a graphical representation to analyze a production line systematically. However, no properties for that production line are proved. In [Mad04] Mader compares two different scheduling algorithms using model checking, for four and eight personalization stations, but the model checking was limited to a maximum of respectively 16 and 40 personalized cards. In contrast to the other studies, Mader does include the graphical treatment in her model. Ruys uses new features of SPIN 4.0 to derive an optimal schedule for four stations and at most five cards [Ruy03]. Nieberg proves in [Nie04] with a mathematical argument that the Super Single Mode is optimal, but does not provide a formal proof that the protocol is safe with respect to the ordering of the cards. Also using model checking, Gebremichael [GV04] is able to derive the Super Single Mode as an optimal schedule for five personalization stations and any number of cards. Gebremichael also extends his model to deal with a possible defective card. None of the studies concerning the smartcard personalization machine combine the rigor of machine checked proof and simulation with a general proof of optimality and safety. In PVS work has been done to integrate model checking and theorem proving for models that have a finite number of states as described in [RSS95]. However, these models must conform to some syntactic restrictions that complicate actually using the model checking part of PVS in practice. Work on verifying algorithms and code generation from PVS has been done by Jacobs, Wichers Schreur and Smetsers in [JSS07], where executable parts PVS specifications are translated into the functional programming language Clean.

8 Future Work

The ad hoc nature of the derivation of the invariant needed for the proof of the properties, suggests a natural direction for future work. More case studies can hopefully give us ideas how to derive invariants more methodically. We have only focused on the scheduling mechanism on a rather abstract level until now. If code that drives the machine is to be generated, more detail will have to be added to the specification. An open question is whether the proof will have to be substantially altered when this is attempted. Another subject of research concerns devising methods to incorporate the context in which the generated code has to be run into the theorem prover itself in a methodical and easy to use fashion.

9 Conclusion

We addressed the Cybernétix smartcard personalization machine as an example of an industry supplied case study for the application of formal methods. We constructed an executable model in the specification language PVS. Since the model is executable it was straightforward to visualize the behavior of the model and construct a simulator that was used to establish that the model that had been created adequately represented the machine. In future work it is possible to use the verified scheduling algorithm to control the machine itself, eliminating any errors that might arise from manually translating the model into code.

Model checking techniques already proved optimality and safety of this machine for a limited number of stations. In typical applications of this machine, the number of stations will be much larger than the amount for which was model checked. This means that no guarantee can be given that the properties will hold generally. By using a theorem prover we have established that the safety and optimality of the scheduling algorithm is guaranteed for any number of personalization stations.

References

[GV04]   Gebremichael, B., Vaandrager, F.W.: Control synthesis for a smart card personalization system using symbolic model checking. In: Larsen, K.G., Niebert, P. (eds.) FORMATS 2003. LNCS, vol. 2791, pp. 189–203. Springer, Heidelberg (2004)

[HKW05]   Harel, D., Kugler, H., Weiss, G.: Some methodological observations resulting from experience using lscs and the play-in/play-out approach. In: Leue, S., Systä, T.J. (eds.) Scenarios: Models, Transformations and Tools. LNCS, vol. 3466, pp. 26–42. Springer, Heidelberg (2005)

[JSS07]   Jacobs, B., Smetsers, S., Schreur, R.W.: Code-carrying theories. Formal
             Aspects of Computing 19(2), 191–203 (2007)
[Mad04]   Mader, A.H.: Deriving schedules for a smart card personalisation sys-
             tem. Technical Report TR-CTIT-04-05, University of Twente, Enschede
             (January 2004)
[Muñ03]   Muñoz, C.: Rapid prototyping in PVS. Report NIA Report No. 2003-
             03, NASA/CR-2003-212418, NIA-NASA Langley, National Institute of
             Aerospace, Hampton, VA (May 2003)
[Nie04]   Nieberg, T.: On cyclic plans for scheduling a smart card personalisation
             system. Technical Report TR-CTIT-04-01, Centre for Telematics and
             Information Technology, University of Twente, Enschede (January 2004)
[ORS92]   Owre, S., Rushby, J.M., Shankar, N.: PVS: A prototype verification
             system. In: Kapur, D. (ed.) CADE 1992. LNCS, vol. 607, pp. 748–752.
             Springer, Heidelberg (1992)
[RSS95]   Rajan, S., Shankar, N., Srivas, M.K.: An integration of model-checking
             with automated proof checking. In: Wolper, P. (ed.) CAV 1995. LNCS,
             vol. 939, pp. 84–97. Springer, Heidelberg (1995)
[Ruy03]   Ruys, T.C.: Optimal scheduling using branch and bound with spin 4.0.
             In: Ball, T., Rajamani, S.K. (eds.) SPIN 2003. LNCS, vol. 2648, pp.
             1–17. Springer, Heidelberg (2003)
[vHPPR98]   von Henke, F., Pfab, S., Pfeifer, H., Rueß, H.: Case studies in meta-
             level theorem proving. In: Grundy, J., Newey, M. (eds.) TPHOLs 1998.
             LNCS, vol. 1479, pp. 461–478. Springer, Heidelberg (1998)

An Action/State-Based Model-Checking Approach for the Analysis of Communication Protocols for Service-Oriented Applications*

Maurice H. ter Beek[1], A. Fantechi[1,2], S. Gnesi[1], and F. Mazzanti[1]

[1] Istituto di Scienza e Tecnologie dell'Informazione "A. Faedo", CNR, Pisa, Italy
{maurice.terbeek,stefania.gnesi,franco.mazzanti}@isti.cnr.it
[2] Dipartimento di Sistemi e Informatica, Università degli Studi di Firenze, Italy
fantechi@dsi.unifi.it

Abstract. In this paper we present an action/state-based logical framework for the analysis and verification of complex systems, which relies on the definition of doubly labelled transition systems. The defined temporal logic, called UCTL, combines the action paradigm—classically used to describe systems using labelled transition systems—with predicates that are true over states—as captured when using Kripke structures as semantic model. An efficient model checker for UCTL has been realized, exploiting an on-the-fly algorithm. We then show how to use UCTL, and its model checker, in the design phase of an asynchronous extension of the communication protocol SOAP, called aSOAP. For this purpose, we describe aSOAP as a set of communicating UML state machines, for which a semantics over doubly labelled transition systems has been provided.

1 Introduction

Complex systems are often modelled according to either a state-based or an event-based paradigm. While in the former case the system is characterized by states and state changes, in the latter case it is characterized by the events (actions) that can be performed to move from one state to another. Both are important paradigms for the specification of complex systems and, as a result, formal methods ideally should cover both. Indeed, this trend is witnessed by the recent widespread use of modelling frameworks that allow both events and state changes to be specified. An example are UML state diagrams, which are used more and more in industry to specify the behaviour of (software) systems, though often without caring much for their formal aspects. Also the specification of Service-Oriented Applications has seen several applications of UML state diagrams [25]. What is missing in order to use in full specification techniques that allow one to specify both events and state changes, is the availability of a formal framework in which desired properties can subsequently be proved over the specification, with the support of specific verification tools.

---

* This work has been partially funded by the EU project SENSORIA (IST-2005-016004) and by the Italian project TOCAI.IT.

S. Leue and P. Merino (Eds.): FMICS 2007, LNCS 4916, pp. 133–148, 2008.

In this paper, we aim to fill this gap by presenting the action/state-based temporal logic UCTL, which allows one to both specify the basic properties that a state should satisfy and to combine these basic predicates with advanced temporal operators dealing with the events performed. As was done for CTL and ACTL in the past, we consider a fragment of a doubly labelled temporal logic, interpreted over doubly labelled structures: This fragment is UCTL, which preserves the property shared by CTL and ACTL of having an explicit local model-checking algorithm in linear time. The semantic domain of UCTL is doubly labelled transition systems [11]. A prototypical on-the-fly model checker, called UMC, has been developed for UCTL: The tool allows the efficient verification of UCTL formulae that define action- and state-based properties.

In recent years, several logics that allow one to express both action-based and state-based properties have been introduced, for many different purposes. An event- and state-based temporal logic for Petri nets is given in [17]. In [16], a modal temporal logic without a fixed-point operator and interpreted over so-called Kripke modal transition systems (a modal version of doubly labelled transition systems) is defined. In [4,6], a state/event extension of LTL is presented, together with a model-checking framework whose formulae are interpreted over so-called labelled Kripke structures (essentially doubly labelled transition systems). Finally, in [5], this linear-time temporal logic is extended to a universal branching-time temporal logic. The latter logics are used extensively to verify software systems. The advantage of all such logics lies in the ease of expressiveness of properties that in pure action-based or pure state-based logics can be quite cumbersome to write down. Moreover, their use often results in a reduction of the state space, the memory use and the time spent for verification. Obviously, the real gain depends—as always—on the specific system under scrutiny.

To conclude, we present a case study that shows the use of UCTL and its model checker UMC in the design phase of aSOAP, which is an asynchronous extension of the web service communication protocol SOAP. Mobile communication networks typically are unstable, since terminal devices can dynamically change reachability status during their lifetime. In Service-Oriented Architectures, asynchronous service invocation is often the more suitable paradigm for the choreography and orchestration of their mobile components. Hence, there is a need for communication protocols that can manage asynchronous communication also in the presence of unstable network connections. Formal modelling and analysis of such protocols is a first step towards the successful implementation and evaluation of reliable Service-Oriented Applications. For this purpose, we describe aSOAP as a set of communicating UML state machines, for which a semantics over doubly labelled transition systems has been provided, express several behavioural properties on this UML model of aSOAP in UCTL and verify them with UMC.

The paper is organized as follows. Some preliminary definitions are given in Section 2. In Section 3, we present the syntax and semantics of UCTL, while in Section 4 we describe its model checker UMC. The case study illustrating their use is presented in Section 4. Finally, Section 5 concludes the paper.

2   Preliminaries

In this section, we define the basic notations and terminology used in the sequel.

Definition 1 (Labelled Transition System). *A* Labelled Transition System *(LTS for short) is a quadruple* (Q, q_0, Act, R), *where:*

- *Q is a set of states;*
- *$q_0 \in Q$ is the initial state;*
- *Act is a finite set of observable events (actions) with e ranging over Act, α ranging over 2^{Act} and ϵ denoting the empty set;*
- *$R \subseteq Q \times 2^{Act} \times Q$ is the transition relation; instead of $(q, \alpha, q') \in R$ we may also write $q \xrightarrow{\alpha} q'$.*

Note that the main difference between this definition of LTSs and the classical one is the labelling of the transitions: we label transitions by sets of events rather than by single (un)observable events. This extension allows the transitions from one state to another to represent sets of actions without the need of intermediate states, which has proved to be useful when modelling, e.g., UML state diagrams.

Another extension is to label states with atomic propositions, like the concept of doubly labelled transition systems [11], again extended as in Definition 1.

Definition 2 (Doubly Labelled Transition System). *A* Doubly Labelled Transition System *($L^2 TS$ for short) is a quintuple* (Q, q_0, Act, R, AP, L), *where:*

- *(Q, q_0, Act, R) is an LTS;*
- *AP is a set of atomic propositions with p ranging over AP; p will typically have the form of an expression like $VAR = value$;*
- *$L : Q \longrightarrow 2^{AP}$ is a labelling function that associates a subset of AP to each state of the LTS.*

The L^2TSs thus obtained are very similar to so-called *Kripke transition systems* [19]. The latter are defined as an extension of Kripke structures by a labelling over transitions.

The usual notion of bisimulation equivalence can be straightforwardly extended to L^2TSs by taking into account equality of labelling of states, and considering the transitions labelled by sets of events.

Definition 3 (Bisimulation). *Let $A_1 = (Q_1, q_{0_1}, Act, \rightarrow_1, AP_1, L_1)$ and $A_2 = (Q_2, q_{0_2}, Act, \rightarrow_2, AP_2, L_2)$ be two $L^2 TSs$ and let $q_1 \in Q_1$ and $q_2 \in Q_2$. We say that the two states q_1 and q_2 are strongly equivalent (or simply equivalent), denoted by $q_1 \sim q_2$, if there exists a strong bisimulation $\mathcal{B}$ that relates q_1 and q_2. $\mathcal{B} \subseteq Q_1 \times Q_2$ is a strong bisimulation if for all $(q_1, q_2) \in \mathcal{B}$ and $\alpha \in 2^{Act}$:*

1. *$L_1(q_1) = L_2(q_2)$,*
2. *$q_1 \xrightarrow{\alpha}_1 q_1'$ implies $\exists q_2' \in Q_2 : q_2 \xrightarrow{\alpha}_2 q_2'$ and $(q_1', q_2') \in \mathcal{B}$, and*
3. *$q_2 \xrightarrow{\alpha}_2 q_2'$ implies $\exists q_1' \in Q_1 : q_1 \xrightarrow{\alpha}_1 q_1'$ and $(q_1', q_2') \in \mathcal{B}$.*

We say that the two L^2TSs A_1 and A_2 are equivalent, denoted by $A_1 \sim A_2$, if there exists a strong bisimulation $\mathcal{B}$ such that $(q_{0_1}, q_{0_2}) \in \mathcal{B}$.

The usual notions of simulation preorder or weak (observational) equivalence can be defined analogously.

LTSs and Kripke structures can be lifted to L^2TSs in a straightforward manner. An LTS $T = (Q, q_0, Act, R)$ can be lifted to an L^2TS A_T, on the same set of states and maintaining the same transition relation, in the following way: $A_T = (Q, q_0, Act, R, \varnothing, L)$, where for all $q \in Q$: $L(q) = \varnothing$.

A Kripke structure $K = (Q, q_0, R, AP, L)$ can be lifted to an L^2TS A_K, on the same set of states and maintaining the same labelling function, in the following way: $A_K = (Q, q_0, \{\epsilon\}, R', AP, L)$, where for all $(q, q') \in R$: $(q, \epsilon, q') \in R'$.

3   The Action/State-Based Temporal Logic UCTL

In this section, we present the syntax and semantics of UCTL. This temporal logic, *action and state based*, allows one to reason on state properties as well as to describe the behaviour of systems that perform actions during their lifetime. UCTL includes both the branching-time action-based logic ACTL [10,11] and the branching-time state-based logic CTL [7].[1]

Before defining the syntax of UCTL, we introduce an auxiliary logic of events.

Definition 4 (Event formulae). *Let Act be a set of observable events. Then the language of event formulae on $Act \cup \{\tau\}$ is defined as follows:*

$$\chi ::= tt \mid e \mid \tau \mid \neg \chi \mid \chi \wedge \chi$$

Definition 5 (Event formulae semantics). *The satisfaction relation $\models$ for event formulae of the form $\alpha \models \chi$ is defined over sets of events as follows:*

$\alpha \models tt$ holds always;
$\alpha \models e$ iff $\alpha = \{e_1, \ldots, e_n\}$ and there exists an $i \in \{1, \ldots, n\}$ such that $e_i = e$;
$\alpha \models \tau$ iff $\alpha = \varnothing$;
$\alpha \models \neg \chi$ iff not $\alpha \models \chi$;
$\alpha \models \chi \wedge \chi'$ iff $\alpha \models \chi$ and $\alpha \models \chi'$.

As usual, *ff* abbreviates $\neg tt$ and $\chi \vee \chi'$ abbreviates $\neg(\neg \chi \wedge \neg \chi')$.

Definition 6 (Syntax of UCTL)

$$\phi ::= true \mid p \mid \neg \phi \mid \phi \wedge \phi' \mid A\pi \mid E\pi$$
$$\pi ::= X_\chi \phi \mid \phi_\chi U \phi' \mid \phi_\chi U_{\chi'} \phi' \mid \phi_\chi W \phi' \mid \phi_\chi W_{\chi'} \phi'$$

---

[1] Note that ACTL is also used to denote the universal fragment of CTL, originally called ∀CTL in [8]. For easy of writing, ∀CTL was changed to ACTL, thus generating a conflict with the previously introduced acronym ACTL for Action-based CTL.

State formulae *are ranged over by* ϕ, path formulae *are ranged over by* π, *A and E are* path quantifiers, *and* X, U *and* W *are the indexed* next, until *and weak* until *operators.*[2]

In linear-time temporal logic (LTL), the formula $\phi\, W\, \psi$ can be obtained by deriving it from the until (U) and the always (G) operators, as follows: $\phi\, U\, \psi \vee G\,\phi$. This way to derive the weak until operator from the until operator is not applicable in UCTL since disjunction or conjunction of path formulae is not expressible according to the UCTL syntax, and the same holds for any pure branching-time temporal logic.

To define the semantics of UCTL, we need the notion of a path in an L²TS.

Definition 7 (Path). *Let* $\mathcal{A} = (Q, q_0, Act, R, AP, L)$ *be an* $L^2\,TS$ *and let* $q \in Q$.

- σ *is a* path *from* q *if* $\sigma = q$ *(the* empty path *from* q*) or* σ *is a (possibly infinite) sequence* $(q_0, \alpha_1, q_1)(q_1, \alpha_2, q_2)\cdots$ *with* $(q_{i-1}, \alpha_i, q_i) \in R$ *for all* $i > 0$.
- *The concatenation of paths* σ_1 *and* σ_2, *denoted by* $\sigma_1\sigma_2$, *is a partial operation, defined only if* σ_1 *is finite and its final state coincides with the first state of* σ_2. *Concatenation is associative and has identities:* $\sigma_1(\sigma_2\sigma_3) = (\sigma_1\sigma_2)\sigma_3$ *and if* q_0 *is the first state of* σ *and* q_n *is its final state, then* $q_0\sigma = \sigma q_n = \sigma$.
- *A path* σ *is said to be* maximal *if it is either an infinite sequence or it is a finite sequence whose final state has no successor states.*
- *The* length *of a path* σ *is denoted by* $|\sigma|$. *If* σ *is an infinite path, then* $|\sigma| = \omega$. *If* $\sigma = q$, *then* $|\sigma| = 0$. *If* $\sigma = (q_0, \alpha_1, q_1)(q_1, \alpha_2, q_2)\cdots(q_n, \alpha_{n+1}, q_{n+1})$, *for some* $n \geq 0$, *then* $|\sigma| = n+1$. *Moreover, the* i^{th} *state in such a path, i.e.* q_i, *is denoted by* $\sigma(i)$.

Definition 8 (Semantics of UCTL). *The satisfaction relation for UCTL formulae is defined as follows:*

$q \models$ *true holds always;*
$q \models p$ *iff* $p \in L(q)$;
$q \models \neg\phi$ *iff not* $q \models \phi$;
$q \models \phi \wedge \phi'$ *iff* $q \models \phi$ *and* $q \models \phi'$;
$q \models A\pi$ *iff* $\sigma \models \pi$ *for all paths* σ *such that* $\sigma(0) = q$;
$q \models E\pi$ *iff there exists a path* σ *with* $\sigma(0) = q$ *such that* $\sigma \models \pi$;
$\sigma \models X_\chi\phi$ *iff* $\sigma = (\sigma(0), \alpha_1, \sigma(1))\sigma'$, *and* $\alpha_1 \models \chi$, *and* $\sigma(1) \models \phi$;
$\sigma \models [\phi_\chi U\phi']$ *iff there exists a* $j \geq 0$ *such that* $\sigma(j) \models \phi'$ *and for all* $0 \leq i < j$:
    $\sigma = \sigma'(\sigma(i), \alpha_{i+1}, \sigma(i+1))\sigma''$ *implies* $\sigma(i) \models \phi$ *and* $\alpha_{i+1} = \epsilon$ *or* $\alpha_{i+1} \models \chi$;
$\sigma \models [\phi_\chi U_{\chi'}\phi']$ *iff there exists a* $j \geq 1$ *such that* $\sigma = \sigma'(\sigma(j-1), \alpha_j, \sigma(j))\sigma''$ *and* $\sigma(j) \models \phi'$ *and* $\sigma(j-1) \models \phi$ *and* $\alpha_j \models \chi'$, *and for all* $0 < i < j$:
    $\sigma = \sigma'_i(\sigma(i-1), \alpha_i, \sigma(i))\sigma''_i$ *implies* $\sigma(i-1) \models \phi$ *and* $\alpha_i = \epsilon$ *or* $\alpha_i \models \chi$;
$\sigma \models [\phi_\chi W\phi']$ *iff either there exists a* $j \geq 0$ *such that* $\sigma(j) \models \phi'$ *and for all* $0 \leq i < j$:
    $\sigma = \sigma'(\sigma(i), \alpha_{i+1}, \sigma(i+1))\sigma''$ *implies* $\sigma(i) \models \phi$ *and* $\alpha_{i+1} = \epsilon$ *or* $\alpha_{i+1} \models \chi$;
    or for all $i \geq 0$: $\sigma = \sigma'(\sigma(i), \alpha_{i+1}, \sigma(i+1))\sigma''$ *implies* $\sigma(i) \models \phi$ *and* $\alpha_{i+1} = \epsilon$ *or* $\alpha_{i+1} \models \chi$;

---

[2] Note that, differently from the original ACTL logic, in UCTL the operator $X_\chi\phi$ can be derived as $false\ _{false}U_\chi\ \phi$.

$\sigma \models [\phi\, _\chi W_{\chi'}\, \phi']$ iff either there exists a $j \geq 1$ such that $\sigma = \sigma'(\sigma(j{-}1), \alpha_j, \sigma(j))\sigma''$ and $\sigma(j) \models \phi'$ and $\sigma(j-1) \models \phi$ and $\alpha_j \models \chi'$, and for all $0 < i < j$: $\sigma = \sigma'_i(\sigma(i-1), \alpha_i, \sigma(i))\sigma''_i$ implies $\sigma(i-1) \models \phi$ and $\alpha_i = \epsilon$ or $\alpha_i \models \chi$; or for all $i > 0$: $\sigma = \sigma'_i(\sigma(i-1), \alpha_i, \sigma(i))\sigma''_i$ implies $\sigma(i-1) \models \phi$ and $\alpha_i = \epsilon$ or $\alpha_i \models \chi$.

It is now straightforward to obtain a set of derived operators for UCTL, such as:

$< \chi > \phi$ stands for $E[true\ _\tau U_\chi\ \phi]$;
$[\chi]\phi$ stands for $\neg < \chi > \neg\phi$;
$EF\phi$ stands for $E[true\ _{true}U\phi]$;
$AG\phi$ stands for $\neg EF\neg\phi$;

Operators $< \chi > \phi$ and $[\chi]\phi$ are the diamond and box modalities, respectively, of the Hennessy-Milner logic [15]. The meaning of $EF\phi$ is that ϕ must be true sometimes in a possible future; that of $AG\phi$ is that ϕ must be true always.

The logic UCTL is *adequate* with respect to strong bisimulation equivalence on L^{2}TSs. Adequacy [21] means that two L^{2}TSs A_1 and A_2 are strongly bisimilar if and only if $F_1 = F_2$, where $F_i = \{\, \psi \in UCTL : A_i \models \psi\,\}$ for $i = 1, 2$. In other words, adequacy implies that if there is a formula that is not satisfied by one of the L^{2}TSs but satisfied by the other L^{2}TS, then the L^{2}TSs are not bisimilar, and—on the other hand—if two L^{2}TSs are not bisimilar, then there must exist a distinguishing formula.

Proof (sketch). Let A_1 and A_2 be two L^{2}TSs. Note that neither the existential nor the universal next operator of a UCTL formula can distinguish the transition $q_1 \xrightarrow{a} q'_1$ in A_1 from the two transitions $q_2 \xrightarrow{a} q'_2$ and $q_2 \xrightarrow{a} q''_2$, with $\{q'_2, q''_2\}$ bisimilar to q'_1, which makes q_1 and q_2 bisimilar as well. The same can be said for the atomic predicates, since the labelling of bisimilar states is the same, as well as for the until operators, which just follow recursively the transition relation. Hence, if two L^{2}TSs are bisimilar, then no distinguishing formula can be found.

On the other hand, if two L^{2}TSs are not bisimilar, then applying recursively the definition of bisimulation to the pair of initial states $\{q_{0_1}, q_{0_2}\}$ of the two L^{2}TSs implies that we eventually end up in at least one pair of states $\{q_1, q_2\}$ with the following characteristics: A sequence $a_1, a_2, \ldots, a_n$ of actions leads from q_{0_1} and q_{0_2} to q_1 and q_2, respectively, and q_1 and q_2 can be differentiated either (but not necessarily exclusively) by their labelling or by an outgoing transition.

In the former case, there exists at least one predicate p such that $p \in L(q_1)$ but $p \notin L(q_2)$ (or vice versa), which means that $X_{a_1}X_{a_2} \cdots X_{a_n}p$ is a distinguishing formula for the two L^{2}TSs.

In the latter case, there exists at least one transition $q_1 \xrightarrow{a} q'_1$, for some action a and state q'_1, while there exists no transition labelled with a from q_2 to some state q'_2 (or vice versa), which means that $X_{a_1}X_{a_2} \cdots X_{a_n}X_a\ true$ is a distinguishing formula for the two L^{2}TSs.   □

Starting from the syntax of UCTL, it is possible to derive both CTL [7] and ACTL [10,11] by simply removing the action or the state component, respectively: Given a Kripke structure $K = (Q, q_0, R, AP, L)$ that has been lifted to an L²TS $A_K = (Q, q_0, Act, R', AP, L)$, a CTL formula ϕ and a state $q \in Q$, it follows that

$$q \models_K \phi \text{ iff } q \models_{A_K} \phi',$$

where ϕ' is a UCTL formula which is syntactically identical to ϕ, apart from the fact that all occurrences of $X\psi'$ have been replaced by $X_{true}\psi'$ and all occurrences of $\psi U\psi'$ have been replaced by $\psi \text{ }_{true}U\psi'$.

Given an LTS $T = (Q, q_0, Act \cup \tau, R)$ that has been lifted to an L²TS $A_T = (Q, q_0, Act, R, AP, L)$, an ACTL formula ϕ and a state $q \in Q$, it follows that

$$q \models_T \phi \text{ iff } q \models_{A_T} \phi',$$

where ϕ' is a UCTL formula which is syntactically identical to ϕ, apart from the fact that all occurrences of $X_{true}\psi$ are replaced by $X_{\neg\tau}\psi$.[3]

4   The UCTL Model Checker UMC

We have developed an on-the-fly model checking tool for UCTL, called UMC [18].

The big advantage of the on-the-fly approach to model checking is that, depending on the formula, only a fragment of the overall state space might need to be generated and analyzed in order to produce the correct result [2,12,24]. This type of model checking is also called local [9], in contrast to global model checking [7], in which the whole state space is explored to check the validity of a formula.

The basic idea behind UMC is that, given a state of an L²TS, the validity of a UCTL formula on that state can be evaluated by analyzing the transitions allowed in that state, and by analyzing the validity of some subformula in only some of the next reachable states, all this in a recursive way. The following simplified schema gives an idea of the algorithmic structure of the evaluation process: F denotes the UCTL formula (or subformula) to be evaluated, **Start** denotes the state in which the (recursive) evaluation of F was started and **Current** denotes the current state in which the evaluation of F is being continued.[4]

---

[3] The original definition of ACTL [10] is based on a definition of LTSs in which a transition label can be a single (un)observable action. Hence, to be precise, we actually need to use here a different definition of lifting an LTS to an L²TS, namely one in which τ-transitions are replaced by ϵ-transitions.

[4] The given schema can be extended to handle also max and min fixpoint operators, by replacing the single **Start** state with a vector of states according to the fixpoint nesting depth of the formula. UMC actually supports this extension, but with drawbacks in the level of optimizations performed.

```
Evaluate (F : Formula, Start : State, Current : State) is
    if we have already done this computation and its result is available,
        i.e. (⟨F, Start, Current⟩ → Result) has already been established then
            return the already known result;
    else if we were already computing the value of exactly this computation,
        i.e. (⟨F,Start,Current⟩ → inprogress) has already been established then
            return true or false depending on max or min fixed point semantics;
    else
        keep track that we started to compute the value of this computation,
        i.e. set (⟨F, Start, Current⟩ → inprogress);
        foreach subformula F′ and next state S′ to be computed do loop
            if F ≠ F (i.e. this is a syntactically nested subformula) then
                call Evaluate(F′, S, S′);
            else if F = F (i.e. this is just a recursive evaluation of F) then
                call Evaluate(F, Start, S′);
            end
            if the result of the call suffices to establish the final result then
                exit from the loop;
            end
        end loop
        At this point we have in any case a final result. We keep track of the
        result of this compuation (e.g. set (⟨F, Start, Current⟩ → Result)).
        return the final result;
    end
end Evaluate;
```

This simplified schema can be extended with appropriate data-collection activities in order to be able to produce, in the end, also a clear and detailed explanation of the returned result.

In case of infinite state spaces, the above schema may fail to produce a result even when a result could actually be deduced in a finite number of steps. This is a consequence of the "depth-first" recursive structure of the algorithm. The solution taken to solve this problem consists of adopting a bounded model-checking approach [3], i.e. the evaluation is started assuming a certain value as limit of the maximum depth of the evaluation. In this case, if a formula is given as result of the evaluation within the requested depth, then the result holds for the whole system; otherwise the maximum depth is increased and the evaluation is subsequently retried (preserving all useful subresults that were already found). This approach, initially introduced in UMC to overcome the problem of infinite state machines, happens to be quite useful also for another reason. By setting a small initial maximum depth and a small automatic increment of this limit at each re-evaluation failure, once we finally find a result then we have a reasonable (almost minimal) explanation for it, and this is very useful also in the case of finite states machines.

Given a formula F, the upper bound on the number of necessary computations steps, identifiable by the triple ⟨subformula, startstate, currentstate⟩ apparently tends to grow quadratically with respect to the number of system states. A linear complexity of the above model-checking algorithm can be achieved by performing several optimizations in the management of the "archive" of performed computations.[5] In particular, we consider the property that if $(\langle \mathtt{F}, \mathtt{State}, \mathtt{State} \rangle \rightarrow \mathtt{Result})$ is true, then for any other $\mathtt{State}'$, $(\langle \mathtt{F}, \mathtt{State}',$ $\mathtt{State} \rangle \rightarrow \mathtt{Result})$ is also true. Moreover, when $(\langle \mathtt{F}, \mathtt{State}, \mathtt{State} \rangle \rightarrow \mathtt{Result})$ is established, for all the recursive subcomputations of F that have the form $(\langle \mathtt{F}, \mathtt{State}, \mathtt{State}' \rangle \rightarrow \mathtt{Result})$ it is also true that $(\langle \mathtt{F}, \mathtt{State}', \mathtt{State}' \rangle \rightarrow \mathtt{Result})$ can be considered to hold.

The development of UMC is still in progress and a prototypical version is being used internally at ISTI–CNR for academic and experimental purposes. Until now, the focus of the development has been on the design of the kind of qualitative features one would desire for such a tool, experimenting with various logics, system modelling languages and user interfaces. So far there has been no official public release of the tool, even if the current prototype can be experimented via a web interface at the address http://fmt.isti.cnr.it/umc/.

UMC verifies properties defined over a set of communicating UML state machines [22,20]. We used UML as particular formal method since it has become the de facto industrial standard for modelling and documenting software systems. The UML semantics associates a state machine to each object in a system design, while the system's behaviour is defined by the possible evolutions of the resulting set of state machines that may communicate by exchanging signals. All these possible system evolutions are formally represented as an L^2TS, in which the states represent the various system configurations and the transitions represent the possible evolutions of a system configuration. In this L^2TS, states are labelled with the observed structural properties of the system configurations (e.g. active substates of objects, values of object attributes, etc.), while transitions are labelled with the observed properties of the system evolutions (e.g. which is the evolving object, which are the executed acions, etc.).

5   aSOAP: A Case Study

The particular case study we describe here has as main objective to define a variant of SOAP [26] supporting asynchronous communications, driven step-by-step by the results of a formal analysis. This approach thus contrasts with the usual approach of performing analysis on an already specified protocol to verify its correctness. The development of aSOAP is ongoing joint work with Telecom Italia. Some initial modelling and verification results have been presented in [1].

The domain of the case study is the definition of a SOAP-based protocol supporting asynchronous interactions, i.e. interactions different from the usual

---

[5] In [1,13,14], a less restricted logic (μ-UCTL) was defined and used in previous versions of UMC. Essentially based on the full μ-calculus, μ-UCTL was still defined over doubly labelled structures, but in that case the system transitions were labelled with sequences of events rather than with sets. Moreover, since the model-checking algorithm lacked the necessary optimizations, the complexity of the evaluation of alternation-free formulae still had a quadratic complexity.

synchronous "request-response" interactions supported by the available SOAP implementations based on HTTP. For the following reasons, asynchronous interactions are highly relevant in the delivery of telecommunication services:

- a service logic is triggered/activated by events produced, in an asynchronous way, by the network/special resources, or must react to such events during the execution of a service instance;
- requests produced by a service logic to a network/special resource may result in long computations (e.g. the set-up of a call), which might also require the involvement of end users;
- some service logic components may not be reachable (e.g. the ones deployed on mobile terminals), e.g. due to the temporary absence of communication.

The final objective is thus to formally define aSOAP as a protocol that is able to address most of these situations. We consider the following requirements.

Backward compatibility
- aSOAP must be compatible with SOAP v1.2 on HTTP;
- aSOAP must have limited impact on clients, i.e. clients that need no support for asynchronous interactions must be usual SOAP clients, working in request-response mode, while clients that do need such support should introduce only very limited variations w.r.t. normal SOAP requests.

Reachability
- aSOAP must be able to deal with the unreachability of the servers (e.g. due to the lack of connectivity);
- aSOAP must be able to deal with the case in which a server cannot return a (provisional or final) response due to the lack of connectivity;
- aSOAP must be able to deal with the case in which a (provisional or final) response cannot be returned to a client due to the lack of connectivity.

Message Exchange Patterns
- aSOAP must be able to deal with requests that require the servers to perform some long-running computation (longer than the HTTP timeout) before producing any results;
- aSOAP must be able to deal with requests with multiple responses.

We envision aSOAP to operate in a Client-Server architecture with an additional web service Proxy placed in between the Client and Server side. This Proxy must guarantee that various attempts to contact either side are made in case of temporary unavailability of the respective side. Moreover, aSOAP requires that a Client, whenever it is willing to accept the possibility of an asynchronous response to its request, sends to the Proxy not only its request but also the URL at which it would like to receive the response. We consider this URL to be the address of a generic "SOAP listener" and we assume the application level to be equipped with a mechanism capable of receiving SOAP messages at this URL.

Before discussing some aspects of our formal specification of aSOAP, we first list the assumptions that are part of the design of aSOAP.

- The Proxy is always reachable by both the Client and the Server, whenever they have an active connection;
- If the Client is willing to accept an asynchronous response to its SOAP invocation, then it inserts in the SOAP header the URL of the SOAP listener where it wants to receive the response;
- The URL in the header of an asynchronous SOAP invocation is the address of a generic SOAP listener and the application level is equipped with a mechanism for receiving SOAP messages at this URL;
- Upon receiving an asynchronous SOAP invocation from the Client, the Proxy generates a request identifier ReqId that uniquely identifies the Client's SOAP invocation in further communications.

During several sessions between ISTI–CNR and Telecom Italia we discussed our design and developed our formalisation of aSOAP in detail. In order to facilitate the discussions about the behaviour of the various use case scenarios of aSOAP, we decided upon a separate message sequence chart for each such a scenario. Finally, all these scenarios were translated into an operational model, in which the following concrete modelling choices were adopted:

- All SOAP invocations are asynchronous, i.e. we abstract from the synchronous SOAP invocations that only serve to guarantee backward compatibility with SOAP v1.2;
- The URL in the header of a SOAP message is identified with the Client, i.e. each Client is seen as just a listener of asynchronous SOAP invocations;
- A system model is constituted by a Server (and its subthreads), a Proxy (and its subthreads) and a fixed (configurable) number of Clients;
- The Proxy and the Server may activate at most a fixed (configurable) number of parallel subthreads;
- With the Client or the Server unreachable, the Proxy attempts to contact them up to a configurable number of times;
- The Client issues a single SOAP invocation and then terminates.[6]

For a complete discussion on these modelling choices, we refer the reader to [1].

Specifying the formal model of aSOAP as a set of communicating UML state machines has allowed us to express behavioural properties of our aSOAP model in UCTL and to verify them with UMC. The reader can consult the full specification online [23]. In Figure 1, the activity of a Client, a Server thread and a Proxy thread are depicted.

The full specification contains also the definition of the statecharts for the classes Server and Proxy. Objects of these classes are very simple (they have just one state) and their role is simply to forward any incoming request to some available subthread, which will then perform all the relevant activities. The actual complexity of the systems which can be built with these components clearly depends on the number of Clients, Servers and Proxies that one wants

---

[6] In the future we do intend to consider Clients that perform a loop of SOAP invocations or issue several SOAP invocations before awaiting the deferred SOAP results.

to deploy, on the number of subthreads one assigns to each Server or Proxy and on the maximum number of times a Proxy thread may retry to contact a Server or a Client before it must give up.

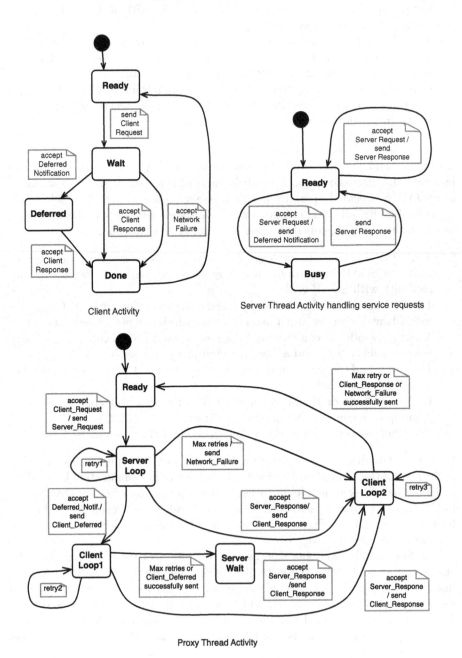

Fig. 1. Activity of a Client, a Server thread and a Proxy thread

The minimal system composed of 1 Client, 1 Proxy and 1 Server (the latter two both with only 1 subthread) and 1 as maximum number of retries, clearly is an example of a small system with only 118 states and 245 transitions. A more complex system can be deployed by using 2 Clients, 1 Server and 1 Proxy (the latter two with 2 subthreads each), and with up to 2 communication attempts. Such a system contains $96,481$ states and $367,172$ transitions. Finally, a system composed of 3 Clients, 1 Server and 1 Proxy (the latter two with 3 subthreads each) instead is too complex to be able to explicitly measure its size (far more than $600,000$ states and well over $1,000,000$ transitions).

5.1   Verification of UCTL Formulae with UMC

In this section, we show the verification with UMC of several behavioural properties expressed in UCTL over our model of the aSOAP protocol. These properties demonstrate the logic's flexibility in dealing with both action- and state-based properties. A different set of behavioural properties is verified in [1]. Property 1:

From every system state a Proxy thread can reach its initial state 'Ready'

can be shown to hold by using UMC to verify the state-based UCTL formula

$$AG\ EF\ PT1.state = Ready,$$

in which *PT1* is a Proxy Thread. This is different for Clients, since Property 2:

A Client C1 may reach a deadlock, i.e.
      there exists a system state from which C1 cannot evolve

can be shown to hold by using UMC to verify the action-based UCTL formula

$$EF\ (\neg EF < C1: > true),$$

in which *C1:* is satisfied by any system evolution in which object *C1* is the one that evolves. This outcome is not so bad as it might seem, because Property 3:

Whenever a Client C1 reaches a deadlock,
      then C1 is either in state 'Wait' or in state 'Deferred'

can be shown to hold by using UMC to verify the action/state-based UCTL formula

$$AG\ (\,(\neg EF < C1: > true) \Rightarrow (C1.state = Wait \vee C1.state = Deferred)\,).$$

The time needed to verify any of the above formulae in the minimal system mentioned above (with 118 states and 245 transitions) is negligible. The situation is different for the system with 2 Clients specified above (with $96,481$ states and $367,172$ transitions). In spite of its higher complexity, the evaluation of the formula EF ($\neg EF < C1 : > true$) (corresponding to Property 2) is still almost immediate, since it requires the analysis of only 1998 states, while the remaining formulae require the analysis of all system states and therefore their evaluation requires about one minute (using a state of the art portable computer).

Finally, none of the above formulae can be verified over more complex systems. However, formulae whose evaluation require the analysis of just a small fraction of all the system states can be evaluated also for such complex systems. Consider, e.g., the formula

$$EF\ EG\ ((PT1.state = ClientLoop2) \wedge < PT1 : > (PT1.state = Ready)),$$

which states that there exists an infinite path along which object $PT1$ always remains in the $ClientLoop2$ state, although the object itself always has the possibility of immediately returning to the state $Ready$ in just one step. This formula can be proved to hold also in case of a complex system composed of 3 Clients, 1 Server and 1 Proxy (but each with 3 subthreads), which has more than $600,000$ states and over $1,000,000$ transitions. It takes just a few seconds, during which only $92,536$ system states are analysed. Clearly it is simply a form of unfairness in the scheduling that prevents the Proxy thread to complete its execution cycle.

6 Conclusions

In this paper, we have presented the action/state-based temporal logic UCTL and its on-the-fly model checker UMC. The need to define an action/state-based logic stems from the fact that in order to verify concurrent (software) systems, it is quite often necessary to specify both state information and the evolution in time by actions (events). As a result, semantic models should take both views into account. The L^2TSs that are at the basis of UCTL are one such semantic model. Given a state of an L^2TS, UMC evaluates the validity of a UCTL formula on that state on the fly by analyzing the transitions allowed in that state, and by analyzing the validity of some subformula in only some of the next reachable states, all this in a recursive way. Some clever "archiving" of performed computations allows UMC to evaluate UCTL formulae in linear time.

UML is a graphical modelling language for object-oriented software (systems). UML models can be used to visualize, specify, build and document several aspects—or views—of such systems. The UML semantics associates to each active object a state machine, and the system's behaviour is defined by the possible evolutions of these communicating state machines. All possible system evolutions can be formally represented as an L^2TS in which the states represent the system configurations and the transitions represent the possible evolutions of a system configuration. As a result, UCTL can be used to express properties of the dynamic behaviour of complex systems described as UML state diagrams. The ability to state structural properties of system configurations (state attributes and predicates) and not just actions (events), opens the door to the modelling and verification of structural properties of parallel systems. Examples include topological issues, state invariants and mobility issues.

Acknowledgements. We thank Corrado Moiso of Telecom Italia for having provided us with the case study mentioned in this paper and for his work on aSOAP.

References

1. ter Beek, M.H., Gnesi, S., Mazzanti, F., Moiso, C.: Formal Modelling and Verification of an Asynchronous Extension of SOAP. In: Bernstein, A., Gschwind, T., Zimmermann, W. (eds.) Proceedings of the 4th IEEE European Conference on Web Services (ECOWS 2006), Zurich, Switzerland, pp. 287–296. IEEE Computer Society, Los Alamitos, CA (2006)
2. Bhat, G., Cleaveland, R., Grumberg, O.: Efficient On-the-Fly Model Checking for CTL*. In: Proceedings of the 10th IEEE Symposium on Logics in Computer Science (LICS 1995), San Diego, CA, USA, pp. 388–397. IEEE Computer Society, Los Alamitos, CA (1995)
3. Biere, A., Cimatti, A., Clarke, E.M., Zhu, Y.: Symbolic Model Checking without BDDs. In: Cleaveland, W.R. (ed.) ETAPS 1999 and TACAS 1999. LNCS, vol. 1579, pp. 193–207. Springer, Heidelberg (1999)
4. Chaki, S., Clarke, E.M., Ouaknine, J., Sharygina, N., Sinha, N.: State/Event-Based Software Model Checking. In: Boiten, E.A., Derrick, J., Smith, G.P. (eds.) IFM 2004. LNCS, vol. 2999, pp. 128–147. Springer, Heidelberg (2004)
5. Chaki, S., Clarke, E.M., Grumberg, O., Ouaknine, J., Sharygina, N., Touili, T., Veith, H.: State/Event Software Verification for Branching-Time Specifications. In: Romijn, J.M.T., Smith, G.P., van de Pol, J. (eds.) IFM 2005. LNCS, vol. 3771, pp. 53–69. Springer, Heidelberg (2005)
6. Chaki, S., Clarke, E.M., Ouaknine, J., Sharygina, N., Sinha, N.: Concurrent software verification with states, events, and deadlocks. Formal Aspects of Computing 17(4), 461–483 (2005)
7. Clarke, E.M., Emerson, E.A., Sistla, A.P.: Automatic Verification of Finite State Concurrent Systems using Temporal Logic Specifications. ACM Transactions on Programming Languages and Systems 8(2), 244–263 (1986)
8. Clarke, E.M., Grumberg, O., Long, D.E.: Model Checking and Abstraction. ACM Transaction on Programming Languages and Systems 16(5), 1512–1542 (1994)
9. Cleaveland, R.: Tableau-Based Model Checking in the Propositional μ-Calculus. Acta Informatica 27(8), 725–747 (1989)
10. De Nicola, R., Vaandrager, F.W.: Actions versus State based Logics for Transition Systems. In: Guessarian, I. (ed.) LITP 1990. LNCS, vol. 469, pp. 407–419. Springer, Heidelberg (1990)
11. De Nicola, R., Vaandrager, F.W.: Three Logics for Branching Bisimulation. Journal of the ACM 42(2), 458–487 (1995)
12. Fernandez, J.-C., Jard, C., Jéron, T., Viho, C.: Using On-The-Fly Verification Techniques for the Generation of test Suites. In: Alur, R., Henzinger, T.A. (eds.) CAV 1996. LNCS, vol. 1102, pp. 348–359. Springer, Heidelberg (1996)
13. Gnesi, S., Mazzanti, F.: On the fly model checking of communicating UML State Machines. In: Dosch, W., Lee, R.Y., Wu, C. (eds.) SERA 2004. LNCS, vol. 3647, pp. 331–338. Springer, Heidelberg (2006)
14. Gnesi, S., Mazzanti, F.: A Model Checking Verification Environment for UML Statecharts. In: XLIII Annual Italian Conference AICA, Udine (2005)
15. Hennessy, M., Milner, R.: Algebraic Laws for Nondeterminism and Concurrency. Journal of the ACM 32(1), 137–161 (1985)

16. Huth, M., Jagadeesan, R., Schmidt, D.A.: Modal Transition Systems: A Foundation for Three-Valued Program Analysis. In: Sands, D. (ed.) ESOP 2001. LNCS, vol. 2028, pp. 155–169. Springer, Heidelberg (2001)
17. Kindler, E., Vesper, T.: ESTL: A Temporal Logic for Events and States. In: Desel, J., Silva, M. (eds.) ICATPN 1998. LNCS, vol. 1420, pp. 365–384. Springer, Heidelberg (1998)
18. Mazzanti, F.: UMC User Guide v3.3. Technical Report 2006-TR-33, Istituto di Scienza e Tecnologie dell'Informazione "A. Faedo", CNR (2006)
19. Müller-Olm, M., Schmidt, D.A., Steffen, B.: Model-Checking—A Tutorial Introduction. In: Cortesi, A., Filé, G. (eds.) SAS 1999. LNCS, vol. 1694, pp. 330–354. Springer, Heidelberg (1999)
20. OMG (Object Management Group), UML (Unified Modeling Language), http://www.uml.org/
21. Pnueli, A.: Linear and Branching Structures in the Semantics and Logics of Reactive Systems. In: Brauer, W. (ed.) ICALP 1985. LNCS, vol. 194, pp. 15–32. Springer, Heidelberg (1985)
22. Rumbaugh, J., Jacobson, I., Booch, G.: The Unified Modeling Language Reference Manual. Addison-Wesley, Reading, MA (1998)
23. Specification of aSOAP, http://fmt.isti.cnr.it/umc/examples/aSOAP.umc
24. Stirling, C., Walker, D.: Local Model Checking in the Modal μ-Calculus. In: Díaz, J., Orejas, F. (eds.) Proceedings of the International Joint Conference on Theory and Practice of Software Development (TAPSOFT 1989), Barcelona, Spain, vol. 354, pp. 369–383. Springer, Berlin (1989)
25. Wirsing, M., Clark, A., Gilmore, S., Hölzl, M., Knapp, A., Koch, N., Schroeder, A.: Semantic-Based Development of Service-Oriented Systems. In: Najm, E., Pradat-Peyre, J.-F., Donzeau-Gouge, V.V. (eds.) FORTE 2006. LNCS, vol. 4229, pp. 24–45. Springer, Heidelberg (2006)
26. W3C (WWW Consortium), Latest SOAP versions, http://www.w3.org/TR/soap/

Model Classifications and Automated Verification

Radek Pelánek*

Department of Information Technologies, Faculty of Informatics
Masaryk University Brno, Czech Republic
xpelanek@fi.muni.cz

Abstract. Due to the significant progress in automated verification, there are often several techniques for a particular verification problem. In many circumstances different techniques are complementary — each technique works well for different type of input instances. Unfortunately, it is not clear how to choose an appropriate technique for a specific instance of a problem. In this work we argue that this problem, selection of a technique and tuning its parameter values, should be considered as a standalone problem (a verification meta-search). We propose several classifications of models of asynchronous system and discuss applications of these classifications in the context of explicit finite state model checking.

1 Introduction

One of the main goals of computer aided formal methods is automated verification of computer systems. In recent years, very good progress has been achieved in automating specific verification problems. However, even automated verification techniques like model checking are far from being a push-button technology. With current verification techniques many realistic systems can be automatically verified, but only if applied to the right level of abstraction of a system and if suitable verification techniques are used and right parameter values are selected.

The first problem is addressed by automated abstraction refinement techniques and received lot of attention recently (e.g., [1,9]). The second problem, however, did not receive much attention so far and there are only few works in this direction. Ruys and Brinksma [38] describe methodology for model checking 'in the large'. Sahoo et al. [39] use sampling of the state space to decide which BDD based reachability technique is the best for a given model. Mony et al. [29] use expert system for automating proof strategies. Eytani et al. [11] give a high-level proposal to use an 'observation database' for sharing relevant information among different verification techniques.

Automation of the verification process is necessary for practical applicability of formal verification. Any self-respecting verification tool has a large number of options and parameters, which can significantly influence the complexity of verification. In order to verify any reasonable system, it is necessary to set these

---

* Partially supported by GA ČR grant no. 201/07/P035.

S. Leue and P. Merino (Eds.): FMICS 2007, LNCS 4916, pp. 149–163, 2008.

parameters properly. This can be done only by an expert user and it requires lot of time. We believe that the research focus should not be only on the development of new automated techniques, but also on an automated selection of an existing technique.

1.1 Verification Meta-search

So far most of the research in automated verification has been focused on questions of the verification problem: given a system S and a property (or specification) φ, determine whether S satisfies φ. This is a *search* problem — an algorithm searches for an incorrect behaviour or for a proof. Research has been focused on solving the problem for different formalisms and optimizing it for the most useful ones.

We believe that it is worthwhile to consider the following problem as well: given a system and a property, find a technique T and parameter values p such that $T(p)$ can provide answer to the verification problem. This can be viewed as a *verification meta-search problem*. Let an entity responsible for the verification meta-search be called a *verification manager*. The manager has the following tasks:

1. Decide which approach to the verification should be used, e.g., symbolic versus explicit approach, whether to use on-the-fly verification or whether to generate the full state space and then perform verification, etc.
2. Combine relevant information obtained from different techniques, see e.g., Synergy approach [18] for combination of over-approximation and testing.
3. Choose among different techniques (implementations) for a particular verification task and set parameters of a chosen technique.

In this work we focus mainly on the third task of the manager. To give a practical example of this task, we provide two specific cases. Firstly, consider on-the-fly memory reduction techniques — the goal of these techniques is to reduce memory requirements of exhaustive finite state verification. Examples of such techniques are partial order reduction, symmetry reduction, state compression, and caching. Each of these techniques has its merits and disadvantages, none of them is universal (see [32] for an evaluation). Moreover, most of these techniques have parameters which can tune a time/memory trade-off. Secondly, consider algorithms for accepting cycle detection on networks of workstations, which are used for LTL verification of large finite state models. Currently there are at least five different algorithms, each with specific disadvantages and parameters [2].

At the moment the verification manager is usually a human expert. Expert can perform this role rather well, however such 'implementation' of the verification manager is far from automated. There has been attempts to facilitate the human involvement, e.g., by using special purpose scripting languages [25], but such an approach automatizes only stereotypical steps during the verification, not decisions.

The problem can be addressed by an expert system, which perform the meta-search with the use of a set of rules provided by experts. Example of such rules may be:

- If the model is a mutual exclusion protocol then use explicit model checking with partial order reduction.
- If state vector is longer then 30 bytes, then use state compression.
- If the state space is expected to contain a large strongly connected component, then use cycle detection algorithm X else use cycle detection algorithm Y.

Another option is to employ an adaptive learning system which remembers characteristics of verification tasks and their results and learns from its own experiences.

1.2   The Need for Classifications

At this moment, it is not clear what rules should the verification manager use. But more fundamentally, it is not even clear what criteria should be used in rules. Whatever is the realization of the manager, the manager needs to make decision based on some information about an input model. The information used for this decision should be carefully chosen:

- If the information was too coarse, the manager would not be able to choose among potentially suitable techniques.
- If the information was too detailed, it would be very hard for the manager to apply its expertise and experiences.

We believe that an appropriate approach is to develop several categorical classifications of models and then use these classification for manager's decisions. To be applicable, it must be possible to determine suitable techniques for individual classes of the classification. Moreover, it must be possible to determine a class of a given model without much effort — either automatically by a fast algorithm or easily by user judgement.

In this work we focus on asynchronous concurrent systems, for the evaluation we use models from the BEEM set [35]. For asynchronous concurrent systems one of the most suitable verification techniques is explicit state space exploration. Therefore, we focus not only on analysis of a model structure, but also on the analysis of state spaces. In this work we propose classifications based on a model structure (communication mode, process similarity, application domain) and also classifications based on properties of state spaces (structure of strongly connected components, shape and local structure of a state space). We study relation of these classifications and discuss how they can be useful for the selection of suitable techniques and parameters (i.e., for guiding the meta-search).

The restriction to explicit model checking techniques limits the applicability of our contribution. Note, however, that even for this restricted area, there is a very large number of techniques and optimizations (there are at least 80 research papers dealing with explicit model checking techniques, see [34] for a list). Moreover, the goal of this work is not to present the ultimate model classification, but rather to pinpoint a direction, which can be fruitful.

2   Background

Used models. For the evaluation of properties of practically used models we employ models from the benchmark set BEEM [35]. This set contains large number of models of asynchronous systems. The set contains classical models studied in academic literature as well as realistic case studies. Models are provided in a low-level specification language (communicating finite state machines) and in Promela [20]. For our study we have used 115 instances obtained by instantiation of 57 principally different models.

State spaces. For each instance we have generated its state space. We view a state space as a simple directed graph $G = (V, E, v_0)$ with a set of vertices V, a set of directed edges $E \subseteq V \times V$, and a distinguished initial vertex v_0. Vertices are states of the model, edges represent valid transitions between states. For our purposes we ignore any labeling of states or edges. We are concerned only with the reachable part of the state space.

Let us define several parameters of state spaces. We use these parameters for classifications. We have also studied other parameters (particularly those reported in [31]), but these parameters do not lead to interesting classification.

An *average degree* of G is the ratio $|E|/|V|$. A *strongly connected component* (SCC) of G is a maximal set of states $C \subseteq V$ such that for each $u, v \in C$, the vertex v is reachable from u and vice versa. Let us consider the breadth-first search (BFS) from the initial vertex v_0. A *level* of the BFS with an index k is a set of states with distance from v_0 equal to k. The *BFS height* is the largest index of a non-empty level, *BFS width* is the maximal size of a BFS level. An edge (u, v) is a *back level edge* if v belongs to a level with a lower or the same index as u. The *length* of a back level edge is the difference between the indices of the two levels.

Reduction techniques. In the following, we often mention two semantics based reduction techniques. Under the notion *partial order reduction* (POR) we consider all techniques which aim at reducing the number of explored states by reducing the amount of interleaving in the model, i.e., we denote by this notion not just the classic partial order reduction technique [16], but also other related techniques, e.g., confluence reduction [5], simultaneous reachability analysis [30], transition compression [24]. *Symmetry reduction* techniques aim at reducing the number of explored states by considering symmetric states as equivalent, see e.g. [22].

3   State Space Classifications

We consider three classifications based on properties of state spaces. Two of them are based on "global" properties (structure of SCC and shape), one is based on "local" features of state spaces.

3.1   Structure of SCC Components

There is an interesting dichotomy with respect to structure of strongly connected components, particularly concerning the size of the largest SCC (see Fig. 1). A state space either contains one large SCC, which includes nearly all states, or there are only small SCCs. Based on this observation, we propose the following classification:

A type (acyclic): a state space is acyclic, i.e., it contains only trivial components with one state,

S type (small components): a state space is not acyclic, but contains only small components; more precisely we consider a state space to be of this type if the size of the largest component is smaller then 50% states.

B type (big component): a state space contain one large component, most states are in this component.

In order to apply the classification for automated verification, we need to be able to detect the class of a model without searching its full state space. This can be done by random walk exploration [36], for example by the following simple method based on detection of cycles by random walk. We run 100 independent random walks through the state space. Each random walk starts at the initial state and is limited to at most 500 steps. During the walk we store visited states, i.e., path through the state space. If a state is revisited then a cycle is detected and its length can be easily computed. At the end, we return the length of the longest detected cycle. Fig. 1 shows results of this method. For the class **A** the longest detected cycle is, of course, always 0. For the class **S** the longest detected cycle is usually between 10 and 35, for the class **B** it is usually above 30. This illustrates that even such a simple method can be used to quickly classify state spaces with a reasonable precision.

What are possible applications of this classification? For the **A** type it is possible to use specialized algorithms, e.g., dynamic partial order reduction [12] or bisimulation based reduction [33, p. 43-47]. The sweep line method [8] deletes from memory states, which will never be visited again. This method is useful only for models with state spaces of the type **A** or **S**.

The performance of cycle detection algorithms[1], which are used for LTL verification, is often dependent on the SCC structure. For example a distributed algorithm based on localization of cycles is suitable only for **S** type state spaces; depth-first search based algorithm [21] can also be reasonably applied only for **S** type state spaces, because for **B** type state spaces it tends to produce very long counterexamples, which are not practical. On the other hand, (explicit) one-way-catch-them-young algorithm [6] has complexity $O(nh)$, where h is height of the

---

[1] Note that cycle detection algorithm are usually executed on the product graph with a formula [42] and not on the state space itself. However, our measurements indicate that the structure of product graphs is very similar to structure of plain state spaces. The measurements were performed on product graphs included in the BEEM [35] set.

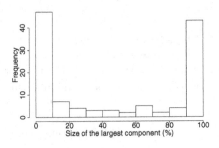 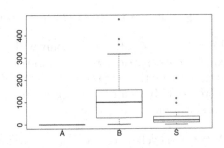

Fig. 1. The first graph shows the histogram of sizes of the largest SCC component in a state space. The second graph shows the longest detected cycle using random walk; results are grouped according to class and presented using a boxplot method (lines denote minimum, 25th quartile, median, 75th quartile and maximum, circles are outliers).

SCC quotient graph, i.e., this algorithm is more suitable for **B** type state spaces. Similarly, the classification can be employed for verification of branching time logics (e.g., the algorithm in [7] does not work well for state spaces consisting of one SCC).

3.2 Shape of the State Space

We have found that several global state space parameters are to certain extent related: average degree, BFS height and width, number and length of back level edges. In this case the division into classes is not so clear as in the previous case. Nevertheless, it is possible to identify two main classes with respect to these parameters[2]:

H type (high): small average degree, large BFS height, small BFS width, few long back level edges.
W type (wide): large average degree, small BFS height, large BFS width, many short back level edges.

This classification can be approximated using an initial sample of the BFS search. The classification can be used in similar way as the previous one. Sweep line [8] and caching based on transition locality [37] work well only for state spaces with short back level edges, i.e., these techniques are suitable only for **W** type state spaces. On the other hand, the complexity of BFS-based distributed cycle detection algorithm [3] is proportional to number of back level edges, i.e., this algorithm works well only on **H** type state spaces.

For many techniques the **H/W** classification can be used to set parameters appropriately: algorithms which exploit magnetic disk often work with individual BFS levels [41]; random walk search [36] and bounded search [23] need to

---

[2] Note that this classification is not complete partition of all possible state spaces. The remaining classes, however, do not occur in practice. The same holds for as several other classifications which we introduce later.

Diamond   3-mond   Diamond 3x3 FFL

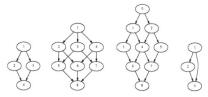

Fig. 2. Illustrations of motifs

estimate the height of the state space; techniques using stratified caching [15] and selective storing of states [4] could also take the shape of the state space into account.

3.3   Local Structure

Now we turn to a local structure of state spaces, particularly to typical subgraphs. Recently, so called 'network motifs' [28,27] were intensively studied in complex networks. Motifs are studied mainly in biological networks and are used to explain functions of network's components (e.g., function of individual proteins) and to study evolution of networks.

We have systematically studied motifs in state spaces. We have found the following motifs to be of specific interest either for abundant presence or for total absence in many state spaces: *diamonds* (we have studied several variations of diamond-like structures, see Fig. 2), which are well known to be present in state spaces of asynchronous concurrent systems due to the interleaving semantics; *chains* of states with just one successor, we have measured occurrences of chains of length 3, 4, 5; *short cycles* of lengths 2, 3, 4, 5, which are not very common in most state spaces; and *feed forward loop* (see Fig. 2), which is a typical motif for networks derived from biological systems [28], in state spaces it is rather rare.

We have measured number of occurrences of these motifs and studied correlations of their occurrences. With respect to motifs we propose the following classes:

D type (diamond): a state space contains many diamonds, usually no short cycles and only few chains of feed forward loops,

C type (chain): a state space contains many chains, very few diamonds or short cycles,

O type (other): a state space either contains short cycles and/or feed forward loops, chains are nearly absent, diamonds may be present, but they are not dominant.

Identification of these classes can be performed by exploration of a small sample of the state space. This classification can be used to choose among memory reduction techniques. For **D** type state spaces it is reasonable to try to employ POR, whereas for **C** type state spaces this reduction is unlikely to yield significant improvement. On the other hand, for **C** type state spaces good memory

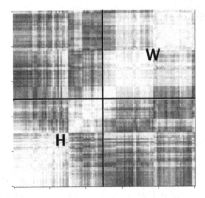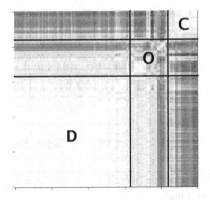

Fig. 3. Correlation matrix displaying correlation of 116 state spaces. Light color means positive correlation, dark color means negative correlation. The first matrix shows correlation with respect to average degree, BFS height and width, number and length of back level edges (all parameters are normalized). The second matrix shows correlations with respect to presence of studied motifs.

reduction can be obtained by selective storing of states [4]. The classification can be also used for tuning parameter values, particularly for technique which employ local search, e.g., random walk enhancements [36,40], sibling caching and children lookahead in distributed computation [26], heuristic search.

3.4   Relation Among State Space Classifications

Table 1. presents number of models in different combinations of classes. Specific numbers presented in the table are influenced by the selection of used models. Nevertheless, it is clear that presented classifications are rather orthogonal, there is just slight relation between the shape and the local structure.

4   Model Classifications

Now we turn to classifications based directly on a model. At first, we study classifications according to model structure, which are relevant particularly with respect to reduction techniques based on semantics (e.g., partial order reduction, symmetry reduction). Secondly, we study models from different application domains and show that each application domain has its characteristics with respect to presented classifications.

4.1   Model Structure

Classifications based on structure of a model are to some extent dependent on a specific syntax of the specification language. There are many specification languages and individual specification languages significantly differ on syntactical level. However, if we restrict our attention to models of asynchronous systems, we find that most specification languages share the following features:

- a model is comprised of a set of processes,
- a process can be viewed as a finite state machine extended with variables,
- processes communicate either via channels or via globally shared variables.

We discuss several possible classifications based on these basic features. Categorization of a model according to these classifications can be determined automatically by static analysis of a model. This issue is dependent on a particular specification language and it is rather straightforward, therefore, we do not discuss it in detail.

Communication Mode. With respect to communication we can study the predominant mean of communication (shared variables or channels) and the communication structure (ring, line, clique, star). It turns out that these two features are coupled, i.e., with respect to communication we can consider the following main classes:

DV type (dense, variable): processes communicate via shared variables, the communication structure is dense, i.e., every process can communicate with (nearly) every other process,

SC type (sparse, channel): processes communicate via (buffered) channels, the communication structure is rather sparse, e.g., ring, star, or tree.

N type (none): no communication, i.e., the model is comprised of just one process.

This classification is related particularly to partial order reduction techniques. The classification is completely orthogonal to state space classifications (see Table 1.).

Process Similarity. A common feature in models of asynchronous systems is the occurrence of several similar processes (e.g., several participants in a mutual exclusion protocol, several users of an elevator, several identical nodes in a communication protocol). By 'similarity' we mean that processes are generated from one template by different instantiations of some parameters, i.e., we do not consider symmetry in any formal sense (cf. [22]). With respect to similarity, a reasonable classification is the following:

S2 type. All processes are similar.

S1 type. There exists some similar processes, but not all of them.

S0 type. There is no similarity among processes.

This classification is clearly related to symmetry reduction. It can also be employed for state compression [19]. This classification is again orthogonal to state space classifications and only slightly correlated with the communication mode classification (**S1** is related to **SC**, **S2** is related to **DV**), for details see Table 1.

Table 1. Relations among classifications. For each combination of classes we state the number of models in the combination. In total there are 115 classified models, all models are from the BEEM set [35]. Reported state space classifications are based on traversal of the full state space.

State space classifications

	all	**H**	**W**	**D**	**O**	**C**
all	115	58	57	75	23	17
A	24	10	14	19	3	2
S	37	18	19	21	9	7
B	54	30	24	35	11	8
H	58			43	3	12
W	57			32	20	5

Model classifications

	all	**S2**	**S1**	**S0**
all	115	41	39	35
DV	44	31	9	4
SC	61	10	30	21
N	10	0	0	10

State space versus model classifications

	all	**A**	**S**	**B**	**H**	**W**	**D**	**O**	**C**
all	115	24	37	54	58	57	75	23	17
S2	41	10	9	22	20	21	37	3	1
S1	39	8	17	14	20	19	20	10	9
S0	35	6	11	18	18	17	18	10	7
DV	44	8	12	24	20	24	33	6	5
SC	61	12	22	27	36	25	40	10	11
N	10	4	3	3	2	8	2	7	1

Other. We briefly mention several other possible classifications and their applications:

- Data/Control intensity of a model (Is a model concerned with data manipulation and arithmetic?); related to abstraction techniques [17,1,9], which focus on reducing the data part of the model.
- Tightly/Loosely coupled processes (What is the proportion of interprocess and intraprocess computation?); important for thread-modular techniques [13].
- Length of a state vector; relevant particularly for state compression techniques [19].

4.2   Application Domain

Finally, we discuss application domains of asynchronous concurrent systems. Table 2. presents relations among application domains and previously discussed classifications. The table demonstrates that models from each application domain have specific characteristics. Knowledge of these characteristics can be helpful for the development of (commercial) verification tools specialized for a particular application domain. Beside that, characteristics of models can be used to develop templates and design patterns [14,10], which can facilitate the modeling process.

Mutual exclusion algorithms. The goal of a mutual exclusion algorithm is to ensure an exclusive access to a shared resource. Models of these algorithms usually consist of several nearly identical processes which communicate via shared

Table 2. Relation of state space classification and model type

	all	SCC struct.			shape		local struct			comm.			proc. sim.		
		A	**S**	**B**	**H**	**W**	**C**	**D**	**O**	**SC**	**DV**	**N**	**S2**	**S1**	**S0**
all	115	24	37	57	58	57	17	75	23	61	44	10	41	39	35
com. protocol	24	0	10	14	15	9	5	18	1	24	0	0	0	7	17
controller	17	1	7	9	15	2	3	12	2	12	5	0	0	13	4
leader el.	12	12	0	0	6	6	0	12	0	8	4	0	9	3	0
mutex	28	0	8	20	13	15	0	25	3	2	26	0	28	0	0
sched.	18	9	3	6	4	14	2	5	11	2	6	10	1	5	12
other	16	2	9	5	5	11	7	3	6	13	3	0	3	11	2

variables; communication structure is either clique or ring; individual processes are usually rather simple. State vectors are relatively short; state space usually contains one big strongly connected component, with many diamonds. POR and symmetry reduction may be useful, but careful modeling may be necessary in order to make them applicable.

Communication protocols. The goal of communication protocols is to ensure communication over an unreliable medium. The core of a model is a sender process, a receiver process, and a bus/medium; the communication structure is therefore usually linear (or simple tree). Processes communicate by handshake; shared variables are not used. Processes are not similar, sender/receiver processes can be rather complicated. State vectors are rather long; state space is not acyclic, it is rather high, often with many diamonds. POR is usually applicable.

Leader election algorithms. The goal of leader election algorithms is to choose a unique leader from a set of nodes. Models consist of a set of (nearly) identical processes, which are rather simple. Processes are connected in a ring, tree, or arbitrary graph; communication is via (buffered) channels. State spaces are acyclic with diamonds. POR, symmetry reduction, and specialized techniques for acyclic state spaces [12] may be applicable.

Controllers. Models of controllers usually have centralized architecture: a controller process communicates with processes representing individual parts of the system. The controller process is rather complex, other processes may be simple. The communication can be both by shared variables and handshake. State vectors are rather long; state spaces are high, usually with diamonds. Due to the centralized architecture semantics-based reduction techniques are hard to apply.

Scheduling, planning, puzzles. Planning and scheduling problems and puzzles are not the main application domain of explicit model checkers. Nevertheless, there are good reasons to consider them together with asynchronous systems (similar modeling formalism, research in combinations of model checking and artificial intelligence techniques). Models often consist of just one process.

Planning, scheduling problems have wide state space without prevalence of diamonds or chains. State spaces are often acyclic.

Other application domains. Similar characterizations can be provided for many other application domains. Examples of other often studied application domains are cache coherence protocols, device drivers or data containers.

5 Conclusions and Future Work

We argue that it is important not just to develop (narrowly focused) techniques for automated verification, but also to automatize the verification *process*, which is currently usually performed by an expert user. To this end, it is desirable to have classifications of models. We propose such classifications for asynchronous systems; these classifications are based on properties of state spaces and on structure of models. We also discuss examples of applications of these classifications; particularly the following two types of application:

- indication of suitable techniques to use for verification of the given model,
- setting suitable parameter values for the verification.

In the paper we provide several specific examples of such application; we note that these are just examples, not a full list of possible applications. The presented classifications are also not meant to be the final classifications of asynchronous systems. We suppose that further research will expose the need for other classification or for the refinement of presented classification. Moreover, for other application domains and verification techniques (e.g., synchronous systems, symbolic techniques, bounded model checking) it will be probably necessary to develop completely new classifications. Nevertheless, we believe that our approach can provide valuable inspiration even for this direction.

This work is a part of a long term endeavour. We are continuously developing the benchmark set BEEM [35]. Using the presented classification, we are working on experimental evaluation of the relation of classes and performance of different techniques. We are also developing techniques for estimation of state space parameters from samples of a state spaces, such estimations (e.g., the size of a state space), can be useful for guiding the verification meta-search. Finally, the long term goal is to develop an automated 'verification manager', which would be able to learn from experience.

References

1. Ball, T., Majumdar, R., Millstein, T.D., Rajamani, S.K.: Automatic predicate abstraction of c programs. In: Proc. of Programming Language Design and Implementation (PLDI 2001), pp. 203–213. ACM Press, New York (2001)
2. Barnat, J., Brim, L., Cerná, I.: Cluster-based ltl model checking of large systems. In: de Boer, F.S., Bonsangue, M.M., Graf, S., de Roever, W.-P. (eds.) FMCO 2005. LNCS, vol. 4111, pp. 259–279. Springer, Heidelberg (2006)

3. Barnat, J., Brim, L., Chaloupka, J.: Parallel breadth-first search LTL model-checking. In: Proc. Automated Software Engineering (ASE 2003), pp. 106–115. IEEE Computer Society, Los Alamitos (2003)

4. Behrmann, G., Larsen, K.G., Pelánek, R.: To store or not to store. In: Hunt Jr., W.A., Somenzi, F. (eds.) CAV 2003. LNCS, vol. 2725. Springer, Heidelberg (2003)

5. Blom, S., van de Pol, J.: State space reduction by proving confluence. In: Brinksma, E., Larsen, K.G. (eds.) CAV 2002. LNCS, vol. 2404, pp. 596–609. Springer, Heidelberg (2002)

6. Černá, I., Pelánek, R.: Distributed explicit fair cycle detection. In: Ball, T., Rajamani, S.K. (eds.) SPIN 2003. LNCS, vol. 2648, pp. 49–73. Springer, Heidelberg (2003)

7. Cheng, A., Christensen, S., Mortensen, K.: Model checking coloured petri nets exploiting strongly connected components. Technical Report DAIMI PB – 519, Computer Science Department, University of Aarhus (1997)

8. Christensen, S., Kristensen, L.M., Mailund, T.: A Sweep-Line Method for State Space Exploration. In: Margaria, T., Yi, W. (eds.) ETAPS 2001 and TACAS 2001. LNCS, vol. 2031, pp. 450–464. Springer, Heidelberg (2001)

9. Clarke, E.M., Grumberg, O., Jha, S., Lu, Y., Veith, H.: Counterexample-guided abstraction refinement. In: Emerson, E.A., Sistla, A.P. (eds.) CAV 2000. LNCS, vol. 1855, pp. 154–169. Springer, Heidelberg (2000)

10. Dwyer, M.B., Avrunin, G.S., Corbett, J.C.: Property specification patterns for finite-state verification. In: Proc. Workshop on Formal Methods in Software Practice, pp. 7–15. ACM Press, New York (1998)

11. Eytani, Y., Havelund, K., Stoller, S.D., Ur, S.: Toward a Framework and Benchmark for Testing Tools for Multi-Threaded Programs. Concurrency and Computation: Practice and Experience 19(3), 267–279 (2007)

12. Flanagan, C., Godefroid, P.: Dynamic partial-order reduction for model checking software. In: Proc. of Principles of programming languages (POPL 2005), pp. 110–121. ACM Press, New York (2005)

13. Flanagan, C., Qadeer, S.: Thread-modular model checking. In: Ball, T., Rajamani, S.K. (eds.) SPIN 2003. LNCS, vol. 2648, pp. 213–224. Springer, Heidelberg (2003)

14. Gamma, E., Helm, R., Johnson, R., Vlissides, J.: Design Patterns: Elements of Reusable Object-Oriented Software. Addison-Wesley Professional, Reading (1995)

15. Geldenhuys, J.: State caching reconsidered. In: Graf, S., Mounier, L. (eds.) SPIN 2004. LNCS, vol. 2989, pp. 23–39. Springer, Heidelberg (2004)

16. Godefroid, P.: Partial-order methods for the verification of concurrent systems: An approach to the state-explosion problem. LNCS, vol. 1032. Springer, Heidelberg (1996)

17. Graf, S., Saidi, H.: Construction of abstract state graphs with pvs. In: Grumberg, O. (ed.) CAV 1997. LNCS, vol. 1254, pp. 72–83. Springer, Heidelberg (1997)

18. Gulavani, B.S., Henzinger, T.A., Kannan, Y., Nori, A.V., Rajamani, S.K.: Synergy: A new algorithm for property checking. In: Proc. of Foundations of software engineering, pp. 117–127. ACM Press, New York (2006)

19. Holzmann, G.J.: State compression in SPIN: Recursive indexing and compression training runs. In: Proc. of SPIN Workshop (1997)

20. Holzmann, G.J.: The Spin Model Checker, Primer and Reference Manual. Addison-Wesley, Reading, Massachusetts (2003)

21. Holzmann, G.J., Peled, D., Yannakakis, M.: On nested depth first search. In: Proc. SPIN Workshop, pp. 23–32. American Mathematical Society, Providence, RI (1996)

22. Ip, C.N., Dill, D.L.: Better verification through symmetry. Formal Methods in System Design 9(1–2), 41–75 (1996)

23. Krčál, P.: Distributed explicit bounded ltl model checking. In: Proc. of Parallel and Distributed Methods in verifiCation (PDMC 2003). ENTCS, vol. 89. Elsevier, Amsterdam (2003)

24. Kurshan, R.P., Levin, V., Yenigün, H.: Compressing transitions for model checking. In: Brinksma, E., Larsen, K.G. (eds.) CAV 2002. LNCS, vol. 2404, pp. 569–581. Springer, Heidelberg (2002)

25. Lang, F.: Compositional verification using svl scripts. In: Katoen, J.-P., Stevens, P. (eds.) TACAS 2002. LNCS, vol. 2280, pp. 465–469. Springer, Heidelberg (2002)

26. Lerda, F., Visser, W.: Addressing dynamic issues of program model checking. In: Dwyer, M.B. (ed.) SPIN 2001. LNCS, vol. 2057, pp. 80–102. Springer, Heidelberg (2001)

27. Milo, R., Itzkovitz, S., Kashtan, N., Levitt, R., Shen-Orr, S., Ayzenshtat, I., Sheffer, M., Alon, U.: Superfamilies of evolved and designed networks. Science 303(5663), 1538–1542 (2004)

28. Milo, R., Shen-Orr, S., Itzkovitz, S., Kashtan, N., Chklovskii, D., Alon, U.: Network motifs: Simple building blocks of complex networks. Science 298(5594), 824–827 (2002)

29. Mony, H., Baumgartner, J., Paruthi, V., Kanzelman, R., Kuehlmann, A.: Scalable automated verification via expert-system guided transformations. In: Hu, A.J., Martin, A.K. (eds.) FMCAD 2004. LNCS, vol. 3312, pp. 159–173. Springer, Heidelberg (2004)

30. Ozdemir, K., Ural, H.: Protocol validation by simultaneous reachability analysis. Computer Communications 20, 772–788 (1997)

31. Pelánek, R.: Typical structural properties of state spaces. In: Graf, S., Mounier, L. (eds.) SPIN 2004. LNCS, vol. 2989, pp. 5–22. Springer, Heidelberg (2004)

32. Pelánek, R.: Evaluation of on-the-fly state space reductions. In: Proc. of Mathematical and Engineering Methods in Computer Science (MEMICS 2005), pp. 121–127 (2005)

33. Pelánek, R.: Reduction and Abstraction Techniques for Model Checking. PhD thesis, Faculty of Informatics, Masaryk University, Brno (2006)

34. Pelánek, R.: Web portal for benchmarking explicit model checkers. Technical Report FIMU-RS-2006-03, Masaryk University Brno (2006), http://anna.fi.muni.cz/models/

35. Pelánek, R.: Beem: Benchmarks for explicit model checkers. In: Bošnački, D., Edelkamp, S. (eds.) SPIN 2007. LNCS, vol. 4595, pp. 263–267. Springer, Heidelberg (2007)

36. Pelánek, R., Hanžl, T., Černá, I., Brim, L.: Enhancing random walk state space exploration. In: Proc. of Formal Methods for Industrial Critical Systems (FMICS 2005), pp. 98–105. ACM Press, New York (2005)

37. Penna, G.D., Intrigila, B., Melatti, I., Tronci, E., Zilli, M.V.: Exploiting transition locality in automatic verification of finite state concurrent systems. Software Tools for Technology Transfer (STTT) 6(4), 320–341 (2004)

38. Ruys, T.C., Brinksma, E.: Managing the verification trajectory. International Journal on Software Tools for Technology Transfer (STTT) 4(2), 246–259 (2003)

39. Sahoo, D., Jain, J., Iyer, S.K., Dill, D., Emerson, E.A.: Predictive reachability using a sample-based approach. In: Borrione, D., Paul, W. (eds.) CHARME 2005. LNCS, vol. 3725, pp. 388–392. Springer, Heidelberg (2005)

40. Sivaraj, H., Gopalakrishnan, G.: Random walk based heuristic algorithms for distributed memory model checking. In: Proc. of Parallel and Distributed Model Checking (PDMC 2003). ENTCS, vol. 89 (2003)
41. Stern, U., Dill, D.L.: Using magnetic disk instead of main memory in the Murphi verifier. In: Y. Vardi, M. (ed.) CAV 1998. LNCS, vol. 1427, pp. 172–183. Springer, Heidelberg (1998)
42. Vardi, M.Y., Wolper, P.: An automata-theoretic approach to automatic program verification. In: Kozen, D. (ed.) Proc. of Logic in Computer Science (LICS 1986), pp. 332–344. IEEE Computer Society Press, Los Alamitos (1986)

An Approach to Formalization and Analysis of Message Passing Libraries*

Robert Palmer, Michael DeLisi,
Ganesh Gopalakrishnan, and Robert M. Kirby

School of Computing, University of Utah
{rpalmer,delisi,ganesh,kirby}@cs.utah.edu

Abstract. Message passing using libraries implementing the Message Passing Interface (MPI) standard is the dominant communication mechanism in high performance computing (HPC) applications. Yet, the lack of an implementation independent formal semantics for MPI is a huge void that must be filled, especially given the fact that MPI will be implemented on novel hardware platforms in the near future. To help reason about programs that use MPI for communication, we have developed a formal TLA+ semantic definition of the point to point communication operations to augment the existing standard. The proposed semantics includes 42 MPI functions, including all 35 point to point operations, many of which have not been formally modeled previously. We also present a framework to extract models from SPMD-style C programs, so that designers may understand the semantics of MPI by exercising short, yet pithy, communication scenarios written in C/MPI. In this paper, we describe (i) the TLA+ MPI model features, such as handling the explicit memory for each process to facilitate the modeling of C pointers, and some of the widely used MPI operations, (ii) the model extraction framework and the simplifications made to the model that help facilitate explicit-state model checking of formal semantic definitions, (iii) a customized model checker for MPI that performs much faster model checking, and features a dynamic partial-order reduction algorithm whose correctness is directly based on the formal semantics, and (iv) an error trail replay facility in the Visual Studio environment. Our effort has helped identify a few omissions in the MPI reference standard document. These benefits suggest that a formal semantic definition and exploration approach as described here must accompany every future effort in creating parallel and distributed programming libraries.

1 Introduction

Progress in high-performance scientific computing (HPC) is fundamental to scientific discovery in virtually all walks of life. The Message Passing Interface (MPI, [1]) library has become a *de facto* standard in HPC, and is being actively developed and supported through several implementations [2,3,4,5] designed to

---

* Supported in part by NSF award CNS-00509379, Microsoft HPC Institutes Program, and SRC Contract 2005-TJ-1318.

S. Leue and P. Merino (Eds.): FMICS 2007, LNCS 4916, pp. 164–181, 2008.

run on a plethora of architectural platforms. MPI is, however, a portable standard for overall behavior, and not performance. Therefore, MPI programs are often manually or automatically (e.g., [6]) re-tuned when ported to another hardware platform, for example by changing its basic primitives (e.g., MPI_Send) to specialized versions (e.g., MPI_Isend). The fact that MPI-1 supports over 128 primitives and MPI-2 supports over 300 is largely to facilitate such transformations.[1] In this context, it is crucial that the designers performing code tuning are aware of the very fine details of the MPI semantics. Unfortunately, such details are far from obvious. For illustration, consider the following MPI pseudo-code involving two processes:

```
P0: if(rank==0){MPI_Irecv(rcvbuf1, from 1); MPI_Irecv(rcvbuf2,from 1);..}
P1: if(rank==1){sendbuf1=6; sendbuf2=7;
                MPI_Issend(sendbuf1, to 0); MPI_Isend(sendbuf2, to  0);..}
```

Process 1 is designed to issue two *immediate mode* sends (the first being a synchronous-mode send) to process 0, while Process 0 is designed to post two immediate-mode receives. Consider some simple questions pertaining to the execution of this program:

1. *Is it guaranteed that* rcvbuf1 *will eventually contain the message sent out of* sendbuf1*?* The answer is 'yes,' since MPI guarantees in-order message delivery.
2. *When can the buffers be accessed?* Since all sends and receives use the immediate mode, the handles that these calls return have to be tested for completion using an explicit MPI_Test or MPI_Wait (suppressed for brevity in our pseudo-code) before the associated buffers are allowed to be accessed (written to or even read from).
3. *Will the first receive always complete before the second?* No such guarantee exists (the second may complete first), as these are *immediate mode* receives which are guaranteed only to be *initiated* in program order.
4. *What is guaranteed about the matching receive when the first send completes?* It is guaranteed that this receive has been *posted*. This is because the first send is a *synchronous* send, which forces a rendezvous with the posting of the first receive.

The MPI reference standard [1] is an informal, non machine-readable document that offers English descriptions of the individual behaviors of MPI primitives. It does not support answering the above kinds of simple questions in any tractable and reliable way. Running test programs, using actual MPI libraries, to reveal answers to the above kinds of questions is also futile, given that various MPI implementations exploit the liberties of the standard by specializing the semantics in various ways.

In this paper, we present a formal, high-level, and executable standard specification for a non-trivial subset of MPI 1.1. In particular, our specification consists

---

[1] It is widely known that MPI programs use only about a dozen or so of the 300 MPI library calls - but the precise dozen chosen depends on the applications being programmed, as well as the hardware platform on which the program runs.

of 42 MPI 1.1 functions. We write this specification in TLA+ [7], a formal specification notation widely used in industry. Our specification is integrated with the verification framework described in this paper. The features of this framework are as follows:

1. It permits designers to explore the MPI semantics in the setting of MPI programs written in C by extracting a TLA+ model of the program, embedding the MPI calls, and linking it to our TLA+ models of MPI functions. The exploration happens through *model checking* [8], and not through concrete executions. Error traces produced by the model checker are, however, displayed in a user-friendly way by driving the Microsoft Visual Studio debugger to walk the original program code following the error trace.
2. The framework includes two model checkers: MPI-TLC, a model checker that works directly off the formal semantic definitions using the TLA+ model checker, TLC [9]; and MPIC [10], a model checker that embodies the communication semantics of MPI directly as C# program code.
3. The communication semantics of a small representative subset of MPI were incorporated into MPIC by faithfully following our TLA+ definitions. In addition, MPIC implements a *dynamic partial-order reduction algorithm* (DPOR) (adapted from [11]) for efficient state-space traversal. The DPOR algorithm avoids commuting independent actions, where the notion of independence was stated and manually proved using a simplified version of our MPI formal semantics.

Experimental results from MPIC are provided in Figure 11. A more detailed coverage of MPIC or our DPOR algorithm are outside the scope of this paper, but may be found in [10].[2]

The questions raised on Page 165 can be answered by writing an MPI program such as the one in Figure 1 and analyzing this program using our framework. The four questions can be answered, in order, as follows:

1. Assert that the data read by process 0 is: `rcvbuf1 == 6&&rcvbuf2 == 7`. If it is possible under the semantics for other values to be assigned to these two variables, then the TLC model checker will find the violation.
2. Move the assertions mentioned in the response to the previous question to any other point before the corresponding `waits`. The model checker then finds violations—meaning that the data cannot be accessed on the receiver until after the `wait`. If one adds an assignment to the variable being transmitted, i.e., after the `MPI_Issend` yet before the `MPI_Wait`, the model checker discovers the violation as the wrong value will be passed to the receiver.
3. We can reverse the order of the `MPI_Wait` commands. If the model checker does not find a deadlock then it is possible for the operations to complete in either order.
4. To answer this question, we employ the program in Figure 1. The MPI semantics for immediate mode ready send requires the corresponding receive to

---

[2] The entire modeling framework described in this paper may be downloaded from http://www.cs.utah.edu/formal_verification/verification_environment

```
1 #include "mpi.h"                        22      data2 = 6;
2                                          23      MPI_Issend(&data1, 1, MPI_INT, 0,
3 int main(int argc, char** argv)          24                 1, MPI_COMM_WORLD, &req1);
4 {                                        25    }
5   int rank, size, data1, data2, data3, flag;  26  if(rank == 1){
6   MPI_Request req1, req2, req3;          27      MPI_Wait(&req1, &stat);
7   MPI_Status stat;                       28      MPI_Irsend(&data2, 1, MPI_INT, 0,
8   MPI_Init(&argc, &argv);                29                 0, MPI_COMM_WORLD, &req2);
9   MPI_Comm_rank(MPI_COMM_WORLD, &rank);  30      MPI_Irsend(&data3, 1, MPI_INT, 0,
10  MPI_Comm_size(MPI_COMM_WORLD, &size);  31                 2, MPI_COMM_WORLD, &req3);
11  if(rank == 0){                         32    } else {
12    data1 = 0;                           33      MPI_Wait(&req2, &stat);
13    data2 = 0;                           34    }
14    MPI_Irecv(&data1, 1, MPI_INT, 1,     35    if(rank == 0){
15            0, MPI_COMM_WORLD, &req1);   36      MPI_Wait(&req1, &stat);
16    MPI_Irecv(&data2, 1, MPI_INT, 1,     37    } else {
17            1, MPI_COMM_WORLD, &req2);   38      MPI_Wait(&req2, &stat);
18    MPI_Irecv(&data3, 1, MPI_INT, 1,     39    }
19            2, MPI_COMM_WORLD, &req3);   40    MPI_Finalize();
20  } else {                               41    return 0;
21    data1 = 7;                           42 }
```

Fig. 1. The C program used to answer Question 4 on Page 165

be posted before the `MPI_Irsend`. We cause the tag of the messages to force the second `MPI_Irecv` to match the `MPI_Issend`. We execute the `MPI_Wait` corresponding to the `MPI_Issend` and then post two `MPI_Irsend` operations. Now we observe that the model checker (in performing a breadth first search) finds the first `MPI_Irsend` posts without error, but the second `MPI_Irsend` violates the semantics. Thus we conclude that when the `MPI_Wait` of process 1 returns, process 0 is guaranteed to have executed the second `MPI_Irecv`, but is not guaranteed to have executed any further.

1.1 Related Work

The idea of writing formal specifications of standards and building executable environments is a vast area. The IEEE Floating Point standard [12] was initially conceived as a standard that helped minimize the danger of non-portable floating point implementations, and now has incarnations in various higher order logic specifications (e.g., [13]), finding routine applications in *formal proofs* of modern microprocessor floating point hardware circuits. Formal specifications using TLA+ include Lamport's Win32 Threads API specification [14] and the RPC Memory Problem specified in TLA+ and formally verified in the Isabelle theorem prover by Lamport, Abadi, and Merz [15]. In [16], Jackson presents a lightweight object modeling notation called Alloy, which has tool support [17,18] in terms of formal analysis and testing based on Boolean satisfiability methods.

Each formal specification framework solves modeling and analysis issues specific to the object being described. In our case, we were initially not sure how to handle the daunting complexity of MPI nor how to handle its modeling, given that there has only been very limited effort in terms of formal characterization of MPI. The architecture of our framework that incorporates solutions that finally worked are described in Section 2.

In [19], Georgelin and Pierre specify some of the MPI functions in LOTOS [20]. In [21], Siegel and Avrunin describe a finite state model of a limited number of MPI point-to-point operations. This finite state model is embedded in [22]. In [23], the authors support a limited partial-order reduction method – one that handles wild-card communications in a restricted manner, as detailed in [10]. In [24], additional 'non-blocking' MPI primitives are modeled in Promela. Our own past efforts in this area are described in [25,26,27,28]. None of these efforts: (i) approach the number of MPI functions we handle, (ii) have the same style of high level specifications (TLA+ is much closer to mathematical logic than finite-state Promela or LOTOS models), (iii) have a model extraction framework starting from C/MPI programs, (iv) incorporate a dynamic partial-order reduction algorithm that handles the difficulties of wildcard communications more generally, and (v) have a practical way of displaying error traces in the user's C code. Section 3 describes the architecture of our implementation.

In the act of writing our formal specification, we noticed serious omissions in the English standard (confirmed by experts [29]). While these omissions were found largely by luck, the *opposite* problem – namely, that of our specification itself not correctly implementing the intent of the MPI English standard writers – needs much more care to avoid. We have taken some precautions to avoid such errors. First, our specification is organized for *easy traceability*: many clauses in our specification are cross-linked with [1] to particular page/line numbers of [1]. Second, the "formal semantic calculator" provided by our approach using familiar programming and debugging environments (*e.g.*, TLC, Phoenix, and Visual Studio) may help engage expert MPI users (who may not be formal methods experts) into experimenting with our semantic definitions.

More work is needed to exploit the full potential of formal semantic definitions, as well as a framework such as ours. One can state and prove theorems that link concepts spread across multiple pages, as is the case with the current reference document [1]. These, and other concluding remarks are provided in Section 4.

2   Communication Semantics Model of MPI

We have tried to make this section intuitive even for those not familiar with MPI: they may focus on the higher level points that we have expressed, as these issues are bound to arise in any such endeavor as this.

The TLA+ model of MPI is intended to capture the semantic details that are both explicitly and tacitly referenced in the natural language standard, while abstracting away the implementation specific issues that are not specified. Our model broadly implements the architecture shown in Figure 2. We preserve the MPI API such that application of an MPI operation has the same external interface as an MPI procedure call in C. The main pieces of the model are point-to-point operations, collective operations, and constants.

Point-to-point and collective operations are coupled using a communicator. We model the communicator as a context and a group (MPI additionally has topologies and attributes, which we consider to be future work). The context

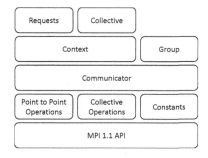

Fig. 2. TLA+ MPI model architecture

MPI_Get_count	MPI_Request_free	MPI_Test_canceled
MPI_Buffer_attach	MPI_Waitany	MPI_Send_init
MPI_Buffer_detach	MPI_Testany	MPI_Bsend_init
MPI_Isend	MPI_Waitall	MPI_Ssend_init
MPI_Ibsend	MPI_Testall	MPI_Rsend_init
MPI_Issend	MPI_Waitsome	MPI_Recv_init
MPI_Irsend	MPI_Testsome	MPI_Start
MPI_Irecv	MPI_Iprobe	MPI_Startall
MPI_Wait	MPI_Probe	
MPI_Test	MPI_Cancel	

Fig. 3. Point-to-point operations included in the TLA+ specification

houses all information about messages that are currently available for communication. Groups define the set of processes allowed to access a communicator and their respective ranks (used for message addressing).

2.1 Modeling Approach

The MPI standard [1] contains some 128 operations that provide a rich collection of communication options. A full 35 of these operations are dedicated to pair-wise exchanges of messages between processes. Our model contains those operations that we could represent using exactly one TLA+ atomic transition (primed variables equated to unprimed variables, as in Figures 6 and 7). The operations included are shown in Figure 3. We model the remaining seven operations as sequential compositions of those shown in Figure 3. Thus MPI_Send becomes MPI_Isend and MPI_Wait issued in that order. Similarly, MPI_Sendrecv becomes MPI_Isend, MPI_Irecv, and two MPI_Wait operations issued sequentially, and so on. The reason for this decision is that the additional overhead involved in modeling these operations *directly* would significantly complicate our model. For example, consider the additional information needed to model MPI_Ssend directly. For doing this, we would require, for each process, a map from the program counter (pc) to the next operation to be performed when MPI_Ssend is enabled. In this manner, we can determine when a corresponding

MPI_Barrier   MPI_Group_size   MPI_Group_rank
MPI_Comm_size MPI_Comm_rank MPI_Comm_compare
MPI_Init   MPI_Finalize   MPI_Initialized
MPI_Abort

Fig. 4. Additional MPI operations modeled to enable tool-based reasoning on MPI based parallel programs

MPI_Recv could be executed by the receiving process, and then cause both processes to jointly execute their state transition steps. However, since there is no restriction on what type of receive could be matched with MPI_Ssend (it could be MPI_Recv, MPI_Irecv, MPI_Sendrecv, *etc.*), nor are there restrictions on the blocking nature of the receives (some block the receiving process while others do not), supporting each of the variants becomes quite laborious, in addition to resulting in unreadable model descriptions.

Additional supporting operations included in the model are shown in Figure 4. Each of the operations has the same parameters in the same order as the MPI standard, with two additions. First, there is no way for TLA+ operations to query the system to discover which process is executing, short of having a globally visible state element. Therefore, the PID of the process executing an MPI call is passed as a parameter, which appears after the parameters specified in the standard. We also have not determined a graceful way to provide return values of MPI function calls. The return address is, therefore, also provided as a parameter (although handling return values other than MPI_SUCCESS remains as future work).

2.2   What Is Not Modeled

It is important to point out that we have not modeled all of the semantics of MPI in our work. In addition to the restrictions stated in the previous section, we have not modeled the following items.

Data: Most data. Data, such as arrays of floating point values, objects, *etc.*, could be modeled using TLA+. It is, however, not necessary in most cases to retain the actual data values of a distributed computation to verify reactive properties of the participating nodes. Therefore we allow a placeholder for data in our formal model in such a way that it can be included when necessary. We currently *do* allow for the preservation of data values, if they are used in assert statements. Similarly, there are many data manipulation operations, and also operations to pack data. These are not currently modeled.

Operations on communicators and topologies: Operations on communicators and topologies are modeled to a limited extent to enable point-to-point communications on intracommunicators. We currently model the operations shown in Figure 4 in addition to the point-to-point operations of Chapter 3 of MPI 1.1 shown in Figure 3. Operations on communicators and topologies are planned to be modeled in the next version of our semantics.

Implementation details: To the greatest extent possible we have avoided asserting implementation-specific details in our formal semantics. One obvious ramification of this omission is that modeling return codes of MPI operations is completely eliminated (cf. [1, Page 11]).

Handling Implementation-dependent Buffer Availability: As far as the standard mode sends (*e.g.*, MPI_Send, MPI_Isend, MPI_Send_init) go, we require the system to either eventually buffer these requests or to not buffer them at all. The standard allows for an implementation to switch between these policies in a time-varying manner; we do not know how to attain such generality without complicating our semantics drastically.

2.3 Modeling Granularity to Preserve the Corner Cases

A formal model for a communications library must model at the right level of granularity in order to not mask corner cases. In order to achieve this objective, we introduced three additional rules that are allowed to interleave with the actions of an individual processes. These rules facilitate message pairing, message buffering, and message transmission.

Figure 5 shows the interleaved rule that transmits messages from one process to another. This rule is enabled when there exists process i, and request j on process i such that the request is started, is globally active, has not been canceled, has not been transmitted, and has already been paired with another request on some other process. It is necessary to pair and transmit messages separately because *there is*

```
1 Transmit ==
2    /\ \E i \in 0..(N-1) :
3        \E j \in 1..Len(requests[i]) :
4        LET m == requests[i][j] IN
5        /\ m.started
6        /\ m.globalactive
7        /\ \lnot m.canceled
8        /\ \lnot m.transmitted
9        /\ m.match /= <<>>
10       /\ requests' = [requests EXCEPT ![i] =
11                          [@ EXCEPT ![j] =
12                             [@ EXCEPT !.transmitted = TRUE]]]
13       /\ IF \lnot requests[m.match[1]][m.match[2]].transmitted
14          THEN
15             IF m.message.state = "recv"
16             THEN Memory' = [Memory EXCEPT ![i] = [@ EXCEPT ![m.message.addr] =
17                    Memory[m.match[1]][requests[m.match[1]][m.match[2]].message.addr]]]
18             ELSE Memory' = [Memory EXCEPT ![m.match[1]] =
19                    [@ EXCEPT ![requests[m.match[1]][m.match[2]].message.addr] =
20                       Memory[i][m.message.addr]]]
21          ELSE
22             UNCHANGED <<Memory>>
23
24       /\ IF m.ctype = "bsend"
25          THEN
26             message_buffer' = [message_buffer EXCEPT ![i] = @ - 1]
27          ELSE
28             UNCHANGED << message_buffer >>
29    /\ UNCHANGED << group, communicator, bufsize, initialized, collective >>
```

Fig. 5. Message transmission

no requirement for ordering of message completion in the MPI standard [1]. Consider the case where two messages are sent from process 1 to process 2 where the first message is very large and the second message is very small. The MPI standard requires that the first message sent be matched with the first receive posted in program order on both processes. However this makes no statement about *when* the messages will complete. In our example, it should be possible for the smaller message to complete first. The use of a separate transmit rule allows us to facilitate the modeling of MPI_Cancel which is used to cancel pending MPI messages. Further discussions are provided in Section 2.5.

Continuing with Figure 5, the final three conjuncts in the model of `MPI_Wait` define the values of `Memory`, `requests`, and the `message_buffer` in the next state. In MPI, the event marking the completion of the transmission on the sender side may become visible before the event on the receiver side, or vice versa. Therefore, in our model, only one request is updated to show that the transmitting step has completed. We do move some data between processes. We currently have abstracted the programs modeled such that the value in only *one memory location* can be transmitted between processes. We also have abstracted the notion of buffering such that a counting semaphore tracks the number of messages that can be buffered using the explicit space provided by the user — rather than modeling the number of bytes being sent per message.

2.4   A Complete Definition: MPI_Wait

Figures 6 and 7 contain the TLA+ model definition of MPI_Wait, commonly used to complete communications. As with all MPI operations (except for MPI_Initialized), MPI_Init must have been called prior to the application of this operation. The model checks this as an assertion on line 3 of the operation. The comments are of two types: *regular* and *cross references* into the natural language version of the standard. The cross references are numbered as "page.line" following the TLA+ comments (*), and allow our assertions to be traced. We now examine a few aspects of the specification of MPI_Wait. The main conjunct in the specification causes the `group`, `communicator`, `bufsize`, `message_buffer`, `initialized`, and `finalized` to remain unchanged in the next state. It then considers two cases: when the request is the special MPI_REQUEST_NULL value, or when it is a non-null request handle. For the non-null case, the operation becomes enabled when (i) the request is locally active — meaning it has not been previously completed by some wait or test, and (ii) the request indicates that the message has been transmitted, canceled, or buffered. In this case, if the source and destination referenced in the request are non-null, the memory of the executing process is updated to indicate that the message has completed by filling the fields of the status object (lines 16–22). Otherwise, the status fields are set to reflect that the completion has occurred on a request referencing MPI_PROC_NULL. In either case the request handle is appropriately set, and we also mark the status fields in memory.

The request sequence for the executing process must also be updated (lines 34–58. When a communication between processes i and j is initiated by i using

```
1 MPI_Wait(request, status, return, proc) ==
2   LET r == requests[proc][Memory[proc][request]] IN
3   /\ Assert(initialized[proc] = "initialized", \* 200.10-200.12
4             "Error: MPI_Wait called with proc not in initialized state.")
5         \* 41.32-41.39 The request handle is not the null handle.
6   /\ \/ /\ Memory[proc][request] /= MPI_REQUEST_NULL
7         /\ r.localactive                        \* The request is active locally.
8         /\ \/ /\ r.message.src /= MPI_PROC_NULL   \* The message src is not null
9               /\ r.message.dest /= MPI_PROC_NULL  \* The message dest is not null
10                             \* 41.32 - Blocks until complete
11            /\ \/ r.transmitted \* The message was transmitted or
12               \/ r.canceled    \* canceled by the user program or
13               \/ r.buffered    \* buffered by the system
14            /\ Memory' =
15               [Memory EXCEPT ![proc] =    \* 41.36
16                 [@ EXCEPT ![Status_Canceled(status)] =
17                                /\ r.canceled
18                                /\ \lnot r.transmitted, \* 54.46
19                     ![Status_Count(status)] = r.message.numelements,
20                     ![Status_Source(status)] = r.message.src,
21                     ![Status_Tag(status)] = r.message.msgtag,
22                     ![Status_Err(status)] = r.error,
23                     ![request] = \* 41.32-41.35, 58.34-58.35
24                        IF r.persist
25                        THEN @
26                        ELSE MPI_REQUEST_NULL]]
27      \/ /\ \/ r.message.src = MPI_PROC_NULL
28            \/ r.message.dest = MPI_PROC_NULL
29         /\ Memory' = [Memory EXCEPT ![proc] =  \* 41.36
30            [@ EXCEPT ![Status_Canceled(status)] = r.canceled,
31                      ![Status_Count(status)] = 0,
32                      ![Status_Source(status)] = MPI_PROC_NULL,
33                      ![Status_Tag(status)] = MPI_ANY_TAG,
34                      ![Status_Err(status)] = 0,
35                      ![request] = \* 41.32-41.35, 58.34-58.35
36                         IF r.persist
37                         THEN @
38                         ELSE MPI_REQUEST_NULL]]
```

Fig. 6. The first half of the TLA+ model of MPI_Wait. The rest of MPI_Wait is shown in Figure 7.

a buffered send (such as MPI_Send) or when using MPI_Cancel, it is possible for the Wait to become enabled before the matching request is posted on process j. This is apparent when r.match $=<<>>$ on line 34. In the true case, the previously paired request is marked globally inactive, in addition to the local request being marked locally inactive and globally inactive. In the false case, only the local request is marked locally inactive. Again, the status fields are marked as required by the standard.

2.5 Issues Raised by Modeling

While creating the model we became aware of some specific issues that had not been discussed in the MPI natural language version of the standard. The following descriptions are helpful in understanding the issues identified. MPI_Probe takes a process rank j and some additional message envelope information, and becomes enabled when there is a matching request posted on process j. MPI_Cancel takes a request handle as an argument and attempts to cancel the corresponding

```
39          /\ requests' =
40              IF r.match /= << >>
41              THEN
42                  [requests EXCEPT ![proc] =   \* 58.34
43                      [@ EXCEPT
44                          ![Memory[proc][request]] =
45                              IF r.persist
46                              THEN
47                                  IF requests[r.match[1]][r.match[2]].localactive
48                                  THEN [@ EXCEPT !.localactive = FALSE,
49                                                 !.globalactive = FALSE]
50                                  ELSE [@ EXCEPT !.localactive = FALSE]
51                              ELSE
52                                  IF requests[r.match[1]][r.match[2]].localactive
53                                  THEN [@ EXCEPT !.localactive = FALSE,
54                                                 !.globalactive = FALSE,
55                                                 !.deallocated = TRUE]
56                                  ELSE [@ EXCEPT !.localactive = FALSE,
57                                                 !.deallocated = TRUE]],
58                          ![r.match[1]] =
59                              [@ EXCEPT ![r.match[2]] =
60                                  IF requests[r.match[1]][r.match[2]].localactive
61                                  THEN requests[r.match[1]][r.match[2]]
62                                  ELSE [@ EXCEPT !.globalactive = FALSE]]]
63              ELSE
64                  [requests EXCEPT ![proc] =   \* 58.34
65                      [@ EXCEPT ![Memory[proc][request]] =
66                          IF r.persist
67                          THEN [@ EXCEPT !.localactive = FALSE]
68                          ELSE [@ EXCEPT !.localactive = FALSE,
69                                         !.deallocated = TRUE]]]
70      \/ /\ \/ Memory[proc][request] = MPI_REQUEST_NULL      \* 41.40-41.41 The
71          \/ /\ Memory[proc][request] /= MPI_REQUEST_NULL \* request handle is
72                  /\ \lnot r.localactive         \* null or the request is not active
73          /\ Memory' = [Memory EXCEPT ![proc] = \* 41.36
74                          [@ EXCEPT ![Status_Canceled(status)] = FALSE,
75                                    ![Status_Count(status)] = 0,
76                                    ![Status_Source(status)] = MPI_ANY_SOURCE,
77                                    ![Status_Tag(status)] = MPI_ANY_TAG,
78                                    ![Status_Err(status)] = 0]]
79          /\ UNCHANGED << requests >>
80  /\ UNCHANGED << group, communicator, bufsize, message_buffer,
81                  initialized, collective >>
```

Fig. 7. The second half of the TLA+ model of MPI_Wait

communication. The standard says the message may still complete, and it is up to the user to program appropriately. A third operation MPI_Rsend, and variants, requires the matching receive operation to have been previously posted, barring which the operation is in error. In this context, here are some specific issues we identified:

- There are numerous ways that MPI_Probe and MPI_Cancel can interact, resulting in an undefined system state. In particular, any time a message is probed successfully, it is not specified whether it is still possible for the message to be canceled or if the message must at that point be delivered.
- MPI_Cancel also creates an undefined system state when used with ready mode send (MPI_Irsend). Consider the following execution trace: "MPI_Irecv; MPI_Irsend; MPI_Cancel; ..." If the ready send is successful, can the receive still be canceled?

- Continuing with Cancel, what happens if the null request is canceled?
- The MPI system allows the user to specify a buffer for outgoing messages. To ensure that all buffered messages have been sent, the user must call MPI_Buffer_detach. What is the state of the system when no buffer has been specified and MPI_Buffer_detach is called?

It is encouraging to note that even a few weeks invested in the process of writing a formal semantics forced us to conduct a thorough walk-through of the MPI standard, spotting the above omissions.

3   Modeling Framework

We have developed a modeling framework based on the Microsoft Phoenix [30] compiler which allows developers to insert a compilation phase between existing compiler phases in the process of lowering a program from language independent MSIL to device specific assembly. We place our phase at the point where the input program has been simplified into a single static assignment form, with a homogenized pointer referencing style, where the instructions are still device independent. Our phase reads the Phoenix intermediate representation and builds from it a state-transition system (the MPIC IR) for each function, similar in spirit to a control flow graph. Control locations in the program are represented by states, and program statements are represented using transitions.

The architecture of the verification framework is shown in Figure 8. From the MPIC IR, we can output different formats, including TLA+, Dot[31], and MPIC. The framework integrates both TLC and a new model checker MPIC to perform the verification tasks. If an error is found, the error trail is then made available to the verification environment, and can be used by our tool to drive the Visual Studio debugger to replay the trace to the error. The remainder of this section describes the simplification and replay capabilities of our framework. We report the MPIC tool primarily in [10].

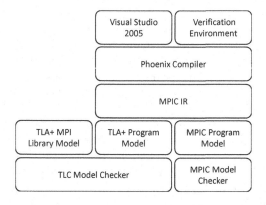

Fig. 8. System architecture

3.1 Simplification

From the extracted state-transition format, it would be possible to emit a TLA+ model directly. However, the TLA+ model would have to have sufficient mechanisms to handle function calls and returns. Although this is possible with TLA+ [32]–the scientific computing applications we have considered would not benefit from the additional functionality. As such we propose the following sequence of transformations, intended to reduce the complexity of model checking while preserving the properties of interest, before applying model checking based analysis. The simplifications are as follows:

- Inline all user defined functions: We assume (i) that all parameters are pass by value, (ii) that there are no function pointers, and (iii) there is no recursion.
- Remove operations foreign to the model checking framework: Examples include `printf`.
- Slice the model with respect to communications and user assertions: The cone of influence of variables is computed using a chaotic iteration over the program graph, similar to what is described in [33].
- Eliminate redundant counting loops: This is a heuristic to handle loops that occur frequently in MPI programs.

3.2 Program Modeling

Our model of MPI is intended to capture the semantics while abstracting away the possible implementation details. However there are some implementation details retained that are common to all present-day computer systems, and that are implied by the standard. The first of these is the notion of memory: it is assumed that each process operates in a disjoint memory space. As such, we allocate an array of TLA+ variables that represent the local store of each process. More formally, memory is modeled as a function $memory : \mathbb{N} \rightarrow \mathbb{N}$ where allocated addresses are mapped onto values. Variable names are represented by an array of address that use symbols, (*i.e.*, strings) for indices. These are again functions that map strings onto addresses. The mention of memory brings to the fore the first of several abstractions that are imposed on the model. Only values in $\mathbb{N}$ are considered valid memory contents. With an explicit notion of memory and addresses, it is possible to have explicit pointers in the model. This we support, allowing for arbitrary dereferences. We also never allocate address 0, allowing for null pointer dereference violations to be discovered.

It is possible to allocate memory using the operator in Figure 9. This operator updates the function representing process memory by changing the function for process i such that there are `size` new memory locations at the end, each having uninitialized memory contents. The operator also writes the address of the first uninitialized location into the memory location of the pointer.

Many constants are used by MPI and consequently in our model. Since the model is automatically extracted from the program while it is being compiled, it is necessary that the constants used in our model match those used by the

```
1  AllocateMemory(ptr, pid, size) ==
2    /\ Memory' = [i \in 0..(N-1) |->
3                    IF i = pid
4                    THEN [j \in 1..(Len(Memory[i]) + size) |->
5                            IF j <= Len(Memory[i])
6                            THEN
7                                IF ptr = j
8                                THEN Len(Memory[pid]) + 1
9                                ELSE Memory[i][j]
10                           ELSE "uninitialized memory space"]
11                   ELSE Memory[i]]
```

Fig. 9. Memory allocation in TLA+

```
\/ /\ pc[pid] = state_pc
   /\ pc' = [pc EXCEPT ![pid] = next_pc]
   /\ guard
   /\ action
   /\ UNCHANGED << variables not mentioned in the action >>
```

Fig. 10. Transition template for TLA+ program model

implementation of MPI used with the program being analyzed. Constants are provided in a separate TLC configuration file. These constant definitions generally match the values used in the corresponding C header files (mpi.h). Since not all values can be used (*e.g.*, no floating point values, *etc.*) we make manual changes to the configuration and corresponding header files when necessary.

The individual transitions are formatted as shown in Figure 10, combined with the initial values of the memory array and the map from variable names to their addresses and written to disk. The constants, program model, and MPI model are then given to the TLC model checker.

Error Trail Generation. In the event that the model contains an error, an error trail is produced by the model checker and returned to the verification environment. To map the error trail back onto the actual program we observe the changes in the error trail to variable values that appear in the program text. For each such change, we step the Visual Studio debugger until the corresponding value of the variable in the debugger matches. We also observe which process moves at every step in the error trail and context switch between processes in the debugger at corresponding points. When the error trail ends, the debugger is within a few steps of the error with the process that causes the error scheduled.

4   Examples

We have applied our semantic evaluation framework to a small number of examples and show the results of a few verification tasks in this section. The two tables shown in Figure 11 shows the number of states generated / execution time for the following examples: (i) an example code from [34], (ii) the 2D

	MPI-TLC	MPIC without DPOR	MPIC with DPOR
Trap	724/2	331/0	66/0
Diffusion 2D	timeout	timeout	19,807,253/623
Scenario 4	310/2	N/A	N/A

Fig. 11. Number of states generated / execution time (seconds)

diffusion example from [35], and (iii) the last scenario described in Section 1, namely "*What is guaranteed about the matching receive when the first send completes?*" Each of the experiments was run on a dual core 2GHz processor with 2GB of memory. When TLC was applied, two worker threads were used.

The Trap example from [34] computes the integral under a curve by application of the trapezoidal integration rule. The program is written in the SPMD style and is typical of "textbook examples" in this area. We verify the example as written for the absence of deadlocks and the default assertions provided by the respective model checkers for two model processes.

The Diffusion 2D example computes the diffusion of a substance through a two dimensional grid of cells. We could not verify the pseudo-code given in [35] because we require actual C program code. To facilitate this requirement, we implemented the program as described. We then optimized the code to overlap the preparation for communication with the actual communication operations. This is accomplished by changing the program to communicate via immediate mode synchronous sends and immediate mode receives (MPI_Issend and MPI_Irecv) coupled with MPI_Wait and then moving the message initiations as far from the completions as possible. We then were able to verify this code using MPIC using dynamic partial-order reduction, for the absence of deadlocks and the default set of assertions for 4 model processes.

The final example requires an additional MPI procedure, namely MPI_Irsend, which requires that the matching receive be posted before the "ready" mode send can be posted. We cause the first send to match the second receive using the tag field of the message. We then post the ready mode send immediately after the MPI_Wait corresponding to the MPI_Issend. We post a second ready mode send that can match only the third receive. Successful posting of the first MPI_Irsend implies that the receiver is guaranteed to be beyond that program point. Failed posting of the second MPI_Irsend implies that no guarantee can be made about further progress: thus the receiver is guaranteed to have posted the corresponding receive and no more (Figure 1). This verification task requires only two model processes.

5   Concluding Remarks

To help reason about programs that use MPI for communication, we have developed a formal TLA+ semantic definition of the point-to-point communication operations to augment the existing standard. We described this formal specification, as well as our framework to extract models from SPMD-style C programs.

We discuss how the framework incorporates high level formal specifications, and yet allows designers to experiment with these specifications, using model checking, in a familiar debugging environment. Our effort has helped identify a few omissions in the original MPI reference standard document. The experience gained so far suggests that a formal semantic definition and exploration approach as described here must accompany every future effort in creating parallel and distributed programming libraries.

Our future plans include overcoming the limitations of our current framework in terms of handling communication topologies. Another area where formal semantic definitions can help is in extensions of MPI to support different levels of threading. As pointed out in [36], even short MPI programs which employ threading can have nasty corner cases. Formal specifications, as well as direct execution methods for these specifications can have maximal impact in these areas, in that we will not be capacity limited in terms of model checking, and yet be able to shed light on the semantic intricacies, and pitfalls to avoid.

References

1. The Message Passing Interface Forum: MPI: A Message-Passing Interface Standard (1995), http://www.mpi-forum.org/docs/mpi-11-html/mpi-report.html
2. Gropp, W., Lusk, E.L., Doss, N.E., Skjellum, A.: A high-performance, portable implementation of the mpi message passing interface standard. Parallel Computing 22(6), 789–828 (1996)
3. Microsoft: Microsoft windows compute cluster 2003 (2006), www.microsoft.com/windowsserver2003/ccs/faq.mspx
4. Squyres, J.M., Lumsdaine, A.: A Component Architecture for LAM/MPI. In: Dongarra, J., Laforenza, D., Orlando, S. (eds.) EuroPVM/MPI 2003. LNCS, vol. 2840, pp. 379–387. Springer, Heidelberg (2003)
5. Gabriel, E., Fagg, G.E., Bosilca, G., Angskun, T., Dongarra, J.J., Squyres, J.M., Sahay, V., Kambadur, P., Barrett, B., Lumsdaine, A., Castain, R.H., Daniel, D.J., Graham, R.L., Woodall, T.S.: Open MPI: Goals, concept, and design of a next generation MPI implementation. In: Proceedings, 11th European PVM/MPI Users' Group Meeting, Budapest, Hungary, pp. 97–104 (2004)
6. Danalis, A., Kim, K.Y., Pollock, L., Swany, M.: Transformations to parallel codes for communication-computation overlap. In: SC 2005: Proceedings of the 2005 ACM/IEEE conference on Supercomputing, Washington, DC, USA, p. 58. IEEE Computer Society, Los Alamitos (2005)
7. Lamport, L.: Specifying concurrent systems with TLA (1999)
8. Clarke, E., Grumberg, O., Peled, D.: Model Checking. MIT Press, Cambridge (1999)
9. Yu, Y., Manolios, P., Lamport, L.: Model checking TLA+ specifications. In: Pierre, L., Kropf, T. (eds.) CHARME 1999. LNCS, vol. 1703, pp. 54–66. Springer, Heidelberg (1999)
10. Palmer, R., Gopalakrishnan, G., Kirby, R.M.: Semantics Driven Dynamic Partial-order Reduction of MPI-based Parallel Programs. In: PADTAD 2007 (2007), http://www.cs.utah.edu/formal_verification/verification_environment

11. Flanagan, C., Godefroid, P.: Dynamic partial-order reduction for model checking software. In: POPL 2005: Proceedings of the 32nd ACM SIGPLAN-SIGACT symposium on Principles of programming languages, pp. 110–121. ACM Press, New York (2005)

12. IEEE: IEEE Standard for Radix-independent Floating-point Arithmetic, ANSI/IEEE Std 854-1987 (1987)

13. Harrison, J.: Formal verification of square root algorithms. Formal Methods in System Design 22(2), 143–154 (2003); Guest Editors: Gopalakrishnan, G., Hunt, W., Jr.

14. Lamport, L.: The Win32 Threads API Specification (1996),
    http://research.microsoft.com/users/lamport/tla/threads/threads.html

15. Abadi, M., Lamport, L., Merz, S.: A tla solution to the rpc-memory specification problem. In: Formal Systems Specification, pp. 21–66 (1994)

16. Jackson, D.: Alloy: A lightweight object modelling notation. ACM Transactions on Software Engineering Methodologies 11(2), 256–290 (2002)

17. Jackson, D., Schechter, I., Shlyahter, H.: Alcoa: The alloy constraint analyzer. In: ICSE 2000: Proceedings of the 22nd international conference on Software engineering, pp. 730–733. ACM Press, New York (2000)

18. Jackson, D.: Alloy: A new technology for software modeling. In: Katoen, J.-P., Stevens, P. (eds.) TACAS 2002. LNCS, vol. 2280. Springer, Heidelberg (2002)

19. Georgelin, P., Pierre, L., Nguyen, T.: A formal specification of the MPI primitives and communication mechanisms. Technical report, LIM (1999)

20. Eijk, P.V., Diaz, M. (eds.): Formal Description Technique Lotos: Results of the Esprit Sedos Project. Elsevier Science Inc., New York, NY, USA (1989)

21. Siegel, S.F., Avrunin, G.: Analysis of mpi programs. Technical Report UM-CS-2003-036, Department of Computer Science, University of Massachusetts Amherst (2003)

22. Holzmann, G.: The model checker SPIN. IEEE Transactions on Software Engineering 23(5), 279–295 (1997)

23. Siegel, S.F., Avrunin, G.S.: Modeling wildcard-free MPI programs for verification. In: SIGPLAN Symposium, A.C.M. (ed.) ACM SIGPLAN Symposium on Principles and Practices of Parallel Programming, Chicago, pp. 95–106 (2005)

24. Siegel, S.F.: Model Checking Nonblocking MPI Programs. In: Cook, B., Podelski, A. (eds.) VMCAI 2007. LNCS, vol. 4349, pp. 44–58. Springer, Heidelberg (2007)

25. Barrus, S., Gopalakrishnan, G., Kirby, R.M., Palmer, R.: Verification of MPI programs using SPIN. Technical Report UUCS-04-008, The University of Utah (2004)

26. Palmer, R., Barrus, S., Yang, Y., Gopalakrishnan, G., Kirby, R.M.: Gauss: A framework for verifying scientific computing software. In: SoftMC: Workshop on Software Model Checking. ENTCS, vol. 953 (2005)

27. Pervez, S., Gopalakrishnan, G., Kirby, R.M., Thakur, R., Gropp, W.: Formal verification of programs that use MPI one-sided communication. In: Mohr, B., Träff, J.L., Worringen, J., Dongarra, J. (eds.) PVM/MPI 2006. LNCS, vol. 4192, pp. 30–39. Springer, Berlin, Heidelberg (2006)

28. Palmer, R., Gopalakrishnan, G., Kirby, R.M.: The communication semantics of the message passing interface. Technical Report UUCS-06-012, The University of Utah (2006)

29. Gropp, W.D.: Personal communication (2006)

30. Microsoft: Phoenix academic program (2007),
    http://research.microsoft.com/phoenix

31. Ellson, J., Gansner, E., Koutsofios, L., North, S.C., Woodhull, G.: Graphviz – open source graph drawing tools. In: Mutzel, P., Jünger, M., Leipert, S. (eds.) GD 2001. LNCS, vol. 2265, p. 483. Springer, Heidelberg (2002)
32. Lamport, L.: A +CAL user's manual (2006),
    http://research.microsoft.com/users/lamport/tla/p-manual.pdf
33. Nielson, F., Nielson, H.R., Hankin, C.: Principles of Program Analysis. Springer-Verlag New York, Inc., Secaucus, NJ, USA (1999)
34. Pacheco, P.S.: Parallel programming with MPI. Morgan Kaufmann Publishers Inc., San Francisco, CA, USA (1996)
35. Siegel, S.F., Avrunin, G.S.: Verification of mpi-based software for scientific computation. In: Graf, S., Mounier, L. (eds.) SPIN 2004. LNCS, vol. 2989, pp. 286–303. Springer, Heidelberg (2004)
36. Gropp, W., Thakur, R.: Issues in developing a thread-safe MPI implementation. In: Mohr, B., Träff, J.L., Worringen, J., Dongarra, J. (eds.) PVM/MPI 2006. LNCS, vol. 4192, pp. 12–21. Springer, Heidelberg (2006)

Analysis of a Session-Layer Protocol in mCRL2*
Verification of a Real-Life Industrial Implementation

Marko van Eekelen[1], Stefan ten Hoedt[2],
René Schreurs[2], and Yaroslav S. Usenko[3,4]

[1] Institute for Computing and Information Sciences, Radboud Universiteit Nijmegen,
P.O. Box 9102, 6500 HC Nijmegen, The Netherlands
[2] Aia Software B.V.
P.O. Box 38025, 6503 AA Nijmegen, The Netherlands
[3] Laboratory for Quality Software (LaQuSo), Technische Universiteit Eindhoven,
P.O. Box 513, 5600 MB Eindhoven, The Netherlands
[4] Centrum voor Wiskunde Informatica,
P.O. Box 94079, 1090 GB Amsterdam, The Netherlands

Abstract. This paper reports the analysis of an industrial implementation of the session-layer of a load-balancing software system. This software comprises 7.5 thousand lines of C code. It is used for distribution of the print jobs among several document processors (workers). A large part of this commercially used software system has been modeled closely and analyzed using process-algebraic techniques. Several critical issues were discovered. Since the model was close to the code, all problems that were found in the model, could be traced back to the actual code resulting in concrete suggestions for improvement of the code. All in all, the analysis significantly improved the quality of this real-life system.

1 Introduction

In this paper we consider the following real-life industrial case study. The ITP Document Platform (developed and marketed by Aia Software BV) enables organizations to produce critical business documents in a scalable and personalized environment. This application has a load-balancer, a process kernel that makes diverse document processors and clients communicate with each other, distribute and execute tasks. This system has been used satisfactorily for several years (in 2007 in over 25 countries by more than 800 customers). However, it comes every now and then in an undesirable state. The goal of the project was to investigate to what extent the inter-process communication and synchronization of this load-balancer could be modeled and analyzed. The desired results had to be detailed enough to give an advice on how to avoid these undesirable situations, and to suggest concrete code changes.

The project has been performed in the following phases: In a discussion with two employees of Aia Software (Stefan ten Hoedt and René Schreurs) we obtained

---

* This research was supported by SenterNovem Innovation Voucher Inv053967. The fourth author has also been supported by NWO Hefboom project 641.000.407.

S. Leue and P. Merino (Eds.): FMICS 2007, LNCS 4916, pp. 182–199, 2008.

the overall idea of the structure and the behavior of the software in general and the parts to be modeled in particular. The relevant parts were modeled in mCRL2 [1]. The session layer of the load-balancer protocol was modeled quite closely to the C code. Both the higher-level application layer and the underlying TCP-socket layer were modeled in an abstract manner. The code and the model were reviewed by the LaQuSo-modeler and the Aia-developer in order to achieve the maximal matching. This led to a number of changes in the model, as well as to a number of questions about the code and a number of concrete desired properties that could be analyzed. The model was analyzed with the help of the model-checking techniques of the mCRL2 toolset w.r.t. deadlock-freedom and a number of other starvation and consistency properties that were formulated together with the client. This revealed 6 problems in the C code. These problems were accepted by Aia Software and incorporated to the production release of the software system.

The type of analysis presented in this paper is as such not new. It was performed before using different kinds of model checkers (e.g. imperative [2] and declarative [1]: see also the related work paragraph below). Noteworthy characteristics of our work are that the model is very close to the code, the code is relatively large (7500 lines), the code has been running within a commercial product for years and it has been improved several times while problems still kept occurring, errors have been found that led to code improvements and finally, problems regarding the code have not occurred since the code was corrected. This project was done with a model checker based on Process Algebra [3]. It is the first time that a project with such characteristics was achieved with a model checker based on Process Algebra.

Related Work. Many projects study the verification of the *design* of a software system. Karl Palmskog in his Master Thesis [4] studied using the SPIN model checker the design of a Session Management Protocol developed at Ericsson Research. He has discovered a design flaw. This study was done on the level of the design without looking carefully at the implemented code. Also on the design level, in [5] Janicki and He present the verification of a Wireless Transaction Protocol design in SPIN. Another verification project concerning model checking of the design of a software system in mCRL2 is the parking garage project done by Mathijssen and Pretorius [6]. In [7] Brock and Jackson prove correctness of an industrial implementation of a 'fault tolerant computer' by creating a small abstract model in CSP.

A real-life *code* example was recently studied by Hessel and Pettersson [8] with nice results. In contrast to our project, they do not model the code but use a black-box testing approach.

In [9] an application of the Verisoft model checking approach to a software system from Lucent is presented. The model checking was applied as a part of the testing procedure during the software development. The paper reports about a large number of revealed errors, most of which indicated incorrect variable initializations.

A framework for C code analysis with CADP [10] is presented in [11], where the methods of process graph extraction and generation of an LTS for a C program are described. In [12] the model checker MOPS was used to model-check safety properties of single-threaded C programs. This paper reports on automatic analysis of a million lines of code.

The Java Pathfinder tool is described in [13] as a tool that is used to find deadlocks and other behavioral properties in java programs. The tool has been used to analyse software systems at NASA. It is also used as the back-end model checker of the Bandera project [14]. The Bandera project uses abstraction techniques based on abstraction-based program specialization: a combination of abstract interpretation and partial evaluation.

Research at Microsoft Corporation led by Thomas Ball has shown significant results for a restricted subset of programs: device drivers. Using an automatic analysis engine - called SLAM - that combines model checking with symbolic execution for the language C, they have successfully found many errors in many real-life industrial device drivers [15]. They do not support analysis of multi-threaded systems.

Probably, the most related work is performed by Holzmann and Smith in [16]. Using SPIN they followed the development of a piece of telephone call processing software of about 1600 lines of C code. They verified successfully so-called feature requirements. They found many errors in different stages of the development.

Organization of the paper. The paper is organized as follows. Section 2 presents the case study and the problems that were to be investigated. Section 3 presents the mCRL2 language and the toolset and the way they were used in the modeling of the case study. Section 4 presents details on the analysis with the mCRL2 toolset and the issues that were detected. Section 5 contains conclusions and possibilities for future work. In the Appendix a part of the C code and the corresponding part of the mCRL2 model are presented. The whole mCRL2 model can be found in the Appendix of [17].

2   Intelligent Text Processing (ITP) and Its Load-Balancer

The Intelligent Text Processing system is used to prepare large quantities of documents to be printed. Sometimes it is done in an interactive way, where additional information is being asked from the client during the processing. In the early versions of the ITP software the *clients* could directly communicate to the *document processors*, but with the increased complexity of the processing jobs a coordinating mechanism was needed. The task of the *load-balancer* is to distribute the jobs of the clients to the available document processors, without actually changing the application layer of the client-server communication protocol too much (see Figure 1).

Due to the evolutionary way the ITP software was developed in the late nineties, the load-balancer has been implemented in C on the Windows platform making use of the Windows Socket Library. The possibility of using a standard

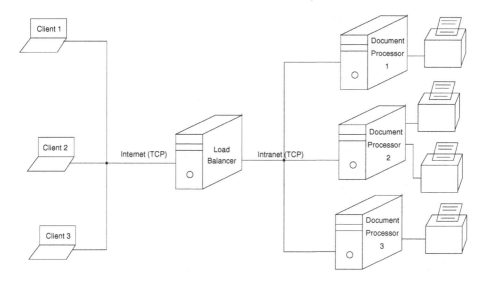

Fig. 1. ITP and a Load-Balancer in it

solution for load-balancing, like the Linux virtual server, has not been used for a number of reasons.

A typical use-case scenario of the load-balancer deployment is presented as a Message Sequence Chart on Figure 2. There, a client of the load-balancer communicates with the client object and a document processor communicates with the document processor object. The client sends a request to print and the document processor sends a request for work. After that the document processor object asks the client object for work and gets the answer. At this point the client and the document processor objects are linked together by a partnership link. Further, the document processor asks for additional data and goes to a sleeping state. The client object gets the data from the client and wakes up the document processor object. The document processor object transfers the data to the document processor.

2.1   Issues and Artifacts

The load-balancer software was developed in the late nineties and has been tested both at AIA and at clients' environments since that time. The system has been in use in production for quite some time now. During testing and maintenance a number of issues with the software have been fixed, but some items remained unsolved till the beginning of our project.

Most of these 'difficult' issues could be classified as follows:

 – the load-balancer would get to a state where it did not respond at all to the requests of neither clients nor document processors;
 – the load-balancer would ignore the document processors that were free and willing to accept jobs;

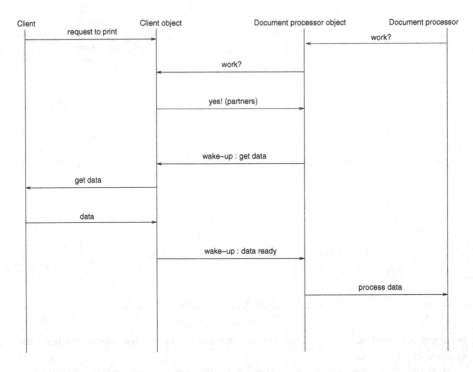

Fig. 2. A typical use-case scenario of the load-balancer

- a client would not get any response from the load-balancer about the status of its jobs.

These issues occurred in rare situations, mostly on particular hardware configurations. Reproducing such errors was very difficult or impossible. Restarting the system solved the issue but it could occur again somewhere in the future.

The company provided the source code in C for Windows (7681 lines) and the application layer protocol documentation. Further information was communicated during meetings, via phone calls and e-mail. Analysis of the artifacts revealed that the system was a multi-threaded Windows application using mutual exclusion primitives (mutexes, semaphores) and multiple event synchronization (WaitForMultipleObjects). For the asynchronous I/O and the network communication the Windows Socket Administration and call-back functions were used. The reverse engineering of the design revealed the structure of the load-balancer (see Figure 3). Here each client and each document processor object has a request queue and a partnership link to a possible partner. Each such object implements a finite state machine that first waits for one of the two events, either a network socket event or a wake-up event from a partner. After that, a certain action is performed and the object proceeds to a new state.

Based on the source code and the revealed architecture of the load-balancer the following properties were considered to be important for the further analysis.

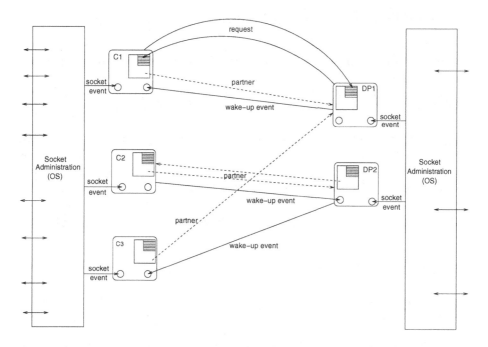

Fig. 3. Architecture of the load-balancer

- The software should be free from *deadlocks*.
- Certain log messages are considered to be of critical importance. These should never occur as they indicate that there is something fundamentally wrong with the system.
- The partnership links should be consistent, e.g., if the partner of A is $B > 0$ (0 means no partner), then the partner of B is either A or 0.
- Waiting for a partner should only be done if the partner link is not 0. This boils down to the fact that a document processor may not be in a sleeping state if it has no partner (except when a request is pending to it).
- The number of times a thread acquires a lock should be limited. In case a lock is acquired a multiple number of times it has to be released the same number of times. If a thread acquires a lock in a loop, a certain bound induced by the operating system can be reached, resulting in an undesired behavior. Moreover, a high number of nested lock acquisitions may indicate a logical error in the program.
- The number of requests that are pending in the system should be limited.

3   Modeling in mCRL2

To check the desired properties part of the system had to be formally modelled in a language that supports model-checking. For the reasons of available expertise we decided to use mCRL2 and its toolset.

3.1   Description of the mCRL2 Language

mCRL2 [1] is a process algebraic language that includes data and time. It is an extension of the language μCRL [18] with multi-actions, built-in data types and local communication functions instead of a single global one. mCRL2 is basically intended to study description and analysis techniques for (large) distributed systems. The abbreviation mCRL2 stands for milli Common Representation Language 2.

An mCRL2 specification consists of two parts. The first part specifies the data types, the second part defines the processes. Data are represented as terms of some sort, for example 2, cos(pi), and concat(L1,L2) could be terms of sort natural number, real number and list, respectively.

The process equations are defined in the following way. Starting from a set Act of actions that can be parameterized with data, processes are defined by means of guarded recursive equations and the following operations.

First, there is a constant δ ($\delta \notin$ Act) that cannot perform any action and is called deadlock or inaction.

Next, there are the sequential composition operation $\cdot$ and the alternative composition operation $+$. The process $x \cdot y$ first behaves as x and if x successfully terminates continues to behave as y. The process $x + y$ can either do an action of x and continue to behave as x or do an action of y and continue to behave as y.

Interleaving parallelism is modeled by the operation $\|$. The process $x \| y$ is the result of interleaving actions of x and y, except that actions from x and y also synchronize to multiactions. So a $\|$ b = a$\cdot$b + b$\cdot$a + a$|$b. The communication operation Γ allows multiactions to communicate: parameterized actions a(d) and b(d') in $\Gamma_{\{a|b \to c\}}$(a(d) $|$ b(d')) communicate to c(d), provided $d = d'$.

To enforce that actions in processes x and y synchronize, we can prevent actions from happening on their own, using the encapsulation operator ∂_H. The process $\partial_H(x)$ can perform all actions of x except that actions in the set H are blocked. So, in $\partial_{\{a,b\}}(\Gamma_{\{a|b \to c\}}(x \| y))$ the actions a and b are forced to synchronize to c. Another way to restrict process behaviour is the allow operation. By specifying a list of multiactions one can prohibit all other multiactions by renaming them to δ. So $\nabla_{\{a|b\}}$(a $\|$ b) = a $|$ b.

We assume the existence of a special action τ ($\tau \notin$ Act) that is internal and cannot be directly observed. The hiding operator τ_I renames the actions in the set I to τ. By hiding all internal communications of a process only the external actions remain.

The following two operators combine data with processes. The sum operator $\sum_{d:D} p(d)$ describes the process that can execute the process $p(d)$ for some value d selected from the sort D. The conditional operator $\_ \to \_ \diamond \_$ describes the *if-then-else*. The process $b \to x \diamond y$ (where b is a boolean) has the behavior of x if b is true and the behavior of y if b is false. The expression $b \to x$ is a syntactic sugar representing the *if-then* construction. It is an abbreviation to $b \to x \diamond \delta$.

3.2   The mCRL2 Toolset

The mCRL2 toolset (`http://www.mcrl2.org`) has been developed at Technical University of Eindhoven to support formal reasoning about systems specified in mCRL2. It is based on term rewriting techniques and on formal transformation of process-algebraic and data terms. At the moment it allows to generate state spaces, search for deadlocks and particular actions, perform symbolic optimizations for mCRL2 specifications and simulate them.

The toolset is constructed around a restricted form of mCRL2, namely the Linear Process Specification (LPS) format. An LPS contains a single process definition of the *linear form*:

$$\texttt{proc}\ \ P(x{:}D) = \sum_{i \in I} \sum_{y_i : E_i} c_i(x, y_i) \rightarrow \alpha_i(x, y_i) \cdot P(g_i(x, y_i))$$

$$\texttt{init}\ \ P(d_0);$$

where data expressions of the form $d(x_1, \ldots, x_n)$ contain at most free variables from $\{x_1, \ldots, x_n\}$, I is a finite index set, and for $i \in I$ the following are:

- $c_i(x, y_i)$ are boolean expressions representing the conditions,
- $\alpha_i(x, y_i)$ is a multiaction $\mathsf{a}_i^1(f_i^1(x, y_i)) \mid \cdots \mid \mathsf{a}_i^{n_i}(f_i^{n_i}(x, y_i))$, where $f_i^k(x, y_i)$ (for $1 \leq k \leq n_i$) are the parameters of action name a_i^k,
- $g_i(x, y_i)$ is an expression of sort D representing the next state of the process definition P;
- d_0 is a closed data expression;
- $\sum_{i \in I} p_i$ is a shorthand for $p_1 + \cdots + p_n$, where $I = \{1, \ldots, n\}$.

The form of the summand as described above is sometimes presented as the *condition-action-effect* rule. In a particular state d and for some data value e the multiaction $\alpha_i(d, e)$ can be done if condition $c_i(d, e)$ holds. The effect of the action on the state is given by the fact that the next state is $g_i(x, y_i)$.

The tool `mcrl22lps` checks whether a certain specification is a well formed mCRL2 and attempts to transform it into a linearized (i.e. LPS) form (See [19] for the detail of the linearization). All other tools use this linearized format as their starting point (see Figure 4).

These tools come in four kinds:

1. a tool (`xsim`) to step through the process specified in the LPS;
2. a tool (`lps2lts`) to generate the labeled transition system (LTS) underlying a given LPS;
3. several tools to optimize the LPSs:
   (a) `lpsrewr`, normalizes an LPS by rewriting the data terms in it;
   (b) `lpsconstelm`, removes data parameters that are constant throughout any run of the LPS;
   (c) `lpsparelm`, reduces the state space of the transition system by removing the data parameters and sum variables that do not influence the behavior of the system,
   (d) `lpsstructelm`, expands variables of compound data types;
4. a tool (`lpspp`) to print the linearized specification.

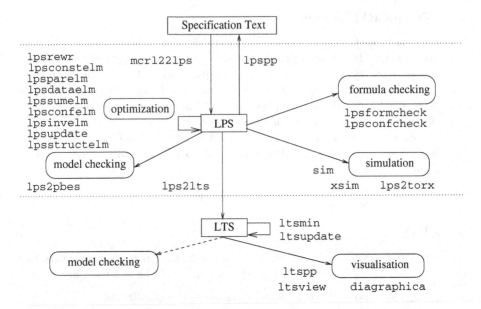

Fig. 4. The mCRL2 Toolset (www.mcrl2.org)

3.3 The Load-Balancer in mCRL2

For the modeling we concentrated on the session layer of the load-balancer protocol. This layer is responsible for controlling the connections with the clients and the document processors, e.g., establishing, breaking the connection, handling non-expected connection breaks and network errors. Sending and receiving of data goes through this layer as well.

The lower-level interface (back-end) of the session layer protocol goes to the Windows Socket Administration (WSA) library. This library is a part of the operating system and is responsible for sending and accepting network socket events from the application. In our mCRL2 model WSA is modelled as a part of the environment.

The high-level interface (front-end) of the session layer performs calls to the application layer of the protocol. This happens when a certain part of data is received from a client or a document processor in a state when data is expected, or a connection is broken and this fact has to be noticed by the application layer (sometimes the session layer can close the session itself and no action from the application layer is required). The code of the application layer happens to be a rather large piece of homogeneous code, a large case distinction so to say. We modelled it by making an over-approximation of all possible behaviors and choosing them in a non-deterministic way. By doing this we ended up with less than ten alternatives for the application layer.

The model of the session layer follows the C code in a way to make it as precise as possible. The model resembles the request handling and the network events handling in most details, following the state-transition paradigm implemented in the code. Appendix B presents a part of the mCRL2 models that corresponds to the request handling session layer part of the C-implementation in Appendix A. The model and the code in these appendices follow each other rather closely. The sizes of the two specifications are more or less the same.

The shared variables and arrays that are used for inter-thread communications are modelled by separate processes. Parts of the operating system are modelled by processes as well. Below an mCRL2 process for the mutual exclusion primitive of Windows (MSDN Mutex objects) is presented. A thread can acquire a mutex a multiple number of times and has to release it the same number of times.

$\mathsf{Lock}(owner{:}Nat, count{:}Nat) =$

$$\sum_{tid:Pos} (owner == 0 \lor owner == tid) \rightarrow \mathsf{lock}(tid) \cdot \mathsf{Lock}(tid, count + 1)$$

$$+ \, (owner > 0) \rightarrow \mathsf{unlock}(Nat2Pos(owner)) \cdot$$
$$\mathsf{Lock}(if(count == 1, 0, owner), Int2Nat(count - 1))$$
$$+ \, (count > nMaxLock) \rightarrow \_\mathsf{error}(MaxLock) \cdot \delta;$$

The process Lock has two natural numbers as parameters. The first one represents the id of the thread that owns the mutex, or is equal to 0 if the mutex is free. The second parameter is used to count how many times the mutex has been acquired.

The actions lock and unlock are parameterized by positive numbers representing the id of the locking/unlocking thread. Such a thread would perform a corresponding $\_\mathsf{lock}$ or $\_\mathsf{unlock}$ action parameterized with its id. The two corresponding actions (with and without the underscore) are then forced to synchronize by the process defining the entire system.

The first summand of the process Lock says that it can be acquired (by performing a $\_\mathsf{lock}$ action) by a thread with its id represented by the variable tid. This is allowed for a thread with any id in case the mutex is free (condition $owner == 0$), or for the owner thread ($owner == tid$). After this acquisition the lock is owned by the thread identified by tid and the acquisition number counter is incremented.

The second summand says that a non-free mutex can be unlocked by the owner. Here we use $Nat2Pos$ to cast the value of the natural variable $owner$ to the positive number. This function maps 0 to 0 and any number bigger than 1 to itself. Given the condition $owner > 0$, this cast is always the identity mapping. The function $Int2Nat$ is used to cast the integral value of $count - 1$ to the natural number. It maps the negative integers to 0 and does not change the non-negative integers. It can be shown that $owner > 0 \implies count > 0$ is an $invariant$ of the Lock process. Therefore, this cast is also an identity mapping.

The third summand lets the process perform an $\_\mathsf{error}$ action if the value of $count$ reaches a certain limit $nMaxLock$. In this way, by checking for absence of $\_\mathsf{error}$ actions, one can prove that the mutex is acquired in a nested way less than $nMaxLock$ number of times.

3.4 Modeling the Properties

It turned out that all the desired properties (except for the deadlock absence) could be modeled as safety properties and checked by adding _error actions to the model and check for them. For example, the partner consistency property from Section 2.1 is modelled as the following summand in the SharedConnection process:

$$\sum_{cid:Nat} \sum_{n:Nat} (n \neq 0 \ \wedge \ getpartner(connections.n) \neq 0 \ \wedge$$
$$getpartner(connections.n) \neq cid) \rightarrow$$
$$\mathsf{setConnectionPartner}(cid, n) \cdot \_\mathsf{error}(WrongPartners) \cdot \delta$$

Here $getpartner(connections.n)$ gives the current partner link value for the connection n. Once an attempt to change the partner of connection cid to the value n is performed by one of the threads (by performing the corresponding _setConnectionPartner action with the actual parameters), the condition is checked and if it is true, the error action is enabled. The condition says that neither n nor the partner of connection n is 0 (meaning 'no partner') and the partner of n is not cid. The latter condition means the actual partnership link inconsistency between n and cid.

4 Analysis and Issues

The model has been analyzed for the absence of deadlocks and for validity of certain properties. These properties were incorporated in the model itself so that an _error action would occur if the property is violated. In this way the verification is performed by the explicit generation of the entire state-space and by looking for the _error actions and the deadlocks. Once one of this is found in a particular state, a minimal trace to this state gives a counterexample.

Performing the analysis takes only a few steps that can be activated from the command line. To give the reader an idea how this is done in practice, we give the actual commands with their actual parameters and options. As the first step, the linearization of the model takes place: with the command `mcrl22lps ITPpatched.mcrl2 ITPpatched.lps` that produces the linearized version of the model. Next, we apply the optimization steps on the LPS: `lpsrewr ITPpatched.lps | lpsconstelm > ITPpatched_opt.lps`. The actual generation of the transition system and checking for the properties is done with the command `lps2lts -vrDt -a _error -R jittyc ITPpatched_opt.lps` where the -D option enables deadlock checking and -a _error enables checking for _error actions. The -t option enables generation of trace files. In case a deadlock or an _error action is found, a trace file is generated with one of the shortest traces to that deadlock state or a state where the _error action is possible. The trace files can be printed out with `tracepp` or simulated in the `xsim` simulator.

4.1   Experiments and Results

The analysis has been performed by an exhaustive generation of the underlying state space using the mCRL2 toolset. The experiments were carried out on a computer with 2.6GHz 64 bit AMD CPUs and 128Gb RAM running Linux. The execution times and the resulting numbers of states and transitions are presented in Table 1. The mCRL2 state space generator uses the depth-first search algorithm (by default), and the levels are the levels of depth reached by performing the search. The cases with the total number of clients+document processors larger than 4 could not be fully analyzed.

4.2   Detected Issues

An early analysis of the model revealed multiple modeling problems. After resolving these initial modeling problems, the model was compared with the original C code by both the modeler and the author of the C code working together. This revealed some essential difference between the code and the model. Once these differences were resolved, the mCRL2 tools were applied and the following issues were detected.

– **Issue 1.** In one case partner links were inconsistent. This was due to the fact that in one place in the C code the 'forward' partner link was set to 0 and the 'backward' one was forgotten. This piece of code was found 'unclear' during the model-code comparison activity, and later was confirmed to be erroneous by the mCRL2 toolset finding a shortest trace to the property violation.
– In two cases a document processor could end-up in a sleeping state without having a partner.
  - **Issue 2.** In one case this happened because the client's partner link was set to 0 before actually waking up the document processor (happened due to an earlier bug 'fix'). This problem was found by the model-code comparison and later confirmed by the mCRL2 toolset.
  - **Issue 3.** In another case it was simply forgotten to wake-up the document processor. This problem can be clearly explained by a use-case

Table 1. Execution time (days, hours, minutes and seconds), number of levels, number of states and number of transitions (thousands, millions and billions) for different numbers of clients and document processors (DPs)

clients	DPs	time	levels	states	transitions
1	1	7m 38s	237	368k	796k
1	2	1h 42m	365	9.8m	21m
2	1	4h 52m	442	28m	61m
1	3	36h	480	209m	455.6m
2	2	7d6h	550	1.5b	31.9b
3	1	9d3h	637	1.8b	38.9b

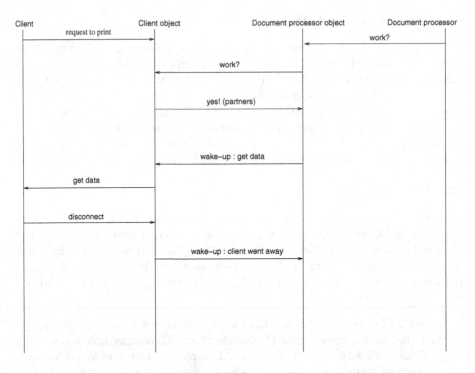

Fig. 5. A faulty scenario

scenario in Figure 5. This use-case scenario is similar to the one presented in Figure 2, with the difference that after sending a request for data to the client this client disconnects, instead of providing the actual data. This problem was found using the tools.

– It also happened that critical logs could occur in the program:
  - **Issue 4.** A client could send a request to disconnect to itself in a wrong state, because changing of a state was forgotten;
  - **Issue 5.** Request to wake up could lead to an inappropriate state change when a document processor was in the middle of a disconnection (found to be non-critical).
– **Issue 6.** The number of requests sent to a client could exceed the preset limit and could possibly be unbounded. This happened when a document processor sent a request to disconnect to its partner client and did not break the partnership afterwards.

These issues were analyzed and accepted by Aia and led to modifications of the original C code. The corresponding modifications, fixing the problems mentioned above, were also brought into the model. The subsequent analysis of the model revealed no more property violations.

Most of the issues were detected in the case of 1 client and 1 document processor, while the rest in 1-2 or 2-1 situations. Analysis of the situations with more clients and document processors did not lead to detection of new issues.

5   Conclusions and Future Work

We modelled the session layer of the ITP load-balancer in mCRL2 such that the model is close to the actual C code. A number of properties were verified using the mCRL2 toolset. This led to the discovery of 6 issues that were easily traced back to the actual C code. The code was repaired and also the corrections were brought into the model. The resulting model was verified with respect to the desired properties by checking the entire state space for several configurations.

mCRL2 could be used successfully in this industrial setting of a load-balancer for document production. A part of the operating system services (sockets, locks, events, etc.) could also be modeled. Unfortunately the verification could only be done on a restricted setting, so an improvement of the toolset is required for bigger cases. Also an automatic conformance checking of the model w.r.t. the code could be of interest.

Lessons Learned: The case study gave the researchers more confidence that real-life examples can actually be dealt with using a close-to-code model. It increases the motivation to further improve the power of the analysis tool and to start investigating code generation from the model (the proximity to the code may simplify code generation).

Aia released the new version with the improved code about half a year ago. While previously it happened now and then that their systems infrastructure came to a standstill and had to be restarted again, this situation never occurred anymore with the new release. The infrastructure (which has the load-balancer as the most critical part) kept running all the time.

They have now a working reference model in mCRL2 of a crucial part of their load-balancer software. In principle, they are able to incorporate code changes into the model and check whether the properties still hold for the new version. In practice, they probably need assistance of the researchers in the beginning. Aia has acquired an increased interest in using formal models for analyzing software quality aspects, in particular for the most critical parts of their system.

Future Work: In the future an improvement of the toolset could lead to model checking of bigger cases. Analyzing more properties of the session layer (e.g. verifying client notification of document processor failures) could lead to certification of the software. If we want to improve the relation between the model and the code, we can consider code generation directly from the model.

References

1. Groote, J.F., Mathijssen, A.H.J., Reniers, M.A., Usenko, Y.S., van Weerdenburg, M.J.: The formal specification language mCRL2. In: Proc. Methods for Modelling Software Systems. Number 06351 in Dagstuhl Seminar Proceedings (2007)
2. Holzmann, G.J.: Software model checking with spin. Advances in Computers 65, 78–109 (2005)
3. Bergstra, J.A., Ponse, A., Smolka, S.A. (eds.): Handbook of Process Algebra. Elsevier, Amsterdam (2001)

4. Palmskog, K.: Verification of the session management protocol. Master's thesis, School of Computer Science and Communication, Royal Institute of Technology, Stockholm (2006)
5. He, Y.-T., Janicki, R.: Verifying protocols by model checking: A case study of the wireless application protocol and the model checker spin. In: CASCON 2004: Proceedings of the 2004 conference of the Centre for Advanced Studies on Collaborative research, pp. 174–188. IBM Press (2004)
6. Mathijssen, A., Pretorius, A.J.: Verified design of an automated parking garage. In: Brim, L., Haverkort, B.R., Leucker, M., van de Pol, J. (eds.) FMICS 2006. LNCS, vol. 4346, pp. 165–180. Springer, Heidelberg (2007)
7. Brock, N.A., Jackson, D.M.: Formal verification of a fault tolerant computer. In: Proc. 11th Digital Avionics Systems Conference (IEEE/AIAA), pp. 132–137 (1992)
8. Hessel, A., Pettersson, P.: Model-based testing of a wap gateway: An industrial case-study. In: Brim, L., Haverkort, B.R., Leucker, M., van de Pol, J. (eds.) FMICS 2006 and PDMC 2006. LNCS, vol. 4346, pp. 116–131. Springer, Heidelberg (2007)
9. Chandra, S., Godefroid, P., Palm, C.: Software model checking in practice: an industrial case study. In: ICSE, pp. 431–441. ACM, New York (2002)
10. Fernandez, J.C., Garavel, H., Kerbrat, R.M.A., Mounier, L., Sighireanu, M.: CADP: A protocol validation and verification toolbox. In: Proceedings of the 8th Conference on Computer-Aided Verification, New Brunswick, New Jersey, USA, pp. 437–440 (August 1996)
11. del Mar Gallardo, M., Merino, P., Sanán, D.: Towards model checking c code with open/cæsar. In: Barjis, J., Ultes-Nitsche, U., Augusto, J.C. (eds.) MSVVEIS, pp. 198–201. INSTICC Press (2006)
12. Chen, H., Dean, D., Wagner, D.: Model checking one million lines of c code. In: NDSS, The Internet Society (2004)
13. Visser, W., Mehlitz, P.C.: Model checking programs with java pathfinder. In: Godefroid, P. (ed.) SPIN 2005. LNCS, vol. 3639, p. 27. Springer, Heidelberg (2005)
14. Iosif, R., Dwyer, M.B., Hatcliff, J.: Translating java for multiple model checkers: The bandera back-end. Formal Methods in System Design 26(2), 137–180 (2005)
15. Ball, T., Bounimova, E., Cook, B., Levin, V., Lichtenberg, J., McGarvey, C., Ondrusek, B., Rajamani, S.K., Ustuner, A.: Thorough static analysis of device drivers. In: Berbers, Y., Zwaenepoel, W. (eds.) EuroSys, pp. 73–85. ACM, New York (2006)
16. Holzmann, G.J., Smith, M.H.: Automating software feature verification. Bell Labs Technical Journal 5(2), 72–87 (2000)
17. van Eekelen, M., ten Hoedt, S., Schreurs, R., Usenko, Y.S.: Modeling and verifying a real-life industrial session-layer protocol in mCRL2. Technical Report ICIS-R07014, Radboud University Nijmegen (June 2007)
18. Groote, J.F., Ponse, A.: The syntax and semantics of μCRL. In: Ponse, A., Verhoef, C., van Vlijmen, S.F.M. (eds.) Algebra of Communicating Processes 1994. Workshop in Computing, pp. 26–62. Springer, Heidelberg (1995)
19. Usenko, Y.S.: Linearization in μCRL. PhD thesis, Eindhoven University of Technology (December 2002)

A   Part of C Code of the Request Handling

```
 1   while (Interface->Request != (REQUEST *) NULL){
       REQUEST *Req = Interface->Request;
       DWORD ID = Req->Connection - Req->Connection->Interface->Connections;
       switch (Req->Request){
       case requestDisconnect:
 6       /* Partner requests a disconnect */
         if (Req->Connection->State != STATE_PENDING &&
             Req->Connection->State != STATE_SLEEP){
           if (Req->Connection->State == STATE_EVENT){
           CancelEvent (Req->Connection);
11         } else if (Req->Connection->State != STATE_DISCONNECT&&
                      Req->Connection->State != STATE_BREAK      ){
           LogMessage (ClassError,
             L"Disconnect: Forcing illegal state switch %s->%s on socket %d",
                        ShowConnState(Req->Connection->State),
16                      ShowConnState(STATE_DISCONNECT),
                        ID);
         }else {
            /*Our own connection was already shutting down. Just confirm it.*/
         }
21       }
         if (Req->Connection->State != STATE_BREAK){
           Req->Connection->State = STATE_DISCONNECT;
         }
         break;
26     case requestSend:
       case requestReceive:
         if (Req->Connection->State != STATE_PENDING &&
             Req->Connection->State != STATE_SLEEP){
           CONNECTION *Partner;
31         if (Req->Connection->State == STATE_BREAK     ||
               Req->Connection->State == STATE_DISCONNECT){
             /* Lost connection to client */
           LogMessage (ClassError,
                   L"Remote host closed connection unexpectedly on socket %d.",
36                 ID);
           /* Detach our connection */
         } else {
          LogMessage (ClassError,
            L"Send/Receive: Forcing illegal state switch %s->%s on socket %d",
41                   ShowConnState(Req->Connection->State),
                     ShowConnState(STATE_TRANSACTION),
                     ID);
         }
           /* Remove our link to the partner */
46         WaitHandle (PartnerLock);
           Partner = Req->Connection->Partner;
           Req->Connection->Partner = (CONNECTION *) NULL;

           /* Wake the partner */
51         if (Partner != (CONNECTION *) NULL){
             if (Partner->Partner == Req->Connection){
               Partner->Partner = (CONNECTION *) NULL;
             }
             WakeConnection (Partner);
56         }
           ReleaseMutex (PartnerLock);
           /* And close our socket */
           if (Req->Connection->State != STATE_BREAK){
             Req->Connection->State = STATE_DISCONNECT;
61         }
           break;
         }
         /* Start the requested operation */
         Req->Connection->State = STATE_TRANSACTION;
```

```
66      Req->Connection->Protocol = Req->NewState;
        Req->Connection->Read = (Req->Request == requestReceive);
        Req->Connection->Write = (Req->Request == requestSend);
        Req->Connection->Size = Req->Size;
        Req->Connection->Buffer = Req->Data;
71      break;
     case requestWakeUp:
        /* Our partner finished its operations and tries to wake us up. */
        if (Req->Connection->State == STATE_TRANSACTION){
           /*
76          * We are already awake and handling transactions.
            * Don't change anything.
            */
        } else if (Req->Connection->State != STATE_PENDING    &&
                   Req->Connection->State != STATE_SLEEP){
81         /* Detach our connection */
           LogMessage (ClassError,
                 L"Wake up: Forcing illegal state switch %s->%s on socket %d",
                      ShowConnState(Req->Connection->State),
                      ShowConnState(STATE_TRANSACTION),
86                    ID);
        } else {
           Req->Connection->State = STATE_TRANSACTION;
           Req->Connection->Read = FALSE;
           Req->Connection->Write = FALSE;
91      }
        break;
     default:
        LogMessage (ClassError, L"INTERNAL ERROR: State %d.", Req->Request);
        break;
96   }
     Interface->Request = Req->Next;
     Free (Req);

     /* Reset event flag so we won't delay processing the requests */
101  SetEvent (Interface->Pending);
  }
```

B   Corresponding Part of the mCRL2 Model

```
   TCP_ProcessRequests(tid:Pos,pending:Bool,nConns:Nat)=
     sum reqs:List(REQUEST).
3     _getRequests(tid,reqs).
      (reqs==[])->_unlockPartner(tid).
                  (pending->_setPendingEvent(tid).
                           TCP_WaitEvent(tid,nConns)
                          <>TCP_WaitEvent(tid,nConns)
8                 )
                 <>_popRequest(tid).
                   TCP_ProcessRequest(tid,head(reqs),nConns);

   TCP_ProcessRequest(tid:Pos,req:REQUEST,nConns:Nat)=
13   % first we need to get the state of the connection in the request:
     sum state:STATE._getConnectionState(tid,getcid(req),state).(

     ( (getname(req)==requestDisconnect &&
         (state==STATE_BREAK ||
18        state==STATE_DISCONNECT)
       )||
         (getname(req)==requestWakeUp &&
          (state==STATE_TRANSACTION ||
          state==STATE_DISCONNECT ||
23        state==STATE_BREAK)
         )
     )-> TCP_ProcessRequests(tid,true,nConns)<> % do nothing in these cases

     (getname(req)==requestDisconnect)->(
```

```
28          (state==STATE_PENDING ||
             state==STATE_SLEEP)
             -> _setConnectionState(tid,getcid(req),STATE_DISCONNECT).
                TCP_ProcessRequests(tid,true,nConns)<>

33          % otherwise log and force.
            (state==SOCK_FREE ||
             state==SOCK_ACCEPT ||
             state==SOCK_READING ||
             state==SOCK_WRITING ||
38           state==SOCK_SHUTDOWN ||
             state==STATE_TRANSACTION)
             -> _log(tid,LogDisconnectForsingIllegalStateSwitch(getcid(req),
                                                        STATE_DISCONNECT)).
                error(CriticalLog).
43              _setConnectionState(tid,getcid(req),STATE_DISCONNECT).
                TCP_ProcessRequests(tid,true,nConns)
          )<>

          (getname(req)==requestSend ||
48         getname(req)==requestReceive)->(
            (state==STATE_PENDING ||
             state==STATE_SLEEP)
             ->  _setConnectionStateProtocolReadWrite(
                    tid,
53                  getcid(req),
                    STATE_TRANSACTION,
                    getnewprotocol(req),
                    getname(req)==requestReceive,
                    getname(req)==requestSend).
58              TCP_ProcessRequests(tid,true,nConns)+
            (state==STATE_BREAK ||
             state==STATE_DISCONNECT)
             -> _log(tid,LogRemoteHostClosedUnexpectedly(getcid(req))).
                TCP_ProcessRequest_Close(tid,getcid(req),nConns)+
63
            (state==STATE_EVENT ||
             state==SOCK_FREE ||
             state==SOCK_ACCEPT ||
             state==SOCK_READING ||
68           state==SOCK_WRITING ||
             state==SOCK_SHUTDOWN ||
             state==STATE_TRANSACTION)
             -> _log(tid,LogSendReceiveForsingIllegalStateSwitch(getcid(req),
                                                        STATE_TRANSACTION)).
73              error(CriticalLog).
                TCP_ProcessRequest_Close(tid,getcid(req),nConns)
          )<>

          (getname(req)==requestWakeUp)->(
78          (state==STATE_PENDING ||
             state==STATE_SLEEP)
             -> _setConnectionStateReadWrite(tid,getcid(req),
                                             STATE_TRANSACTION,false,false).
                TCP_ProcessRequests(tid,true,nConns)<>
83          (state==STATE_BREAK ||
             state==STATE_EVENT ||
             state==SOCK_FREE ||
             state==SOCK_ACCEPT ||
             state==SOCK_READING ||
88           state==SOCK_WRITING ||
             state==SOCK_SHUTDOWN)
             ->_log(tid,LogWakeUpForsingIllegalStateSwitch(getcid(req),state)).
                error(CriticalLog).
                TCP_ProcessRequests(tid,true,nConns)
93        )
      );
```

Automatic Certification of Java Source Code in Rewriting Logic[*]

Mauricio Alba-Castro[1,2], María Alpuente[1], and Santiago Escobar[1]

[1] Universidad Politécnica de Valencia, Spain
{alpuente,sescobar}@dsic.upv.es
[2] Universidad Autónoma de Manizales, Colombia
malba@autonoma.edu.co

Abstract. In this paper we propose an abstract certification technique for Java which is based on rewriting logic, a very general *logical and semantic framework* efficiently implemented in the functional programming language Maude. Starting from a specification of the Java semantics written in Maude, we develop an abstract, finite-state operational semantics also written in Maude which is appropriate for program verification. As a by-product of the abstract verification, a dependable safety certificate is delivered which consists of a set of (abstract) rewriting proofs that can be easily checked by the code consumer using a standard rewriting logic engine. Our certification methodology extends to other programming languages by simply replacing the concrete semantics of Java by a semantics for the programming language at hand. The abstract proof-carrying code technique has been implemented and successfully tested on several examples, which demonstrate the feasibility of our approach.

1 Introduction

As an emerging research field, code mobility is generating a growing body of scientific literature and industrial development. Proof-carrying code (PCC), originated by Necula [18,19], is a mechanism for ensuring the safe behavior of programs that is useful for general software development, and particularly advantageous for the development of mobile code. In PCC, a program contains both the code and an encoding of an easy–to–check proof whose validity entails compliance with a predefined safety policy supplied by the code consumer. The safety certificate is automatically generated by the software producer, and then packaged along with the verified code. The crucial issues for a practical realization of PCC are: (i) the expresiveness of the language used to specify the policies, (ii) the size of the transmitted certificate, and (iii) the performance of validation at the consumer side. The main technologies commonly applied in PCC are type

---

[*] This work has been partially supported by the EU (FEDER) and the Spanish MEC, under grants TIN2004-7943-C04-01 and TIN2007-68093-C02-02, Integrated Action HA 2006-0007, LERNet AML/19.0902/97/0666/II-0472-FA, and Generalitat Valenciana GV06/285.

S. Leue and P. Merino (Eds.): FMICS 2007, LNCS 4916, pp. 200–217, 2008.
© Springer-Verlag Berlin Heidelberg 2008

analysis [2,13], and theorem proving [3,21]. Recently, abstract interpretation has been also proposed as an enabling technology for PCC [1,3].

Rewriting logic [16] is a flexible and expressive *logical framework* in which a wide range of logics and models of computation can be faithfully represented. It also provides an easy and inexpensive way to develop formal definitions of programming languages which are *directly executable* [17] as interpreters in a rewriting logic language such as Maude [7]. The verification of embedded and reactive systems in rewriting logic offers a good number of advantages, an important one being the maturity, generality and sophistication of the formal analysis tools available for it (see e.g. [7]).

In this paper, we develop an abstraction-based, PCC technique for the certification of Java source code which exploits the automation, expressiveness and genericity of rewriting logic. We focus on safety properties, i.e., properties of a system that are defined in terms of certain events not happening, which we characterize as unreachability problems in rewriting logic: given a concurrent system described by a term rewriting system and a safety property that specifies the system states that should never occur, the unreachability of all these states from the considered initial state allows us to infer the desired safety property. The safety policy is expressed in JML [15], a standard property specification language for Java modules. In order to provide a decision procedure, we enforce finite-state models of programs by using abstract interpretation [8]. The code consumer annotates each variable in the Java code with an abstract domain.

Our methodology is as follows. Starting from a definition of the Java semantics in rewriting logic formalized in [10], we develop an analysis technique for source code certification which is parametric w.r.t. the abstract domains. The key idea for the analysis is to test the unreachability of Java states that represent the counterpart of the safety property fulfilment using the standard Maude (breadth-first) search command, which explores the entire (finite) state space of the program. In the case when the test succeeds, the corresponding rewriting proofs demonstrating that those states are indeed never reachable are delivered as the expected outcome certificate. In order to lower the computational costs of validation and avoid specification burdens to the experts, certificates are encoded as (abstract) rewriting sequences that, together with an encoding in Maude of the abstraction, can be checked by standard reduction. As far as we know, the use of rewriting logic for the purpose of Java certification has not been investigated to date. Moreover, our methodology extends to other mainstream conventional languages or lower level languages (e.g. Java bytecode) by simply replacing the concrete semantics by a semantics for the programming language at hand (for instance, a rewriting logic semantics for Java bytecode can be found in [11]).

Our approach differs from other PCC approaches based on abstract interpretation in several aspects. With regard to the *abstraction carrying code* ACC approach of [1] for constraint logic programs, we share the high flexibility due to the parametericity on different abstract domains, the lightness of the (static analysis) proof checker on the consumer side, and the fact that both techniques are defined at the source-level (which is Ciao-Prolog in the case of ACC).

However, their certificate is produced by means of a static analizer, and takes the form of a particular subset of the (fixpoint) analysis result that the consumer validates by means of a simpler abstract interpreter. Our certificate is mainly an encoding of the unreachability (abstract) rewriting proofs, which is closer to the original PCC [18,19] where the safety certificate was a proof in first-order logic. [3] also focuses on abstract interpretation without relying on any theorem prover or type analysis tool, but their certificates take the form of strategies for reconstructing a fixpoint. Abstract interpretation is used in this case to reduce the proofs that are generated and checked by the theorem prover Coq for (a subset of) Java bytecode by a technique for fixpoint compression. It is worth noting that, in our framework, the abstract Java semantics is directly available to the code consumer, which can be verified once for all and trusted henceforth.

Let us motivate our work by focusing on some simple Java programs borrowed from the related literature, that we want to certify. A brief explanation of the JML notation used in the examples is found in Section 2.

Example 1. Consider a simple Java program, borrowed from [22], with the requirement to produce an even number as a result. We express this requirement as a safety policy in the assertion language JML by using the **ensures** clause and the operator \result. Namely, we require that the Java outcome is not an odd number when the execution of the method is completed.

```
static int even16()
{ /*@   Safety Specification:
  @       ensures \result % 2 != 1; @*/
      int x = 4; int y = x + 8;
      return x+y;
}
```

A dedicated, standard verification tool for Java such as JavaFAN [11] can help verify the program above since there is only one initial state and its space state is finite. This can be done either by symbolic simulation or by explicit-state model checking of the property (specified in linear temporal logic). Unfortunately, no safety certificate would be delivered that could be inexpensively tested at the consumer side.

Example 2. Consider a more elaborated Java program together with a similar "even" safety policy required on both, the input and the output of the function.

```
static int evenOdd(int j)
{ /*@  Safety Specification:
  @      ensures ((j % 2) == 0) ==> ( \result % 2 == 0); @*/
      int u = 3; int v,z = 4;
      z += 30;
      v = u*8 + j;
      return z - v;
}
```

Here an infinite number of initial states is considered, although the search space is finite for each of them. Existing Java verification tools such as JavaFAN do not support program abstraction. Thus, for the infinite-state program of Example 2 above, JavaFAN can only be used as a semi-decision procedure to look for safety violations starting from specific initial states.

Our last example is more realistic, involving loops and conditionals, as follows.

Example 3. Consider a more realistic Java program, requiring a more involved condition on the input to ensure the fulfillment of the considered safety property. The parity of the output is again required to be "even" under a more complex "modulo 4" safety policy on the input parameter.

```
static int summation(int n)
{ /*@  Safety Specification:
   @        ensures  ((n % 4) == 0 | (n % 4) == 3)
   @                    ==> ( \result % 2 == 0);      @*/
   int sum ; int i = 0;
   while (i<=n) { sum += i; i++; }
   return sum;
 }
```

Other safety properties that are routinely checked in PCC include data shape/ size, bounds on resource consumption, and procedure level properties such as termination. In all these cases, PCC has the advantage to replace a (potentially) costly re-verification process by an easy–to–check proof at the consumer side. In this paper we do not address these different policies, which we consider as future work. Nevertheless, some of them are still plausible in the abstract interpretation framework and clearly not difficult to define in our setting, since all the necessary Java state elements such as memory, stacks, I/O, etc. are explicitly considered; see Section 3.

In Section 2 we briefly introduce the Java Modeling Language. In Section 3 we describe the rewriting logic semantics of Java considered in this paper and in Section 4 we present its abstract version, discussing all the difficulties that we have found and their solutions. Finally, in Section 5 we present our certification methodology, in Section 6 we demonstrate the practicality of our proposal with some experimental results, and conclude with some related work and future work in Section 7.

2   The Java Modeling Language

The Java Modeling Language [15] is a behavioral interface specification language that allows Java programmers to write specifications of Java classes, interfaces and modules without the difficulty of learning a language-independent formal specification language like OCL [5]. JML has been designed as an easily accessible specification language that combines the design by contract method and the model-based approach to specification to guarantee that a program satisfies its specification at execution time. That is, it contributes to the idea of including specifications into the code and then pre-compiling them into runtime checks embedded in the Java code. Java developers can specify with JML the functional properties of their programs in a generalization of Hoare logic, tailored to Java. As an interface specification language, JML can describe the names and static information found in Java declarations of Java modules with preconditions (in **requires** clauses), normal postconditions (in **ensures** clauses), invariants and exceptional preconditions (with the **signals** clauses), that express first-order logic statements. JML notation includes quantifiers \forall and \exists and specification-only fields and methods that allow more precise and complete specifications. As a behavior specification language, JML can also describe how the module will behave when used with assertions intermixed with the Java code. JML comes with a library with Java types that can be used for describing behavior mathematically like sets, sequences and relations. In this paper, we consider the simplest JML clauses: the `ensures` clause to indicate the result of a function expected by the code consumer and the `requires` clause to indicate any precondition on an input parameter of a function.

The JML specifications of a Java program can either be written as code annotations in Java program files or in separate files. The JML specifications as code annotations are treated like Java comments that are ignored by the compiler. The text of an annotation could be either in one line, after the marker //@ or, in many lines enclosed between the markers /*@ and @*/.

```
/*@  requires <precondition>;
  @  ensures <postcondition if no exception raised>;
  @  signals(E) <postcondition when exception E raised>;
  @  assignable <modified fields and variables>         @*/
```

3   The Rewriting Logic Semantics of Java

We assume some basic knowledge of term rewriting [20] and rewriting logic [16]. In the following, we briefly describe the rewriting logic semantics of Java given in [10] and used by the JavaFAN verification tool [11,12]. Its novelty and interest are based on the following four advantages: (i) formal specifications provide a rigorous semantic definition for a language that can be mathematically scrutinized; (ii) such formal specifications can be developed with relatively little effort, even for large languages like Java [11] and the JVM [12]; (iii) the Maude programming language [7], which implements rewriting logic, provides a formal analysis infrastructure, so that its formal analysis tools (such as state-space breadth-first search and LTL model checking) become available for free for each programming language that is specified in Maude; and (iv) in spite of their generality, those formal analyses can be performed with competitive performance (see [11]).

The specification of Java operational semantics is a rewrite theory, that is, a triple $\mathcal{R}_{\text{Java}} = (\Sigma_{\text{Java}}, E_{\text{Java}}, R_{\text{Java}})$, with Σ_{Java} an order-sorted signature, $E_{\text{Java}} = \Delta_{\text{Java}} \uplus B_{\text{Java}}$ a set of Σ_{Java}-equational axioms where B_{Java} are axioms such as associativity, commutativity and identity and Δ_{Java} are a set of terminating and confluent (modulo B_{Java}) set of Σ_{Java}-rewrite rules, and R_{Java} a set of Σ_{Java}-rewrite rules. Intuitively, the sorts and function symbols in Σ_{Java} describe the static structure of the Java program state space as an algebraic data type, the equations in Δ_{Java} describe the operational semantics of its deterministic features, and the rules in $\mathcal{R}_{\text{Java}}$ describe its concurrent features. Following the rewriting logic framework [20,16], we denote by $u \rightarrow^r_{\text{Java}} v$ the fact that concrete terms u, v, denoting Java program states, are rewritten (at the top position, see [10]) by using r, which is either a rule in R_{Java} or an equation in Δ_{Java} both applied modulo B_{Java}. We simply write $u \rightarrow_{\text{Java}} v$ when no confusion can arise. We denote by $\rightarrow^*_{\text{Java}}$ the extension of $\rightarrow_{\text{Java}}$ to multiple rewrite steps, i.e., $u \rightarrow^*_{\text{Java}} v$ if there exist $u_1, \ldots, u_k$ such that $u \rightarrow_{\text{Java}} u_1 \rightarrow_{\text{Java}} u_2 \cdots u_k \rightarrow_{\text{Java}} v$. Associativity, commutativity and unity (written ACU) axioms of binary operations in B_{Java} allow us to elegantly and effectively define (and implicitly implement) the crucial infrastructure of the Java programming language, including environments, threads, memory, input/output, synchronization information, and stores as well as the lookup operations on them; all of them implemented as a multiset union operation that builds up a "soup" of elements; see [10]. The rewrite theory $\mathcal{R}_{\text{Java}}$ is defined as terms of a concrete sort State, with the main state attributes (i.e., constructors of the algebraic type State) such as in, out, mem, or store. They define an algebraic structure which is parametric on a generic sort Value that defines all the possible values returned by Java functions, or stored in the memory, etc. For instance, the int and bool constructors describe Java, integer and boolean values and are defined in Maude as "op int : Int -> Value ." and "op bool : Bool -> Value .", where Int and Bool are the internal built–in Maude sorts to define integers and booleans. Intuitively, equations in Δ_{Java} and rules in R_{Java} are used to specify the changes to the program state, i.e., the changes to the memory, threads, input/output, etc.

In [10], a sufficiently large subset of full Java 1.4 language is specified in Maude, including multithreading, inheritance, polymorphism, object references, and dynamic object allocation. However, Java native methods and many of the Java built-in libraries available are not supported. The semantics of Java is defined modularly, i.e., different features of the language are defined in separate Maude modules so to ease extensions and maintenance. See [10] for further details.

The semantics of Java is defined in a *continuation-based style*. Continuations maintain the control context of each thread, which explicitly specifies the next steps to be performed by the thread. Continuations are a typical technique to transform the uncontrollable control context into controllable data context, by stacking the sequence of actions that still need to be executed. Once the expression e on the top of a continuation (e -> k) is evaluated, its result will be passed to the remaining continuation k. Continuations significantly ease the definition of flow-control instructions, such as break, continue, return, and exceptions. For instance, the Java addition operation on Java integers is specified[1] in Figure 1 using continuations, where k is the constructor symbol used to denote a continuation in a thread, -> is the constructor symbol used to concatenate continuations, int is the constructor symbol used to denote a Java integer, and + with[2] arity 2 and inside the constructor int is the Maude addition symbol, whereas + with arity 2 but outside the constructor int is the Java addition symbol, and + with arity 0 is a continuation symbol used to remember that the Java addition action is being stacked. The Java less-or-equal boolean operation on Java integers is specified in a similar way in Figure 2.

---

[1] The Maude syntax is almost self-explanatory. The general point is that each item: a sort, a subsort, an operation, an equation, a rule, etc., is declared with an obvious keyword: sort, subsort, op, eq, rl, etc., with each declaration ended by a space and a period. We use uppercase letters to denote Maude variables and lowercase letters to denote Maude constructor symbols. See [7] for details.

[2] The Maude syntax allows overloading of operators, with different arities.

```
--- First evaluate arguments
eq k((E + E) -> K) = k((E, E) -> (+ -> K)) .
--- Once arguments are evaluated to integers, compute addition
eq k((int(I), int(I)) -> (+ -> K)) = k(int(I + I) -> K) .
```

Fig. 1. Continuation-based equations for Java addition operator on integers

```
--- First evaluate arguments
eq k((E <= E') -> K) = k((E, E') -> (<= -> K)) .
--- Once arguments are evaluated to integers, compute boolean
eq k((int(I), int(I')) -> (<= -> K)) = k(bool(I <= I') -> K) .
```

Fig. 2. Continuation-based equations for Java less-or-equal operator on integers

A relevant construction in the Java semantics is the `buildEnv` continuation symbol shown in Figure 3, that gives a new location in the memory store to each new variable. It involves the following four elements of the Java state: the thread adding new variables (denoted by constructor `t`), the environment inside the thread (denoted by constructor `env`), the store shared by all threads (denoted by constructor `store`), and a counter for the last used location in the store (denoted by constructor `nextLoc`).

Another important aspect of the semantics is the use of Java variables. In Figure 4 we show how the content of a Java variable is retrieved from the store in the Java state. The assignment operator for Java variables is specified in Figure 5. Note that the relative order among assignment and retrieval operations is relevant since multiple threads can try to concurrently assign a value to a variable or read its value from the store; hence a rule, instead of an equation, is used to represent the physical assignment as well as the physical retrieval from the store. In other words, the assignment operator and the retrieval of a variable value are non-deterministic due to the presence of different threads and are specified with Maude rules instead of Maude equations.

The state space associated to a rewrite theory is determined in Maude only by the program rules, since equations are deterministic. That is, rules and equations are applied in the same way but Maude only keeps track of the rules applied and omits the information about the equations applied. Therefore, the number of rules and equations is relevant and the smaller the number of rules, the more efficient the verification analysis, since the search space is smaller. According to [10], the Java operational semantics contains about 424 equations and only 7 rules, which considerably saves memory and execution time.

The following example illustrates the mechanization of the Java semantics.

```
--- No new variable, end buildEnv continuation
eq k(buildEnv(noParameters, noValues) -> K) = k(K) .
--- New variable with name Var and value Val assigned to Location I' + 1
eq t(k(buildEnv(((T d(Var)), P1), (Val, V1)) -> K) env(Env) TC)
   store(ST) nextLoc(I')
 = t(k(buildEnv(P1, V1) -> K) env([Var, l(I' + 1)] Env) TC)
   store([l(I' + 1), Val] ST) nextLoc(I' + 1) .
```

Fig. 3. Continuation-based equations for building the environment

```
--- First obtain location in store from variable name
eq k(Var -> K) env([Var, Loc] env) = k(#(Loc) -> K) env([X, Loc] env) .
--- Then obtain value stored in such location
rl t(k(#(Loc) -> K) TC) store([Loc, Value] Store)
=> t(k(Value -> K) TC) store([Loc, Value] Store) .
```

Fig. 4. Continuation-based equations for variable content retrieval

```
--- First obtain location in store of the variable
--- while keeping expression in the continuation
eq k((Var = E) -> K) = k(getLocation(Var) -> (=(E) -> K)) .
--- Once the location is obtained, evaluate expression
--- while keeping location in the continuation
eq k(Loc -> (=(E) -> K)) = k(E -> (=(Loc) -> K)) .
--- Once the expression is computed, assign to location
eq k(Value -> (=(L) -> K)) = k([Value -> L] -> (V -> K)) .
--- General procedure to update a location in the shared memory
rl t(k([Value -> L] -> K) TC) store([L, Value'] ST)
=> t(k(K) TC) store([L, Value] ST) .
```

Fig. 5. Continuation-based equations and rules for Java assignment operator

Example 4. Consider the Java program of Example 1 together with the following Java main function:

```
void main() { System.out.println(addition()); }
```

The Maude command **search** provides us built–in breadth-first search, i.e., it provides all the sequences of rules (recall that the application of equations is omitted within the search space) from an initial term (without variables) to a final term (possibly with variables) [7]. Note that the initial term (without variables) describes a concrete initial Java state and the final term (possibly with variables) describes a (possibly infinite) set of final Java states. In the search command below we ask for all possible values returned by the **main** Java function of Example 1 and, therefore, a variable term denotes the goal state to be reached. Note that the code of the two Java functions **addition** and **main** is embedded within the search command, as well as the initial call to **main** (see [10] for details on how to build an initial Java state).

```
search in PGM-SEMANTICS : java((preprocess(default class 'Safe1Even1
extends Object implements none {
  (default static) int 'addition(noPara)throws(noType)
  {int d('x) = i(4) ; int d('y) = 'x + i(8) ; 12 @ return 'x + 'y ;}
  (public static) void 'main(t('String)[] d('args))throws(noType)
  {5 @ ('System . 'out . 'println < 'addition < noExp > > ;)}
})
t('Safe1Even1) . 'main < new string [i(0)] > noVal))
=>! X:ValueList .

Solution 1 (state 0)
X:ValueList --> int(16)
```

The search command returns that one unique possible Java execution trace is possible, which leads to the Java value 16 as the outcome of the Java instruction "System.out.println(addition());". The whole rewriting sequence leading to this Java value is also delivered by Maude.

4   The Abstract Rewriting Logic Semantics of Java

In this section, we develop an abstract version of the rewriting logic semantics of Java, described by the rewrite theory $\mathcal{R}_{\text{Java}^\#} = (\Sigma_{\text{Java}^\#}, E_{\text{Java}^\#}, R_{\text{Java}^\#})$, $E_{\text{Java}^\#} = \Delta_{\text{Java}^\#} \uplus B_{\text{Java}^\#}$ and its corresponding $\rightarrow_{\text{Java}^\#}$ rewriting relation. Recall that the rewrite theory $\mathcal{R}_{\text{Java}}$ is defined on a generic sort Value. Our approach consists in extending $\mathcal{R}_{\text{Java}}$ (taking advantage of its modularity) by creating abstract domains as subsorts of the sort Value and adding the appropriate versions of the Java constructions and operators for the abstract domains.

An *abstract interpretation* (or abstraction) [8] of the program semantics is given by an *upper closure operator* $\alpha : \wp(\text{State}) \rightarrow \wp(\text{State})$, that is *monotonic* (for all $SSt_1, SSt_2 \in \wp(\text{State})$, $SSt_1 \subseteq SSt_2$ implies $\alpha(SSt_1) \subseteq \alpha(SSt_2)$), *idempotent* (for all $SSt \in \wp(\text{State})$, $\alpha(SSt) \subseteq \alpha(\alpha(SSt))$), and *extensive* (for all $SSt \in \wp(\text{State})$, $SSt \subseteq \alpha(SSt)$). The intuition of this definition is that each Java program state $St \in \text{State}$ is abstracted by its closure $\alpha(\{St\})$. Closure operators have many interesting properties. For instance, when the considered domain is a complete lattice, e.g. $\langle \alpha(\text{State}), \subseteq \rangle$, each closure operator is uniquely determined by the set of its fixed points. In the context of abstract interpretation, closure operators are important because abstract domains can be equivalently defined by using them or by Galois insertions, as introduced in [9]. Let $\iota : \alpha(\wp(\text{State})) \rightarrow A$ be an isomorphism. Then, given an upper closure operator $\alpha : \wp(\text{State}) \rightarrow \wp(\text{State})$, the structure $(\wp(\text{State}), \alpha \circ \iota, \iota^{-1}, A)$ is a Galois insertion, where $\alpha \circ \iota$ and ι^{-1} are the abstraction and concretization functions, respectively (see [9] for further details).

In our approach, the code consumer can assign a different abstract domain to each variable in the Java code to obtain a finite-state model of the program. This is an important point, since a potential user of the tool only has to select some source variables to be abstracted together with the selected abstraction. A graphical interface equipped with user–friendly advisory facilities can help her in this process. Furthermore, the user could simply annotate the source code with JML assertions encoding the required safety policy so that the critical variables (together with their appropriate abstract domains) might be automatically inferred, although in this case the abstraction might be less accurate.

For the process of assigning an abstract domain to a source variable, we have a twofold situation, considering the theoretical and practical levels. On the theoretical level, we define an abstract function for each Java variable name x, e.g., $\alpha_{\text{x}} : \wp(\text{Int}) \rightarrow \wp(\text{Int})$, and homomorphically extend those abstract functions to an abstract function $\alpha : \wp(\text{State}) \rightarrow \wp(\text{State})$. Indeed, for each variable x, α abstracts the values stored in the Java memory for x using α_{x}, which can be the identity function if no abstract domain is selected. As mentioned before, these assignments of an abstract domain to a source variable can be inferred from the JML annotations, e.g. "\result % 2" or "n % 4", in the Java source code. The following example shows some abstract domains which are relevant for this work.

Example 5. Let us consider an abstract function that classifies Java integers into even and odd classes, i.e., $\text{mod2} : \wp(\text{int}(\text{Int})) \rightarrow \wp(\text{int}(\text{Int}))$ where $\text{int}(\text{Int})$

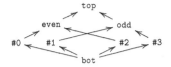

Fig. 6. Lattice of integers for the *mod2* and *mod4* abstractions

denotes the Maude terms of sort Value that correspond to the Java integers. This abstraction is relevant for Examples 1, 2, and 3. We can choose the following abstract symbols $A = \{$even, odd, top, bot$\}$ to denote the following subsets top $=$ int (Int), bot $= \emptyset$, even $= \{$int $(n) \mid n \bmod 2 = 0\}$, and odd $= \{$int $(n) \mid n \bmod 2 = 1\}$. We can even refine such abstract domain by including the abstraction for Java integers modulo 4, i.e., mod4 $: \wp(\text{int (Int)}) \rightarrow \wp(\text{int (Int)})$. This abstraction is relevant for Example 3. We can have the following abstract symbols $A = \{$top, bot, #0, #1, #2, #3$\}$ where #k $= \{$int $(n) \mid n \bmod 4 = k\}$ for $k \in \{0, 1, 2, 3\}$. The lattice induced by the relation $\subseteq$ on sets of Java integers is shown in Figure 6.

On the practical level, we have to supplement the original Java semantics with a new Maude function, called inAbsDomain, that records the abstract domain associated to each variable name and that it will be used in two points: when the variable is initially created in the Java memory and everytime its value is updated in the memory. For instance, Figure 7 shows the code of inAbsDomain for variables x,y of Example 1 according to the JML annotations, together with the Maude code for the abstract functions mod2 and mod4. We also have to add a call to the inAbsDomain function in the buildEnv continuation symbol of Figure 3 and the Java assignment operator of Figure 5; all these modifications are shown in Figure 8. Obviously, we have to provide abstract versions of all the Java operators in the Java semantics dealing with such kind of values, e.g., we must provide an approximation of integer addition, less-or-equal boolean operator, etc. dealing with the new abstract domains for integers. For instance, given the abstract function mod2, the addition operation on integers is specified in Figure 9.

```
--- Define abstract domains
sorts Mod2 Mod4 . subsort Mod2 Mod4 < Value .
ops even odd : -> Mod2 .
op #_: Int -> Mod4 .
--- Define abstraction functions
op mod2 : Value -> Mod2 .
eq mod2(int(I)) = if (I rem 2 == 0) then even else odd fi .
op mod4 : Value -> Mod4 .
eq mod4(int(I)) = #(I rem 4) .
--- Equations for abstracting concrete values
op inAbsDomain : Qid Value -> Value .
eq inAbsDomain('x,int(I)) = mod2(int(I)) .
eq inAbsDomain('y,int(I)) = mod2(int(I)) .
eq inAbsDomain(Var,Value) = Value [owise] .
```

Fig. 7. Abstract domain and association of abstract domain to variable name

```
--- BuildEnv modified equation
eq t(k(buildEnv(((T d(Var)), Pl), (Value, Vl)) -> K) env(Env) TC)
   store(ST) nextLoc(I')
 = t(k(buildEnv(Pl, Vl) -> K) env([Var, l(I' + 1)] Env) TC)
   store([l(I' + 1), inAbsDomain(Var,Value)] ST) nextLoc(I' + 1) .
--- Assignment modified equations
op = : Exp Qid -> Continuation . --- new definition
op = : Location Qid -> Continuation . --- new definition
eq k((Var = E) -> K) = k(getLocation(Var) -> (=(E,Var) -> K)) .
eq k(Loc -> (=(E,Var) -> K)) = k(E -> (=(Loc,Var) -> K)) .
eq k(Val -> (=(Loc,Var) -> K)) = k([inAbsDomain(Var,Val) -> Loc] -> (Val -> K)) .
```

Fig. 8. Modified continuation-based equations for building environment and Java assignment

```
--- Execute abstract mod2 values
eq k((even, even) -> (+ -> K)) = k(even -> K) .
eq k((even, odd) -> (+ -> K)) = k(odd -> K) .
eq k((odd, even) -> (+ -> K)) = k(odd -> K) .
eq k((odd, odd) -> (+ -> K)) = k(even -> K) .
--- Combine with standard integer values
eq k((int(I), Val) -> (+ -> K)) = k((mod2(int(I)), Val) -> (+ -> K)) .
eq k((Val, int(I)) -> (+ -> K)) = k((Val, mod2(int(I))) -> (+ -> K)) .
```

+	even	odd
even	even	odd
odd	odd	even

Fig. 9. Abstract definition and equations for abstract Java addition operator

In abstract interpretation, it is common to compress several computation steps into one abstract computation step, to reflect the fact that several distinct behaviors are mimicked by an abstract state. Consider for instance the Java less-or-equal operator <= of Figure 2 and the abstract function mod2. For the case of comparing two even expressions with <=, an (inaccurate) approximation of the result is the union of true and false, which is denoted by the symbol top. A naïve implementation of this idea would mean including the following equation in the abstract Java semantics $\mathcal{R}_{\text{Java}\#}$ (following the definition of operator <= in Figure 2):

```
eq k((even, even) -> (<= -> K)) = k(top -> K) .
```

This instrumentalization of the Java semantics to deal with abstraction implicitly means too many modifications, since completely different Java states could be generated that have to be packed together into a unique abstract state. For instance, consider a Java expression "if eb then et else ef" such that the expression eb returns top so that we have to represent within a single Java state both, the case when we reach a Java state continued by executing instruction et and also the case when we reach a Java state continued with the instruction ef. This would amount to a deep modification of the whole Java semantics, in order to cope with sets of Java states. Therefore, we adopt a different approach. When several $\rightarrow_{\text{Java}}$ rewrite steps are mimicked by an abstract Java state and those rewrite steps apply different rules or equations, we use concurrency at the Maude level. That is, we add rules to $\mathcal{R}_{\text{Java}\#}$ to reflect the different possible evolutions of the system. Following this approach, the Java less-or-equal operator is defined as follows, describing that the comparison operator <= can return true or false indifferently:

```
rl k((even, even) -> (<= -> K)) = k(bool(true) -> K) .
rl k((even, even) -> (<= -> K)) = k(bool(false) -> K) .
```

Now, we are ready to formalize the abstract rewriting relation $\rightarrow_{\text{Java}\#}$, which intuitively develops the idea of applying only one rule or equation from the concrete Java semantics to an abstract Java state while exploring the different alternatives in a non-deterministic way. By abuse, we denote the abstraction of a rule $\alpha(\{l\}) \rightarrow \alpha(\{r\})$ by $\alpha(\{l\} \rightarrow \{r\})$.

Definition 1 (Abstract rewriting). *Let $\alpha : \wp(\text{State}) \rightarrow \wp(\text{State})$ be an abstraction. We define the approximated version of rewriting $\rightarrow_{\text{Java}\#} \subseteq \wp(\text{State}) \times \wp(\text{State})$ by:*

$$SSt_1 \rightarrow_{\text{Java}\#} SSt_2 \text{ using } \alpha(\{l\} \rightarrow \{r\}) \in (R_{\text{Java}\#} \cup \Delta_{\text{Java}\#})$$
$$\text{iff } \forall u \in \alpha(SSt_1), \exists v \in SSt_2 \text{ s.t. } u \rightarrow_{\text{Java}} v, \text{ using } l \rightarrow r \in R_{\text{Java}} \cup \Delta_{\text{Java}}.$$

We denote by $\rightarrow_{\text{Java}\#}^*$ the extension of $\rightarrow_{\text{Java}\#}$ to multiple rewrite steps. The following result follows straightforwardly by monotonicity, idempotency, and extensitivity of the upper closure operator α.

Theorem 1 (Correctness & Completeness). *Let $\alpha : \wp(\text{State}) \rightarrow \wp(\text{State})$ be an abstraction. Let $SSt_1, SSt_2 \in \wp(\text{State})$. If $SSt_1 \rightarrow_{\text{Java}\#}^* SSt_2$, then for all $u \in \alpha(SSt_1)$, there is $v \in SSt_2$ such that $u \rightarrow_{\text{Java}}^* v$. Let $St_1, St_2 \in \text{State}$. If $St_1 \rightarrow_{\text{Java}}^* St_2$, then there exists $SSt_3 \subseteq \wp(\text{State})$ s.t. $\alpha(St_1) \rightarrow_{\text{Java}\#}^* SSt_3$ and $St_2 \in SSt_3$.*

The breadth-first search for the abstract finite state system (finite due to the use of finite abstract domains) gives us a useful tool for symbolic execution, while keeping simple the modifications of the Java semantics in Maude. Actually, verification simply boils down to the exploration of all the rewriting sequences.

Example 6. Consider the Java functions `addition` and `main` of Example 4 and the abstract Java semantics shown above with the `inAbsDomain` function of Figure 7. The call to function `main` is now as follows. Note that, for the search command, the only change we need in this case is the replacement of `PGM-SEMANTICS` with `PGM-SEMANTICS-ABSTR`, since the considered Java function `addition` of Example 1 has no input parameters.

```
search in PGM-SEMANTICS-ABSTR : java((preprocess(default class 'Safe1Even1
extends Object implements none
{(default static) int 'addition(noPara)throws(noType)
  {((int d('x) = i(4) ;) (int d('y) = 'x + i(8) ;)) 12 @ return 'x + 'y ;}
(public static) void 'main(t('String)[] d('args))throws(noType)
  {5 @ ('System . 'out . 'println < 'addition < noExp > > ;)}})
t('Safe1Even1) . 'main < new string [i(0)] > noVal))
=>! X:ValueList .
```

This search command now returns the following result, meaning that exactly one abstract Java execution trace is proven, which returns the abstract value **even** as a result of the Java instruction "`System.out.println(addition());`":

```
Solution 1 (state 0)
X:ValueList --> even
```

and therefore every real execution of the Java program of Figure 1 also returns an even value, according to Theorem 1.

However, the abstraction defined in Example 5 is not accurate enough for the Java program of Example 3, as shown in the following example.

Example 7. Consider the code of Example 3 with the following function `main`:

```
void main() { System.out.println(sum(0)); }
```

We provide the following assignment of abstract domains for the variables in the Java program:

```
op inAbsDomain : Qid Value -> Value .
eq inAbsDomain('n,int(I)) = mod4(int(I)) .
eq inAbsDomain('i,int(I)) = mod4(int(I)) .
eq inAbsDomain('sum,int(I)) = mod2(int(I)) .
eq inAbsDomain(Var,V) = V [owise] .
```

When we search for all the results of the function `main`

```
search in PGM-SEMANTICS-ABSTR : java((preprocess(default class 'Safe1Even1
extends Object implements none {
(default static) int 'sum(int d('n))throws(noType)
  {(((int d('sum) ;) (int d('i) = i(0) ;)) 17 @ (while 'i <= 'n
  17 @ {(15 @ ('sum += 'i ;)) 16 @ ('i ++ ;)}})) 18 @ return 'sum ;}
(public static) void 'main(t('String)[] d('args))throws(noType)
  {7 @ ('System . 'out . 'println < 'sum < i(0) > > ;)}})
t('Safe1Even1) . 'main < new string [i(0)] > noVal))
=>! X:ValueList .
```

Maude delivers the following two results

```
Solution 1 (state 2)              Solution 2 (state 5)
X:ValueList --> even              X:ValueList --> odd
```

which are useless since both, an even and an odd output value are possible. The problem is that the boolean condition (`i <= n`) returns both `true` and `false` (in a non-deterministic way) under the `mod2` and `mod4` abstraction operators in too many situations.

In order to improve accuracy, we define a new, more precise abstract domain $\text{leq}^{\#}_{x,y}$ that is parametric w.r.t. two Java variable names x, y (which have different abstraction domains). For the previous example, this can be used to abstract variable i w.r.t. n. On the theoretical level, there are two abstract domains $\alpha_x, \alpha_y : \wp(\text{Int}) \to \wp(\text{Int})$ that are used for the values stored in the Java memory for variables x, y, respectively. The extension $\text{leq}^{\#}_{x,y} : \wp(\text{State}) \to \wp(\text{State})$ takes those abstract domains α_x, α_y and captures also whether $x \leq y$ or $x > y$. On the practical level, we use the abstract symbols `leq#` and `gt#` defined in Maude as "`leq# : Abst Qid -> AbstLeqN`" and "`gt# : Abst Qid -> AbstLeqN`" where the first argument denotes the abstract domain for variable x (i.e., α_x) and the second argument is just y (the name of the second variable), e.g. for the previous example we will have an abstract expression for variable i such as `leq#(#0,'n)` denoting that the current value of variable i modulo 4 is 0 and that variable i is less or equal to variable n, whatever value n has been assigned in the execution. The appropriate version of the Java operators relevant for this new

<=	any value
leq#(Val,V)	true
gt#(Val,V)	false

++	
leq#(#(I),V)	leq#(mod4(I + 1),y) if $y = $#(I') $\wedge$ I $<$ I'
leq#(#(I),V)	gt#(mod4(I + 1),y) if $y = $#(I') $\wedge$ I $\geq$ I'
gt#(#(I),V)	gt#(mod4(I + 1),y)

```
--- Two equations for the Java less-or-equal operator on integers
eq k((leq#(Val1,Var),Val2) -> <= -> K) = k(bool(true) -> K) .
eq k((gt#(Val1,Var),Val2) -> <= -> K) = k(bool(false) -> K) .
--- This equation is the core of the new abstract domain
--- The value of Var in memory has to be obtained before incrementing
ceq t(k(leq#(#(I),Var) -> ++'(Loc) -> K) env([Var, Loc'] Env) TC)
     store([Loc',#(I')] Store)
  = t(k([NewVal -> Loc] -> leq#(#(I),Var) -> K) env([Var, Loc'] Env) TC)
     store([Loc',#(I')] Store)
  if NewVal := if (I + 1 <= I') then leq#(mod4(int(I + 1)),Var)
                                else gt#(mod4(int(I + 1)),Var) fi .
--- This other equation complements the previous one
eq k(gt#(#(I),Var) -> ++'(Loc) -> K)
  = k([gt#(mod4(int(I + 1)),Var) -> Loc] -> gt#(mod4(int(I + 1)),Var) -> K) .
```

Fig. 10. Continuation-based equations for Java less-or-equal operator on integers

abstract domain are shown in Figure 10. Note that we cannot use the abstract domain above for the second variable instead of its name, since the value of this variable can change dynamically. Consider, for instance, the following variant of Example 3 where the loop therein contains the assignment n -= 1, and thus variable n changes in each iteration.

Example 8. Let us reconsider now Example 7. The code of function inAbsDomain for Example 3 is as follows, denoting that variables i and n have domains mod4, variable sum has domain mod2 and that the relation $i \leq n$ is also represented in the abstract domain:

```
op inAbsDomain : Qid Value -> Value .
eq inAbsDomain('n,int(I)) = mod4(int(I)) .
eq inAbsDomain('i,int(I)) = leq#(mod4(int(I)),'n) .
eq inAbsDomain('sum,int(I)) = mod2(int(I)) .
eq inAbsDomain(Var,V) = V [owise] .
```

When we search for solutions for the Java function main using the following command

```
search in PGM-SEMANTICS-ABSTR : java((preprocess(default class 'Safe1Even1
extends Object implements none {
(default static) int 'sum(int d('n))throws(noType)
  {(((int d('sum) ;) (int d('i) = i(0) ;)) 17 @ (while 'i <= 'n
  17 @ {(15 @ ('sum += 'i ;)) 16 @ ('i ++ ;)})) 18 @ return 'sum ;}
(public static) void 'main(t('String)[] d('args))throws(noType)
  {7 @ ('System . 'out . 'println < 'sum < i(0) > > ;)}})
t('Safe1Even1) . 'main < new string [i(0)] > noVal))
=>! X:ValueList .
```

we get the following unique output, meaning that exactly one abstract Java execution trace is proven, which returns the abstract value even as a result of the Java instruction "System.out.println(sum(0))":

```
Solution 1 (state 2)
X:ValueList --> even
```

This certifies that every possible Java execution starting with an integer n such that $n \bmod 4 = 0$ does always return an even value. Indeed, we can verify that initial calls "System.out.println(sum(0))" and "System.out.println(sum(3))" always return **even** whereas "System.out.println(sum(1))" and "System.out.println(sum(2))" return **odd**.

5   Certifying Java

Examples 4, 6, 7, 8 above illustrate how our methodology generates a safety certificate which essentially consists of the set of (abstract) rewriting proofs of the form $t_1 \rightarrow^{r_1}_{\text{Java}\#} t_2 \cdots \rightarrow^{r_{k-1}}_{\text{Java}\#} t_k$ that describe the program states which can and cannot be reached from a given (abstract) initial state. Since these proofs correspond to the execution of the abstract Java semantics specification, which is made available to the code consumer, the certificate can be unexpensively checked on the consumer side by any standard rewrite engine by means of a rewriting process that can be very simplified. Actually, it suffices to check that each abstract rewriting step in the certificate is valid and no other valid rewritings have been disregarded, which essentially amounts to use the matching infrastructure within the rewriting engine. Note that, according to the different treatment of rules and equations in Maude, where only transitions caused by rules create new states in the space state, an extremely reduced certificate can be delivered by just recording the rewrite steps given with the rules, while the rewritings with the equations are omitted.

The certification methodology presented here has been implemented in Maude and is publicly available at http://www.dsic.upv.es/~sescobar/JavaACC/. In developing and deploying the system, we fixed the following requirements: 1) define a system architecture as simple as possible, 2) make the certification

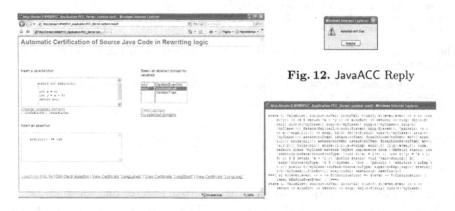

Fig. 12. JavaACC Reply

Fig. 11. JavaACC Snapshot   **Fig. 13.** JavaACC Certificate

Table 1. Sizes of source code and certificates, and times ofcertificate generation and validation times

Code example	Source Size (bytes)	Full Cert. Size (Kbytes)	Red Cert. Size (Kbytes)	F/R	Full Cert. Gen. Time (ms)	Red Cert. Gen. Time (ms)	Full Cert. Val. Time (ms)	Red Cert. Val. Time (ms)
even16	562	117	0.93	126	~0	~0	~0	~0
even16*	767	401	3.58	112	6	4	4	2
evenOdd	671	312	1.08	288	~0	~0	~0	~0
summation	870	1551	39.03	40	2294	146	1628	103

service available to every Internet requestor, and 3) hide the technical details from the user. The prototype system JavaACC offers a rewriting-based program certification service, which is able to analyze safety properties of Java code which are related to the safe use of types. A snapshot of JavaACC is shown in Figures 11, 12, and 13.

6 Experiments

In Table 1, we study two key points for the practicality of our proposal: the size of the reduced versus full certificates and the relative efficiency of checking certificates w.r.t. their generation. The experiments have been performed on a MacBook with 2 Gb RAM. Programs even16, evenOdd, and summation are the Java programs of Examples 1, 2, and 3, respectively. Program even16* performs more involved arithmetic computations than even16, including subtraction and multiplication, while returning the same result. The first column contains the size (in bytes) of the source code for each benchmark program. The three columns for Full Cert. show the size in Kbytes, the generation time, and the validation time, respectively, for the full certificates. Similarly for the three columns of Red. Cert. Running times are given in milliseconds and were averaged over a sufficient number of iterations. Our figures demonstrate that the reduction in size of the certificate is very significant in all cases, ranging the quotient F/R (Full Cert. Size/Red. Cert. Size) from 288 in even16* to 40 for summation. When we compare the time employed to generate the (full and reduced) certificates w.r.t. the corresponding validation time, we have that the validation time is reduced by a factor up to 50%. Thus we conclude that, by minimizing the number of equations in the certificate, we achieve a simpler and indeed superior certificate that can be verified much more efficiently.

7 Conclusions and Related Work

Correctness of JML specifications can be verified either during runtime or statically. The most basic static tool support for JML is type checking and parsing (see [5]). At runtime an exception is raised if a JML condition fails.

There are several tools for static verification of Java programs using JML as specification language. The main differences between these tools regard its soundness, its level of automation, its language coverage and whether they are proof tools or just validation tools. The ESC/Java tool [14] offers a higher level of automation without any user interaction and relies on a complete (but unsound [4]) automatic prover to check null pointers or array bounds limits which uses its own specification language. The ESC/Java2 tool [6] extends ESC/Java to support more of the JML syntax and to add other functionality but it is also unsound and incomplete. It supports Java 1.4 code with JML annotations but we can not generate certificates whenever the validation succeds. Another drawback is that there is no arithmetic axiomatization that enables reasoning within ESC/Java2 about programs with integer computation [5].

As a conclusion, as far as we know our approach is the first sound and complete, fully automatic certification tool that applies to the verification of source Java code. The proposed methodology features quality attributes (notably reliability and security, but also good performance) through rigorous mechanisms which integrate a wide range of well-established programming language techniques (abstract interpretation, program semantics, meta-programming, etc). Our approach is based on a rewriting logic semantics specification of the full Java 1.4 language [10], and thus works with the full Java 1.4 language. Our certification methodology extends to other programming languages by simply replacing the concrete semantics by a semantics for the programming language at hand. Different safety policies can be defined using different (abstract) terms denoting the states that should not be reached. Such safety policies are certified by the code producer and easily checked by the code consumer using a rewriting process that can be very simplified. Certificates are encoded as (abstract) rewriting sequences which can be checked in the abstract Java semantics written in Maude on the consumer side by standard reduction. We are currently investigating how other formal verification techniques such as (abstract) model checking can be fruitfully combined with the abstraction methodology presented here to produce a more powerful methodology.

Acknowledgments. We thank Andrea Schiavinato for developing a useful web interface for our PCC tool.

References

1. Albert, E., Puebla, G., Hermenegildo, M.V.: Abstraction-carrying code. In: Baader, F., Voronkov, A. (eds.) LPAR 2004. LNCS (LNAI), vol. 3452, pp. 380–397. Springer, Heidelberg (2005)
2. Appel, A.W., Felty, A.P.: A semantic model of types and machine instuctions for proof-carrying code. In: POPL, pp. 243–253 (2000)
3. Besson, F., Jensen, T.P., Pichardie, D.: Proof-carrying code from certified abstract interpretation and fixpoint compression. Theor. Comput. Sci. 364(3), 273–291 (2006)
4. Burdy, L., Requet, A., Lanet, J.-L.: Java applet correctness: A developer-oriented approach. In: Araki, K., Gnesi, S., Mandrioli, D. (eds.) FME 2003. LNCS, vol. 2805, pp. 422–439. Springer, Heidelberg (2003)
5. Burdy, L., Cheon, Y., Cok, D., Ernst, M., Kiniry, J., Leavens, G.T., Rustan, K., Leino, M., Poll, E.: An overview of JML tools and applications. International Journal on Software Tools for Technology Transfer 7(3), 212–232 (2005)

6. Chalin, P., Kiniry, J.R., Leavens, G.T., Poll, E.: Beyond assertions: Advanced specification and verification with JML and ESC/Java2. In: de Boer, F.S., Bonsangue, M.M., Graf, S., de Roever, W.-P. (eds.) FMCO 2005. LNCS, vol. 4111, pp. 342–363. Springer, Heidelberg (2006)
7. Clavel, M., Durán, F., Eker, S., Lincoln, P., Martí-Oliet, N., Meseguer, J., Talcott, C.: All About Maude - A High-Performance Logical Framework. LNCS, vol. 4350. Springer, Heidelberg (2007)
8. Cousot, P., Cousot, R.: Abstract interpretation: A unified lattice model for static analysis of programs by construction or approximation of fixpoints. In: Conference Record of the Fourth ACM Symposium on Principles of Programming Languages, pp. 238–252 (1977)
9. Cousot, P., Cousot, R.: Systematic Design of Program Analysis Frameworks. In: Proc. of Sixth ACM Symp. on Principles of Programming Languages, pp. 269–282 (1979)
10. Farzan, A., Chen, F., Meseguer, J., Rosu, G.: JavaRL: The rewriting logic semantics of Java (2007),
    http://fsl.cs.uiuc.edu/index.php/Rewriting_Logic_Semantics_of_Java
11. Farzan, A., Chen, F., Meseguer, J., Rosu, G.: Formal analysis of Java programs in JavaFAN. In: Alur, R., Peled, D.A. (eds.) CAV 2004. LNCS, vol. 3114, pp. 501–505. Springer, Heidelberg (2004)
12. Farzan, A., Meseguer, J., Rosu, G.: Formal JVM code analysis in JavaFAN. In: Rattray, C., Maharaj, S., Shankland, C. (eds.) AMAST 2004. LNCS, vol. 3116, pp. 132–147. Springer, Heidelberg (2004)
13. Felty, A.P.: A tutorial example of the semantic approach to foundational proof-carrying code. In: Giesl, J. (ed.) RTA 2005. LNCS, vol. 3467, pp. 394–406. Springer, Heidelberg (2005)
14. Flanagan, C., Leino, K.R.M., Lillibridge, M., Nelson, G., Saxe, J.B., Stata, R.: Extended static checking for Java. In: PLDI, pp. 234–245 (2002)
15. Leavens, G., Baker, A., Ruby, C.: Preliminary design of JML: A behavioral interface specification language for Java. ACM SIGSOFT Software Engineering Notes 31(3), 1–38 (2006)
16. Meseguer, J.: Conditional rewriting logic as a unified model of concurrency. Theor. Comput. Sci. 96(1), 73–155 (1992)
17. Meseguer, J., Rosu, G.: The rewriting logic semantics project. Theor. Comput. Sci. 373(3), 213–237 (2007)
18. Necula, G.C.: Proof carrying code. In: Proceedings of the 24th ACM SIGPLAN-SIGACT Annual Symposium on Principles of Programming Languages POPL 1997, Paris, France, pp. 106–119. ACM Press, New York, NY, USA (1997)
19. Necula, G.C., Lee, P.: Safe kernel extensions without run time checking. In: Proc. of the second USENIX symposium on Operating systems design and implementation OSDI 1996, pp. 229–243. ACM Press, New York (1996)
20. TeReSe (ed.): Term Rewriting Systems. Cambridge University Press, Cambridge (2003)
21. Wildmoser, M., Nipkow, T., Klein, G., Nanz, S.: Prototyping proof carrying code. In: Lévy, J.-J., Mayr, E.W., Mitchell, J.C. (eds.) 3rd Int'll Conf. on Theoretical Computer Science (TCS 2004), pp. 333–348. Kluwer, Dordrecht (2004)
22. Wu, D., Appel, A., Stump, A.: Foundational proof checkers with small witnesses. In: Proceedings of the 5th ACM SIGPLAN international conference on Principles and practice of declarative programming PPDP, pp. 264–274. ACM Press, New York (2003)

Reverse Engineered Formal Models for GUI Testing[*]

Ana C.R. Paiva[1], João C.P. Faria[1,2], and Pedro M.C. Mendes[1]

[1] Engineering Faculty of the University of Porto, [2] INESC Porto
Rua Dr. Roberto Frias, s/n, 4200-465 Porto, Portugal
{apaiva, jpf, pedro.mendes}@fe.up.pt
http://www.fe.up.pt

Abstract. This paper describes a process to reverse engineer structural and behavioural formal models of a GUI application by a dynamic technique, mixing
manual with automatic exploration. The goal is to diminish the effort required
to construct the model and mapping information needed in a model-based GUI
testing process. A skeleton of a state machine model of the GUI, represented in
a formal pre/post specification language, is generated automatically by the exploration process. Mapping information between the model and the implementation is also generated along the way. The model extracted automatically is
then completed manually in order to get an executable model which can be used
as a test oracle. Abstract test cases, including expected outputs, can be generated automatically from the final model and executed over the GUI application,
using the mapping information generated during the exploration process.

Keywords: Reverse engineering; model-based GUI testing.

1 Introduction

GUI testing, with the purpose of finding bugs in the GUI or in the overall application,
is a necessary but very time consuming V&V activity. The application of model-based
testing techniques and tools can be very helpful to systematize and automate GUI testing. An example of a model-based GUI testing approach, based on the Spec# pre/post
specification language [1] and extensions to the Spec Explorer model-based testing
tool [2], is described in [8,9,10].

However, the effort required to construct a detailed and precise enough model for
testing purposes (in order to be able to generate not only test inputs but also expected
outputs), together with mapping information between the model and the implementation (in order to be able to execute abstract test cases derived from the model on a
concrete GUI), are obstacles to the wide adoption of these techniques. One way to
relief the effort mentioned is to produce a partial "as-is" model, together with mapping information, by an automated reverse engineering process. This model will have
to be validated and detailed manually, in order to obtain a complete" should-be"

[*] Work partially supported by FCT (Portugal) and FEDER (European Union) under contract
POSC/EIA/56646/2004.

S. Leue and P. Merino (Eds.): FMICS 2007, LNCS 4916, pp. 218–233, 2008.

model at the level of abstraction desired. Some defects in the application can be discovered in this stage. Overall, the goal is to automate the interactive exploratory process that is commonly followed by testers to obtain a model for an existing application.

In this paper we present a dynamic GUI reverse engineering approach to achieve such goal. The application under test (AUT) is automatically explored through its GUI to discover as much as possible the GUI structure and behaviour and to generate a corresponding GUI model in Spec#, together with mapping information between the model and the implementation. Automatic exploration can be intermixed with manual exploration to allow accessing functionalities that are protected by a key or are in some other way difficult to access automatically. During the exploration process, the intermediate code of the AUT is instrumented with Aspect-Oriented Programming (AOP) techniques in order to be able to recognize and capture a wider range of GUI controls and events, beyond native ones. The model generated automatically is subsequently validated and completed manually.

An "Address Book" application (Fig. 1) built in Java with the Standard Widget Toolkit (SWT) provided by the Eclipse/Rich Client Platform (RCP) will be used as an example to illustrate the approach proposed.

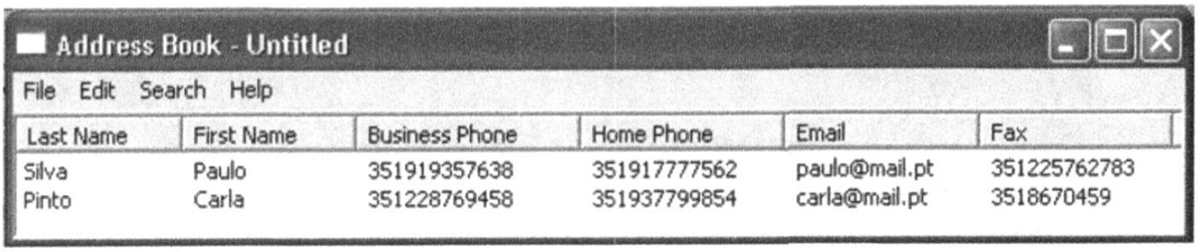

Fig. 1. Address Book main window

This paper is structured as follows: next section gives an overview of the reverse engineering and model-based GUI testing process; section 3 describes the desired characteristics of the target GUI model; section 4 describes the GUI reverse engineering process, while the details of the generation of the GUI model and mapping information are presented in section 5; section 6 describes model validation techniques; section 7 describes related work and the last section presents the conclusions and future work.

2   Overview of the Reverse Engineering and Model-Based GUI Testing Process

The goal of model-based testing is to check the conformity between the implementation and the specification (model) of a software system. The main activities of the model-based GUI testing process proposed are presented in Fig. 2.

The starting activity proposed is the construction of a preliminary GUI model by a reverse engineering process supported by the new REGUI2FM tool. This tool produces a preliminary GUI model in Spec# [1] and mapping information between the model and the implementation.

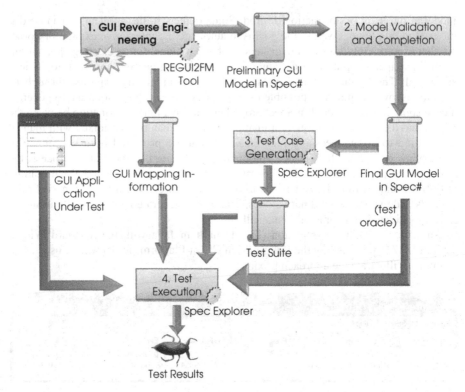

Fig. 2. Overview of the model-based GUI testing process with reverse engineering

The model obtained by the reverse engineering process captures structural information about the GUI (the hierarchical structure of windows and interactive controls
within windows and their properties) and some behavioural information. The model
describes at a high-level of abstraction the state of each window and window control
(enabled/disabled status, content of text boxes, etc.) and the actions the user can perform on the window controls (e.g., press a button, fill in a text box). Besides the signature of each action, some pre and post-conditions are also generated, describing the
states where each action is available (in the pre-condition) and navigation among
windows caused by user actions (in the post-condition).

The mapping information comprise a XML file (GUI object map), describing
physical properties of the GUI objects, and adaptor C# code with methods that simulate the user actions over the GUI, which are automatically bound to model actions.
This information is needed to execute abstract test cases derived from the model on a
concrete GUI.

In order to assure that the model is consistent with the application requirements
and can be effectively used for test case generation and test output evaluation (as a
test oracle), the preliminary model obtained by the reverse engineering process must
be validated and completed manually with additional behaviour specifications.

Typically, executable method bodies must be added manually. Completeness and correctness of the model can be checked visually by defining views with the help of the Spec Explorer tool.

The final GUI model is then used to generate a test suite automatically, using the Spec Explorer tool [2]. Spec Explorer automatically generates test cases from a Spec# specification in two steps. In the first step, a finite state machine (FSM) is generated from the given Spec# specification. In the second step, a test suite that fulfils some coverage criteria is generated from the FSM (e.g., full transition coverage, shortest path or random walk). A test suite is a set of test segments with sequences of operations that model user actions (with input parameters) interleaved with operations to check the outcomes of those actions.

Test execution is also supported by the Spec Explorer tool. Conceptually, during test case execution, related actions (obtained from the mapping information) run in both the specification and implementation levels, in a "lock-step" mode, being their results compared after each step. Whenever an inconsistency is detected, it is reported.

3 Characteristic of the Target GUI Model

In the approach proposed, the main output of the reverse engineering process is a preliminary GUI model in Spec#, which is subsequently refined and provided as input to the Spec Explorer model-based testing tool. Hence, before explaining in more detail the reverse engineering process, it is important to describe how GUIs can be adequately modelled in Spec#, for model-based testing purposes.

Spec# is a pre/post specification language that extends the C# programming language with pre-conditions (written as *requires* clauses), post-conditions (written as *ensures* clauses), invariants, logical quantifiers, and other high-level constructs. A specification written in Spec# is executable: besides method pre/post conditions, one can write executable method bodies (also called model programs). This allows the specification to be used as a test oracle. Models written in Spec# can be the input for the Spec Explorer model-based testing tool.

For conformance testing purposes, a model written in Spec# can be seen as a description of a possibly infinite transition system. The states of the transition system are given by the values of the state variables. The transitions are executions of methods annotated as *Action*. Method pre-conditions indicate which actions are enabled in each system state. Spec# provides four kinds of actions: *controllable*, *probe*, *observable* and *scenario*. *Controllable* actions (the default ones) describe actions that are controlled by the user (or test driver) of the AUT; these actions may update the system state. *Probe* actions describe actions that only read the system state; they are invoked by the test harness in every state where their pre-condition holds, to check the actual AUT state against the model state. *Observable* actions are asynchronous and describe the spontaneous execution of an action in the AUT possibly caused by some internal thread; they are not used in the context of this work. *Scenario* actions describe composite actions; they are useful to drive the system into a desired initial state or to reduce the size of the test suite. When a scenario action is explored for test case generation, Spec Explorer records the sequence of atomic actions called and the intermediate states traversed.

Spec# can be used to model the GUI structure and behaviour at any level of abstraction desired. We describe next a choice of level of abstraction that we found appropriate for most form-based GUIs. Top-level windows of the AUT are modelled as separate classes or modules (namespaces). The internal state of each top-level window (content of text fields, etc.) is modelled by state variables. The actions available to the user inside each top-level window (enter a string into a text field, press a button, select a menu option, etc.) are modelled as *Action* methods. Pre-conditions describe the states in which the actions are available to the user. Post-conditions and method bodies describe the effect of the user actions on the system state. *Probe* methods are used to model the observation of GUI state by the user. *Scenario* methods are optionally used to model typical usage scenarios – sequences of steps (execution of lower level scenarios and atomic actions) the user should follow to achieve a goal. These scenarios need not represent end-to-end usage sequences, because scenario actions and atomic actions can be intermixed in the test cases generated.

An example of part of a Spec# model of the "Find" dialog box (Fig. 3) of the Address Book application is shown in Fig. 4. The "*Find what*" text box is modelled by a state variable (findWhat) and set and get action and probe methods. Check boxes are modelled by Boolean state variables (matchCase and matchWholeWord) and associated set and get methods. The *"Direction"* radio group and the *"Column"* combo box (with a closed list of options) are modelled by state variables (direction and column) of enumerated types and associated set and get methods. The "*Find*" button is modelled by an action method. All methods modelling user actions over GUI objects have a pre-condition that checks if their container window is enabled, and may have additional pre-conditions. For example, the *Find* button has an additional pre-condition to represent the fact that it is enabled only when the "*Find what*" text box is filled in. The example also includes calls to a reusable window management library that keeps track of the collection of windows open and of their enabled/disabled status (when a modal window is opened the other windows of the AUT are disabled).

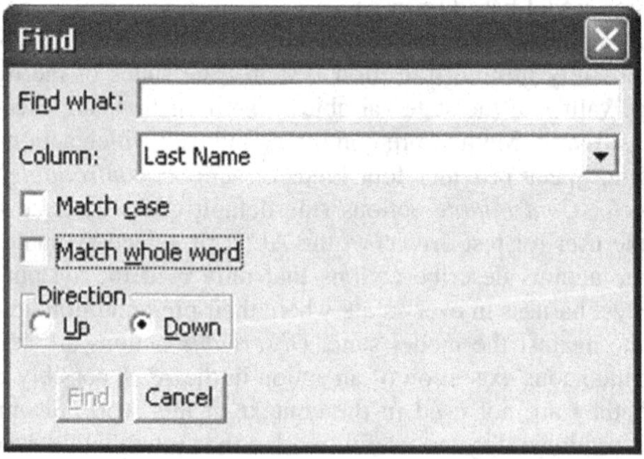

Fig. 3. "Find" dialog window of the Address Book application

```
namespace Find;

enum DirectionEnum { "Up", "Down" };
enum ColumnEnum {"Last Name", "First Name",
        "Business Phone", "Home Phone", "Email", "Fax"};

var string findWhat = "";
var bool matchCase = false;
var bool matchWholeWord = false;
var DirectionEnum direction = "Down";
var ColumnEnum column = "Last Name";

public string FindWhat {
  [Action(kind=Probe)] get
  requires IsEnabled("Find"); { return findWhat; }
  [Action] set
  requires IsEnabled("Find"); { findWhat = value; }
}

// similar properties for Column, MatchCase, MatchWholeWord
// and Direction

[Action] public void Find()
requires IsEnabled("Find") && findWhat != ""; {
  AddressBookWnd.FindNext(findWhat, column, matchCase,
                    matchWholeWord, direction);
}

[Action] public void Cancel()
requires IsEnabled("Find");
ensures IsClosed("Find"); {
    RemoveWindow("Find");
}
```

Fig. 4. Spec# model for the "Find" dialog window of the Address Book application

4   The GUI Reverse Engineering Process

The aim of the GUI reverse engineering tool (REGUI2FM) is to reduce the effort involved in the construction of the GUI model. As already mentioned in the overview, the GUI reverse engineering tool extracts structural and behavioural information about the GUI under test by a dynamic exploration process that mixes automatic and manual exploration. Its architecture is depicted in Fig. 5. The tool provides a front-end that gives access to a GUI Spy&Act tool, for automatic exploration (exploration mode), and a GUI Record tool, for manual exploration (record mode).

The GUI Spy&Act tool captures information about the GUI objects that are present in the AUT, in a way similar to the Spy++ tool that ships with Microsoft Visual Studio, and, based on that information, acts on the GUI objects simulating a user (e.g., click a button, select a menu option, or fill in a textbox), in a way similar to a smart monkey testing [7] tool. Since the Spy&Act tool interacts with the AUT through the operating system window manager, it is independent of the development language of the AUT.

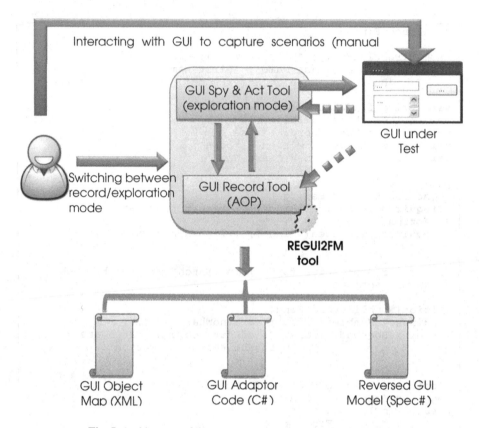

Fig. 5. Architecture of the reverse engineering tool (REGUI2FM)

A preliminary GUI model in Spec# is abstracted from the GUI states and transitions observed (in response to the actions performed), together with mapping information between the model and the physical GUI. Each window gives rise to a Spec# module. Interactive controls give rise to instance variables (e.g., there is a string variable for each text box) and methods (e.g., methods to read/write the text from/to a textbox), following the modelling style described in section 3 and illustrated in Fig. 4.

The Spec# state variables and actions (either *controllable* or *probe*) that the GUI Spy&Act tool should generate for each kind of GUI object can be configured in a XML file, as illustrated in Fig. 6. In this example, it will be generated a string instance variable and associated *set* and *get* methods for each textbox found, and a method corresponding to the *Click* action for each button found. This configuration information is also used by the tool to determine which kind of actions it should execute over physical GUI objects during the exploration. This file needs to be constructed only once and may be reused by other GUI reverse engineering processes.

```
<InteractiveObjects>
  <obj>
    <ClassName>TextBox</ClassName>
    <statevariable>string</statevariable>
    <controllable>set</controllable>
    <probe>get</probe>
  </obj>
  <obj>
    <ClassName>Button</ClassName>
    <controllable>Click</controllable>
  </obj>
  <obj> ... </obj>
  ...
</InteractiveObjects>
```

Fig. 6. XML configuration file

The GUI Spy&Act tool might not be able to reach application functionality that is protected by a key or is in any other way difficult to access without further knowledge. Two solutions are available to overcome this problem:

- the first one is to provide in advance some domain values that can be used during the automatic exploration process when interacting with controls;
- the other one is to switch to manual exploration mode, so that the user can interact with the GUI to supply the data or perform the steps required to access the hidden functionality, and switch back to automatic exploration thereupon.

The GUI Record tool captures the actions performed by the user, together with the GUI states traversed, in a way conceptually similar to a capture-replay tool. The sequence of actions performed by the user is abstracted to a Spec# method annotated as *scenario*.

At the end, the following files are generated:

- a XML file (GUI Object Map) gathering information about the windows and interactive controls detected, including physical identifying properties and logical names assigned;
- a Spec# file with the reversed GUI model, describing possible user actions over the GUI (behaviour model);
- a C# file (adaptor code) with methods to simulate concrete user actions over the GUI under test, corresponding to the abstract actions described in the Spec# model (needed for conformance checking during test execution).

The main activities and artifacts involved will be explained in next sections.

4.1 Automatic Exploration

The exploration starts from the application main window. In each step, it is captured information about interactive controls inside windows of the AUT. The information captured comprises: the hierarchical structure of GUI objects (windows and controls within windows); the type of each GUI object (window, button, textbox, etc.); values of identifying properties (e.g., parent window and id), control state properties (e.g., enabled/disabled), and data state properties (e.g., text content) for each GUI object. The set of properties that should be captured for each type of GUI object can be configured by the user.

After identifying the interactive controls existing in an AUT window, the tool starts interacting with them simulating a user, e.g., click on buttons and menus, send text to textboxes, and select combo box options. The actions to explore upon each type of control and their input values can be configured by the user.

Some of the actions performed may cause navigation among windows (open a new window, close the current window and return to a previously visited window, etc.). In each step, the tool acts upon the window that has the input focus.

The tool keeps track of the collection of windows already reached and of the controls detected in those windows, using their identifying properties to avoid duplicates, as well as of the actions already performed on those controls.

The exploration process stops when all the relevant actions in all the windows reached have been explored, or when it is unable to make progress for some reason.

4.2 Manual Exploration

When the exploration algorithm stops before capturing information about all the windows of the application (e.g., there is a part of the application which is protected by a key), the user can switch to record mode.

In record mode it is assumed that the AUT runs on an AO (aspect oriented) enabled virtual machine and that it was built using the object-oriented programming paradigm [4,11]. When running the application in such an environment, the developed aspects extend the GUI object's "construction" process, by adding extra event listeners. These listeners are enabled only when an environment variable indicates that the current exploration mode is manual mode. The listeners intercept all possible user actions on standard GUI objects. Interaction with customized GUI objects extending standard ones requires adding some extra advice code using the chosen AO programming language for the purpose at hand. The advantage of this AOP technique is the ability to recognize a wide range of GUI controls, beyond native ones.

The advice code is responsible for logging user actions while interacting with GUI controls saving them in a Spec# scenario action such as the one that can be seen in Fig. 8.

5   Generation of the GUI Model and Mapping Information

5.1   Generation of the GUI Object Map (XML)

The GUI object map (Fig. 7) enumerates the GUI objects (windows and controls) of the AUT, and relates logical GUI object names with physical identifying properties. It is stored in a XML file. Logical names are assigned based on some heuristics (caption, nearest label, etc.).

```
<window name="Find">
  <caption>Find</caption>
  <class>#32770</class>
    <control name="Cancel">
      <caption>Cancel</caption>
      <class>Button</class>
      <id>2</id>
      <childPos>8</ChildPos>
    </control>
    <control ...>
      ...
    </control>
  ...
</window>
```

Fig. 7. GUI object map (XML)

5.2 Generation of the GUI Model (Spec#)

A preliminary GUI model in Spec# is generated by the REGUI2FM tool as explained in the next sub-sections.

5.2.1 Generation of the Overall Model Structure and Pre/Post Conditions

As already mentioned in section 3, the top-level windows of the application are modelled in separate namespaces or classes (for modularity reasons).

Inside each module (namespace or class) corresponding to a top-level window, state variables are used to model its abstract state and the state of the controls inside it. Each action that can be performed by the user within each top-level window (set/get the content of a control, press a button, etc.) is represented in Spec# by an *Action* method with a pre-condition that checks if the container window is enabled. In the case of actions that cause navigation among windows, it is also generated a post-condition that checks the open/closed and/or enabled/disabled status of the affected windows and a default method body (see the *Cancel* method in Fig. 4).

Besides keeping track of window navigation effects caused by the actions explored, the reverse engineering tool also keeps track of enabling/disabling and content update effects on GUI controls. Some of these dependencies among GUI controls can also be represented through pre and post-conditions, according to the type of dependency:

− "Setting the content of an object *A* to some condition enables an object *B*" – e.g., in the *Find* dialog shown in Fig. 4, the *Find* button is enabled when the *findWhat* text box is filled in. This dependency may be represented in Spec# by adding a pre-condition that checks the state of *A* to the methods that describe possible actions on object *B*. This avoids the addition of an extra state variable to represent the enabled/disabled status of *B*.

```
[Action] ... BMethods(...)
requires IsEnabled("WindowOfB") && A.State == S_A;
...
```

– "Performing an action on an object *A* updates the content of an object *B*" – e.g., pressing a *Clear* button may erase the fields in a form. This dependency may be represented in Spec# by a post-condition of the method that describes that specific action on *A*. A default method body is also generated.

```
[Action] ... AMethod(...)
ensures B.state == S_B;
{  B.state = S_B; ... }
```

In some cases, these dependencies can be discovered automatically by the exploration process. That would be the case of buttons that are only enabled when some text box is filled in, and buttons that erase the context of text boxes.

5.2.2 Generation of Default Method Bodies

Default method bodies are generated for set/get methods (see Fig. 4), and methods that cause navigation (see Cancel method in Fig. 4). Those method bodies must be checked and completed by the user, to take into account complex behaviours and side effects. For example, the method body of the *Find* action in Fig. 4 has to be constructed manually. All the other method bodies are generated automatically.

5.2.3 Generation of Scenario Methods

The sequences of actions performed by the tester while in record mode are captured by the REGUI2FM tool as *scenario* actions (Fig. 8) supported by Spec Explorer, as explained before. If desired, the scenarios generated can be subsequently edited by the modeller/tester. E.g., concrete values can be replaced by parameters to make the scenarios more generic and reusable.

Scenarios are useful for testing purposes in different ways: as a technique to drive the application into a desirable specific state, overcoming the problem of functionality protected by a key (Fig. 8), as explained before; as a way to describe test conditions that would be covered by manual tests and that can be seen as the minimum set of conditions to automatically test; and as a technique to prune the model exploration and test case generation process [2].

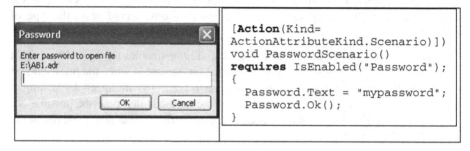

Fig. 8. Manual exploration sequence of a password dialog box recorded as a scenario action

5.3 Generation of the GUI Adapter Code (C#)

The C# code needed to execute the abstract test suit upon the real GUI, simulating the user actions, has a method for each (abstract) action described in the Spec# model. As an example, Fig. 9 illustrates the C# code generated for the portion of the Find namespace shown in Fig. 4.

The C# code generated is based on calls to a reusable GUI Test Library that provides methods to simulate the actions of a user interacting with a GUI application and observe the content of GUI objects. This library was constructed in C# extending a previous existing library to best fit our needs.

```
#region automatically generated code
  class GUIAdapter {
  public static void Find_SetFindWhat(string p0){
    UserEvents.SetText("Find.FindWhat, p0);
  }
  public static string Find_GetFindWhat(){
   return UserEvents.GetText("Find.FindWhat");
  }
  public static void Find_matchCase(bool p0) {
    UserEvents.SelectCheckBok("Find.MatchCase", p0);
  }
  public static void Find_matchWholeWord(bool p0) {
    UserEvents.SelectCheckBok("Find.MatchWholeWord", p0);
  }
  public static void Find_Find() {
    UserEvents.Click("Find.Find");
  }
  public static void Find_Cancel() {
    UserEvents.Click("Find.Cancel");
  }
  //...
}
#endregion
```

Fig. 9. C# code to simulate user actions for test execution

6 Model Validation

After completing the GUI model manually, it is possible to construct a view [10] of the navigation map using Spec Explorer (Fig. 10). Visual inspection of this map is a way to validate the model obtained.

Each state in Fig. 10 indicates the windows of the GUI that are enabled. In the presence of modeless windows, there may be more than one window enabled at the same time, in which case, a state may have more than one window name. This is the case of the *Find&AddressBook* state. While a modal dialog window is opened, as is the case of *Open*, *Save* and *Contact* windows in Fig. 10, user interaction with all other currently open windows of the same application is disabled.

The transitions visible at this level of abstraction are transitions that open/close windows of the GUI application. All transitions that occur inside a window/dialog are abstracted as one transition from the state that represents the dialog/window to itself.

This view can be expressed mathematically as the projection of the model states onto the state variable that holds the set of enabled windows.

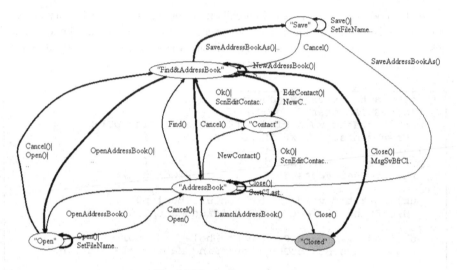

Fig. 10. Navigation map graph

7   Related Work

Reverse engineering is the process of analyzing a subject system to create representations of the system at a higher level of abstraction [3]. It may be performed by static and dynamic analysis. Static analysis is performed on software code and does not involve its execution. Dynamic analysis extracts information from software by executing it.

Reverse engineering can be useful in several contexts like documentation, maintenance and specification-based testing. Another common application of reverse engineering is within a re-engineering process, for instance, to exchange legacy systems to different newer technologies.

The world is full of legacy systems. The technology is in constant change and some companies need to update their old systems. Reverse engineering tools can be used to build the model of existing applications that can be used by UIMSs to generate new GUIs with the same functionality of the older ones, but implemented in more recent technologies, or to be accessed from other computer platforms with specific characteristics.

One common example is the migration of legacy user interfaces to web-accessible platforms in order to support e-commerce activities. Stroulia et al. describe the CelL-EST system within which a new process for migrating legacy systems for the Web was developed [12,13].

Vanderdonckt et al. describe a reverse engineering process of Web user interfaces [14]. The goal is to extract models of Web applications that were not constructed using a model-based approach and then use those models to generate UIs for other computer platforms, like palms, pocket computers, and mobile phones, without losing the effort deployed in the construction of the initial application.

The use of reverse engineering techniques to extract models to be used in a specification-based testing process is not so common. However, there is at least one example of this approach developed by Memon [5]. Memon claims that constructing a GUI model that can be used for test case generation is difficult, so he developed an approach to reverse engineer a model directly from an executable GUI. A so-called GUI ripping process opens automatically all the windows of the GUI under test and extracts their widgets, properties, and values. In the end, it is generated a GUI model that represents the GUI structure as a GUI forest, and its execution behaviour as an event-flow graph and an integration tree. However, the tool does not allow editing the model generated. Memon reports experiences where the ripping process is applied to extract a model from a correct GUI; the model extracted is then used to test an incorrect GUI. In industrial environments, such approach is helpful for regression testing.

Our approach distinguishes from the Memon's approach [5] mainly because of the expressiveness of the behavioural model that can be obtained, which is not limited to describe dependencies between pairs of user events (by an event-flow graph), but comprises also an explicit representation of the GUI state and pre/post conditions expressing dependencies between user events and the GUI state. This allows the same model to be used for the generation of valid test input sequences and outputs expected. In the Memon's approach, a separate pre/post model might be used as a test oracle, i.e., for the generation of the outputs expected [6], and the test sequences generated in first hand may not be valid because of state dependencies that are not taken into account.

8 Conclusions and Future Work

It was presented a dynamic GUI reverse engineering process, mixing automatic and manual exploration, with the goal of diminishing the effort required in constructing a GUI model for model-based testing purposes. Manual exploration mode is used to overcome situations when the automatic exploration process cannot progress because of dependencies that it cannot discover or because of functionalities that are protected by a password.

The outcome of the reverse engineering process is a preliminary behavioural GUI model in Spec#, together with mapping information between the model and the implementation (needed for test execution). The Spec# model describes at a high level of abstraction the actions available to the user and their effect on the GUI state. The mapping information comprises a XML file that stores information about the physical properties of the GUI objects, and a C# code file that bridges the gap between the abstract actions described in the model and simulated user actions upon the physical GUI objects.

The model generated automatically by the reverse engineering process has to be validated and completed manually so that it can be used as a test oracle. Test cases are generated from this model and then executed to check the conformity between the model and an implementation with the help of the Spec Explorer tool.

Preliminary results of using the reverse engineering tool (REGUI2FM) in small GUI applications show that the majority (around 70%) of the model can be built automatically.

We are currently enhancing the REGUI2FM tool to deal with more complex GUI applications and to use in the automatic exploration mode the same AOP mechanisms that are used to record user actions in manual exploration mode. By proceeding with this evolution, the scope of recognizable objects is expected to broaden, and the effort required to build the models is expected to be further reduced.

References

1. Barnett, M., Leino, K.R.M., Schulte, W.: The Spec# Programming System: An Overview. In: Barthe, G., Burdy, L., Huisman, M., Lanet, J.-L., Muntean, T. (eds.) CASSIS 2004. LNCS, vol. 3362. Springer, Heidelberg (2005)
2. Campbell, C., Grieskamp, W., Nachmanson, L., Schulte, W., Tillmann, N., Veanes, M.: Model-Based Testing of Object-Oriented Reactive Systems with Spec Explorer, Microsoft Research, MSR-TR-2005-59 (May 2005)
3. Chikofsky, E.J., Cross, J.H.: Reverse Engineering and Design Recovery: A Taxonomy. IEEE Software 7(1), 13–17 (1990)
4. Kiczales, G., Lamping, J., Menhdhekar, A., Maeda, C., Lopes, C., Loingtier, J.-M., Irwin, J.: Aspect-Oriented Programming. In: M. A. a. S. M. (eds.) Proceedings of the European Conference on Object-Oriented Programming (1997)
5. Memon, A., Banerjee, I., Nagarajan, A.: GUI Ripping: Reverse Engineering of Graphical User Interfaces for Testing. In: Proceedings of the WCRE 2003 - The 10th Working Conference on Reverse Engineering, Victoria, British Columbia, Canada, November 13–16 (2003)
6. Memon, A.M., Pollack, M.E., Soffa, M.L.: Automated Test Oracles for GUIs. In: Proceedings of the FSE (2000)
7. Nyman, N.: In Defense of Monkey Testing (conferred in May 2006)
8. Paiva, A.C.R.: Automated Specification-Based Testing of Graphical User Interfaces, Ph.D, Engineering Faculty of Porto University (Ph.D thesis), Department of Electrical and Computer Engineering (2007), http://www.fe.up.pt/~apaiva/PhD/PhDGUITesting.pdf
9. Paiva, A.C.R., Faria, J.C.P., Tillmann, N., Vidal, R.F.A.M.: A Model-to-implementation Mapping Tool for Automated Model-based GUI Testing. In: Lau, K.-K., Banach, R. (eds.) ICFEM 2005. LNCS, vol. 3785. Springer, Heidelberg (2005)
10. Paiva, A.C.R., Tillmann, N., Faria, J.C.P., Vidal, R.F.A.M.: Modeling and Testing Hierarchical GUIs. In: Proceedings of the ASM 2005 - 12th International Workshop on Abstract State Machines, Paris - France, March 8–11 (2005)
11. Sabbah, D.: Aspect-Oriented software development. In: Proceedings of the Third International Conference on Aspect-oriented Software Development, Lancaster, UK (2004)

12. Stroulia, E., El-Ramly, M., Iglinski, P., Sorenson, P.: User Interface Reverse Engineering in Support of Interface Migration to the Web. Automated Software Engineering 10, 271–301 (2003)
13. Stroulia, E., El-Ramly, M., Kong, L., Sorenson, P., Matichuk, B.: Reverse Engineering Legacy Interfaces: An Interaction-Driven Approach. In: Proceedings of the WCRE 1999 (1999)
14. Vanderdonckt, J., Bouillon, L., Souchon, N.: Flexible Reverse Engineering of Web Pages with VAQUISTA. In: Proceedings of the IEEE 8th Working Conf. on Reverse Engineering (2001)

Automatic Interoperability Test Case Generation Based on Formal Definitions

Alexandra Desmoulin and César Viho

IRISA/Université de Rennes 1, Campus de Beaulieu, 35042 Rennes Cedex, France
{alexandra.desmoulin,viho}@irisa.fr

Abstract. The objective of this study is to provide methods for deriving automatically interoperability tests based on formal definitions. First, we give interoperability formal definitions taking into account both objectives of interoperability: the implementations must interact correctly and the expected service must be provided. Based on these definitions, a method for generating interoperability test cases is described. This method is equivalent to classical methods in terms of non-interoperability detection and avoids state-space explosion problem. Classical and proposed methods were implemented using the CADP Toolbox and applied on a connection protocol to illustrate this contribution.

1 Introduction

In the domain of network protocols, implementations are tested to ensure that they will correctly work in an operational environment. These implementations are developed based on specifications, generally standards. Different kinds of tests exist. Among these tests, conformance and interoperability testing considers the behaviour of these implementations at their interfaces to verify that they will work correctly in a real network. The aim of conformance tests [1] is to verify that a single implementation behaves as described in its specification. Interoperability testing objectives are to check both if different implementations communicate (or interact) correctly and if they provide the services described in their respective specification during this interaction.

Conformance testing has been formalized [1, 2]. A formal framework exist together with testing architectures, formal definitions and methods for writting conformance tests. Moreover, this formalization leads to automatic test generation methods and tools like TGV [3] or TorX [4].

In the interoperability testing situation, there is no precise characterization of interoperability for the moment. However, some attemps to give formal definitions of interoperability exists [5, 6]. Some studies also give methods for automatically deriving interoperability tests [7, 8]. These methods are generally based on fault models or on the search of some particular kinds of error. But there is still no method for the moment describing how to generate interoperability test cases based on formal definitions.

In a previous study [5], we give some formal definitions of the notion of interoperability together with some clues for test generation. In this study, we

S. Leue and P. Merino (Eds.): FMICS 2007, LNCS 4916, pp. 234–250, 2008.

complete these formal definitions to take into account all the objectives of interoperability testing. Thus, the so-called "interoperability criteria" describe the conditions that two implementations must satisfy to be considered interoperable and follow the main objectives of interoperability: providing the expected service while interacting correctly. Based on these definitions and using the clues given in [5], we develop a complete interoperability test derivation method. Moreover, we implement this method using the CADP Toolbox. Its application on a connection protocol allows us to verify both that it can generate interoperability test case equivalent to test cases that would have been obtained manually or with classical methods, and that it avoids state-space explosion problem that generally occurs with classical methods [6].

This paper is decomposed as follows. First, Section 2 describes notions used in the paper including interoperability testing architectures and formal models. Then, Section 3 is aimed at providing formal definitions of interoperability. Section 4 describes a method for deriving automatically interoperability tests based on these definitions. Section 5 describes the results of the application of the proposed interoperability test generation method on a connection protocol. Finally, conclusion and future work are in Section 6.

2   Preliminaries

In this Section, we present the different notions that are used in this study. First, we define interoperability testing and interoperability testing architecture in Section 2.1. Then, we describe the model of IOLTS used for interoperability formal definitions in Section 2.2. The proposed method for interoperability test generation reuses some aspects of conformance testing. Few words are said in Section 2.3 on the state of the art in automatic test generation.

2.1   Interoperability Testing

We consider here the context of protocol testing. Protocol implementations are developped based on specifications, generally protocol standards. They must be tested to ensure that thay will work correctly in an operational environment. We consider here the context of black-box testing: the implementations are known by the events executed on their interfaces, generally sending and receiving messages. Among the different kinds of protocol testing contexts, we consider here interoperability testing that puts in relation different implementations (generally from different manufacturers) to verify that they are able to work together.

Interoperability testing has two goals. It verifies that different protocol implementations can communicate correctly, *and* that they provide the services described in their respective specification while communicating. In this study, we consider a context with two implementations under test (IUT for short): this is the one-to-one context (see Figure 1). In an interoperability testing architecture [9, 10], we can differentiate two kinds of interfaces: Lower Interfaces (used for the interaction) and Upper Interfaces (used for the communication with

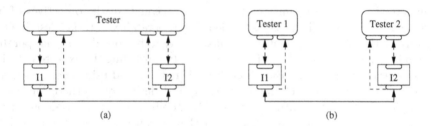

Fig. 1. Interoperability testing architectures

upper layer). Testers are connected to these interfaces but they can *control* (send message) only the upper interfaces. The lower interfaces are only *observable*.

Depending on the access to the interfaces, different architectures can be distinguished. For example, the interoperability testing architecture is called *unilateral* if only the interfaces of one IUT are accessible during the interaction, *bilateral* if the interfaces of both IUTs are accessible but separately (Figure 1(b)), or *global* if the interfaces of both IUTs are accessible with a global view (Figure 1(a)).

2.2 IOLTS Model

We use IOLTS (Input-Output Labeled Transition System) to model specifications. As usual in the black-box testing context, we also need to model IUTs, even though their behaviors are unknown. They are also modeled by an IOLTS.

Definition 1. *An IOLTS is a tuple $M=(Q^M, \Sigma^M, \Delta^M, q_0^M)$. Q^M is the set of states and $q_0^M \in Q^M$ the initial state. Σ^M denotes the set of observable events on the interfaces: $p?m \in \Sigma^M$ (resp. $p!m \in \Sigma^M$) stands for an input (resp. output) where p is the interface and m the message. Δ^M is the transition relation.*

Other Notations. Σ^M can be decomposed: $\Sigma^M = \Sigma_U^M \cup \Sigma_L^M$, where Σ_U^M (resp. Σ_L^M) is the set of messages exchanged on the upper (resp. lower) interfaces. Σ^M can also be decomposed to distinguish input (Σ_I^M) and output messages (Σ_O^M). Based on this model, $Traces(q)$ is the set of executable traces (successions of events) from the state q. $\Gamma(q)$ is the set of executable events (on the interfaces of M) from the state q and $\Gamma(M, \sigma)$ the set of executable events for the system M after the trace σ. In the same way, $Out(M, \sigma)$ (resp. $In(M, \sigma)$) is the set of possible outputs (resp. inputs) for M after the trace σ. Considering a link between lower interfaces l_i of M_i and l_j of M_j, we also define $\bar{\mu}$ as $\bar{\mu}=l_i!a$ if $\mu = l_j?a$ and $\bar{\mu} = l_i?a$ if $\mu = l_j!a$.

Quiescence. An implementation can be *quiescent* in three different situations: either the IUT can be waiting on an input, either it can be executing a loop of internal (non-observable) events, or it can be in a state where no event is executable. For an IOLTS M_i, a quiescent state q is modeled by $(q, \delta(i), q)$ where $\delta(i)$ is treated as an observable output event (practically with timers). The IOLTS M with quiescence modeled is called suspensive IOLTS and is noted $\Delta(M)$.

Interaction and Projection. To give a formal definition of interoperability, two operations need to be modeled: asynchronous interaction and projection.

The *asynchronous interaction* is used to calculate the behavior - modeled by an IOLTS - of a system composed by two communicating entities. For two IOLTS M_1 and M_2, this interaction is noted $M_1\|_A M_2$. The way to obtain $M_1\|_A M_2$ is described in [5]. First, M_1 and M_2 are transformed into IOLTS representing their behavior in an asynchronous environment (as in [11, 12]). Then, these two IOLTS are composed to obtain $M_1\|_A M_2$ via the rules usually used for synchronous interaction. These rules (see for example [6, 13]) are "mapping" events on lower interfaces and propagating quiescence and events on upper interfaces.

The *projection* of an IOLTS on a set of events is used to represent the behavior of the system reduced to some events (such as events observable on specific interfaces). For example, the projection of M on the set of events executable on its lower interfaces Σ_L^M is noted M/Σ_L^M. It is obtained by hiding events (replacing by τ-transitions) that do not belong to Σ_L^M, followed by determinization. In the same way, $Out_X(M, \sigma)$ corresponds to a projection of the set of outputs $Out(M, \sigma)$ on the set of events X.

2.3   State of the Art in Automatic Test Generation

Some methods for generating automatically interoperability tests exists in [7, 14, 15, 16, 17]. However, these methods are not based on formal definitions. On the contrary, conformance testing is a kind of test for which a formal framework was developed. It determines to what extent a single implementation of a standard conforms to its requirements. Conformance testing architectures and formal definitions [1, 2] were described. Among these formal definitions, the **ioco** conformance relation [2] says that an implementation I is **ioco**-conformant to a specification S if I can never produce an output which could not be produced by its specification S after the same trace. Moreover, I may be quiescent only if S can do so. Formally : I **ioco** $S = \forall \sigma \in Traces(\Delta(S)), Out(\Delta(I), \sigma) \subseteq Out(\Delta(S), \sigma)$. This relation is the most used in practice for conformance tests. Defining formally conformance also allows automatic conformance test generation: conformance test generation tools like TGV [3] or TorX [4] are based on ioco-theory. Even though conformance and interoperability are two different kinds of test, they have in common to be based on traces of the specifications. Thus, part of the existing concepts of conformance testing can be reused for interoperability testing. However, the ioco-theory does not fit all objectives of interoperability testing (verification that the implementations communicate correctly and that they provide the expected services while interacting: see Section 3.2).

3   Formalizing Interoperability

3.1   Specification Model

As we are concerned with interoperability testing, the considered specifications must allow interaction. We call this property the interoperability specification compatibility property (iop-compatibility for short). Two specifications are iop-compatible iff, for each possible output on the interfaces used for the interaction after any trace of the interaction, the corresponding input is foreseen in the other specification. Formally, $\forall \sigma \in Traces(S_1 \|_A S_2)$, $\forall \sigma.a.\sigma' \in Traces(S_1 \|_A S_2)$, $a \in Out_{\Sigma_L}(S_1 \|_A S_2, \sigma)$, $\sigma' = \beta_1...\beta_l$, $\Rightarrow \exists \beta_i$ such that $\beta_i = \bar{a}$. Practically, this property can be verified by a parallel search of both specifications -without constructing the specification interaction. This means that the traces of one specification must be compatible with possible execution of the other specification. Notice that this notion of iop-compatibility is different from the one described in [18] where authors consider that "two components are compatible if there is *some* environment that make them work together, simultaneously satisfying both of their environment assumption".

In some situations (underspecification of input actions particularly), the two specifications need to be completed to verify this property. It is done by adding transitions leading to an error trap state and labeled with the inputs corresponding to messages that can be sent by the interacting entity (input m added in $In(S_j, \sigma/\Sigma_j)$ if $\bar{m} \in Out_{\Sigma_L}(S_i, \sigma/\Sigma_i)$). Indeed, this method considers the reception of an unspecified input as an error. This is the most common definition of unspecified inputs in network protocols. In the following, we will consider that specifications are iop-compatible.

3.2   Formalization of Interoperability Principles

The purpose of interoperability testing is to verify that the two interconnected implementations communicate successfully **and** that they provide the expected services during their interaction. Interaction verification corresponds to the verification that outputs sent by an IUT on its lower interfaces are foreseen in the specification and that the interacting IUT is able to receive these messages. Service verification corresponds to the verification that outputs (and quiescence) observed on the upper interfaces of the IUTs are described in their respective specification. Thus, outputs must be verified on both upper and lower interfaces, while inputs are managed on lower interfaces.

Output verification is done by comparing output observed, after a particular trace, on the interfaces of the IUTs with the outputs foreseen in the specifications after the same trace. This part of interoperability testing can reuse ioco-theory. However, during test execution, there is an important difference between interoperability and conformance testing context also for output verification. Indeed, the lower interfaces are controllable in conformance context but during interoperability tests, these interfaces are only observable.

One of interoperability testing purposes is to verify that the two implementations communicate correctly, that is to say that messages sent by one implementation must be correct (this is done by the output verification) and actually received by the other implementation. The verification of this reception corresponds to input management. However only outputs can be observed by testers. Thus, verifying that an input μ is actually received implies to determine the set of outputs that can happen only if this reception is actually executed. This set of outputs is calculated based on causal dependencies. The set of outputs (*without quiescence*) on S that causally depend on the input μ after the trace σ is noted $CDep(S, \sigma, \mu)$ and defined by $CDep(S, \sigma, \mu) = \{\alpha_i \in \Sigma_O^S | \forall (q, q'), q_0^S \overset{\sigma}{\Rightarrow} q \overset{\mu}{\rightarrow} q', \exists q_i, q' \overset{\sigma_i.\alpha_i}{\Longrightarrow} q_i, \sigma_i \in (\Sigma^S \setminus \Sigma_O^S)^* \cup \{\epsilon\}\}$, where $\sigma_i \in (\Sigma^S \setminus \Sigma_O^S)^* \cup \{\epsilon\}$ is the path associated to the output $\alpha_i \in CDep(S, \sigma, \mu)$.

Based on causal dependency events, a condition for input verification can be defined. We give here the condition for the verification of the execution of an input $\bar{\mu}$ by I_2 (the corresponding output is μ sent by I_1). This condition considers each output μ executed by I_1 after a trace σ of the interaction. This trace can be decomposed into σ_1 (events of I_1) and σ_2 (events of I_2). The input management condition says that the reception of $\bar{\mu}$ by I_2 implies the observation of an output that causally depends on $\bar{\mu}$. Some events may be executed between μ and $\bar{\mu}$ (noted by trace $\sigma' \in ((\Sigma^{S_1} \cup \Sigma^{S_2}) \setminus \bar{\mu})^* \cup \{\epsilon\}$) and between $\bar{\mu}$ and the output that causally depends on $\bar{\mu}$ (trace $\sigma_i \in (\Sigma_I^{S_2})^* \cup \{\epsilon\}$). Formally, the condition is described by:

$$\forall \sigma \in Traces(S_1 \|_A S_2), \sigma_1 = \sigma/\Sigma^{S_1} \in Traces(\Delta(S_1)), \sigma_2 = \sigma/\Sigma^{S_2} \in Traces(\Delta(S_2)), \forall \mu \in Out_{\Sigma_L^{I_1}}(\Delta(I_1), \sigma_1),$$
$$\forall \sigma' \in ((\Sigma^{S_1} \cup \Sigma^{S_2}) \setminus \bar{\mu})^* \cup \{\epsilon\}, \sigma.\mu.\sigma'.\bar{\mu} \in Traces(S_1 \|_A S_2),$$
$$\bar{\mu} \in In(I_2, \sigma_2.(\sigma'/\Sigma^{I_2})) \Rightarrow$$
$$Out(I_2, \sigma_2.(\sigma'/\Sigma^{I_2}).\bar{\mu}.\sigma_i) \subseteq CDep(S_2, \sigma_2.(\sigma'/\Sigma^{I_2}), \bar{\mu}) \text{ with } \sigma_i \in (\Sigma_I^{S_2})^* \cup \{\epsilon\}.$$

3.3 Interoperability Formal Definitions

Even though some formal definitions exist in [5, 8], there is no precise characterization for interoperability (*iop* for short in the following). Here, we present some formal definitions, called *iop criteria*. They consider different possible architectures (see Section 2.1) for testing the interoperability of two IUTs.

The **unilateral iop criterion** iop_U (point of view of I_1) considers interfaces of IUT I_1 while interacting with I_2. It says that, after a trace of S_1 observed during the interaction, all outputs (and quiescence) observed in I_1 must be foreseen in S_1, and that I_1 must be able to receive outputs sent by I_2 via its lower interfaces.

Definition 2 (Unilateral iop criterion iop_U). $I_1 iop_U I_2 =$
$\forall \sigma_1 \in Traces(\Delta(S_1)), \forall \sigma \in Traces(S_1 \|_A S_2),$
$\sigma/\Sigma^{S_1} = \sigma_1 \Rightarrow Out((I_1 \|_A I_2)/\Sigma^{S_1}, \sigma_1) \subseteq Out(\Delta(S_1), \sigma_1)$
and $\forall \sigma_1 = \sigma/\Sigma^{S_1} \in Traces(\Delta(S_1))$ such that $\sigma \in Traces(S_1 \|_A S_2), \forall \mu \in Out(I_2, \sigma/\Sigma^{I_2}), \forall \sigma' \in [(\Sigma^{S_1} \cup \Sigma^{S_2}) \setminus \bar{\mu}]^* \cup \{\epsilon\}, \sigma.\mu.\sigma'.\bar{\mu} \in Traces(S_1 \|_A S_2), \bar{\mu} \in In(I_1, \sigma_1.(\sigma'/\Sigma^{I_1})) \Rightarrow Out(I_1, \sigma_1.(\sigma'/\Sigma^{I_1}).\bar{\mu}.\sigma_i) \subseteq CDep(S_1, \sigma_1.(\sigma'/\Sigma^{I_1}), \bar{\mu}),$
$\sigma_i \in (\Sigma_I^{S_1})^* \cup \{\epsilon\}$

The **bilateral total iop criterion** iop_B is verified iff both (on I_1 point of view and I_2 point of view) unilateral criteria are verified: $I_1 \ iop_B \ I_2 \ (= I_2 \ iop_B \ I_1)$ $= I_1 \ iop_U \ I_2 \land I_2 \ iop_U \ I_1$.

The **global iop criterion** considers both kinds of interfaces and both IUTs globally. It says that, after a trace of the specification interaction, all outputs (and quiescence) observed during the interaction of the implementations must be foreseen in the specifications, and that outputs sent by one IUT via its lower interfaces must be effectively received by the interacted IUT. Contrary to iop_U and iop_B that are used in specific contexts where some interfaces are not accessible, this iop criterion iop_G corresponds to the most used testing architecture.

Definition 3 (Global iop criterion iop_G). $I_1 iop_G I_2 =$
$\forall \sigma \in Traces(S_1 \|_A S_2),\ Out(I_1 \|_A I_2, \sigma) \subseteq Out(S_1 \|_A S_2, \sigma)$
and $\forall \{i, j\} = \{1, 2\},\ i \neq j$,
$\forall \sigma \in Traces(S_i \|_A S_j),\ \sigma_i = \sigma / \Sigma^{S_i} \in Traces(S_i),\ \sigma_j = \sigma / \Sigma^{S_j} \in Traces(S_j),$
$\forall \mu \in Out(I_i, \sigma / \Sigma^{S_i}),\ \forall \sigma' \in [(\Sigma^{S_i} \cup \Sigma^{S_j} \cup \{\delta(i), \delta(j)\}) \setminus \bar{\mu}]^* \cup \{\epsilon\},\ \sigma.\mu.\sigma'.\bar{\mu} \in$
$Traces(S_i \|_A S_j),\ \bar{\mu} \in In(I_j, \sigma_j.(\sigma' / \Sigma^{I_j})) \Rightarrow Out(I_j, \sigma_j.(\sigma' / \Sigma^{I_j}).\bar{\mu}.\sigma_k) \subseteq CDep($
$S_j,\ \sigma_j.(\sigma' / \Sigma^{I_j}),\ \bar{\mu}),\ \sigma_k \in (\Sigma_I^{S_j})^* \cup \{\epsilon\}$

In [5], we prove the equivalence of the global criterion with the so-called bilateral iop criterion iop_B in terms of non-interoperability detection. However, the iop criteria defined in [5] only consider the output verification, that is the first part of the definition of iop_B and iop_G of this study. These latter criteria are still equivalent in terms of non-interoperability detection. Indeed, the causal-dependency based condition is defined with a bilateral point of view in both criteria. In next Section, we focus in the way to use this equivalence for developing methods to derive automatically iop test cases.

4   Interoperability Test Generation Methods

In this section, we investigate the way to generate interoperability (iop for short in the following) tests based on the defined iop criteria. Applications of these methods are described in Section 5.

4.1   Test Purposes, Test Cases and Verdicts

Iop Test Purpose. In practice, interoperability test case derivation is done based on test purposes. These test purposes are used by testers to describe the properties they want to test. An iop test purpose is an informal description of behaviors to be tested, in general an incomplete sequence of actions. Formally, a test purpose TP can be represented by a deterministic and complete IOLTS equipped with trap states used to select targeted behaviors. Complete means that each state allows all actions. In this study, we consider simplified iop test purposes with only one possible action after each state ($\forall \sigma,\ |\Gamma(TP, \sigma)| \leq 1$) and one $Accept^{TP}$ trap state used to select the targeted behavior.

Iop Test Cases. During interoperability tests, three kinds of events are possible: sending of stimuli to the upper interfaces of the IUTs, reception of inputs from these interfaces, and observation of events (input and output) on the lower interfaces. Thus, an iop test case TC can be represented by $TC = (Q^{TC}, \Sigma^{TC}, \Delta^{TC}, q_0^{TC})$, an extended version of IOLTS. $\{PASS, FAIL, INC\}$

$\subseteq Q^{TC}$ are trap states representing interoperability verdicts. q_0^{TC} is the initial state. $\Sigma^{TC} \subseteq \{\mu | \bar{\mu} \in \Sigma_U^{S_1} \cup \Sigma_U^{S_2}\} \cup \{?(\mu) | \mu \in \Sigma_L^{S_1} \cup \Sigma_L^{S_2}\}$. $?(\mu)$ denotes the observation of the message μ on a lower interface. Notice that in interoperability testing μ can be either an input or an output. Δ^{TC} is the transition function.

Iop Verdicts. The execution of the iop test case TC on the system composed of the two IUTs gives an iop verdict: PASS, FAIL or INC. The meanings of the possible iop verdicts are PASS: no interoperability error was detected during the tests, FAIL: the iop criterion is not verified and INC (for Inconclusive): the behavior of the SUT seems valid but it is not the purpose of the test case.

4.2   Global Interoperability Test Generation Method

The global interoperability test generation method is based on the first part of the global iop criterion iop_G. This part focuses on the comparison between outputs (and quiescence) observed during the interaction of the implementations and outputs (and quiescence) foreseen in the specifications in the same situation. This method corresponds to what is done practically when writing iop test cases "by hand". It also corresponds to most approaches for automatic interoperability test generation (as in [7, 8, 14, 15, 16, 17]) even if these methods generally do not compute the complete specification interaction graph. This is why we also call it classical interoperability test generation method.

The global interoperability test generation method (see Figure 2(a)) begins with the construction of the asynchronous interaction $S_1 \|_A S_2$ to have a model of the global system specification. Then $S_1 \|_A S_2$ is composed with the test purpose TP. During this operation, two main results are calculated. First TP is validated. If the events composing TP are not found in the specifications (or not in the

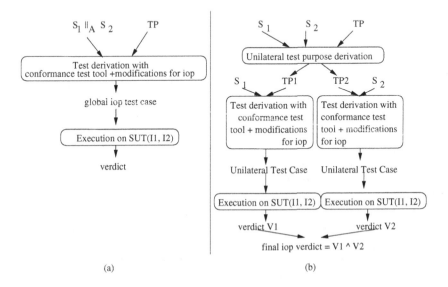

(a)   (b)

Fig. 2. Interoperability test generation: global and bilateral approaches

order described in TP), TP is not a valid Test Purpose. The composition is also used to keep only the events concerned by the Test Purpose (in the interaction of the two specifications). It calculates the different ways to observe/execute TP on the System Under Test (SUT) composed of the two IUTs.

A conformance test tool takes as entries a test purpose and a specification and computes the paths of the specification executing the test purpose. Thus, such a tool can be used for computing the paths executing TP in the specification interaction. In this case, the tool entries are TP and $S_1 \parallel_{\mathcal{A}} S_2$. However, some modifications needs to be applied to the test case obtained with this tool to derive interoperability test cases. Events on lower interfaces are not controllable in the interoperability context, contrary to the case of conformance testing.

One problem with this method (classical method) is that we can have state space explosion when calculating the interaction of the specifications [6]. Indeed, the state number of the specification asynchronous interaction is in the order of $O((n.m^f)^2)$ where n is the state number of the specifications, f the size of the input FIFO queue on lower interfaces and m the number of messages in the alphabet of possible inputs on lower interfaces. This result can be infinite if the size of the input FIFO queues is not bound. However, the equivalence -in terms of non-interoperability detection- between global and bilateral iop criteria (cf. theorem 1 in [5]) suggests that iop tests derived based on the bilateral iop criterion will detect the same non-interoperability situations as tests generated using the global interoperability test generation method.

4.3   Bilateral Interoperability Test Generation Method

The bilateral interoperability test generation method (see Figure 2(b)) is based on the first part of the iop_B criterion. This part focuses on the comparison between outputs (and quiescence) observed on the interfaces of the interacting implementations -each test case considering one IUT during the interaction- and outputs (and quiescence) foreseen in the corresponding specification.

Unilateral iop Test Purpose Derivation. The first step of the bilateral interoperability test generation method derives automatically two unilateral iop test purposes TP_{S_i} from the global iop test purpose TP. The algorithm of figure 3 shows how to derive these two unilateral iop test purposes. Let us consider an event μ of the iop test purpose TP and the construction of TP_{S_i}. If μ is an event of the specification S_i, μ is added to the unilateral iop test purpose TP_{S_i}. If μ is an event from the specification S_j, there are two possibilities. Either the event is to be executed on lower interfaces: in this case, the mirror event $\bar{\mu}$ is added to TP_{S_i}; or, the event is to be executed on the upper interfaces: in this case, the algorithm searches a predecessor of μ, such that this predecessor is an event to be executed on lower interfaces. The algorithm adds the mirror of this predecessor to the unilateral iop test purpose TP_{S_i}.

Some additional functions are used in the algorithm of figure 3. Let us consider a trace σ and an event a. The function *remove_last* is defined by : remove_last$(\sigma.a) = \sigma$. The function *last_event* is defined by : last_event$(\sigma) = \epsilon$

Input: S_1, S_2: specification, TP: iop test purpose
Output: $\{TP_{S_i}\}_{i=1,2}$;
Invariant: $S_k = S_{3-i}$ (* S_k is the other specification *); $TP = \mu_1...\mu_n$
Initialization: $TP_{S_i} := \epsilon\ \forall i \in \{1,2\}$;
for $(j = 0; j \leq n; j++)$ **do**
    if $(\mu_j \in \Sigma_L^{S_i})$ **then** $TP_{S_i} := TP_{S_i}.\mu_j$; $TP_{S_k} := TP_{S_k}.\bar{\mu}_j$ **end(if)**
    if $(\mu_j \in \Sigma_L^{S_k})$ **then** $TP_{S_i} := TP_{S_i}.\bar{\mu}_j$; $TP_{S_k} := TP_{S_k}.\mu_j$ **end(if)**
    if $(\mu_j \in \Sigma_U^{S_i})$ **then** $TP_{S_i} := TP_{S_i}.\mu_j$; $TP_{S_k} :=$add_precursor(μ_j, S_i, TP_{S_k}) **end(if)**
    if $(\mu_j \in \Sigma_U^{S_k})$ **then** $TP_{S_k} := TP_{S_k}.\mu_j$; $TP_{S_i} :=$add_precursor(μ_j, S_k, TP_{S_i}) **end(if)**
    if $(\mu_j \notin \Sigma^{S_k} \cup \Sigma^{S_i})$ **then** error(TP not valid: $\mu_j \notin \Sigma^{S_1} \cup \Sigma^{S_2}$) **end(if)**
end(for)

function add_precursor(μ, S, TP): **return** TP
    $\sigma_1 := TP$; $a_j =$last_event(σ_1)
    while $a_j \in \Sigma_U^S$ **do** $\sigma_1=$remove_last(σ_1); $a_j =$last_event(σ_1) **end(while)**
    $M = \{q \in Q^S; \exists\ q'|(q, \bar{a}_j, q') \wedge \sigma = \bar{a}_j.\omega.\mu \in Traces(q)\}$
    if $(\forall q \in M, \sigma \notin Traces(q))$ **then** error(no path to μ) **end(if)**
    while $(e=$last_event$(\omega) \notin \Sigma_L^S \cup \{\epsilon\})$ **do** $\omega=$remove_last(ω) **end(while)**
    if $(e \in \Sigma_L^S)$ **then** $TP_S = TP_{S_i}.\bar{e}$ **end(if)**

Fig. 3. Algorithm to derive TP_{S_i} from TP

if $\sigma = \epsilon$ and last_event$(\sigma) = a$ if $\sigma = \sigma_1.a$. The *error* function returns the cause of the error and exits the algorithm.

Unilateral iop Test Case Generation. The second step of the bilateral interoperability test generation method is the generation of two unilateral test cases from the unilateral test purposes and the specifications. The same test generation algorithm is executed for TP_{S_1} with S_1 and for TP_{S_2} with S_2. This algorithm calculates on-the-fly the interaction between the unilateral iop test purpose and the corresponding specification to find in the specification the paths executing the test purpose. This step can be done by using a conformance test generation tool (for example TGV).

However, as lower interfaces are not controllable in interoperability testing (contrary to conformance testing), controllable conformance test cases can not always be reused for interoperability. Indeed, a test case is controllable if the tester does not need to choose arbitrarily between different events. In conformance, inputs on lower interfaces correspond to outputs of the tester: a controllable conformance test case only considers one of the possible inputs on lower interfaces. In interoperability testing, inputs on lower interfaces are sent by the other implementation. An interoperability test case must take into account *all* possible inputs on lower interfaces. The complete test graph is an IOLTS which contains all sequences corresponding to a test purpose: all the inputs of the implementation that correspond to the test purpose are considered. Thus, to have test cases usable in interoperability context, the conformance tool used in this step for interoperability test generation must compute the complete test graph.

Moreover, some modifications are needed on the test cases TC_1' and TC_2' generated by the conformance test tool to obtain the unilateral iop test cases TC_1 and TC_2 that will be executed unilaterally on the corresponding IUT in the SUT. These modifications are needed because lower interfaces are only observed (not controlled) in interoperability context. For example, if an event $l!m$ exists in the test case obtained from TGV (which means that the tester connected to interface l must send the message m to the lower interface of the IUT), this will correspond to $?(l?m)$ in the interoperability test case. This means that the interoperability tester observes that a message m is received on the interface l. No changes are made on the test cases for events on the upper interfaces as these interfaces are observable and controllable: a message can be sent (and received) by the tester to the IUT on these interfaces.

The execution of both interoperability test cases return two verdicts. The "bilateral" verdict is obtained by combining these local verdicts with the following obvious rules: $PASS \wedge PASS = PASS$, $PASS \wedge INC = INC$, $INC \wedge INC = INC$, and $FAIL \wedge (FAIL \vee INC \vee PASS) = FAIL$.

Complexity. The first step of the bilateral interoperability test generation method is linear in the maximum size of specifications. Indeed, it is a simple path search algorithm. The second step is also linear in complexity, at least when using TGV [19]. Thus, it costs less than the calculation of $S_1\|_A S_2$ needed in the global interoperability test generation method. Moreover the bilateral interoperability test generation method can be used to generate iop test cases in situations where generating test cases with the global interoperability test generation method is impossible due to state-space explosion problem.

4.4   Causal Dependency Based Algorithm Completing Both Methods

One objective of interoperability is to verify the communication between the IUTs. Moreover, iop test purposes may end with an input. This latter situation occurs, for example, in the unilateral test purposes derived by bilateral method. For example, if the iop test purpose ends with an output on the lower interface, its mirror event (an input) is added -as last event- to one of the derived test purpose. In this case, the conformance test tool (TGV) generates a test case without postamble: the last event of the test case is the input given as objective by the test purpose. However, this input is not observable. An algorithm based on input-output causal dependencies is used to know if this input was actually executed. It completes iop test cases obtained by bilateral method (or test cases generated by classical method based on an iop test purpose ending with an input) by producing outputs that help in verifying that the input is actually executed. Thus, the algorithm based on causal dependencies completes and refines iop test cases generated by bilateral (or global) method. It takes as entry the iop test case to complete: the last event of this test case is the input μ. It returns the outputs that are causally dependent of this input μ. For computing the set of causal dependency events (associated with the paths to these events), this algorithm,

Input: S_1: Specification, σ: Trace of event (after projection on S_1), μ: input of S_1
Output: $CDep(S_1, \sigma, \mu)$, $\{\sigma'\}$: set of traces between μ and an output, m: number of events in $CDep$
Initialization: $\Gamma := \Gamma(S_1, \sigma.\mu)$; $m :=$nb_event(Γ)
for $(i := 0; i \le m; i++)$ **do**
   create(find[i]); find[i]=false; create(σ'[i]); σ'[i] $:= \epsilon$ **end(for)**
BEGIN
while $\exists x(x < n)$, find[x]:=false **do**
   for $(i := 0; i < m; i++)$ **do**
      if (find[i]=false) **do** $Evt := \Gamma(S_1, \sigma.\mu.\sigma'[i])$
         if $(Evt(0) \in \Sigma_O^{S_1})$ **do** find[i]:=true; Add(Evt(0), $CDep(S_1, \sigma, \mu)$)
         else $\sigma'[i] := \sigma'[i].$Evt(0) **end(if)**
         if (nb_event(Evt)> 1) **do**
            for$(j := 1; j \le$ nb_event$(Evt); j++)$ **do**
               m++; create(σ'[m]); σ'[m] $:= \sigma'$[i]
               create(find[m]); find[m]:=false
               if $(Evt(j) \in \Sigma_O^{S_1})$ **do** find[m]:=true; Add(Evt(j), $CDep(S_1, \sigma, \mu)$)
               else σ'[m] $:= \sigma'$[m].Evt(j) **end(if)**
            end(for)
         end(if)
      end(if)
   end(for)
end(while)
END

Fig. 4. Exploration of S_1 to find causally dependent outputs of input μ

see Figure 4, considers each event of the set $\Gamma(S_1, \sigma.\mu)$ to find an output in each trace following the considered input. The obtained outputs are used to verify the actual reception of the input μ and thus, to complete test cases based on the iop test purpose containing this input.

4.5 Implementation of iop Test Generation Methods

In [5], we show the equivalence that allows the definition of the bilateral algorithm. However, the definitions and methods were not complete as inputs were not verified (there was no condition and no algorithm based on causal-dependencies) and the algorithms presented were not tested practically.

The methods presented in this Section were implemented using the CADP toolbox [20]. The conformance test generation tool TGV (Test Generation using Verification techniques) [3] is integrated in this toolbox which also contains an API for manipulating IOLTS. These methods were applied to the generation of iop test cases for a connection protocol. It is described in next Section.

5 Application on a Connection Protocol

Figure 5 describes three specifications for a connection protocol. S_1 and S_2 are respectively the specifications of the client and server. $U1?CNR$ is a connection

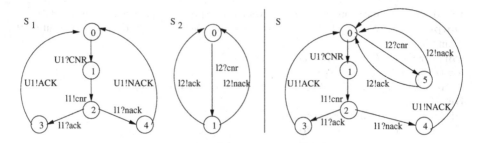

Fig. 5. Examples of specifications: S_1, S_2 and S

request from the upper layer, $l1!cnr$ (resp. $l2?cnr$) the request sent (resp. received) to the peer entity, $l2!ack/l2!nack$ the positive or negative response, and $U1!ACK/U1!NACK$ the response forwarded to the upper layer. The specification S represents both client and server parts.

5.1   A Client/Server Example

Let us consider the three iop test purposes of figure 6(a). These iop test purposes are applicable for the System Under Test (SUT) composed of two IUTs implementing respectively S_1 and S_2. For example, TP_1 means that, after the reception by I_1 (implementing S_1) of a connection demand on its upper interface $U1$, this IUT must send a connection acknowledgment on its upper interface $U1$.

In figure 6 (b1), TP_1^1 and TP_1^2 are the unilateral test purposes derived using the algorithm of figure 3 for TP_1 and respectively specifications S_1 and S_2. In the same way, TP_2^1 and TP_2^2 of figure 6 (b2) (resp. TP_3^1 and TP_3^2 of figure 6 (b3)) are derived from TP_2 (resp. TP_3). The same notation will be used for test cases in the following.

When deriving the unilateral iop test purposes, for events on lower interfaces, the returned event is either the event itself, or its mirror. For event $U1!ACK$, as its predecessor is $\mu = l1?ack$, the returned event is $\bar{\mu} = l2!ack$ (TP_1^2 and TP_3^2) or $U1!ACK$ (TP_1^1 and TP_3^1). The difficulty is for deriving an event from $U1?CNR$ for TP_1^2 and TP_2^2. In S_1, this event is the first possible event after the initial

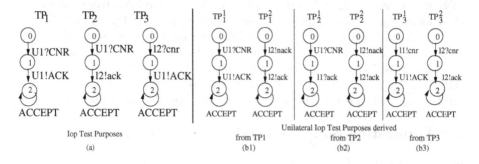

Fig. 6. Iop test purpose TP_1, TP_2 and TP_3, and derived Unilateral Test Purposes

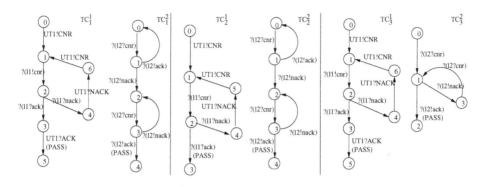

Fig. 7. Test Cases by bilateral method for specifications S_1 and S_2

state. Its predecessor must be found in the paths that bring back the entity in its initial state after some execution. The first predecessor found is $U1!NACK$. As this event is not an event of the interaction, the algorithm continues one more step to find $l1?nack$ as predecessor, and then returns its mirror $l2!nack$.

The second step of the bilateral iop test generation method corresponds to the use of TGV conformance test tool on a unilateral test purpose and the corresponding specification. Figure 7 gives the test cases obtained for the test purposes of figure 6. The results on Figure 7 gives the test cases modified for interoperability. $UT1$ is the tester connected to upper interface $U1$.

Now, let us see what happens when using the classical approach for iop test generation to compare test cases generated by both methods. The first step of the classical method is the calculation of the specification interaction. Then, we can use TGV to generate test cases for test purposes of Figure 6. The obtained global iop test cases are in Figure 8. We can remark that, for the three situations (comparing traces in Figures 7 and 8), the same execution paths lead to the same verdicts. Thus, the iop test cases generated with both methods are equivalent in terms of verdicts.

For TP_2, we can remark that $TC_2^1\|_A TC_2^2$ ends with an input ($l1?ack$) that is not in TC_2 (excluding this event, TC_2 and $TC_2^1\|_A TC_2^2$ contain the same traces). This is due to the test purpose derivation (cf. Section 4.4): the unilateral test purpose generated for S_1 ends with an input. To complete this iop test case (TC_2^1), we can either add a postamble returning to the initial state, either use the causal dependency based algorithm. In this simple example (specification S_1), only the event $U1!ACK$ will be added with causal dependency event method.

To summarize, the application of both method on this connection protocol confirms the equivalence in terms of verdicts. Even though the generated iop test cases are not the same, the execution of the same traces leads to the same verdicts. Thus, the same non-interoperability situation are detected with both our method and the classical method.

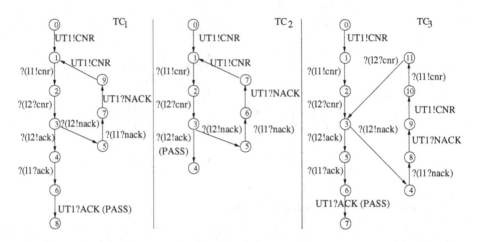

Fig. 8. Test Cases from TGV for the interaction of S_1 and S_2

5.2   Specification Describing Both Entities as Client and Server

Both methods were also applied on the specification S (Figure 5) describing both client and server parts (same test purposes). The interaction $S\|_A S$, calculated for classical approach, is composed of 454 states and 1026 transitions with input queues of each system bounded to one message. The following table gives the number of states s and transitions t (noted s/t in the table) of results derived considering a queue size of 3. Line 1 and 2 give the state and transition numbers for unilateral test cases derived by bilateral method considering S as specification for both systems (lines 1 and 2: S as specification respectively for systems 1 and 2). The third line gives numbers for the interaction of these unilateral test cases TC^1 and TC^2. Finally line 4 gives results for global methods. With a queue size of 3, the specification interaction has 47546 states and 114158 transitions.

	TP_1	TP_2	TP_3
Unilateral iop test case TC^1	9/17	8/16	9/17
Unilateral iop test case TC^2	13/24	13/24	12/22
$TC^1\|_A TC^2$	19546/57746	19468/57614	19405/57386
Global test case TC	54435/120400	18014/40793	54456/120443

We observe that we can derive iop test cases considering a queue size of 3 via both classical and bilateral methods. However, due to the difference in state and transition number between both methods, unilateral test cases obtained by bilateral method are more usable, for example for controlling the execution of the interoperability test cases. Moreover, state space explosion problem can occur when using the global method: results in the previous table are finite only because we consider bounded FIFO queues. We were not able to compute $S\|_A S$ for a queue size limited to 4 places. But the bilateral method gives iop test cases with the same state and transition numbers as in the previous table. This shows that the bilateral method can be used to generate iop test cases even for specifications that produce state space explosion problem. Moreover, these test cases are not dependent of the queue size.

6   Conclusion

In this paper, we present interoperability formal definitions that deal with both purposes of interoperability: implementations must interact correctly and the expected service must be provided. A new interoperability test generation method is proposed based on these formal definitions. This method has been implemented using the CADP toolbox. It avoids the well-known state-space explosion problem that occurs when using classical methods. This is the important result of our study and it is confirmed by the application on a connection protocol. Moreover, we show that the so-called bilateral interoperability test derivation method allows us to generate interoperability test cases in situations where it would have been impossible with the traditional method because of state space explosion problem.

As future work, we will study the generalization of the formal interoperability definitions and test generation methods to the much more complex context of more than two implementations. We will also study how to apply the described method to a distributed testing architecture.

References

[1] ISO. Information Technology - Open Systems Interconnection Conformance Testing Methodology and Framework - Parts 1-7. International Standard ISO/IEC 9646/1-7 (1992)

[2] Tretmans, J.: Testing concurrent systems: A formal approach. In: Baeten, J.C.M., Mauw, S. (eds.) CONCUR 1999. LNCS, vol. 1664, pp. 46–65. Springer, Heidelberg (1999)

[3] Jard, C., Jéron, T.: Tgv: Theory, principles and algorithms. STTT 7(4), 297–315 (2005)

[4] Tretmans, J., Brinksma, E.: Torx: Automated model based testing. In: Hartman, A., Dussa-Zieger, K. (eds.) Proceedings of the First European Conference on Model-Driven Software Engineering, Nurnberg, Germany (December 2003)

[5] Desmoulin, A., Viho, C.: Formalizing interoperability for test case generation purpose. In: IEEE ISoLA Workshop on Leveraging Applications of Formal Methods, Verification, and Validation, Columbia, MD, USA (September 2005)

[6] Castanet, R., Koné, O.: Deriving coordinated testers for interoperability. In: Rafiq, O. (ed.) Protocol Test Systems, Pau-France, vol. VI C-19, pp. 331–345. IFIP, Elsevier Science B.V., Amsterdam (1994)

[7] Seol, S., Kim, M., Kang, S., Ryu, J.: Fully automated interoperability test suite derivation for communication protocols. Comput. Networks 43(6), 735–759 (2003)

[8] Castanet, R., Kone, O.: Test generation for interworking systems. Computer Communications 23, 642–652 (2000)

[9] Walter, T., Schieferdecker, I., Grabowski, J.: Test architectures for distributed systems: State of the art and beyond. In: Petrenko, Yevtushenko (eds.) Testing of Communicating Systems, IFIP, Kap, pp. 149–174 (September 1998)

[10] Barbin, S., Tanguy, L., Viho, C.: Towards a formal framework for interoperability testing. In: Kim, M., Chin, B., Kang, S., Lee, D. (eds.) 21st IFIP WG 6.1 International Conference on Formal Techniques for Networked and Distributed Systems, Cheju Island, Korea, Août, pp. 53–68 (2001)

[11] Jard, C., Jéron, T., Tanguy, L., Viho, C.: Remote testing can be as powerful as local testing. In: Wu, J., Chanson, S., Gao, Q. (eds.) Formal methods for protocol engineering and distributed systems, FORTE XII/ PSTV XIX 1999, Beijing, China, pp. 25–40. Kluwer Academic Publishers, Dordrecht (1999)

[12] Verhaard, L., Tretmans, J., Kars, P., Brinksma, E.: On asynchronous testing. In: Bochman, G.V., Dssouli, R., Das, A. (eds.) Fifth inteernational workshop on protocol test systems, pp. 55–66. North-Holland, Amsterdam (1993) IFIP Transactions

[13] Desmoulin, A., Viho, C.: Quiescence Management Improves Interoperability Testing. In: 17th IFIP International Conference on Testing of Communicating Systems (Testcom), Montreal, Canada (May-June 2005)

[14] El-Fakih, K., Trenkaev, V., Spitsyna, N., Yevtushenko, N.: Fsm based interoperability testing methods for multi stimuli model. In: Groz, R., Hierons, R.M. (eds.) TestCom 2004. LNCS, vol. 2978, pp. 60–75. Springer, Heidelberg (2004)

[15] Griffeth, N.D., Hao, R., Lee, D., Sinha, R.K.: Integrated system interoperability testing with applications to voip. In: FORTE/PSTV 2000: Proceedings of the IFIP TC6 WG6.1 Joint International Conference on Formal Description Techniques for Distributed Systems and Communication Protocols and Protocol Specification, Testing and Verification. Kluwer, B.V., Dordrecht (2000)

[16] Bochmann, G., Dssouli, R., Zhao, J.: Trace analysis for conformance and arbitration testing. IEEE transaction on software engeneering 15(11), 1347–1356 (1989)

[17] Gadre, J., Rohrer, C., Summers, C., Symington, S.: A COS study of OSI interoperability. Computer standards and interfaces 9(3), 217–237 (1990)

[18] de Alfaro, L., Henzinger, T.A.: Interface automata. In: ESEC/FSE-9: Proceedings of the 8th European software engineering conference held jointly with 9th ACM SIGSOFT international symposium on Foundations of software engineering. ACM Press, New York, NY, USA (2001)

[19] Fernandez, J.-C., Jard, C., Jéron, T., Viho, C.: Using on-the-fly verification techniques for the generation of test suites. In: Alur, R., Henzinger, T.A. (eds.) CAV 1996. LNCS, vol. 1102. Springer, Heidelberg (1996)

[20] Garavel, H., Lang, F., Mateescu, R.: An overview of cadp 2001. Technical Report 0254, INRIA (2001)

Author Index

Lecture Notes in Computer Science

Sublibrary 2: Programming and Software Engineering

For information about Vols. 1– 4344
please contact your bookseller or Springer

Vol. 4652: D. Georgakopoulos, N. Ritter, B. Benatallah, C. Zirpins, G. Feuerlicht, M. Schoenherr, H.R. Motahari-Nezhad (Eds.), Service-Oriented Computing ICSOC 2006. XVI, 201 pages. 2007.

Vol. 4640: A. Rashid, M. Aksit (Eds.), Transactions on Aspect-Oriented Software Development IV. IX, 191 pages. 2007.

Vol. 4634: H. Riis Nielson, G. Filé (Eds.), Static Analysis. XI, 469 pages. 2007.

Vol. 4620: A. Rashid, M. Aksit (Eds.), Transactions on Aspect-Oriented Software Development III. IX, 201 pages. 2007.

Vol. 4615: R. de Lemos, C. Gacek, A. Romanovsky (Eds.), Architecting Dependable Systems IV. XIV, 435 pages. 2007.

Vol. 4610: B. Xiao, L.T. Yang, J. Ma, C. Muller-Schloer, Y. Hua (Eds.), Autonomic and Trusted Computing. XVIII, 571 pages. 2007.

Vol. 4609: E. Ernst (Ed.), ECOOP 2007 – Object-Oriented Programming. XIII, 625 pages. 2007.

Vol. 4608: H.W. Schmidt, I. Crnković, G.T. Heineman, J.A. Stafford (Eds.), Component-Based Software Engineering. XII, 283 pages. 2007.

Vol. 4591: J. Davies, J. Gibbons (Eds.), Integrated Formal Methods. IX, 660 pages. 2007.

Vol. 4589: J. Münch, P. Abrahamsson (Eds.), Product-Focused Software Process Improvement. XII, 414 pages. 2007.

Vol. 4574: J. Derrick, J. Vain (Eds.), Formal Techniques for Networked and Distributed Systems – FORTE 2007. XI, 375 pages. 2007.

Vol. 4556: C. Stephanidis (Ed.), Universal Access in Human-Computer Interaction, Part III. XXII, 1020 pages. 2007.

Vol. 4555: C. Stephanidis (Ed.), Universal Access in Human-Computer Interaction, Part II. XXII, 1066 pages. 2007.

Vol. 4554: C. Stephanidis (Ed.), Universal Acess in Human Computer Interaction, Part I. XXII, 1054 pages. 2007.

Vol. 4553: J.A. Jacko (Ed.), Human-Computer Interaction, Part IV. XXIV, 1225 pages. 2007.

Vol. 4552: J.A. Jacko (Ed.), Human-Computer Interaction, Part III. XXI, 1038 pages. 2007.

Vol. 4551: J.A. Jacko (Ed.), Human-Computer Interaction, Part II. XXIII, 1253 pages. 2007.

Vol. 4550: J.A. Jacko (Ed.), Human-Computer Interaction, Part I. XXIII, 1240 pages. 2007.

Vol. 4542: P. Sawyer, B. Paech, P. Heymans (Eds.), Requirements Engineering: Foundation for Software Quality. IX, 384 pages. 2007.

Vol. 4536: G. Concas, E. Damiani, M. Scotto, G. Succi (Eds.), Agile Processes in Software Engineering and Extreme Programming. XV, 276 pages. 2007.

Vol. 4530: D.H. Akehurst, R. Vogel, R.F. Paige (Eds.), Model Driven Architecture - Foundations and Applications. X, 219 pages. 2007.

Vol. 4523: Y.-H. Lee, H.-N. Kim, J. Kim, Y.W. Park, L.T. Yang, S.W. Kim (Eds.), Embedded Software and Systems. XIX, 829 pages. 2007.

Vol. 4498: N. Abdennahder, F. Kordon (Eds.), Reliable Software Technologies - Ada-Europe 2007. XII, 247 pages. 2007.

Vol. 4486: M. Bernardo, J. Hillston (Eds.), Formal Methods for Performance Evaluation. VII, 469 pages. 2007.

Vol. 4470: Q. Wang, D. Pfahl, D.M. Raffo (Eds.), Software Process Dynamics and Agility. XI, 346 pages. 2007.

Vol. 4468: M.M. Bonsangue, E.B. Johnsen (Eds.), Formal Methods for Open Object-Based Distributed Systems. X, 317 pages. 2007.

Vol. 4467: A.L. Murphy, J. Vitek (Eds.), Coordination Models and Languages. X, 325 pages. 2007.

Vol. 4454: Y. Gurevich, B. Meyer (Eds.), Tests and Proofs. IX, 217 pages. 2007.

Vol. 4444: T. Reps, M. Sagiv, J. Bauer (Eds.), Program Analysis and Compilation, Theory and Practice. X, 361 pages. 2007.

Vol. 4440: B. Liblit, Cooperative Bug Isolation. XV, 101 pages. 2007.

Vol. 4408: R. Choren, A. Garcia, H. Giese, H.-f. Leung, C. Lucena, A. Romanovsky (Eds.), Software Engineering for Multi-Agent Systems V. XII, 233 pages. 2007.

Vol. 4406: W. De Meuter (Ed.), Advances in Smalltalk. VII, 157 pages. 2007.

Vol. 4405: L. Padgham, F. Zambonelli (Eds.), Agent-Oriented Software Engineering VII. XII, 225 pages. 2007.

Vol. 4401: N. Guelfi, D. Buchs (Eds.), Rapid Integration of Software Engineering Techniques. IX, 177 pages. 2007.

Vol. 4385: K. Coninx, K. Luyten, K.A. Schneider (Eds.), Task Models and Diagrams for Users Interface Design. XI, 355 pages. 2007.

Vol. 4383: E. Bin, A. Ziv, S. Ur (Eds.), Hardware and Software, Verification and Testing. XII, 235 pages. 2007.

Vol. 4379: M. Südholt, C. Consel (Eds.), Object-Oriented Technology. VIII, 157 pages. 2007.

Vol. 4364: T. Kühne (Ed.), Models in Software Engineering. XI, 332 pages. 2007.

Vol. 4355: J. Julliand, O. Kouchnarenko (Eds.), B 2007: Formal Specification and Development in B. XIII, 293 pages. 2006.

Vol. 4354: M. Hanus (Ed.), Practical Aspects of Declarative Languages. X, 335 pages. 2006.

Vol. 4350: M. Clavel, F. Durán, S. Eker, P. Lincoln, N. Martí-Oliet, J. Meseguer, C. Talcott, All About Maude - A High-Performance Logical Framework. XXII, 797 pages. 2007.

Vol. 4348: S. Tucker Taft, R.A. Duff, R.L. Brukardt, E. Plödereder, P. Leroy, Ada 2005 Reference Manual. XXII, 765 pages. 2006.

Vol. 4346: L. Brim, B.R. Haverkort, M. Leucker, J. van de Pol (Eds.), Formal Methods: Applications and Technology. X, 363 pages. 2007.